Global Tobacco Control

Also by Paul Cairney

UNDERSTANDING PUBLIC POLICY: Theories and Issues

SCOTTISH POLITICS (*with Neil McGarvey*)

THE NEW SCOTTISH POLITICAL SYSTEM

Global Tobacco Control

Power, Policy, Governance and Transfer

Paul Cairney
Senior Lecturer and Head of Department of Politics and International Relations, University of Aberdeen, UK

Donley T. Studlar
Eberly Family Distinguished Professor of Political Science, West Virginia University, USA

Hadii M. Mamudu
Assistant Professor of Public Health, East Tennessee State University, USA

palgrave
macmillan

First published 2012 by
PALGRAVE MACMILLAN

Palgrave Macmillan in the UK is an imprint of Macmillan Publishers Limited, registered in England, company number 785998, of Houndmills, Basingstoke, Hampshire RG21 6XS.

Palgrave Macmillan in the US is a division of St Martin's Press LLC,
175 Fifth Avenue, New York, NY 10010.

Palgrave Macmillan is the global academic imprint of the above companies and has companies and representatives throughout the world.

Palgrave® and Macmillan® are registered trademarks in the United States, the United Kingdom, Europe and other countries

ISBN 978-0-230-20004-3

This book is printed on paper suitable for recycling and made from fully managed and sustained forest sources. Logging, pulping and manufacturing processes are expected to conform to the environmental regulations of the country of origin.

A catalogue record for this book is available from the British Library.

A catalogue record for this book is available from the Library of Congress.

10 9 8 7 6 5 4 3 2 1
21 20 19 18 17 16 15 14 13 12

Printed and bound in Great Britain by
CPI Antony Rowe, Chippenham and Eastbourne

Contents

List of Figures

List of Tables

List of Abbreviations

ACF	Advocacy Coalition Framework
ACOSH	Australian Council on Smoking and Health
ACP	African, Caribbean and Pacific
ACS	American Cancer Society
AGOA	African Growth and Opportunity Act
AIDS	Acquired Immunodeficiency Syndrome
AHA	American Heart Association
ALA	American Lung Association
AMA	American Medical Association
ANRF	American Non-Smokers' Rights Foundation
APACT	Asia Pacific Association for the Control of Tobacco
AP	Asia Pacific
ASH	Action on Smoking and Health
BASP	Bureau of Action on Smoking Prevention
BAT	British American Tobacco
BATF	Bureau of Alcohol Tobacco and Firearms
BMA	British Medical Association (UK)
BUGA UP	Billboard Utilising Graffitists Against Unhealthy Promotions
CAP	Common Agricultural Policy (EU)
CATAP	Coalition Against Tobacco Advertising and Promotions
CDC	Centres for Disease Control and Prevention
CEE	Central and Eastern Europe
CICAD	Inter-American Drug Abuse Control Commission
CLAA	Cigarette Labelling and Advertising Act
COP	Conference of the Parties
COSH	Coalition on Smoking and Health
CRUK	Cancer Research UK
DHHS	Department of Health and Human Services
DHSS	Department of Health and Social Security (UK)
DNP	Duty Not Paid
DTI	Department for Trade and Industry (UK)
EAC	European Action on Cancer
ECJ	European Court of Justice
ECOSOC	UN Economic and Social Council
EEA	European Economic Area
ENSP	European Network for Smoking and Tobacco Prevention
EP	European Parliament
EPA	Environmental Protection Agency
ETS	Environmental Tobacco Smoke

EU	European Union
FAA	Federal Aviation Administration
FAO	Food and Agricultural Organisation
FCA	Framework Convention Alliance
FCC	Federal Communications Commissions
FCTC	Framework Convention on Tobacco Control
FDA	Food and Drug Administration
FOREST	Freedom Organisation for the Right to Enjoy Smoking Tobacco
FPTCA	Family Protection and Tobacco Control Act
FTC	Federal Trade Commission
GATT	General Agreement on Trade Tariffs
GAO	(US) Government Accountability Office
GDP	Gross Domestic Product
GTC	Global Tobacco Control
IARC	International Agency For Research in Cancer
ICC	Interstate Commerce Commission
IDRC	International Development Research Corporation
IGR	Intergovernmental Relations
IMF	International Monetary Fund
INFOTAB	International Tobacco Information Center
INGCAT	International Non-governmental Against Tobacco
INWAT	International Network of Women Against Tobacco
IOCU	International Organisation of Consumer Unions
ISCS	Independent Scientific Committee on Smoking (UK)
ISCSH	Independent Scientific Committee on Smoking and Health (UK)
IT/A	Imperial Tobacco/Altadis
ITCN	The International Tobacco Control Network
ITGA	International Tobacco Growers Association
IUATLD	International Union Against Tuberculosis and Lung Diseases
JTI	Japan Tobacco International
LAC	Latin America and the Caribbean
LDP	Liberal Democratic Party (Japan)
MENA	Middle East and North Africa
MEPs	Members of the European Parliament
MLG	Multi-level Governance
MOP UP	Movement Opposed to Promotions of Unhealthy Products
MPs	Members of Parliament
MRC	Medical Research Council
MSA	Master Settlement Agreement
NAFTA	North Atlantic Free Trade Area
NGO	Nongovernmental Organisations
NHMRC	National Health and Medical Research Council
NHS	National Health Service (UK)

NRT	Nicotine Replacement Therapy
NSMA	Non Smokers Movement of Australia
NSRA	Nonsmoker's Rights Association
OAS	Organization of American States
OECD	Organisation for Economic Co-operation and Development
ONS	Office for National Statistics (UK)
OSH	Office of Smoking and Health
OSHA	Occupational Health and Safety Administration
PAHO	Pan American Health Organisation
PM	Phillip Morris
PPACA	Patient Protection and Affordable Care Act
SCHIP	State Children's Health Insurance Program
SCOTH	Scientific Committee on Tobacco Health
SES	Socio-Economic Status
SHS	Second-hand Smoke
SSA	Sub-Saharan Africa
TAC	Tobacco Advisory Council (UK)
TAD1	Tobacco Advertising Directive (first one)
TAD2	Tobacco Advertising Directive (second one)
TFI	WHO Tobacco Free Initiative
TIOJ	Tobacco Institute of Japan
TMA	Tobacco Manufacturers' Association (UK)
TPCA	Tobacco Products Control Act
TTC	Transnational Tobacco Companies
UICC	International Union Against Cancer
UK	United Kingdom
UN	United Nations
UNITAB	International Union of Tobacco Growers
US	United States
USDA	US Department of Agriculture
USDHHS	US Department of Health and Human Services
USTR	US Trade Representative
WCTOH	World Conference on Tobacco and Health
WHA	World Health Assembly
WHO	World Health Organisation
WW II	World War II

Preface and Acknowledgements

This book represents the culmination of a long journey by its authors, who have investigated tobacco policy for varying lengths of time. Donley Studlar initiated some of the first research on the topic from a political science perspective in 1994. Hadii Mamudu completed his Ph.D. on the topic under Studlar's supervision at West Virginia University in 2005. Paul Cairney began investigating tobacco policy in 2004 as part of a wider project examining devolution in the UK. In sum, they have conducted over 300 semi-structured research interviews in 39 countries with experts and participants in tobacco policy. The study is based on those interviews, a quantitative analysis of policy instruments and extensive documentary analysis.

Paul Cairney

Paul Cairney would like to thank his co-authors, and Amber Stone-Galilee and Liz Blackmore at Palgrave, for their patience. For him, the book started as an article applying multiple theories to tobacco control in the journal *British Politics*. He proposed a book-length treatment of the subject to Palgrave, and Steven Kennedy soon convinced him to write two books: *Understanding Public Policy* (UPP) (2012) and what turned out to be this book when Studlar and Mamudu agreed to be co-authors and extend the focus from the UK to the globe. The original plan was to complete this book in 2009, but his work on UPP took much longer than expected. Paul would also like to thank Greg Gordon for his invaluable legal advice.

Paul would like to dedicate his portion of the book to his still-lovely partner Linda, their still-beautiful children Evie, Alfie and Frankie, their still-smelly but handsome dog (who can be seen here – http://smallvillage-bigdog.wordpress.com/).

Donley Studlar

In a time span stretching over almost 20 years, many debts have been incurred to people and organisations that have supported the research and helped it progress. Unfortunately only a few of them can be mentioned here. There were the many people with specialist knowledge – government officials, policy advocates, and academic experts – who agreed to be interviewed on various topics and/or to supply documents and references. Studlar has enjoyed the services of a string of excellent research assistants provided by the Department of Political Science at West Virginia University, including Mark Lehman, Arnita Sitasari, William Harrison, Carl Taylor, and Andrew Wassmann. Ph.D. students and collaborators at WVU who provided knowledge and inspiration were Bossman Asare, Frederick Appah, Edward Brenya, Kyle Christensen, Stephanie J. Frisbee, and Rebecca Klase. Outside WVU, he benefited from collaborations at the Ontario Tobacco Research Unit, Centre for Addiction and Mental Health, University of Toronto.

Several grant agencies and universities provided financial and intellectual support, including the Eberly College of Arts and Sciences through its sabbatical and faculty development programs, the West Virginia University Faculty Senate, the Embassy of Canada, the National Health Research and Development Program (Canada), the University of Toronto Political Science Department, the Faculty of Business Administration at the University of Regina, the Research School of Social Sciences at the Australian National University, the Department of Politics and International Relations at the University of Aberdeen, the Political Science Department at University of Aarhus, the Nordic Social Science Council, and the Fulbright Senior Scholar Programs for Canada and for European Union Affairs. Among the scholars who made his visits to foreign universities so rewarding, Paul Cairney, Christopher Green-Pedersen, Anne Lavack, Ian McAllister, and Marian Sawer stand out.

In addition, various conferences, international and domestic, over the years provided opportunities to present portions of the work. Parts of it also have appeared in a variety of political science, public policy and public health journals and edited books.

Ronny Thompson, Administrative Secretary in Political Science at West Virginia University, has been an unflagging contributor in helping to produce the final version of the manuscript. Finally, Susan Moyle Studlar has been good-humored in tolerating her husband's often-diverted attention to the book.

Hadii Mamudu

Hadii Mamudu would like to thank his parents, Zuwerah Mamudu and Abdul Mamudu; Uncle, Issah Cobbinah; his wife, Lapri Mamudu; his in-laws, Antoinette Arnold and Kay Arnold; and his mentors, Professor Stanton A. Glantz of the University of California in San Francisco, Professor Donley Studlar of West Virginia University, and Professor Thomas Novotny of San Diego State University for their support throughout the years. Institutionally, he would like to thank the College of Public Health of East Tennessee State University, the Center for Tobacco Control Research and Education of the University of California in San Francisco, and Department of Political Science of West Virginia University. Additionally, Hadii would like to express his gratitude to Legacy Foundation and the US National Institutes of Health for the financial support provided for his postdoctoral fellowship at University of California in San Francisco. Moreover, Hadii would like to express his appreciation to people at the Tobacco Free Initiative of WHO and particularly, the Executive Director Dr. Douglas Bettcher for supporting his research and being responsive to his numerous inquiries. Finally, while many people in East Tennessee State University have supported Hadii's research, he would particularly like to thank Dr. Wilsie Bishop, Vice President of Health Affairs and Chief Operating Office; Dr. Randolph Wykoff, Dean of College of Public Health, Dr. Robert Pack, Associate Dean of College of Public Health, and Dr. Amal Khoury, Interim Chair of the Department of Health Services Administration.

1
Political Science and Tobacco Policy

Tobacco policy has long been recognised as a major concern in public health. It is also a key issue in political science and public policy research for four main reasons. First, as a policy problem it has some unusual features. Smoking is legal, but represents the number one preventable cause of premature death and disease in the world. Second, tobacco policy contains elements of both stability and instability. It provides one of the most significant examples of major policy change in the developed world. A post-war picture characterised by limited governmental intervention (to control tobacco) has been replaced, in many countries, by a comprehensive set of measures designed to reduce smoking and limit the activities of tobacco companies and, at the global level, by a major public health treaty – the Framework Convention on Tobacco Control (FCTC) of the World Health Organisation (WHO). Third, it provides one of the most important examples of power and politics in the modern world. We can link initial levels of stability and continuity to a great imbalance of power and resources in favour of transnational tobacco companies at the expense of anti-smoking groups. Fourth, it provides an extensive source of information on comparative public policy processes and outcomes. In particular, it allows us to examine the policy divide between developed and developing countries (as categorised by the United Nations).[1] Policy has changed markedly, albeit unevenly, in the former, but it has generally lagged in the latter, prompting many government leaders, international organisations and NGOs to try to bridge the gap through international agreements and policy transfer. While there is some evidence of policy transfer success, and a significant shift to global tobacco control policy, there is also evidence that tobacco companies still have a strong hold on global policy and are often supported by governments. This prompts us to ask two key questions:

1. Why is there often such a wide gap between the size of the policy problem and the government response?

2. Why, if the problem is the same across the globe, does policy vary so markedly across political systems?

This book represents the first major attempt by political scientists, writing from a unified perspective, to explain global tobacco policy. This approach sets it apart from public health accounts more interested in what public policy *should be* rather than what it is and why policy decisions were made. It also sets it apart from edited social science volumes which present useful contributions on individual countries from a range of disciplines, but without a central unifying theme or a means to compare policy development systematically across different political systems over time.

The plan of this chapter is as follows. First, we identify the size of the policy problem. Second, we introduce the argument that there has been a delay between the onset of the problem, recognition of the problem in policy circles, and the policy response, by drawing on the public health advocacy literature. This literature is relatively extensive and displays a highly critical assessment of the policy records of governments and the power and behaviour of tobacco companies. Third, we outline a political science approach to tobacco policy. We initially relate the delay in policy response to classic discussions of power within political systems. For example, drawing on the 'second-face' (Bachrach and Baratz, 1962) discussion of power, we suggest that tobacco industry power is exercised to maintain barriers to policy change – initially to reinforce the dominant social attitude that treated smoking and tobacco companies in a positive light and, subsequently, to influence the policy process to keep the issue of tobacco control off the policy agenda.

This discussion of power and policy sets the scene for the remainder of the book. In Chapter 2 we introduce a framework, based on contemporary theories of public policy, to study policy stability and change. We use this framework to analyse tobacco policy change at different, complementary, levels of detail and breadth: across the globe; in particular developed countries; in groups of developed countries; and, across developing regions. We identify the nature of tobacco policy, examine how we measure policy change and explain stability and change with reference to five main factors: institutions, agenda setting, policy networks, the socioeconomic context and the role and transfer of ideas. Finally, we synthesise the empirical content of each chapter and outline the potential for the tobacco policy experience to inform contemporary theories of public policy.

The tobacco problem

The medical and public health literature suggests that few health conditions have had as catastrophic long-term consequences as tobacco use. It contributes to one in ten deaths worldwide, over six million per year. On current trends, the number of deaths is expected to increase to between eight and ten million by 2030 (Guindon and Boisclair, 2003: vii; Mathers and Loncar, 2006; WHO, 2011b). In the 20th century, tobacco use killed over 100 million people and the WHO estimates that the death toll in the 21st century could reach one billion. Tobacco kills an estimated one-third to one-half of its regular users, which means that of the 1.3 billion smokers today, 390 to 650 million will eventually die from this behaviour (WHO, 2008, 2011b). The US Surgeon General (2006, 2010) indicates that tobacco use is hazardous to almost all parts of the human body. Cigarette smoking especially leads to cancer, respiratory and cardiovascular diseases. In other words, it undermines life and the quality of life (Chapman, 2007: 9). In the US, tobacco accounted for 18% of 1.2 million deaths in 2000, compared to 17% from poor diet/physical inactivity, 4% from alcohol and less than 1% from illegal drugs (Mokdad et al, 2004). The proportions are similar in countries, such as Canada, New Zealand and Australia (Corrao et al, 2000: 378, 410). Tobacco-related diseases, especially lung cancer, have declined since the mid-1990s to reflect a drop in smoking. Nevertheless, in the US, deaths resulting from the direct consumption of tobacco (excluding 'passive' smoking from 'second-hand smoke', SHS) are almost twice as high as the combined total for alcohol, cocaine, heroin, homicide, suicide, car accidents, fire, and AIDS. Yet, the resources spent on tobacco control are relatively low, especially in comparison to the costs of treatment in the healthcare system (CDC, 2009).

Tobacco is increasingly a developing country problem. By 2030, over 80% of tobacco-related deaths may occur in the developing world (Guindon and Boisclair, 2003: vii; Jha and Chaloupka, 1999; WHO, 2008, 2011b). Of the over 1.3 billion smokers in the world, almost half live in China (30%) and India (17%). The increasing rate of tobacco use has resulted in an increasing rate of tobacco-induced morbidity and mortality (Ezzati and Lopez, 2003; Jamison et al, 2006; Lopez et al, 2006; WHO, 2008). With a long gestation period for some tobacco-related diseases, countries, such as China and India have been experiencing dramatically higher death rates from smoking since the 1990s. Tobacco-attributable mortality for males in China was 12% in 1998 (Liu et al, 1998; Niu et al, 1998) and that of India is expected to reach 13% of total deaths by 2020 (Kumar, 2000; Shimkhada and Peabody, 2003: 48). Although India is a relatively poor country with a greater number of sources of death (related, for example, to sanitation), its mortality rate is already markedly higher among tobacco users than non-users (Gupta and Mehta, 2000). The number of cigarettes consumed in the developing world has risen from 1.1 billion in 1970 to 3.4 billion in 2000 (compared to 1.5 billion in the developed world in 1970 and 2000) (Guindon and Bosclair, 2003: 11). While the per capita rate of consumption is still much higher in developed countries (Table 1.1), that figure is falling. In developing countries, the figure is not only rising, but also set to rise much more significantly in line with the 'tobacco epidemic model'.

Table 1.1 Per Capita Cigarette Consumption, Developed and Developing Countries, 1970–2000

	1970	1975	1980	1985	1990	1995	1996	1997	1998	1999	2000
Developing Countries	712	792	960	1091	1147	1081	1086	1074	1076	1047	1041
Developed Countries	2811	3021	2991	2762	2484	2363	2298	2254	2220	2188	2148

Source: adapted from Guindon and Boisclair (2003: 10)

The tobacco epidemic model

The tobacco epidemic in the developed world has unfolded over approximately a century, providing information to public health researchers seeking to prevent a similar epidemic in developing countries. This research is utilised by tobacco control advocates as a learning tool for countries to avoid the life cycle of the epidemic, and move more rapidly to the reduced smoking rates that are occurring in the developed countries today (Lopez et al, 1994).

As Figure 1.1 suggests, the model consists of four stages. In Stage 1, lasting 1–2 decades, male and female smoking prevalence starts at very low levels

Figure 1.1 The Tobacco Epidemic Model

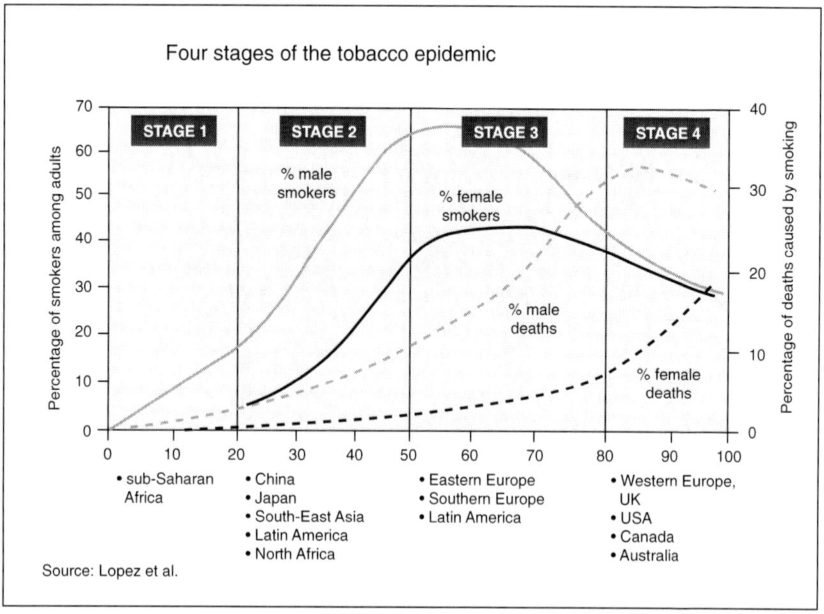

Source: World Bank, 1999 (adapted from Lopez et al, 1994)

before rising rapidly, and before any tobacco-related deaths are evident. In Stage 2, lasting 2–3 decades, male smoking prevalence rises rapidly and reaches levels far higher than female, peaking at 50–80% of the male population. By the end of this stage, illness and deaths attributable to tobacco are rising rapidly, accounting for 10% of all male deaths. Tobacco restrictive activities in this stage are poorly developed, and cessation support activities are uncommon. In Stage 3, the prevalence of male smoking begins to decline and the prevalence of female smoking plateaus, though smoking prevalence among younger women can reach levels close to that of males. Knowledge of smoking health hazards is also more widespread. However, during this stage, the incidence and prevalence of tobacco-attributable disease continues to rise rapidly and peak at 25–30% of male mortality, with tobacco-proportionate mortality even higher in the middle-age groups because of the time lag between tobacco exposure and the related illness and death. As knowledge of smoking hazards spreads, the receptivity for tobacco control increases, and tobacco control activities become more organised, successful, and comprehensive. In the final stage of the model, smoking prevalence for both sexes continues to decline at slow but similar rates, but smoking-attributable death rates remain high at 30–35% of all male deaths (smokers and non-smokers combined) and 40–45% of male deaths in middle age. While smoking-attributable male death rates begin to decline in the latter phases of this stage, smoking-attributable female death rates continue to rise, as female smoking prevalence peaked after that for males.

Developing regions are at different stages of the epidemic. Countries in Sub-Saharan Africa (SSA) are in Stage 1, where the smoking rate is low among men and women and they are yet to experience the harmful effects of tobacco use. Those in Asia Pacific (AP), Latin America and the Caribbean (LAC), and Middle East and North Africa (MENA) are at Stage 2 and have started experiencing the harmful effects of tobacco use (Shafey et al, 2009).

Tobacco use is still primarily a male practice throughout developing countries (CICAD and OAS, 2008; Waldron et al, 1988; WHO, 2001a). The gender gap is widest in AP and least in LAC (WHO, 2008). In AP countries, such as China and Vietnam, over two-thirds of men and less than 10% of women smoke (WHO, 2008). However, in South Asian countries, such as Bangladesh, India, and Nepal, a large proportion of women indulge in traditional forms of tobacco use (Jha et al, 2002; WHO, 1997, 2001a). The generally low rate of tobacco consumption among women in developing countries is rising, especially in AP countries, such as the Philippines, partly because tobacco companies are specifically targeting them as a vast potential market for their products (Sasco, 1992; Waldron et al, 1988; WHO, 2001b; Lam et al, 2004; Morrow and Barraclough, 2003; WHO, 2001a; Amos and Margaretha, 2000; Bansal et al, 2005). A few countries in LAC, such as Argentina and Chile, have reached Stage 3, where the smoking rate among women approximates or even exceeds that of men.

The evidence suggests that developing countries are also following trends based on the socioeconomic status of the tobacco user. Traditional forms of tobacco use are more common in lower income groups. Cigarette smoking is more prevalent among the relatively affluent, a pattern consistent with historical patterns in developed countries – smoking rises when people can more easily afford cigarettes and then falls as they become more aware of the health effects (Chapman and Wong, 1990; FAO, 2003; USDHHS, 1992). In South Asian countries, such as Bangladesh, India, and Pakistan, poor people mostly use bidis; Kretek is used in Indonesia and chewing and hand-rolled tobacco in Latin America. In AP countries, such as the Philippines, educated and higher income young women continue to take up cigarette smoking partly because it is promoted as a symbol of feminine liberation and westernisation (Morrow and Barraclough, 2003). The result is that people in urban areas, where the income levels are relatively higher, smoke cigarettes more than those in rural areas (FAO, 2003).

According to the model, higher GDP leads to increased affordability and consumption of cigarettes until there is widespread awareness of the health consequences of tobacco use. In developed countries, disease rates for men have stopped rising due to the decline in smoking over the past half century, but rates for women continue to increase because of their large uptake in smoking from the 1960s. Once again smoking has become a class-related behaviour and is now a major contributor to health inequalities. In developing countries, the model suggests that cigarette use will increase in line with a rise in income, with the most significant rises in cigarette use and tobacco-related deaths still to occur.

The public health view

The 'public health view' refers to the identification of five key ideas developed from the evidence and arguments produced in the past 50 years by scientists and public health groups:

1. There are clear health dangers related to tobacco use and SHS exposure ('passive smoking').
2. Tobacco is an addictive product and nicotine is an addictive drug.
3. Tobacco use causes an economic burden on individuals, employers and governments.
4. The tobacco industry is responsible for the use and spread of tobacco worldwide and its activities need to be controlled.
5. A 'comprehensive' approach to tobacco control – a composite of measures and programmes that reinforce each other to reduce the use and spread of tobacco – is required (Mamudu et al, 2011b).

A key concern of the public health literature is the extent to which powerful tobacco companies are responsible for the large time lag between the size of the tobacco problem, its recognition within government (and the media and public) and the policy response. The argument can be summarised as follows: if former governments knew the true morbidity and mortality costs of tobacco, they would have banned its growth, manufacture, and consumption – but these health consequences only became known after smoking rates in the Western world were approximately 50% of the overall population. By this time, the political economy of tobacco was well entrenched in industrialised countries: the manufacturing (and, in many cases, tobacco growing) industry was generating income, jobs, and taxes; and, major sectors of the economy – advertising, private media, arts, sports, vendors, the hospitality sector – became reliant on the tobacco industry for their own economic welfare. Therefore, all governments faced significant resistance to tobacco control: smokers, addicted to cigarettes, opposed or ignored restrictions; the tobacco industry pursued alternatives to an enforced comprehensive tobacco control regime and challenged the scientific evidence on tobacco use and exposure to SHS that underpinned such policies.

In this light, the public health view is that it is incumbent on governments to do all they can to reduce smoking in developed countries and prevent a rise in smoking in developing countries (one of the best exponents of this view, and how to influence governments, the media and the public, is Chapman, 2007). The greatest impacts on human longevity come not from the major breakthroughs of medical research and technology, but from much less expensive advances in public health, such as clean water, sanitation, immunisation, and improved living conditions (Blank and Burau, 2007; Nathanson, 2007). Tobacco is the only 'normal' or legal consumer product that, if used as intended, results in the premature death of 50% of its users and disease for many others (European Commission, 2004: 56). Despite the huge expenditures supporting medical research on cancer, there is no better way of reducing this disease than by preventive measures, chief among them a reduction of smoking in the population. In the public health view, it is a moral duty of governments to introduce comprehensive tobacco control measures in their own countries and to collaborate to produce a global tobacco control regime.

A comprehensive tobacco control programme combines a population-based approach, such as advertising bans and smoke-free environments, with an individual-based approach to help tobacco users to quit through cessation programmes, such as Nicotine Replacement Therapy (NRT) and counseling. The WHO (2008: 10–11) identifies six key tobacco control measures: 1) 'monitor tobacco use and prevention policies'; 2) 'protect people from tobacco smoke'; 3) 'offer help to quit tobacco'; 4) 'warn about the dangers of tobacco'; 5) 'enforce bans on tobacco adverting, promotion and sponsorship', and 6) 'raise taxes on tobacco'.

Transnational Tobacco Companies (TTCs)

The public health literature extends to a detailed analysis of the nature and behaviour of the major tobacco companies, highlighting their growth and income, their increasing share of the global tobacco market and their practices that public health advocates argue should be curbed by governments (including, most notably, the sale and marketing of cigarettes). Tobacco agriculture originated in the Americas, then spread to countries in AP, MENA, and SSA through European exploration and colonisation between the 16th and 18th centuries. In spite of this long history of tobacco growth and use in many countries in these developing regions, the tobacco companies were primarily concentrated in developed countries in Europe and North America prior to World War II. From World War II onwards, state monopolies emerged across these developing regions, as did the TTCs. In fact, the largest tobacco company in the world is the China National Tobacco Company, which in 2007 controlled 32% of the global cigarette market. Even as the TTCs have penetrated all markets in the developing world, state monopolies continue to persist in countries in MENA, such as Egypt and Iran and in AP countries, such as Cambodia, China, Myanmar, Thailand, and Vietnam. For this reason, the tobacco industry network in these developing countries consists of the state monopolies, the TTCs, and the growers (Figure 1.2).

Figure 1.2 Global Cigarette Companies Market Share, 2007

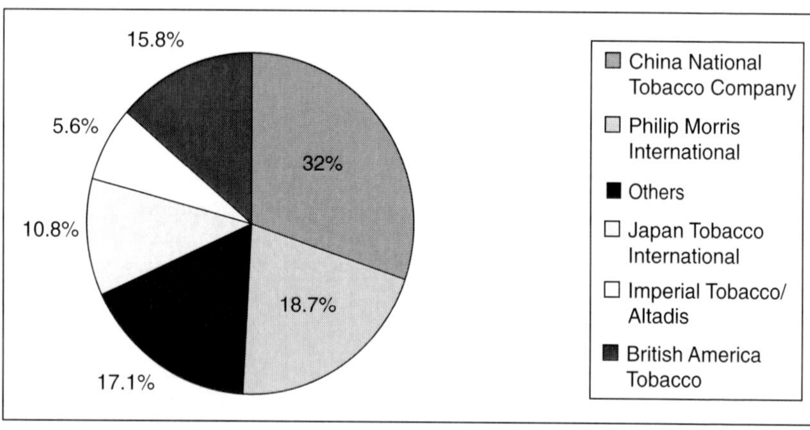

Source: Shafey et al, 2009

Over the past four decades, the TTCs extended their activities into developing countries through mergers, acquisitions and joint ventures with governments. They operate in markets and have factories throughout the developing world. British American Tobacco (BAT), Philip Morris (PM), and Imperial Tobacco/Altadis (IT/A) are the leading tobacco companies in AP, LAC, MENA and SSA, while Japan Tobacco International (JTI), the third largest TTC in the world, continues to increase its market share. Several factors facilitated this extension of TTCs into developing countries, including the pursuit of new markets amidst increasing tobacco regulation and declining consumption in developed countries (Satcher, 2001; Muller, 1978, 1983; Frey, 1997; Taylor, 1984; Crofton, 1990; Chapman and Wong, 1990; World Bank, 1989; USDHHS, 1992). LAC first experienced the influx of the TTCs in the 1950s and the 1960s because of its proximity to North America and the availability of cheaper labour (APACT, 1995; USDHHS, 1992). By the 1980s, the TTCs had expanded their activities further, notably in Asia (USDHHS, 1992; APACT, 1995).

The TTC expansion in developing countries was aided by factors, such as trade liberalisation (Yach, 2000; Bettcher, 2001; Jha, 2000), cultural diffusion (Yach, 2000; WHO Expert Committee, 1983; Yach, 1996), and low levels of literacy in developing countries (Yach, 1996). For example, the US government's post-World War II Food for Peace Program included tobacco (Taylor, 1984), while US Trade Representatives made threats of economic reprisals against Asian countries for failure to open their markets to US-based tobacco companies in the 1980s (Chitanondh, 2001; Connolly, 1993; Chaloupka, 1996; USDA, 1994; Hammond, 1998). Moreover, international organisations, such as the World Bank and the UN encouraged tobacco projects as part of post-World War II and post-independence development programmes in these countries (Muller, 1978; Yach, 1996). The World Bank only ended its support for tobacco projects in 1992 (Ramin, 2006; Mamudu, 2008b).

Bilateral and multilateral trade agreements between developed and developing countries, such as African, Caribbean and Pacific (ACP) partnership agreements with the European Union and the US, the North Atlantic Free Trade Area (NAFTA), and the African Growth and Opportunity Act (AGOA) continue to aid the TTCs in the extension of their activities (Otanez, 2007). This liberalised world trade regime, combined with the decline of state monopoly tobacco manufacturing companies in countries, such as France, Italy, and Spain, the collapse of communism in the 1990s which led to privatisation programmes in Central and Eastern Europe (Gilmore and McKee, 2004a, 2004b, 2005), and expansion in Asia, helped produce a market dominated by transnational companies. Only ten years after the Uruguay Round of trade negotiations began in 1986, the accessible market for TTCs had moved from 40% to 90%. In essence, the TTCs' successful penetration of developing countries was aided by governments in developed countries even as the latter introduced domestic tobacco controls.

The public health literature identifies two main consequences of this shift in the market. First, these companies have remained powerful enough to oppose tobacco control successfully, particularly in developing countries. Tobacco companies are some of the most profitable industries in existence, far wealthier than most of their developing country hosts. According to the WHO, in 2002a, the combined revenue of the top three TTCs – BAT, PM, and JTI – was US$121bn, more than the combined GDP of 27 developing countries (WHO, 2004). In 2006, the profit of these TTCs was more than the GDP of most countries in these developing regions. Second, tobacco companies have contributed successfully to the rise in smoking prevalence in these countries, with a combination of practices: making cigarettes addictive by using nicotine when making cigarettes (European Commission, 2004; IOM, 2007; WHO, 2000b); challenging the evidence regarding the adverse health consequences of smoking; and, aggressively marketing cigarettes. Tobacco consumption tends to increase whenever the TTCs enter a developing country (Chaloupka and Laixuthai, 1996; Mendelowitz, 1990), particularly among women (Samet and Yoon, 2001). The globalisation of the tobacco industry has led to increasing tobacco use and tobacco-induced morbidity and mortality (Yach, 2000: 38; Jha, 2000: 71). This problem has generated the need for global tobacco control.

A political science approach to tobacco: Non-decisionmaking and the un-politics of smoking

The key argument of this chapter is that there is often a wide gap between the size of the tobacco problem and the policy response. This may have arisen initially because not enough people were aware of the problem, but this is no longer the case. Instead, we can now link a lack of policy response to the exercise of power to maintain the status quo. This is effectively a normative argument, made most strongly in the public health literature. There is also a long and important history of normatively-infused studies of power within the public policy literature. This early post-war literature on power underpins the contemporary theories of public policy that we introduce in Chapter 2 to help explain tobacco policy continuity and change (Cairney, 2012: 7). Tobacco would have made an excellent case study of power and policymaking in the debates of the 1960s and 1970s had it been recognised fully by political scientists as a problem back then (in the same way that Bachrach and Baratz, 1970 studied poverty and Crenson, 1971 examined air pollution; but see Fritschler, 1969). Our 'second best' solution is to show in this chapter how the issue of tobacco, and policy theories, are informed by classic debates about power and then use modern theories of policymaking, outlined in Chapter 2, to guide our empirical studies.

Much of the early public policy literature represents an attempt to demonstrate the disproportionate power of elites and the effects of that unequal distribution of power within politics and society. For example, Schattschneider (1960) argues that the pressure group system is not pluralistic; a small proportion of the population – the well educated and upper class – is active and well represented by groups. In particular, the group-government system is largely the preserve of the business class seeking to minimise attention to 'private' disputes. In other words, businesses are at their most effective when they succeed in minimising government (and media and public) attention to their power struggles with other actors. Schattschneider (1960: 12, 119) highlights the need for government to counteract such imbalances based on economic power: 'Democratic government is the greatest single instrument for the socialisation of conflict ... big business has to be matched by ... big democracy'. However, there are more potential conflicts than any government or public can pay attention to. Therefore, most issues are ignored and the people are 'semisovereign' – only able to exercise their power in a few areas. In this light, our attention shifts to the exercise of power to determine the issues most worthy of government attention: 'All forms of political organisation have a bias in favour of the exploitation of some kinds of conflict and the suppression of others because *organisation is the mobilization of bias*. Some issues are organized into politics while others are organized out' (Schattschneider, 1960: 69).

This point reminds us of the famous 'second-face' of power, in which the less powerful face two major barriers to engagement (Bachrach and Baratz, 1962). First, they may be disadvantaged by the dominant view within society that favours some beliefs over others. For example, most may feel that an issue is not a legitimate problem for governments to solve or that the solution proposed is not worth considering. Power may be exercised to maintain this view of an issue in the knowledge that if an issue was more widely debated then more people would support government intervention (Crenson, 1971: 180–1). Second, their grievances may be kept off the agenda by governing organisations and institutional procedures. For example, a government may fill unelected posts with people committed to the status quo or the most powerful may discourage the formal discussion of certain issues (Bachrach and Baratz, 1970: 54–9, 70; Hay, 2002: 175).

Overall, important issues are kept off the political agenda either by powerful interests who reinforce social attitudes and manipulate decisionmaking procedures, or (in effect) by the powerless who pay minimal attention to an issue or feel unable to engage (Bachrach and Baratz, 1970: 105–6). The relevance to our study can be demonstrated by a discussion of the most established case studies in the power literature. First, Bachrach and Baratz (1970) linked non-decisionmaking to the issue of poverty. Too many people thought that poverty was the fault of the individual and too few thought that it was exacerbated by conditions (such as insufficient access to education, housing, transport and healthcare) that the government could address. Power could be exercised to reinforce these attitudes and minimise the opportunities for activists to raise the issue on the public or media agenda. Further, even when attitudes began to change, and those opportunities arose more frequently, opponents of policy change were able to manipulate the procedures of government to reduce the chances of an issue reaching the policy agenda (although in this case the barriers were overcome eventually – 1970: 98).

There are clear parallels with tobacco policymaking in the same era (and indeed during most of the 20th century). The initial barrier to policy change was that most people saw tobacco in a positive light: smoking was a glamorous, enjoyable activity rather than a health hazard; tobacco companies were providers of jobs, export revenue, and arts and sports sponsorship. Tobacco companies were able to reinforce this attitude by, for example, funding advertising campaigns, appealing to notions of civil liberties (the right to smoke) and commissioning scientific studies challenging the links between smoking and illness (a strategy on evidence that has served as a model for more recent activity on issues, such as global warming; see Oreskes and Conway, 2010). Further, even when such attitudes began to change, tobacco companies were often able to exploit their position within government to minimise attention and the government response. For example, their links with finance, trade and agriculture departments helped to minimise the role of departments of health. Also, they were able to challenge major attempts at comprehensive tobacco control by proposing more limited measures or alternatives. The classic example in several countries is the successful push for voluntary agreements, between the industry and government, which were generally ill-enforced. More recent examples include the industry's work on youth smoking prevention and corporate social responsibility.

Second, Crenson (1971) identifies a wide gap, in some US cities, between the size of the environmental problem and the policy response. His three main points are that: (a) post-war levels of public attention to air pollution were low compared to the problem; (b) attention varied in different cities; and (c) some cities had passed legislation to regulate air pollution during manufacturing, but others had not. Crenson (1971: 5) seeks to establish if this inaction was 'politically enforced'. For example, 'machine' politicians (who dispense favours to groups to reinforce their power base) may have ensured that air pollution stayed off the policy agenda as a favour to local industries (1971: 19). Thus, in the case study of Gary, Indiana (in which US Steel is the major employer), we find evidence of 'non-decisionmaking'. The Mayor delayed publication of a major study of air pollution, the study's authors (funded by local industries) underplayed the contribution of manufacturing to air pollution and recommended weak enforcement policies, and the City Council delayed its ruling on legislative proposals (1971: 64–5). However, Crenson (1971: 177) is better known for his conclusions on 'unpolitics', identifying US Steel's power even when it did not act: 'the mere reputation for power, unsupported by acts of power, can be sufficient to restrict the scope of local decision making'. In this case there may be a less observable 'political climate' that is not conducive to new understanding of the policy problem, largely in this case because people assumed that US Steel was against new regulations even though it did not articulate its opposition (Crenson, 1971: 23). Instead, the local population, which was almost entirely dependent on US Steel as a source of employment, took its cue from the corporation and stayed silent on this issue. The conclusion is that, while we observe a situation in which all parties appear content to pay no attention to the issue, the manufacturer is powerful. It benefits at the expense of the local population, whose powerlessness is demonstrated by the fact that it is not acting in its real, demonstrable interests (Lukes, 2005: 48; compare with Polsby, 1980: 97). The most relevant aspect for our purposes is the subsequent debate on how to identify power in instances where it is not readily observable: one identifies a problem that *should* be addressed and deduces a degree of powerlessness when it is not. In our case, when tobacco control policies do not follow closely the identification of tobacco harm, tobacco companies profit at the expense of the smoking (and passive smoking) population.

Such arguments prompted lengthy debates about how to demonstrate power and powerlessness in these situations. Crenson's (1971: 26–8) approach is to compare levels of attention to the same problem by similar populations in different jurisdictions, asking why it is important in one but not the other. It predicts what a jurisdiction's population *would* do by establishing the actions of an equivalent jurisdiction's population in the absence of un-politics (1971: 33). This is a problematic approach to some extent because populations may pay less attention to some issues for other reasons, based, for example, on the different weight they place on the importance of some issues over others. There is no objective way to determine the relative importance of a policy problem. They may also pay attention to an issue and then decide quite reasonably not to legislate or rarely push hard for change. Indeed, we generally identify no more than a 'permissive consensus' for tobacco control, even in jurisdictions with comprehensive control programmes.

However, these are still reasonable questions to ask: does the existence of weaker tobacco controls in some countries suggest that their populations are relatively powerless? In turn, does it suggest that tobacco companies are still relatively powerful in some countries? Such questions form the basis for the rest of the book. We identify radical policy change in some countries and limited change in others, using contemporary theories of policymaking (outlined in Chapter 2) to explain both processes. We then relate the evidence to these fundamental questions regarding power and powerlessness in political systems.

Tobacco and public policy

There are few areas that can match tobacco policy as a source of both public enmity between policy participants (pro- and anti-tobacco groups) and normative academic work geared towards a change in public policy. However, it is not our primary aim to make policy recommendations and criticise governments for not adopting them. Rather, our aim is to outline the policy problem and analyse the nature of the response, using theories of public policy. We go beyond the identification of the power of tobacco companies to challenge policy change because, in many countries, a degree of profound policy change has now occurred. Both non-decisionmaking barriers have been overcome in many countries. We employ contemporary theories to explain this policy shift and to explain why it has not occurred in other countries. Our explanation of policy continuity and change focuses on five related factors: the role of institutions, the agenda-setting context for policy choices, the balance of power within subsystems, the socioeconomic context and the role and transfer of ideas (Chapter 2).

What is tobacco policy?

Our first task is to identify what the policy response has been in each country or region. This is easier said than done. In fact, much of the public policy literature is dubious about reaching firm conclusions concerning the extent and speed of policy change (Cairney, 2012: 28–30). Further, the singular reference to tobacco *policy* may be misleading because it involves a wide range of *policies*. We also make the distinction between tobacco policy in general and tobacco *control* policy (the latter does not include measures, such as agricultural subsidies and trade agreements, designed to encourage the production of tobacco). As Table 1.2 suggests, tobacco policy can be broken down into at least five categories and 14 sub-categories of policy 'instruments' which are more precise

Table 1.2 Tobacco Policy Instruments

I. **Regulation (through legislation or voluntary agreements)**
   1. Tobacco advertising and promotion.
   2. The sale of tobacco, including domestic and export restrictions.
   3. Smoking in public places (second-hand smoke).
   4. Ingredients, such as the levels of tar in cigarettes.
   5. Customs enforcement on smuggling and counterfeit cigarettes.

II. **Finance**
   6. Taxation and other levies.
   7. Spending on directed health services, including smoking cessation services and nicotine replacement therapy.
   8. Economic incentives, including agricultural incentives and tax expenditures on arts and sports sponsorship by tobacco companies.
   9. Litigation against tobacco companies.

III. **Capacity building**
   10. Funding for community development programs and organisations to combat tobacco use.

IV. **Education**
   11. Health warning labels on cigarette and tobacco packs.
   12. Health education campaigns.

V. **Learning and information tools**
   13. Legislative hearings and executive reports.
   14. Funding scientific research.

Source: adapted from Studlar, 2005

and measurable (Schneider and Ingram, 1997; Jordan et al, 2000). The same basic types of policy (such as regulation, finance and education) can be identified in most country discussions, while some governments adopt some different strategies. For example, recourse to the courts is most notable in the US, replacing tobacco sponsorship of the arts and sports with health promotion foundation sponsorship (of the same events) using public health funds is most notable in Australia, and the UK has often placed great importance on setting smoking targets. This is also a fast-moving area, with recently proposed innovations including: restrictions on smoking in cars with children; limits on the ability of smokers to foster children; the refusal of public services to allow workers in homes where smoking occurs; and, the discouragement of diplomats and foreign embassies from attending events promoting tobacco.

Narratives of policy change

The implication of Table 1.2 is that when we seek to define tobacco policy and to gauge the speed and nature of change, we are faced with a range of measures that may give different answers. In some cases these contradictions are relatively clear, such as when the US and European Union (EU) subsidise the production of tobacco at the same time as restricting tobacco use. However, in many cases the implications of each measure are less clear. The classic problem is the use of voluntary agreements between governments and the tobacco industry which may undermine the development of more effective measures (Mamudu et al, 2008). While these were defended for decades in many countries (from the early post-war period) as the best way to regulate an activity that is not illegal, they became increasingly criticised by public health activists dissatisfied with their lack of scope and enforcement (Read, 1996; Pollay, 1994).

There also are problems in gauging the aim or seriousness of intent of some policies. For example, we may be more interested in health education spending not as an absolute figure, but as compared to the level of tobacco advertising, which has often been much higher. We may chart variations in the tone of health education messages, ranging from 'stating the facts' and letting individuals decide, to harm reduction (promoting 'low tar' cigarettes), to absolutism (there is no safe level of tobacco smoking – Berridge and Loughlin, 2005: 960; Cairney, 2007a: 50). We may question the implications of policies to allow tobacco companies to co-fund major scientific research into the links between smoking and illness. The establishment of a new unit within government may represent a reclassification rather than a redistribution of resources (Peters and Hogwood, 1985: 242). We may question the intent behind some policies, such as the use of taxation on tobacco to raise revenue rather than to regulate behaviour, or the ban on smoking on trains as a safety rather than a health measure. We may gauge the effect of policy in terms of the interests of tobacco companies. For example, policy to tackle the illicit trade of tobacco products or curb tobacco advertising may help maintain the market share of domestic tobacco firms. Finally, some policies may highlight the competition for power within or across different levels of government. For example, the funding of anti-smoking group Action on Smoking and Health (ASH) by the United Kingdom's (UK) Department of Health may reflect its desire to lobby or criticise the actions of other departments when it is not in the position to do so itself.

In this light, each empirical chapter outlines a wide range of policy instruments to construct careful analyses of tobacco policy, recognising that different narratives of policy change can be produced. It is possible to produce more than one narrative regarding the type, tempo and nature of change in the same policy issue. This may be particularly the case in a politically charged field, such as tobacco that often provides competing accounts by policymakers and other participants in the process (Cairney, 2007b: 75). These narratives may provide competing accounts of policy change based on the explanatory weight we attach to different policy instruments and the following factors:

- *Time*. Sabatier and Jenkins-Smith (1993) study policy change over a 'decade or more', while Baumgartner and Jones (2009) chart change over several decades. Others may study key episodes to identify crucial periods of change in a short period of time (Cairney, 2007a). The choice of timeframe is crucial to determine if policy change was incremental over a long period and/or if one short period was pivotal.
- *Organisational Focus*. A focus on the policy decisions made from the 'top-down' may exaggerate change by measuring policy formulation rather than implementation. Conversely, a 'bottom-up' study of implementation may find more limited change in particular organisations but not provide a systematic assessment of the use of policy instruments across government as a whole. The picture is blurred further when there is a sharing of policy responsibility by several levels or types of government, each with the ability to introduce different policy instruments and therefore complement or undermine the policies of their counterparts (see Chapter 2, *Who has responsibility for tobacco policy?*).
- *Expectations*. Evaluations of policy change are influenced by the degree of change we expect and therefore how fast change is in relation to this standard. This involves a combination of empirical and normative evaluations, particularly in the area of tobacco control, which is characterised by widespread disagreement between public health groups and tobacco interests. For example, public health interests bemoan the lack of policy progress on the 'most important preventable cause of premature mortality' (Lagiou and Trichopoulos, 2007: 121) while civil liberties groups may criticise the extent to which governments now interfere with individual behaviour (Leichter, 1991; Feldman and Bayer, 2004).
- *The Facts*. Disagreements extend to the facts of tobacco, including the date in which the scientific evidence on passive smoking was 'set in stone'

(Cairney, 2007a: 50) and therefore the time lag between government acceptance of the evidence and subsequent action. Similarly, the scientifically established relationship between smoking and illness has long been considered as the key battle ground in the fight against tobacco control although the tobacco industry now challenges the addictive nature of nicotine and the carcinogenic effect of tar in tobacco less frequently (ASH, 1998). The strategy of many public health activists has been to discredit any scientific evidence based on funding from tobacco sources. This, combined with contradictory interview evidence and unclear data on the nature and appropriateness of policy change, places the *politics of evidence* at centre stage in our study (indeed, even the language of tobacco is contentious, with some debate about the use of 'environmental tobacco smoke', ETS, or second-hand smoke, SHS, to describe passive smoking; we use 'SHS' throughout the book).
- *Power.* Our assessments of the nature of policy change are inextricably linked to power and the causes of change. For example, there is an increasing focus in the policy literature on the shift from what Heclo (1978: 94, 97) describes as the simple 'clubby days' of central government politics towards 'complex relationships' among 'issue networks', or collections of huge, politically active populations. However, this may produce two different responses – the network becomes more pluralistic and difficult to control, or subsystems become smaller, more specialised and more able to exclude the participation of a wider network (Baumgartner and Jones, 1993: 45; Read, 1996).

Each chapter draws on at least one of four discussions of policy change narratives:

1. *Incremental versus sudden or radical change?* In many chapters we identify profound policy change since the post-war period, but when and how did it occur? While flagship legislation (such as recent bans on smoking in public places) may signal a sea change in tobacco control, an overall description of policy instruments may qualify this picture. The shift from voluntary agreements towards legislation may be a complete break from the past (representing a shift in power from tobacco to public health interests) or a logical conclusion to previous policies (if the aim was to pilot and evaluate the success of voluntary measures before 'going nuclear').
2. *Voluntary versus enforced change?* While many sources of external pressure to introduce tobacco controls exist, we may also identify a pre-existing direction of travel, and willingness to learn, within the importing country. Further, the balance between domestic and external forces for change may vary by country. For example, the UK faced external pressure but often acted before (and went beyond the requirements of) the EU. In contrast, policy change in most developing countries has followed a recent global tobacco control agenda (although this does not necessarily suggest *enforced* change).

3. *Leaders or laggards?* Our selection of timeframes may determine the extent to which one country is, or has been, a leader or follower in tobacco control. Some countries may lead the way in, for example, the use of taxation, but follow the lead on smoking in public places.
4. *Agenda setting versus policy formulation and implementation?* Change in the global tobacco policy environment has put tobacco control on the agenda, but there is often a lag in policy development and implementation, particularly in developing countries, where only a few have developed comprehensive tobacco control laws.

Global tobacco policy?

There are two main qualifications to this idea that policy change is difficult to determine. First, we can identify a broad direction of travel among a high proportion of developed countries through similarities in the use and timing of many policy instruments. Most developed countries have gone from minimal tobacco control (or a contradictory tobacco policy, controlling consumption while at the same time encouraging tobacco production and manufacturing) to adopting a wide range of instruments. Most have: warning labels on cigarette packets; health education campaigns; advertising restrictions on TV and radio; taxation as a major policy instrument in the past 20–30 years; and, more recently, regulations on smoking in public and workplaces (Studlar, 2004).

As Chapter 3 recounts in more detail, early instruments consisted mainly of educational campaigns, health warning labels on tobacco products, and removal of tobacco advertising from broadcast and telecast airwaves. The easiest advertising and sponsorship restrictions to legislate and enforce have been those on direct television and radio advertising. Other forms of advertising, mainly print and billboard, were for a long time governed through voluntary agreements between governments and the tobacco industry in several countries. Problems of enforcement prompted an increasing number of countries to legislate on the topic, but often with delays and exceptions that were either explicitly permitted or overlooked. Point-of-sale advertising restrictions are a relatively new but growing phenomenon in many countries. Most advanced industrial democracies have either maintained or raised the sales age in recent years, and some have added substantial fines and better enforcement of these provisions. Controls on SHS (and hence passive smoking) in public places have been ever more stringent in recent years. Outright bans have been extended from selected enclosed public transportation to government buildings, places of employment, and even restaurants, bars, and gaming facilities as well as outdoor public places in some jurisdictions.

Only in the past three decades has taxation been considered a major instrument for reduced tobacco usage (combined with measures to limit cross-border smuggling) as well as a revenue producer. Rather expensive programmes to help people quit – including nicotine replacement therapy (NRT), prescribed smoking cessation medicine (such as Chantix) and counselling – have become more popular, but also raised complex issues regarding, for example, health insurance in many countries. Since the mid-1960s, mass media campaigns have been a major component of tobacco control programmes in several countries. In recent years these campaigns have become even more aggressive in their graphic depiction of the perils of smoking, reflecting an increase in the acceptance of the scientific evidence on smoking. There has also been selective litigation by individuals and governments against tobacco manufacturers in a small number of countries (most notably the US, Canada, and Australia), producing some specific penalties and regulatory decisions but also the release of tobacco industry documents through the discovery process. Thus, information from tobacco company files has become widely available to policymakers.

As a consequence of these and other measures, smoking behaviour is less common and the image of tobacco companies and their products has been tarnished (Studlar, 2007a: 1). From being a 'legal' and 'normal' part of everyday life and a relatively unexamined part of the political agenda, tobacco consumption became a public health issue that all governments in developed countries have to consider, however belatedly. The product, then the behaviour, and finally the tobacco industry became largely 'denormalised'; tobacco is more widely recognised as dangerous and addictive, while the industry is viewed increasingly as conspiratorial and law-breaking.

In some ways it is remarkable that the transformation has gone so far, considering the social and political status of tobacco in the 1950s and the legal, political, and social constraints on government regulation of business and individual behaviour in liberal capitalist states (see Feldman and Bayer, 2004). The fall in consumption and increase in government regulation of cigarettes have also occurred during an era (especially since the 1980s) of deregulation and international market liberalisation. The latter trend has led to governments, such as those in the US and Canada working to open markets for their cigarette producers abroad at the same time they increased regulation of tobacco consumption at home (but see Yang and Novotny, 2009 for recent restrictions in the US following the 'Doggett Amendment' in 1997). As Chapter 9 discusses, this combination of fragmented policies, which has led to tobacco manufacturers seeking smokers in the economically developing world to replace those lost in the developed world, also produced an international reaction: the negotiations that resulted in the adoption of the FCTC in 2003 and its ratification by 174 countries through September 2011 (Mamudu, 2008; see endnote 9 for the distinction between 174 parties and 168 signatories).

Second, there is also some evidence that public health activists are addressing the problem of policy change measurement by setting the agenda for tobacco control. One major attempt is the 'Tobacco Control Scale' (described further in Chapter 4) derived from a survey of activity in around 30 European countries by Joossens and Raw (2006, 2007, 2008, 2011; compare with Studlar, et al, 2011) on behalf of a range of public health organisations (including the

European Network for Smoking Prevention and the Association of European Cancer Leagues). It presents a tobacco control score based on the six main instruments promoted by the World Bank: 'price increases through higher taxes on cigarettes and other tobacco products; bans/restrictions on smoking in public and work places; better consumer information, including public information campaigns, media coverage, and publicising research findings; comprehensive bans on the advertising and promotion of all tobacco products, logos and brand names; large, direct health warning labels on cigarette boxes and other tobacco products; [and] treatment to help dependent smokers stop, including increased access to medications' (Joossens and Raw, 2007: 1; see also Jha and Chaloupka, 1999).

This approach has been extended globally by the WHO (2008) to argue that few countries are doing enough to protect their populations. In both cases, such networks are increasingly able to define the nature of the policy problem and gauge, in their terms, the extent to which individual countries are addressing it. This agenda appears to be increasingly successful. The most dramatic policy changes have now begun to occur at the global level over the first decade of the 21st century – the FCTC has been adopted and the 'Conference of the Parties' (COP, the governing body of the FCTC) continues to develop international norms for tobacco control through the guidelines for the FCTC provisions.

The structure of the book

Chapters 2 and 10 provide the theoretical focus and conclusions of the book. Chapter 2 introduces a wide range of theories of public policy and considers how best to combine their merits. It argues that the most useful approach is to break these theories down into their five major concerns: how policy is shaped by its institutional context; the agenda-setting process that underpins how policymakers understand and seek to solve policy problems; the balance of power between participants within policy networks or subsystems; the socio-economic context; and the role of ideas, from the production and dissemination of the scientific knowledge on smoking, to the spread and transfer of policy solutions.

Chapters 3–9 provide the empirical material, combining a focus on in-depth case study with broad comparative analysis. Chapter 3 outlines the main policy developments across the globe, with a time-line of major events since the 1950s. It identifies, in developed countries, a profound shift of approach: from minimal and often contradictory tobacco policy in the post-war period towards a more comprehensive tobacco control policy in many countries. However, as Chapters 4–7 demonstrate, the timing and substance of policy varies significantly. Chapter 4 focuses on policy developments in Europe, outlining a clear picture of leaders and laggards in tobacco control that has prompted the EU to exert influence in the name of policy harmonisation. Chapter 5 focuses on the UK, a country that was once a policy laggard but now has one of the most restrictive tobacco policy regimes in the world. Examining the UK as a case study allows us to track in detail how and why policy has changed so profoundly. We then devote a full chapter (Chapter 6) to the unusual US experience – a country that often leads the way in the production of the scientific evidence, and influences the global tobacco policy agenda, is also a country that lags behind some others in the comprehensive adoption of tobacco control instruments. In Chapter 7 we compare the policies of three English-speaking developed countries that lead in some dimensions of tobacco control (Australia, New Zealand and Canada) to those in Japan, with perhaps the most limited tobacco control of any developed country.

With the exception of Japan and perhaps a few laggards in Europe, the developed country experience contrasts with that of developing countries, as discussed in Chapter 8. This has prompted a range of countries, individuals and organisations to promote global tobacco control, in the form of the FCTC, to bridge the gap between developed and developing country policy (Chapter 9). Until such global developments, policy change has been either slow or non-existent in most developing countries. As a result, we see two broad processes of policy change: a slow but significant process caused by shifts in domestic policy processes in developed countries, largely followed by a more recent and quicker process, at least in terms of policy choices, prompted by international pressure in developing countries.

Chapter 10 brings together the theoretical framework and empirical conclusions to consider how best to interpret and explain global tobacco policy change. It considers theories and approaches that address one or more aspects of the policy processes we describe – institutionalism, governance, federalism – and outlines in more detail the three main theories of the policy process that attempt to explain the interaction between the five causal factors we identify – punctuated equilibrium theory (as presented by Baumgartner and Jones, 2009), the advocacy coalition framework and multiple streams analysis. Chapter 10 suggests that a combination of theories may be most useful in our analysis of the policy processes of developed countries. In most cases, consideration of policy transfer is necessary to gain a full understanding of the developing country picture. In other words, we may be moving towards an era of 'global governance' in which the domestic policies of countries are supplemented by international agreements that all signatories are expected to fulfil.

2
Theories of Policy Change

In this chapter we outline the value of a framework based on political science theories. In particular, we promote the use of multiple theories as a means to consider different perspectives and to highlight complementary sources of evidence. However, our approach immediately throws up two problems. First, there are at least three ways to apply multiple theories when engaging in empirical research: produce a hybrid model synthesising the most valuable aspects of each theory; use each theory independently to highlight different aspects of the policy process; or establish the extent to which these theories are contradictory and engage in a 'policy shootout' (Eller and Krutz, 2009) to determine the best approach (Cairney, 2012: 266). Second, a full analysis and application of each theory is beyond the scope of one book, particularly one that presents so much empirical data on a global scale. Therefore, we must find a way to derive insights from a range of theories under a single, more manageable, research framework.

Our solution to these problems is twofold. First, in this chapter, we break these theories down into their component parts to focus on what John (2003: 488) calls, 'the relationship between the five core causal processes'. We present a modified account of John's (2003: 488) focus on 'institutions, networks, socioeconomic process, choices, and ideas'. While John (2003) uses the term 'choices' to explore the value of rational choice theory, we use it to explore the agenda-setting context in which policy choices are made. We identify the key policy choices in each empirical chapter (in the *What is Policy?* sections) and consider how they relate to the way that the policy problem was framed or understood by policymakers. Our aim is to examine the relationships among five main explanatory factors – institutions, agenda-setting, networks, socioeconomic and ideas – and to use them as a focus to guide the empirical chapters. Second, in the concluding chapter, we draw on the empirical evidence to inform our theoretical concerns. We consider how the main theories of public policy would explain our empirical results and return to the idea that their explanations may be complementary or contradictory.

This approach helps provide a comprehensive account of policymaking. When we identify policy choices, we seek to illuminate the agenda-setting process that underpins how policymakers understand and seek to solve policy problems. We identify the role of individual policymakers, but also situate their actions within an institutional context and consider the rules followed by organisations, such as bureaucracies, interest groups (within policy networks or subsystems) and political parties (although tobacco is a non-partisan issue in many countries). In particular, we consider which organisations have responsibility for policy and how this affects the rules of policymaking. In most cases, we identify a shift in policy responsibility from one department to another, changing the rules of consultation and information processing within central government. In some cases, we also highlight a degree of shared responsibility between different levels of government, prompting to some extent the need for rules of intergovernmental relations, but also highlighting 'multi-level governance' (MLG). The term 'MLG' describes a situation in which power is dispersed from central government to other levels of government and non-governmental actors, blurring the dividing lines between formal policy responsibility and informal influence. In other words, several venues or organisations may be responsible for, or able to influence, aspects of tobacco policy; this includes international organisations to coordinate policy across many countries. We highlight the importance of socioeconomic influences on these actors, such as shifting public opinion and the economic costs of policy decisions, as well as factors specific to tobacco studies, such as smoking prevalence and the value of the tobacco trade to the economy. Finally, we consider the role of ideas, focusing in particular on, first, the promotion and acceptance within government of the scientific evidence on the health dangers of tobacco use and exposure to SHS and, second, the transfer of policy solutions from one political system to another.

The plan of Chapter 2 is as follows. First, it explores the key questions regarding tobacco policy that can be derived from the political science literature. Second, it identifies the main ways in which public policy theories conceptualise policy change. Both sections set the context for our substantive chapters, which use these insights to guide empirical research.

Global tobacco policy and the key questions in political science

This section produces a series of questions to guide the remainder of our study:

- *Institutions*: who has responsibility for tobacco policy?
- *Agendas*: how is the problem framed and how important is tobacco control as a policy issue?
- *Networks*: has there been a shift in power among pressure participants?[2]

- *Socioeconomic factors*: what is the role of social and economic factors and have they contributed to shifts in power and agenda-status?
- *Ideas*: what is the role of medical or scientific knowledge and to what extent is policy driven by the transfer of ideas?

Institutions: Who has responsibility for tobacco policy?

'New institutionalism' is the umbrella term to describe a range of approaches to the study of institutions, including historical, normative, and constructivist institutionalism. A common aim is to associate institutions with regular patterns of behaviour and the rules, norms, practices and relationships that influence such behaviour (Cairney, 2012: 69). The aim is to link policy outcomes to the rules associated either with a single institution or, in most cases, the multiple institutions that could influence a policy's progress. The rules associated with institutions can be formal, such as the constitution of a political system, or informal, based perhaps on a common understanding of how actors should behave.

For example, Lijphart (1999: 2) highlights the role of formal institutional structures by arguing that there are two basic models of democratic political system design: those that concentrate power in the hands of a few who claim to represent the many (majoritarian) and those that 'share, disperse, and limit power' (consensus). In a majoritarian democracy the first-past-the-post voting system can result in a majority of seats in the legislature to a party with only a plurality of the popular vote. Lijphart (1999: 2–3) associates majoritarian democracies with an 'exclusive, competitive and adversarial' mentality in which parties compete within parliament, interest groups are more likely to compete with each other than cooperate, and governments are more likely to impose policy from the top down than to seek consensus. In a consensus democracy, the proportional electoral system is unlikely to produce an overall majority of legislators for one party; power is dispersed across parties, encouraging the formation of coalitions based on common aims. This spirit of 'inclusiveness, bargaining and compromise' extends to group-government relations, with groups more likely to cooperate with each other and governments more willing to form broad corporatist alliances.

However, pluralism or corporatism are not the inevitable consequences of certain voting systems, and the group-government system (and the policy outcomes they tend to produce) is generally a more open empirical question. In this context, we may merely be interested in the specific consequences of different arrangements. For example, pluralist systems may have a more open competition for group influence on government than in corporatist systems, where the close alliance between governments and a few major, internally unified producer groups (usually business and labour, sometimes agriculture) makes it difficult for new groups to access the inner circle. Studies of corporatism in Europe have found that these relationships between government and groups often persist for long periods (Siaroff, 1999; Lijphart, 1999). A corporatist structure enhances the institutional centralisation of power and normally hinders the progress of outside interests and new agendas. Nevertheless, in cases where all interests agree on the need for change, new policies can be put into place more swiftly than under more pluralist arrangements (Lundqvist, 1980; Green-Pedersen and Wolfe, 2009).

Historical institutionalism focuses on path dependency. When a commitment to an institution and its associated policies have been established and resources have been devoted to them, over time these arrangements produce 'increasing returns' and effectively become increasingly difficult to change (Pierson, 2000). Therefore, institutions, and the practices they encourage, may remain stable for long periods of time. Since institutions develop in different ways in different countries, historical institutionalism tends to identify 'policy continuities over time within countries and policy variation across countries' (Thelen and Steinmo, 1992: 10). Similarly, normative institutionalism highlights the norms, principles and standards that are followed and passed on by members of institutions (March and Olsen, 1984: 739). The norms of particular institutions are caused in part by 'internal dynamics' (rather than just the external environment and the problems they were designed to address), also suggesting that different institutions in different political systems produce different behaviour (March and Olsen, 1996: 256). Overall, a comparative focus on institutions may help explain why tobacco policy varies across political systems.

The main complication to such arguments is that institutions are not entirely fixed and predictable. Further, formally different political systems may produce similar policy styles and similar outcomes (Richardson, 1982). Although the political structures and electoral systems of each country vary, they may also share a 'standard operating procedure' based on two factors: an incremental approach to policy and an attempt to reach consensus with interest groups, not to impose decisions. The latter is based on two factors common to political systems. First, the size and scope of the state is so large that it is in danger of becoming unmanageable. Consequently, its component parts are broken down into policy sectors and sub-sectors, with power spread across government and shared with interest groups. Ministers (or other policymakers) and senior civil servants devolve the bulk of decisionmaking to less senior officials who consult with groups and exchange access for resources, such as expertise. Second, this exchange is based on the 'logic of consultation' with the most affected interests; it encourages group 'ownership' of policy and maximises governmental knowledge of possible problems and solutions (Richardson and Jordan, 1979; Jordan and Maloney, 1997; see also section entitled *Has there been a shift in power within policy networks?* below).

We may also be interested in institutional differences *within* political systems; policy similarities or differences may depend as much on the choice of institution (for example, a particular government department with its own rules of decisionmaking) within a political system as much as on the system itself. Our analysis of policy instruments in Chapter 1 suggests that tobacco policy responsibility may extend to a variety of levels, types, and different departments of government, each with its own clientele, rules and norms of behaviour. In particular, we may identify in tobacco policy a recent tendency for policy responsibility to shift from treasury and trade departments to departments of health (Chapter 3). This is a crucial development, because the norm for health departments in many countries is to treat tobacco as a pressing health problem and to develop relatively close links to medical and public health professions at the expense of links with tobacco companies. It suggests that we can use a focus on institutions within political systems to identify *common* policy outcomes.

The idea of multiple institutional involvement and 'venue' shift is addressed in four main ways in the literature. First, the advocacy coalition framework (ACF) places the policy issue at centre stage and situates actors at all levels and types of government within a policy subsystem (Sabatier and Jenkin-Smith, 1993; Weible et al, 2009). The ACF is based on a critique of the policy cycle literature's artificial distinctions between stages of the policy process (agenda-setting, formulation, adoption, implementation, evaluation) and construction of artificial boundaries regarding the stages at which these actors become involved. Instead, the ACF divides or groups actors together according to their beliefs (rather than interests), which represent the basis for their action. Beliefs act as the glue which binds actors together within coalitions. In turn, different coalitions compete with each other to secure policy outcomes consistent with their beliefs. For example, we may divide tobacco policy into pro- and anti-tobacco control coalitions (Sato, 1999a, 1999b; Farquharson, 2003; Cairney, 2007a) and each coalition may have supporters (or their influence may vary) at multiple levels and in different types of government.

Second, punctuated equilibrium theory and MLG examine the extent to which different actors become involved and how this involvement changes over time. Baumgartner and Jones (1993: 43) argue that in most cases there is no natural jurisdiction for policy problems and no 'iron clad logic' for an issue to be considered at a particular level of government. It is also common for responsibility to shift among venues (1993: 32–3). This flexibility provides the potential for interest groups, dissatisfied with policy in one venue, to pursue 'aggressive venue shopping' (Jones and Baumgartner, 2005) in the search for a receptive audience. For example, in the US, the strongest tobacco control measures before the 1990s were achieved through semi-independent central agencies, states, and local governments; only later did some organisations within the core central government act as well (Studlar, 2002).

The potential to venue shop is increasingly apparent in Europe, as the vertical power of the EU in relation to member states becomes more significant and the horizontal power of central EU institutions remains fragmented. The more supra-state oriented institutions, such as the European Parliament (EP), the European Court of Justice (ECJ), and the European Commission have demonstrated a high level of independence from the more state-centred ones, the Council of Ministers and the European Council (Asare et al, 2009: 84). Theories of MLG have been developed to describe the fragmented nature of EU public policy. In the absence of a clear EU constitution, the separation of powers is often unclear and the overlap of jurisdictions has developed incrementally over time. Thus, we have not only a range of governments and organisations responsible for different policy instruments, but also unclear boundaries between policy responsibilities, particularly in tobacco where: (a) there is a degree of horizontal competition to control policy outcomes; (b) the EU now shares responsibility for issues, such as health warnings, advertising, ingredients and taxation, that were formerly the sole responsibility of member states; and (c) member states have begun to devolve authority for some policy instruments to sub-central governments while maintaining some amount of central control (Asare et al, 2009: 94).

MLG draws on the policy networks literature that stresses the role of interest groups and the porous boundaries between governmental and non-governmental action. This blurring of authority is extended to the roles of government actors at various levels, with informal influence and variations in the propensity to exercise power often more relevant than formal jurisdictions. Like neofunctionalism (Haas, 1975), it contends that states and international organisations are caught in a web of interdependence that allows supra-state organisations and affected interests to shape policy. It establishes the variable significance of three tiers of actors in decisionmaking – supra-state, central state and sub-state – depending on degrees of Europeanisation, the strength of the regional policy agenda, and the existing allocation of policy responsibilities entrenched in the laws of member states (Marks, 1993; Mamudu and Studlar, 2009). MLG processes can be explored empirically in two contrasting ways: as a relatively stable set of relationships, with policy responsibility allocated according to territory and overlaps between jurisdictions minimised (Type 1) or as a relatively complex and fluid process, with the delegation of responsibility related to the nature of the policy rather than territory (Type 2) (Hooghe and Marks, 2003).

Third, the literature on federalism and intergovernmental relations (IGR) places greater emphasis on the means employed to *resolve* issues of overlap. It highlights country-level differences according to institutional structures, power and the recourse to established authority and formal resolution (Agranoff, 2004). This includes a discussion, across different levels of government, of the role of institutions (for example, a reliance on executives rather than legislatures or the courts to resolve IGR issues is common in parliamentary systems), political parties (ranging from Canada with a devolved party structure and territorially-differentiated party competition to Germany, which has integrated parties and formal links to coordinate policy – Horgan, 2004) and the courts (general supreme courts are used in the US, Canada and Australia, while specialised constitutional courts are employed in Germany and Belgium – Watts, 2007).

While variations in political structures across countries may complicate international comparisons, there have been attempts to treat political systems, such as the EU as quasi-federal systems. For example, Kelemen's (2004) argument is twofold. First, the vertical relationship (or the 'politics of competence') is similar in most federal and quasi-federal systems: policymaking takes place at the federal (or central) level, while the responsibility for most implementation rests with the states (or sub-central authorities). Second, the extent to which the centre allows sub-central authorities the freedom to implement federal policy (the 'politics of discretion') depends on the levels of horizontal fragmentation within the central government. A highly fragmented system 'encourages an adversarial, litigious approach' (2004: 2). The competition among institutions makes them more protective of their authority and more likely to write detailed laws for the provinces to follow ('regulatory federalism'). In contrast, a concentration of power at the centre encourages 'discretionary federalism' or a 'less judicialised' approach (2004: 2). Written laws are broad, allowing flexibility in application by lower-level jurisdictions. Thus, according to Kelemen, the policymaking process is centralised in federal systems while the implementation process varies, depending on the separation of, and competition among, institutions (compare with Studlar, 2010 and Asare et al, 2009).

Fourth, issues of policy responsibility, resolution and governance may be complicated by the wider international dimension. Indeed, a key concern in both the policy and international relations literature is whether we are entering an era of 'global governance'. Global governance, 'refers to collective efforts to identify, understand, or address worldwide problems that go beyond the capacities of individual states to solve; it reflects the capacity of the international system ... to provide government-like services' (Weiss, 2000: 257; see also Finkelstein, 1995; Slaughter, 2004). We explore these various uses of the term 'governance' – to describe (a) unclear boundaries between formal policy responsibility and informal influence at multiple levels of government; and (b) a shift of emphasis from government and authority, to governance, persuasion and negotiation – throughout most of the empirical chapters, before reconsidering its meaning and value in Chapter 10.

An important related term is 'international regime complexity'. While a huge number of 'regimes' (or sets of rules to be adhered to by their signatories) have developed to coordinate policy activity across a range of countries, they are marked by the absence of hierarchy, 'making it harder to resolve where political authority over an issue resides' (Alter and Meunier, 2009: 13). International regime complexity thus describes, 'the presence of nested, partially overlapping, and parallel international regimes that are not hierarchically ordered' (2009: 13). In the absence of such formal authority, we may be interested not only in how each regime developed but also how it can possibly be enforced, as well as the extent to which a range of parallel regimes complement or compromise each other (2009: 14). Such enforcement may derive primarily from the establishment of norms and, in some cases, the threats of powerful countries (most notably the US) to punish departure from them (Axelrod, 1986). Yet, the study of international regimes followed an identification of the diminishing ability of individual states to exercise power, at least when we shift our attention from military power to economic and social issues in which there is greater interdependence (Krasner, 1983: vii). This suggests that while international regimes are increasingly important and may demonstrate that some countries are leaders and others followers, the effect of the collective process is difficult to predict and, more importantly, difficult to track empirically when we move from a study of rule adoption to implementation (Cairney, 2012: 260). In Chapter 9 we explore this process of international cooperation through the WHO Framework Convention on Tobacco Control (FCTC).

Agendas: How is tobacco framed? How important is tobacco control as a policy issue?

Agenda-setting refers to, 'an ongoing competition among issue proponents to gain the attention of media professionals, the public, and policy elites' (Dearing and Roger, 1996: 1). It includes what Kingdon (1984: 3–4) calls the 'governmental agenda' (the problems that decisionmakers 'are paying some serious attention at any given time') and the 'decision agenda' (the problems 'that are up for an active decision') (we consider the public agenda and public opinion below). Agenda-setting can be summed up with two statements:

1. There is an almost unlimited amount of policy problems that *could* reach the top of the policy agenda. Yet, very few issues do.
2. There are many potential solutions to those policy problems. Yet, few policy solutions will be considered (Cairney, 2012: 183).

Problem definition is central to both cases. It refers to 'what we choose to identify as public issues and how we think and talk about these concerns' (Rochefort and Cobb, 1994: vii). Problems do not receive the most attention simply because they are the most important or immediate. There are no objective indicators to determine which problems are the most deserving of our attention. Further, the ability of decisionmakers to receive and act on information about the severity of policy problems is imperfect. Instead attention is marked by periods of negative feedback, in which issues are ignored, and positive feedback, in which issues receive unusual attention (Jones and Baumgartner, 2005: 8). Attention is linked strongly to the ability of issue proponents to convince enough people that 'their' issues are the most worthy of discussion (or, as we discuss in Chapter 1, to make sure that certain issues do *not* receive attention). This may not involve a battle over the accuracy of 'facts', but the direction of attention to other facts that support a rival policy image (Baumgartner and Jones, 1993: 107–8, 113). Attention-grabbing strategies draw on the ability to 'frame' issues (to define a policy's image; how issues are portrayed and categorised), the assignment of blame (or identification of a problem's cause and solution), the measure of the size of the problem and the ability to point to a policy crisis which requires immediate resolution (Cairney, 2012: 186; Larsen, 2008).

We can detect two related trends to suggest that the issue of tobacco control has risen on the policy agenda. First, in most developed countries, smoking behaviour has become denormalised and therefore more likely to be viewed as a problem to be solved. Second, denormalisation is linked to an increasing ability of medical and public health groups to frame tobacco as a health problem. Widespread acceptance of the scientific evidence on smoking and, more recently, SHS (Feldman and Bayer, 2004: 1) has shifted the post-war debate from the uncertain links between smoking and illness towards: (a) government acceptance of the evidence but uncertainty about the need to act; to, more recently, (b) the question: given that we need to act, what tobacco controls work best (Cairney, 2009a: 473)? For many developing countries, the question is increasingly becoming: where can we find resources to build capacity and implement tobacco control policies? In many countries we can track the symbiotic relationship between policy choices and problem definition: the reframing of tobacco sets the new context for increased tobacco control, and policy changes related to tobacco control reinforce the definition of tobacco as a health issue.

For example, Baumgartner and Jones (1993: 114, 210) identify in the US in the early 20th century a positive policy image for tobacco, based on the economic benefits of production (in agriculture, exports, jobs, revenues). Tobacco consumption was high and media coverage was very low and generally positive, particularly during and immediately after World War II when smoking had a glamorous image. However, from the 1950s there was significant 'issue expansion', with anti-tobacco groups increasingly setting the media agenda with a negative policy image. Tobacco consumption began to fall from the 1950s, then the 1964 Surgeon General's report, combined with a huge rise in the number of negative articles on tobacco, cemented a new image based on ill-health. Congressional attention followed in the mid-1970s, with health committee hearings outnumbering agriculture meetings, and a range of public health groups increasingly involved and able to reframe the debate (1993: 114, 210). By the 1980s, this new image was pursued through a series of high profile court cases and by innovative states providing best practices and the scope for policy diffusion (Studlar, 2002). Broadly similar agenda-setting trends can be identified in other countries, such as the UK, where a series of scientific reports combined with changing government and private sector responses shifted the image of tobacco from positive to negative (Cairney, 2007a, 2007b).

This trend can also now be identified in developing countries, where domestic and international governmental institutions and non-governmental organisations have focused resources on promoting the negative image of tobacco.

This rise in negative attention to the issue leads to a reappraisal of the positive aspects. For example, the economic benefits have become undermined by a focus on rising healthcare costs and decreasing worker productivity (Baumgartner and Jones, 1993: 114). Similarly, the evidence on passive smoking (exposure to SHS) has shifted attention from the 'right to smoke' to the 'right to clean air' as a justification for smoking bans. As we discuss in Chapter 3, this agenda has been furthered by public health groups drawing on morality arguments to highlight the need to prioritise tobacco on the policy agenda; to argue that it would be wrong not to act immediately to halt preventable deaths.

Networks: Has there been a shift in power within policy networks?

This change in problem definition and attention can be linked to a shift in the balance of power among subsystem participants. The literature on 'policy networks' or 'subsystems' links periods of policy continuity to stable group-government relations and, in particular, the ability of some groups to dominate consultation with government at the expense of others. The European term 'policy community' ('iron' or 'cozy' triangle in the US) often suggests a close, stable and consensual relationship between a small number of groups and government (Jordan and Maloney, 1997). In contrast, 'issue network' suggests a wider variety of links between the government and many groups, in which there is less agreement and less stability (Heclo, 1978). 'Issue network' captures what Heclo (1978: 94) describes as an end to the 'clubby days of Washington politics' and Jordan (1981: 96–100) depicts, in other countries, as a shift from corporatism, in which group-government relations are centralised and exclusive, towards a more fragmented system with more policy participants. Issues which were once 'quietly managed by a small group of insiders' have become 'controversial and politicised' (Heclo, 1978: 105; Cairney, 2012: 180). Combined, we have two different pictures of the policy environment (Marsh and Rhodes, 1992). On the one hand, it is a source of instability: populated by many participants, potentially with different values, perceptions and preferences (Sabatier, 2007a: 3–4). On the other, groups often share close and stable relationships with government officials, often operating out of the public spotlight.

Contemporary theories seek to capture and explain these contrasting pictures. For example, Baumgartner and Jones (1993: 6) argue that certain groups have established a relatively insulated policy community by maintaining a 'policy monopoly', or a dominant image of the policy problem. This requires a common adherence to the same image and an ability to exclude groups who do not adhere. When government officials and certain interest groups form relationships, they recognise the benefits, such as group-government stability and policy continuity, of attempting to insulate their decisions from the wider political process (Richardson and Jordan, 1979). In some accounts, this stability hinges on socialisation. Inclusion within the policy community depends on the gaining of personal trust, through an awareness of, willingness to follow, and reproduction of the 'rules of the game'. The learning process involves immersion within a 'common culture', in which there exists a great deal of agreement on the nature of and solutions to policy problems (Wilks and Wright, 1987: 302–3; McPherson and Raab, 1988: 55). This explains the insulation of these communities from the wider political process. First, policies are disaggregated to a level at which few actors are interested or have the time and resources to become involved. Second, a 'rule of the game' is that participants resolve issues within the network rather than seeking change elsewhere. Participants know that while they may not agree with all decisions taken, it is counterproductive to highlight grievances in other venues where involvement by other actors may dilute their influence. Third, the lack of wider political interest is furthered by defining issues as humdrum or technical, often because they appear to have been 'solved' (Baumgartner and Jones, 1993, 2009); a technical focus, in which only the experts need be involved to help implement policy, also limits the ability of other groups to participate (Jordan and Maloney, 1997).

If the attempt to maintain a policy monopoly is unsuccessful, the participants cannot insulate the decisionmaking process from a wider audience, and there is effective competition to define the policy's image. More groups become involved, with greater competition for access to government and consequent political instability. The breakdown of a policy monopoly involves movement away from a closed policy community (or cozy triangle) towards an issue network. The ability of groups to set the policy agenda and control the policy image is linked strongly to their ability to restrict participation. Those excluded from monopolies have an interest in challenging the policy image. This may come from within, by ensuring that new ideas or evidence force a shift in government attention. If that attention is stifled, groups attempt to expand the scope of conflict and promote their definition of a problem to a more sympathetic venue. Policy change follows a mutually-reinforcing process of increased attention, venue shift and shifting policy images. As people come to understand the nature of a policy problem in a different way, then more groups become interested and involved. The more external involvement there is, then the greater likelihood of a further shift of the policy image, as new ideas are discussed and different policy solutions are proposed by a larger array of participants.

Chapter 3 identifies this broad shift within tobacco policy networks in most developed countries, while Chapter 5 outlines the process in detail for the case study of the UK. Tobacco company dominance in the first half of the 20th century has been challenged successfully by public health groups. Indeed, the latter now often dominate group-government relations, particularly since health departments have become more central to the tobacco policy process. This is also the case at the international level. The formal exclusion of pro-tobacco groups during the FCTC negotiations contrasts with the much stronger status that tobacco promotion groups enjoy within many developing countries.

What is the role of social and economic factors in this process?

The term 'policy conditions' refers to the nature or structure of the policy environment and hence the specific problems that policymakers face (Cairney, 2012: 111). The policy environment may represent what policymakers take into account when identifying problems and deciding how to address them. Relevant contextual factors include a political system's size, demographic structure, economy and mass attitudes and behaviour. While few accounts suggest that the policy environment determines policy, there is a long history of studies, based on systems theory, that employ a simple model in which socio-economic factors produce demands that feed into the political system (see Blomquist, 2007: 266). For example, more urbanised populations may demand more social welfare policies, while wealthier jurisdictions are better able to afford them (Dawson and Robinson, 1963: 285). In tobacco policy, a number of socioeconomic conditions may help explain both global policy convergence (when the context of the problem is similar) and divergence (when it is different). Possible factors include:

- Public behaviour, including the prevalence of smoking and overall consumption (as a whole, but also disaggregated by demographics, such as gender, age and class).
- The economic benefits of tobacco, including the number of jobs and tax revenues (which may be undermined by the illicit trade of tobacco), and the economic burdens caused by smoking.
- Public attitudes to smoking, smokers, and tobacco companies (and their knowledge of, and reactions to, tobacco control policies).

As a rule of thumb, we would expect the willingness of policymakers to introduce tobacco control to be relatively high when: smoking prevalence and consumption is low; tobacco provides a dwindling source of tax revenue and jobs (and the health and economic burdens of tobacco are high); and, when opinion polls highlight a reduction in public opposition to tobacco control (or a more general trend towards the 'denormalisation' of smoking and its proponents). As Chapter 3 discusses, this development can be identified in most developed countries (although the effect may be stronger in countries, such as the UK and weaker in countries, such as Germany and Spain), but is less marked in developing countries with high levels of smoking and, in some cases, a strong tobacco industry presence.

Indeed, socioeconomic and policy change in developed countries may have produced unanticipated consequences in other countries. For example, a significant drop in tobacco consumption in developed countries, combined with increasing tobacco control measures, was followed by attempts by tobacco companies to market tobacco consumption more strongly in developing countries. This shift, combined with fewer tobacco control measures, helps explain why smoking prevalence in developing countries rose consistently from the 1970s to 1990s while in developed countries it has fallen since the 1980s (Jha, 1999: 14–15). We may also identify differences in smoking prevalence according to the life cycle of smoking habits among populations (see Chapter 1 on the tobacco epidemic model).

In each case, the nature of the problem changes over time, presenting policymakers with a new context in which to make policy choices. In developed countries, the changing socioeconomic context (reduced smoking, reduced tobacco tax revenues, public opinion more in favour of tobacco control) may be particularly advantageous for pro-tobacco control groups. In developing countries, these changes may not have occurred (at least to the same extent) and pro-tobacco control groups may have fewer socioeconomic resources on which to draw.

Ideas: What is the role of knowledge and beliefs in this process? How much policy transfer has taken place?

When we seek to explain how actors exercise power, we also need to examine the role of ideas – or the knowledge, beliefs, world views, policy solutions, language and ideologies shared and promoted by policy participants (for a discussion of the wide range of definitions of 'ideas', see Cairney, 2012: 223; Campbell, 2002; John, 1998: 144; 2003: 487). Policy choices follow argumentation and persuasion, and the substance or status of ideas may represent a key resource for participants. Similarly, if policymakers need a consistent political message to command support and motivate those who carry out public policy, then the 'vision' or set of ideas underpinning that message is crucial (Cairney, 2012: 223; Majone, 1989: 2; Kingdon, 1984: 131; Hall, 1993: 291; Reich, 1988: 4). As Cairney (2009a: 474) suggests, the role of ideas seems particularly strong in tobacco policy. It is tempting when conducting research on tobacco control to treat ideas as strong independent variables; tobacco control as a policy solution represents an 'an idea whose time has come', an 'irresistible movement that sweeps over our politics and our society' (Kingdon, 1984: 1) or a 'virus' (Richardson, 2000) which infected and destroyed previously closed policy communities.

Yet, ideas are rarely discussed purely as independent variables without some qualification regarding their *use* by participants and the *receptivity* to ideas within political systems. In particular, we demonstrate that ideas, such as the scientific knowledge on tobacco-related ill-health, were used to challenge closed policy communities and to alter the balance of power from pro-tobacco to public health interests. While Chapter 3 suggests that this process has taken place within developed countries, and that the scientific evidence on smoking and passive smoking is now generally accepted by their governments, it also highlights the significant time lag between acceptance of the ideas (or, in other words, the successful dissemination of the knowledge that helped change the beliefs of policymakers) and the policy changes that followed.

The promotion of tobacco knowledge is increasingly performed internationally by an 'epistemic community', or a network of knowledge-based experts, such as medical practitioners and public health officials providing the scientific basis for tobacco control (Haas, 1992: 3; Mamudu, 2008; Mamudu et al, 2011b), combining with a much broader 'advocacy coalition' (Sabatier and Jenkins-Smith, 1993) of anti-smoking interest groups, public officials and interested individuals (Farquharson, 2003; Cairney, 2007b; Mamudu and Glantz, 2009). Such activity provides the impetus to reframe the image of tobacco policy and contribute to a new world view on tobacco, with the idea of tobacco control taken for granted and the agenda shifting to solutions rather than problems. In short, we may identify, internationally, a process of denormalisation, followed by the establishment of new norms in favour of tobacco control. These norms increasingly place limits on policy debate. In other words, it becomes more difficult to argue successfully that tobacco control should be limited. This international shift focuses our attention on 'policy transfer', an umbrella term used to describe the policy convergence, diffusion and lesson-drawing that take place among different jurisdictions.

The transfer literature seeks to explain why policy change occurs and to gauge the extent to which change is common throughout the world. The diffusion literature originally asked why some US states innovate and others emulate (Walker, 1969), but comparable processes of diffusion can be studied in other political systems, particularly the EU with strong supranational institutions to foster learning and diffusion. Policy convergence refers to the evidence for similarities in policy across jurisdictions over time. The literature invites us to consider what causes this convergence and who pursues such similarities (Bennett, 1991). This *may* involve policy transfer from one jurisdiction to another. If so, we may ask a further series of questions, including: is the transfer of policy voluntary; which actors are involved; how much policy is transferred; and how do we explain variations in levels of transfer (Dolowitz and Marsh, 1996)? The answers vary. Transfer can involve a wide range of international actors, or a small professional network. It can relate to the wholesale transfer of policy programmes, broad ideas, minor administrative changes or even the decision to learn negative lessons and *not* to follow another jurisdiction. As a result, policy transfer is often viewed as a vague term rather than a theory of action, producing the need for us to demonstrate in detail if, how and why transfer took place.

As Chapter 3 suggests, the level of global tobacco policy transfer seems impressive; there is a high degree of international policy change driven by the promotion and sharing of ideas. Policy diffusion is a well known phenomenon in tobacco control. Faced with an unprecedented issue, jurisdictions within countries (Berry and Berry, 1999; Shipan and Volden, 2006; Cairney, 2007a) and across countries (Studlar, 2002, 2005, 2007; Farquharson, 2003) learn from each other and apply the experiences of others to their problems. This may occur through government-to-government policy transfer or lesson drawing through the work of epistemic communities, non-governmental advocacy groups, and policy entrepreneurs. Diffusion can occur in three ways: top-down, horizontal (among similar jurisdictions), and bottom-up (Mossberger, 2000; Shipan and Volden, 2006; Studlar, 2007).

However, the response by individual countries to the international tobacco control agenda varies markedly, according to the vested economic interests, cultural practices, institutions and other political factors in each (Studlar, 2004, 2007). In most countries there are significant time lags between the proposal and acceptance of scientific knowledge and the introduction of solutions; some countries have become 'leaders' and others 'laggards'. Thus, our focus shifts from the inevitability of the transfer of ideas to: (a) the role of policy promotion; (b) the conditions that have to be met before a country is receptive to policy transfer; and (c) the positive and negative roles that existing ideas play in this process. In other words, while new ideas may represent a driver for policy change, they must contend with an established set of ideas that may limit their effect.

This relationship between *new* and *established* ideas is a key concern of academic public policy literature. It is perhaps captured best by Hall (1993), who highlights the ability of ideas to *cause* or *inhibit* first, second and third order changes in policy. First order change is incremental (changes in policy calibrations), with current policy based on the lessons of past decisions. Second order change is also based on adapting to past experience while maintaining overall goals, but with major changes in the prioritisation of policy instruments. Third order change refers to a radical, not incremental, shift in policy, involving profound changes to the way that the policy is understood and, therefore, how policy instruments are used to address it. This is rare and can be compared to 'paradigm shift' (Kuhn, 1962). A paradigm is a set of ideas that is so accepted that it is 'taken for granted and unamenable to scrutiny' (Hall, 1993: 279). Third order change involves a major alteration in the way that policymakers think and act. It often follows significant policy failures that command the attention of the wider political arena, call into question current thinking and undermine the position of its advocates. This produces a shift of power within government, with new personnel taking over and introducing radically different policies, or existing policymakers rejecting the advice of one set of experts in favour of another. In other words, those closest to the existing paradigm are only likely to make incremental changes, adapting and 'stretching' their theories to accommodate new information. At the brink of third order change, their concepts are so stretched that they cannot meaningfully explain and address policy problems. This prompts a 'first principles' battle of ideas (in which current assumptions are challenged and much less is taken for granted) which ends 'when the supporters of a new paradigm secure positions of authority over policymaking and are able to rearrange the organisation and standard operating procedures of the policy process so as to institutionalise the new paradigm' (Hall, 1993: 281).

In other words, we can ascribe two main roles to ideas. First, they can act as a source of resistance to policy change. Policymakers establish a language and a set of policy assumptions that excludes most participants. Radical change is rare and only occurs when policy failures are so significant that they produce shifts in power that displace existing policymakers and cause previously recognised experts to fall out of favour. Second, when new ideas are adopted, they can sweep aside existing policy monopolies (Baumgartner and Jones, 1993: 237) and cause a complete change in the way that policy is understood and made within government (Hall, 1993: 287). The policy process is characterised by 'the presence of a policy paradigm [generating] long periods of continuity punctuated occasionally by the disjunctive experience of a paradigm shift' (Hall, 1993: 291). The privileged status of a paradigmatic set of ideas ensures that most alternative ideas are ignored or rejected, only to be revisited in rare cases of third order change (following policy failure) or policy punctuations (following intense levels of 'external' attention and positive feedback).

Kingdon's (1984) multiple streams analysis places similar limits on the adoption or transfer of ideas. Ideas are not accepted, and policy does not change significantly, unless three separate streams come together at the same time: problems (policy issues deemed to require attention), policies (ideas or solutions proposed by pressure participants) and politics (changes in the political system that affect the receptivity to new ideas). While solutions already exist, their proponents must wait for the right opportunity to present them and have them adopted. This window of opportunity opens when the streams come together: 'A problem is recognized, a solution is developed and available in the policy community, a political change makes it the right time for policy change, and potential constraints are not severe' (Kingdon, 1995: 165–6).

Since a policy window does not stay open very long, an 'idea's time comes, but it also passes', particularly if the reasons for a particular level of attention to the policy problem fade before a coalition behind policy change can be mobilised (Kingdon, 1995: 169). This shifts our attention from the power of ideas to the significance of the *receptivity* to ideas within government (for an application to tobacco policy, see Cairney, 2009a).

The ACF also gives considerable prominence to ideas. The competition between coalitions involves: 'not only interest group leaders, but also agency officials, legislators from multiple levels of government, applied researchers, and perhaps even a few journalists' (Sabatier, 1998: 103). This suggests that ideas can be produced from, and promoted by, a wide range of sources. However, the glue that binds these actors together is 'belief systems' which circumscribe the effects of new information. These range from 'core' beliefs to 'policy core' and secondary aspects. Core values are the least susceptible to change. Policy core beliefs may only change following 'shocks' to the subsystem, such as sudden changes in socioeconomic conditions, that either prompt a dominant coalition to revisit their beliefs or help another coalition (with different beliefs) take a stronger position in the subsystem. Secondary aspects of beliefs are more subject to change following policy-learning (for example, coalitions may shift their beliefs about the best way to *deliver* policy). These beliefs are refined according to new information based on the evidence from the policy cycle and the 'enlightenment function' of actors, such as journalists or policy analysts. Advocacy coalitions compete for position within subsystems by learning from past policy and revising their strategic positions based on new evidence and the need to react to events. Change can come from two main sources: first, from within a coalition which adapts to its policy environment and engages in policy learning to protect its position, or second from a shift in power following a 'shock' to the political system or a more successful period of policy learning by a competing coalition. In either case, the role of ideas is not straightforward. In rare cases, ideas can be used to overcome the position of a previously dominant coalition (or that coalition has an internal crisis of confidence). However, the more likely scenario is that information is merely assimilated and interpreted selectively by coalitions (according to their policy core beliefs) in an attempt to maintain their policy positions and world views. This process may be identified in tobacco policy. In particular, while anti-tobacco coalitions may *now* dominate the subsystem in many developed countries, we can identify several strategies used successfully by pro-tobacco coalitions to adapt to new circumstances and maintain their positions for much of the post-war period (Cairney, 2007a: 57).

Overall, these models suggest that the ability of radically new ideas to 'catch fire' is unusual (Baumgartner and Jones, 1993). Extending this argument to policy transfer suggests that lesson-drawing from other jurisdictions merely forms one part of a much larger set of domestic ideas which compete for the attention of governments, while receptivity to these new ideas may be more important than the ideas themselves. In other words, the fact that the medical knowledge exists, and solutions (derived from the experience of other countries) to the tobacco problem are available, does not lead inevitably to the acceptance of that knowledge and those solutions. Instead, established ideas and ways of thinking may act as a hindrance to learning and lesson-drawing.

However, a discussion of voluntary and coercive policy transfer qualifies these conclusions. This is best demonstrated by the policy transfer continuum (Dolowitz and Marsh, 2000: 13). At one end we find voluntary transfer. In such cases, transfer is not inevitable. Rather, it follows some level of internal dissatisfaction with existing policy that cannot be addressed adequately by the ideas in the domestic political process. Only then do decisionmakers widen their search for ideas elsewhere (Dolowitz and Marsh, 1996: 347). At the other end, we find direct coercive transfer. This refers to the influence exerted by an organisation, jurisdiction or supra-national body to make another jurisdiction adopt a policy. For Dolowitz and Marsh (1996: 348; 2000: 10–11) direct imposition by another country is rare. In most cases there is still some degree of choice within the importing country. Coercion therefore refers to the *agenda* for transfer being set elsewhere and the adverse consequences if the importing jurisdiction does not cooperate. The third main category – indirect coercive transfer – refers to a process of voluntary transfer in which the importing jurisdiction *perceives* the need to change. While there are still coercive elements involved, this refers mostly to the role of externalities (Dolowitz and Marsh, 1996: 348–9). Countries react to a range of external pressures in the shape of norms (some jurisdictions adopt the same behaviour and expect others to follow suit), embarrassment or peer pressure (a feeling of being left behind) and economics (when countries react to the decisions made in competitor countries either because they expect benefits or wish to avoid harm by such an adjustment) (Hoberg, 1991: 110).

Coercion may be a key influence on the supply, demand and transfer of new ideas. This insight can be used to create a hybrid theory of the transfer of ideas – adapting Kingdon's (1984) focus on the role of problems, policies and politics. In the 'policy transfer window' (Cairney, 2012: 269) the power to be more or less receptive to new ideas often gives way to the power to oblige importing governments to consider one policy problem and its solution more than another. The window of opportunity now depends on the ability of other jurisdictions to set the agenda of the importing one, the comparability and applicability of their ideas, and the level of domestic receptivity to those ideas (or the ability to resist transfer). For example, in EU tobacco policy this can take at least two forms: (1) directives, potentially backed by judicial authority; and (2) recommendations to promote policy diffusion among member states, or the insistence that new members adopt current EU policies as a condition of accession (Asare et al, 2009; Frisbee et al, 2009). We may also identify indirect coercion in the FCTC process: ideas from developed countries are placed on the agenda by the WHO with the support of a broad coalition of countries and NGOs (Mamudu, 2008, 2011b). The agreement by other countries to sign up to the FCTC (Chapter 9) may be based on a perceived need to adhere to international norms (although we question the strength of such motives in Chapter 10).

How much policy change?

If we use multiple theories to highlight different aspects of the policy process, then we can identify a wide range of sources of policy continuity or change. The common link to most theories is a departure from 'comprehensive rationality' which represents an ideal description of the power of a central decisionmaker to research and articulate a series of consistent policy aims and then make sure that they are carried out. The assumptions necessary to demonstrate this power – that organisations can analyse information comprehensively, separate values from facts, rank policy preferences and make policy in a linear fashion – are unrealistic. Therefore, we describe what happens when these assumptions are relaxed or rejected: the search for knowledge is limited by capacity and ideology; problem definition is determined by both facts and values; policymakers have multiple, and often unclear or conflicting, objectives which are difficult to rank in any meaningful way; and, the policy process is difficult to separate into stages and may not be linear (Cairney, 2012: 96–7). Most theories adopt Simon's (1976: xxviii) term 'bounded rationality', which suggests that policymakers and organisations 'satisfice' (or seek 'a course of action that is satisfactory or "good enough"') rather than maximise their utility, and use simple rules of thumb (such as trial-and-error) because they cannot research and consider the effects of all options (see also Schlager, 2007: 299–302).

Much of the literature also follows Lindblom's (1959, 1979) argument that policymakers rarely pursue non-incremental change, because: (a) they need to build on past policies; and (b) too much effort has already been invested in seeking an agreed position among a wide range of interests. For example, the literature on policy communities suggests that incrementalism transcends formal political structures. Regular changes of government do not necessarily cause wholesale shifts in policy, even in the 'majoritarian UK'. In part, this is because most policy decisions are effectively beyond the reach of ministers. The sheer size of government necessitates breaking policy down into more manageable issues involving a smaller number of interested and knowledgeable participants. Therefore, most public policy is conducted primarily through policy communities which process 'technical' issues at a level of government not particularly visible to the public or parliament, and with minimal ministerial involvement (Richardson and Jordan, 1979; Jordan and Maloney, 1997; Cairney, 2008b).

Rose (1990; Rose and Davies, 1994) extends the discussion of incrementalism to inertia. The effect of cumulative policies is that policymakers inherit a huge government with massive commitments. Since governments are more likely to introduce new than terminate old policies, the cumulative effect is profound. Similarly, Hogwood and Peters (1983) argue that the size and scope of the state is such that any 'new' policy is likely to be a revision of an old one following a degree of policy failure; last year's solution is this year's problem. Policy succession is more likely than innovation because the issue already has legitimacy, institutions exist and policy has an established clientele. More significant innovations also require policy termination to reduce costs before committing new resources. Yet, complete termination also has immediate costs (financial and political), may smack of failure without direct replacement, may be opposed by groups and interests associated with the policy, and may be undermined by organisations seeking new ways to justify their existence (Geva-May, 2004).

Other approaches extend Lindblom's focus on the diffusion of power. MLG suggests that large, fragmented governments lack a powerful centre (Kooiman, 1993: 4). Policy outcomes result from the complex interplay between government and non-governmental actors at a variety of levels. Similarly, a 'street-level bureaucracy' approach to implementation suggests that although legislation is made at the 'top', it is influenced heavily by the public sector professions who deliver it. Policy is effectively made by bureaucrats at the 'bottom' when dealing with their clients. Since they are subject to an immense range of (often unclear) requirements laid down by regulations at the top, they are powerless to implement them all successfully. Instead, they establish routines and use rules of thumb to satisfy a proportion of central government objectives while preserving a sense of professional autonomy necessary to maintain morale (Lipsky, 1980).

Yet, many theories use the same starting point to predict a *greater* likelihood of non-incremental change in some cases. For example, MLG identifies a number of dynamic elements, including: the potential for innovation in devolved jurisdictions, followed in some cases by policy learning across a wider territory; and, the ability of supra-national organisations, such as the EU to make member states introduce policies that they would otherwise not entertain.

Similarly, punctuated equilibrium modifies the policy communities approach to show that bounded rationality produces incremental *and* radical change. Since policymakers have limited resources, they cannot deal with the full range of policy problems; they ignore most and promote few to the top of their agenda. This lack of attention to most issues helps explain why most policies do not change dramatically, while intense periods of attention to some issues may prompt new demands for change. Since it is impossible to separate facts from values, the nature of policy problems is subject to interpretation and debate. Therefore, by reframing issues, policy actors can draw the attention of policymakers, the media and the public towards new ways of looking at (and a pressing need to solve) old problems. When successful, this produces positive feedback, in which policymakers pay disproportionate attention to the issue (Jones, 1999, 2003; Baumgartner and Jones, 1993; Jones and Baumgartner, 2005). In some cases venue shopping, combined with a reframing of the policy issue, produces a 'bandwagon effect', in which multiple actors in the policy process all pay attention to, and seek to influence, the same issue. However, in most cases we may witness inertia, particularly in the US whose separation of powers (executive, legislative and judicial) and overlapping jurisdictions (between institutions or between federal, state and local government) suggest a political system 'conservatively designed to resist many efforts at change' (True et al, 2007: 157).

Kingdon's multiple streams analysis draws on the 'garbage can' model (Cohen et al, 1972), which strongly rejects the assumption in comprehensive rationality of linearity and suggests that the three processes – problem definition, solution, choice – appear to act almost independently, often with the potential for a different order. This may begin with solutions that already exist and then 'chase problems'; policymakers select a solution that already exists to a problem defined for them! Kingdon's (1984) model suggests that a 'window of opportunity' for significant policy change opens only when these three independent streams come together. In most cases policy does not change radically because a policy problem does not receive enough attention, an adequate idea or solution is not available and/or policymakers are not receptive to the idea. Yet, in some cases these streams *do* come together to produce radical change. The model therefore combines an overall assumption of policy continuity with an often random or unpredictable process of non-incremental change.

Finally, theories of policy diffusion demonstrate that non-incremental change may be consistent with the logic of incrementalism. Boundedly rational decisionmakers develop rules of thumb to provide focus to their policy analysis and make the best use of their limited resources. One such rule of thumb, particularly among US states, is diffusion. Diffusion studies suggest that some states merely emulate rather than learn in detail from others, on the assumption that the innovating state was successful. Therefore, although bounded rationality may place limits on the ability of states to innovate, it may also encourage states to emulate. The policy transfer continuum suggests that this process may also follow coercion. While the degree of 'rationality' diminishes as coercion increases (jurisdictions appear forced to change policy without full consideration), this does not preclude significant change (Berry and Berry, 1999; Dolowitz and Marsh, 2000).

While these theories provide ways to explain both policy continuity and change, there is still some ambiguity in the literature regarding how we measure, characterise and interpret change. We return to this broad conceptual issue in Chapter 10 after identifying continuity and change in the empirical chapters. Our study suggests that radical policy change has taken place in many countries over 50 years, but that it has often happened in the absence of a big bang event or profound policy failure highlighted by key theories.

Conclusion

Using multiple theories of public policy, we construct a research agenda for our empirical chapters, asking the following questions:

Who has responsibility for tobacco policy? Institutions have their own norms and rules of behaviour and policy outcomes are influenced by the institution responsible for tobacco policy. We identify a basic shift in policy responsibility from treasury and trade departments towards departments of health. In many cases, since tobacco policy is the responsibility of more than one institution, we also identify issues of overlap, the importance of intergovernmental relations, and the fluid nature of multi-level governance.

How is the tobacco problem framed and how high is it on the policy agenda? Policy choices are underpinned by the way that policymakers understand, and therefore seek to solve, policy problems and the levels of attention that policymakers devote to them.

What is the balance of power between tobacco and public health interests and how has this changed in the post-war period? Policymakers rely on interested participants for information and advice. Therefore, the dominance of that consultation process by one group of participants, at the expense of another, influences how policymakers frame and address problems.

What effect do socioeconomic conditions have on the propensity of governments to pursue tobacco control policies? The policy environment influences how policymakers understand and seek to solve policy problems. For example, they may be more likely to introduce or bolster tobacco control if the policy conditions are conducive to change; if, for example, there have been reductions in tobacco consumption, opposition to tobacco regulation, and/or the economic value of the tobacco trade.

What is the role of ideas and to what extent is tobacco policy driven by the transfer of ideas? Policymaking is not just about people exercising power to pursue their interests. It is also about the role of ideas: shared beliefs that give people a common aim; paradigms, or forms of thought that are taken for granted and acted upon with little further thought; norms or standards of behaviour; and the knowledge accumulated within political systems and used to make policy decisions. Ideas, in the form of policy solutions, may also be exported and adopted by other governments. Policy transfer is a key part of global tobacco policy, with international organisations, such as the EU and the WHO acting as major sources of diffusion and policy coordination.

These five factors can be separated analytically but, in practice, they interact with each other to produce an overall outcome: a shift in policy responsibility may cause, or be caused by, a change in problem definition; the successful promotion of new ideas may shift, or follow a shift in, the balance of power within policy networks; socioeconomic conditions may facilitate, and be caused by, public policy (these links are explored further in Chapter 3).

All five combine, in many cases, to produce major policy change. The public policy literature can guide us, to some extent, on how to characterise and explain such change. For example, bounded rationality may encourage incremental policymaking in most cases, but radical policy change in some. However, it does not provide a definitive means to *measure* the level and nature of policy change. As we discuss in Chapter 1, it is possible to produce two competing narratives on tobacco policy change in most developed countries. The first suggests that major change has occurred. The difference between post-war and current tobacco policy is fundamental, and most of it has occurred in the past 25 years. Limited and ineffective governmental intervention has been replaced by comprehensive tobacco control in many cases. The second suggests that policy change has been incremental. It has become stronger as the evidence has become more established, and most current measures are based largely on a trial-and-error process involving earlier measures.

These uncertainties are complicated further when we recognise that the rate of policy change varies by region. In particular, we make a simple distinction between developed and developing countries (see endnote 1) and identify different policy processes and types of policy change. In general, policy has changed more quickly in developed countries, particularly since the 1980s when limited tobacco controls were replaced by more extensive measures. In turn, this has increased pressure on developing countries to follow their lead. As we discuss in Chapter 10, such issues prompt us to consider the varying ability of theories to explain policy change. In short, theories that explain change primarily with reference to (often US) domestic processes may be less applicable to countries in which international developments set the agenda for action and 'short circuit' domestic processes that might otherwise take decades to develop. Further, theories that distinguish between incremental and radical change need to be clear on what radical change actually looks like. A series of incremental steps that produces major change may suggest that a punctuation has occurred and that a fundamental decision on the direction of policy has been made in the past.

3
The Global Policy Context

This chapter outlines the main policy developments across the globe, with a detailed time-line of major events since the 1950s. It identifies two key eras to demonstrate that tobacco policy has changed radically since the 19th century. An era in which political economy was the dominant frame for policy choice, and the tobacco industry was encouraged by governments to grow and sell tobacco to improve the economy, has been replaced by an era in which moral, socioeconomic and public health arguments are used to justify increasingly restrictive tobacco controls. The chapter seeks to characterise the degree and tempo of global tobacco policy change, making the simple distinction between experiences in developed and developing countries (see endnote 1 on the distinction). In our analysis of developed countries we seek to qualify, to some extent, the idea of a sudden transition to tobacco control by focusing on the wide range of tobacco policy instruments that have been introduced in the past 20 years. A succession of developed countries have now signalled what appears to be a sharp break from the past by introducing bans on smoking in public and work places (clean indoor air policies). However, these developments may often be characterised as an incremental progression of, rather than a radical departure from, policies already in place. Many developed countries had already introduced a range of policies designed to reduce smoking prevalence in the population – including regulations on the content of cigarettes, health warnings on cigarette packs, bans on tobacco advertising, taxing tobacco, funding health education and smoking cessation services and building up public health capacity – before strengthening rather than shifting their stance on tobacco control.

The analysis of policy change in developed countries is important for two-main reasons. First, by taking a long-term view based on a wide range of policy measures, we find that the causal factors outlined in Chapter 2 reinforce each other over time. For example, health departments have generally replaced trade or agriculture departments as the main source of policy innovation and interest group pressure. This power shift can be linked to changes in problem definition, from tobacco production as an economic benefit to tobacco consumption as a public health crisis. The policy image of tobacco has been influenced by government-funded scientific research and public health promotion (which has also helped reduce smoking). Second, our discussion here informs our explanations of change explored in the concluding chapter. For example, models of public policy which explain change with reference to punctuated equilibrium may only have value if we can identify something that can be meaningfully described as a policy punctuation.

As Chapter 1 suggests, our broad analysis of developing countries does not present a different tobacco problem as such, but we can identify significant differences in the policymaking context. While countries exhibit differences in smoking behaviour (based on influences related to gender, religion and class), and are at different stages of the 'tobacco epidemic model' (Chapter 1), the overall size of the 'epidemic' is well known, and the stated aim of most governments is to reduce smoking prevalence. However, we identify key differences in the way that tobacco control policies have developed in these two sets of countries. In developed countries we identify a process of reinforcement among policy choices, the way that domestic institutions and public health groups frame policy, the scientific knowledge and social attitudes and behaviour. In contrast, few domestically driven policy measures were apparent in developing countries until the 1990s (with the exceptions of Singapore and Thailand) and domestic public health capacity is relatively low. We suggest that an unintended consequence of tobacco control in developed countries was the decision of transnational tobacco companies (TTCs) to widen their market activities, focusing on developing countries with less restrictive tobacco control regimes (although the phenomenon was also a natural extension of an industry in search of new markets for its products). As in earlier phases of policy in developed countries, TTCs faced relatively low levels of opposition from medical-state interests and public health pressure groups, a rising market for tobacco and low levels of knowledge diffusion regarding the links between smoking and illness.

The rise of tobacco control in developing countries is therefore better explained with reference to a two-stage process of policy transfer. First, the declining presence of TTCs in developed countries further strengthened the ability of their governments to restrict tobacco use and construct a 'comprehensive' package of measures from which lessons could be drawn. We can track an impressive degree of policy convergence between developed countries, based on the prominent position of public health interests and their strong transnational policy networks. Second, the widening gap between tobacco controls in different regimes led to a focus on policy learning led by governmental actors in the European Union (EU) and US and a range of organisations, such as the World Bank, the WHO, United Nations (UN) and NGOs, leading to the development of the WHO FCTC. As a result, transnational actors have become major force in policy development in developing countries.

What is tobacco policy? Phases and eras of tobacco control

There have been five phases of tobacco control policy in the developed world since the late 19th century, with perhaps a sixth currently emerging. Table 3.1 outlines the major themes and approximate dates of these phases, although they vary somewhat by country.

Table 3.1 The Phases of Tobacco Control Policy, 1885–2010

Period	Events
	Paradigm: Tobacco Promotion (Political Economy)
Phase 1: 1885–1914	Consolidation of the Cigarette Industry and Early Controversies over Morality and Public Health
Phase 2: 1914–1950	Tobacco Growing and Manufacturing Promoted by Governments
Phase 3: 1950–1964	The Gathering Storm of Health Concerns
	Paradigm: Tobacco Restriction (Public Health)
Phase 4: 1964–1984	Regulatory Hesitancy; Tobacco Control seen as a Developed World Issue
Phase 5: 1984–2010	Tobacco as a Social and Global Menace
Phase 6: the future?	Neo-prohibitionism vs. Harm Reduction and/or Decommercialization?

Source: Adapted from Studlar 2002

Broadly, we can divide these phases into two eras. From 1884 to 1950 the dominant paradigm, political economy, was positive towards tobacco and related mostly to the benefits of tobacco production for the economy. There were tobacco controls in some countries, but these were limited and ineffective. The rise of tobacco as an issue of political economy began a century ago with the mass production of cigarettes; the invention of the Bonsack machine for mass cigarette production, purchased by James B. Duke in 1885, along with the invention of the small safety match, mass communication and transportation. In 1890 Duke formed the American Tobacco Company and attempted to gain a monopoly of manufacturing and sales in the US and Canada. This attempt was frustrated in 1911 by the US Supreme Court, but cigarette production remained an oligopoly of a few companies in most countries (Brandt, 2007). During this period, US and British tobacco companies began investing in Asia, particularly China. BAT was particularly prominent in these efforts and controlled much of the Chinese market until the Communist Revolution in 1949 (Mackay and Crofton, 1996; Wu, 2008).

Cigarettes gradually gained in popularity and displaced chewing tobacco, cigars, and pipe tobacco as a means of tobacco consumption, spreading from the upper to lower classes (Ferrence, 1989). Cigarettes rose from 1% of the market in the US in 1880 to 85% of total tobacco sales in the mid-1960s (Tate, 1999; McGowan, 1995; by 2009, cigarettes' share of the market has declined to 80% – GAO, 2011). The pattern for other industrialised countries was similar. Although the use of commercial tobacco in developing countries lagged behind developed ones by about half a century, the patterns of tobacco consumption have been converging. Today cigarettes are the most prevalent form of tobacco use, except for a few countries in South East Asia (primarily India where bidis constitute a significant proportion of tobacco use). From the 1970s, cigarette use in developing countries became more prevalent among people with higher socioeconomic status (SES). However, the situation is also changing in developing countries, where cigarette use is increasingly becoming concentrated in those with lower SES (Muller, 1978: 83; Chapman, 1990; FAO, 2003; WHO, 2008).

The increase in cigarette consumption did not proceed completely unopposed. The anti-tobacco movement of the late 19th and early 20th centuries was allied to the alcohol prohibition movement and criticised cigarettes as morally and physically corrupting, especially for the young, as well as being a nuisance. It was strongest in English-speaking regimes, Nordic countries and Japan, and had some political effects, resulting in the passage of legislation banning sales to young people (and, in some state/provincial jurisdictions, broader prohibitions forbidding the manufacture, sales, and/or purchase of cigarettes) (Hilton, 1995; Tate, 1999). However, in the wake of the growing popularity of cigarettes during and after World War I, all of these provisions were repealed or largely ignored for over a half century. The industrialised world entered the promotional stage of tobacco policy, and anti-tobacco political activity almost completely ceased. Demand for cigarettes rose, and it was considered a patriotic duty to supply the troops with smokes to relieve the stress of battle. Cigarettes had an advantage over drink in wartime, as any deleterious health effects and impairment to a soldier's performance were not immediately evident. The political economy of cigarette promotion flourished.

In the wake of World War I, cigarette sales accelerated domestically. Governments in tobacco leaf growing countries came to view tobacco crops as a desirable source of income for their rural populations, and some subsidised tobacco growing and exports. Countries switched from considering banning cigarettes to taxing them, which became a reliable revenue raiser. Some governments, such as in Denmark, even had an agreement with their domestic tobacco companies for high cigarette taxes in order to maintain government revenue and discourage foreign producers from entering the market (Albaek, 2004). TTCs tried to expand their markets through advertising, such as proclaiming the benefits of smoking over the eating of sweets. Meanwhile, the anti-tobacco movement was stymied everywhere, and in most countries it completely disappeared except for a few health promoters and physicians.

Table 3.2 Major Tobacco Control Events and Decisions, 1885–2010

Year	Activity
1885	James B. Duke acquires license for Bonsack cigarette machine
1890	American Tobacco Company formed from four tobacco companies
1890–1921	Morality and health arguments against cigarettes; legislative action against sales to minors, possession, sales in United States (US), Canada, Australia, New Zealand, and United Kingdom (UK); anti-cigarette movements in Nordic countries
1895	Anti-cigarette League formed
1908	The British parliament passed one of the first age limitations for cigarette purchase in the world
1911	US Supreme Court anti-trust decision in US v. American Tobacco Company
1914	World War I promotes cigarettes as relief for troops
1921	First US state cigarette taxes
1920s	Tobacco advertising boom Government aids to tobacco growers and manufacturers in several countries
1933	US Agriculture Adjustment Act rations and subsidises tobacco growing
1933–1945	Nazis limit smoking; German publications document health effects
1939–1945	World War II leads to greatest ever growth in cigarette sales in US
1950	US and UK scientific publications on health effects of cigarette smoking
1952	'Cancer by the Carton' (Reader's Digest in US and abroad) launches public cancer/health scare and prompts introduction of filtered cigarettes
1953–4	US and Canadian Studies on smoking and lung cancer
1962	Report of Royal College of Physicians
	Italy is first country to ban televised cigarette advertising
1963–1964	Voluntary industry codes in several countries
1964	US Surgeon General's Report on the health effects of cigarette smoking

Table 3.2 Major Tobacco Control Events and Decisions, 1885–2010 – *continued*

Year	Activity
1964–1965	US ban on television advertising of cigarettes, emphasis on education
	US Interagency Group on Smoking established; similar organizations in other countries
1967	First World Conference on Tobacco and Health (WCTOH), New York City
1970	First World Health Assembly (WHA) resolution on tobacco control, Health Consequences of Smoking
1970s	First US subcentral limits on smoking; wave of government limits on smoking on common carriers
1974	Lalonde Report in Canada, launching a movement for disease prevention and health promotion (Healthy Public Policy)
1975	First WHO Expert Committee on Smoking and its Effects on Health
	Sweden: First rotating health warnings on packages (i.e. different warnings were put on packages at different times)
1979	Fourth WCTOH, Stockholm, Sweden focused on tobacco in developing countries
1980	WHO creates Smoking and Health programme
1980s	Wave of countries and EU become more active in tobacco control
	More countries adopt health warnings on packages
	Tax increases on cigarettes; government financial aid to anti-tobacco groups in some English-speaking countries
	The US forces Asian countries to open their markets to the TTCs
1981	Japanese studies on effects of second-hand smoke (SHS)
1983	WHO Expert Committee on Smoking Control in Developing Countries
1985	US Special Trade Representative negotiates for US cigarette markets abroad
1986	Surgeon General's Report on the effects of SHS
	WHA Resolution establishes Tobacco or Health programme
	European Action on Cancer (EAC) programmes starts
1986–1994	Uruguay round of trade talks makes tobacco a tradeable commodity
1988	Surgeon General's Report on cigarettes as addictive
	California Proposition 99 for tobacco tax for health promotion
	Canadian Tobacco Products Control Act passes, banning advertising and mandating health warnings

Table 3.2 Major Tobacco Control Events and Decisions, 1885–2010 – *continued*

Year	Activity
1988	WHO 'World No Tobacco Day'
1989	First EU Tobacco Products Labelling Directive mandates health warnings Smoking banned on many air carriers
1992	US federal aid to state tobacco control coalitions begins
1991	World Bank decides not to support tobacco projects
1992	US Environmental Protection Agency report on dangers of second hand smoke EU tax harmonisation for cigarettes The UN Focal Point created by United Nations Conference on Trade and Development An international meeting in Harare, Zimbabwe, begins focus on economics of tobacco control
1994	Maastricht Treaty expands EU role in health US tobacco company chief executives testify before House Subcommittee US state lawsuits over Medicaid expenses A panel of General Agreement on Trade and Tariffs (GATT) ruled in a case between the US and Thailand on non-discrimination of foreign tobacco
1996	US Food and Drug Administration (FDA) claims regulation over tobacco products Initiation of the negotiations of the WHO Framework Convention on Tobacco Control (FCTC), the first international public health treaty
1997	US National Settlement of states with tobacco industry over Medicaid costs First EU general ad ban approved British Labour government begins anti-tobacco activities
1998	US Senate rejects National Settlement; replaced by Master Settlement Agreement for 46 states and four individual state settlements with tobacco companies; tobacco companies forced to release their internal documents WHO Tobacco Free Initiative created to focus global attention on tobacco control
1999	World Bank publishes the *Curbing the Epidemic: Governments and Economics of Tobacco Control*, providing economic justification for tobacco control and followed by several country-level analysis The UN Ad Hoc Interagency Task Force on Tobacco Control was created

Table 3.2 Major Tobacco Control Events and Decisions, 1885–2010 – *continued*

Year	Activity
2000	US Supreme Court rules FDA has no authority over tobacco Canadian federal government adopts graphic cigarette warnings, 50% of pack EU Tobacco Products Advertising Directive overturned by European Court of Justice Negotiations of the FCTC begin
2001	EU Tobacco Products Regulation Directive Iceland: First complete cigarette products display ban UK bans tobacco advertising
2002	New EU Tobacco Advertising Directive
2003	The 191 members of the WHO unanimously adopt the FCTC Ireland becomes first country to adopt non-smoking in pubs and restaurants Ten new Accession countries join EU under aquis communautaire India becomes the first country to regulate characters smoking in the movies
2004	Scotland becomes first UK jurisdiction to adopt indoor non-smoking, England follows in 2006 The FCTC becomes international law
2007	The FCTC Conference of the Parties (governing body) begins work to develop guidelines for the FCTC provisions
2008	US federal court finds tobacco companies guilty of racketeering
2009	US federal legislation raises federal cigarette taxes by largest amount ever US FDA received authority for limited regulation of ingredients and marketing of cigarettes
2010	Australia approves first plain packaging First United Nations resolution on non-communicable diseases
2011	First United Nations ministerial meeting on non-communicable diseases in Moscow, Russia

What is tobacco policy? The development of policy control instruments

The old tobacco promotion paradigm contrasts sharply with the new tobacco control paradigm now present in many countries. Over the past two decades many developed countries, and increasing numbers of developing countries, have accepted a 'comprehensive approach' to tobacco control (although note the gulf between policy preferences and implementation, particularly in developing countries). The problems in comparing data across countries, and the similar timing and interaction of various policy instruments within countries, make it difficult for tobacco control advocates to calculate the relative effect of different instruments (Jha and Chaloupka, 2000; Licari, 2002). Instead, many countries adopt a package of instruments designed to reinforce each other. The cumulative impact of sustained and enforced measures is considered to be most effective over time, particularly when viewed as a process of 'denormalisation' of smoking and tobacco products (Studlar, 2002).

The trajectory of policy development has often been piecemeal even in countries now deemed to be tobacco control leaders. The development of a new approach, based on public health and the need for government to control tobacco, accelerated in 1964 and only began to achieve dominance from the 1980s (Studlar, 2004). Only in the period starting in 1990 did the number of measures employed by several countries begin to accumulate in a manner that could be called 'comprehensive' (Studlar et al, 2011). While several elements of this approach to tobacco control were initiated in developed countries, they diffused worldwide eventually. Some developing countries, such as Brazil, Singapore, Thailand, and Venezuela, have also become innovative in tobacco control.

The eventual replacement of political economy as the dominant paradigm began slowly from the 'health scare' in the 1950s, widely publicised through the dramatically-titled article 'Cancer by the Carton' in *Reader's Digest* (Norr, 1952) (Table 3.2). However, governments did little to combat smoking in the 1950s beyond sporadic and highly targeted educational campaigns warning against 'excessive smoking'. Some governments did engage in cooperative research activities with tobacco companies, as well as with cancer societies, on the tobacco-health link. Even after the publication of two major reports on the health effects of smoking – by the UK Royal College of Physicians in 1962 and the US Surgeon General in 1964 – government responses were restrained. In the 1960s only a few countries went beyond introducing voluntary restrictive agreements with the tobacco industry, an idea the tobacco companies exported to developing countries in the 1980s. There were some educational measures and bans on televised advertising. There was little government investment in tobacco control, according to the three major empirical indicators of policy: laws, personnel, and finance (Rose, 1987). Most countries lacked even one official in the health ministry working full time on the issue.

In the 1980s some countries, such as Canada, Australia, and Ireland joined the ranks of former tobacco control leaders Finland, Sweden, Norway, France, and, more erratically, the US. But others, including many on the continent of Europe, remained laggards. Until the mid-1980s, only a few countries had such instruments as high taxation, educational campaigns, health warning labels on packages, broadcast bans, and other advertising restrictions. The latter three, however, were often based on voluntary agreements with the tobacco industry, which were unsatisfactory because of various loopholes and violations (Pollay, 1994). These early restrictive policies grew gradually. The total number of countries having some tobacco control legislation increased from less than 30 in 1976 (WHO, 1976) to 57 in 1982 and 91 in 1995 (Roemer, 1982, 1993, 1995). The type and scope of instruments also increased, with some countries passing legislation and regulations banning print advertising, enacting stronger and more prominent health warnings, underwriting media campaigns, and requiring reports of cigarette ingredients.

Taxes above that on ordinary consumer products (often called 'excise taxes' or 'sin taxes' – Meier, 1994) have been an instrument long applied to tobacco, and all countries have some form of special taxation on cigarettes. However, until the mid-1980s it was almost universally perceived in fiscal terms alone, as a source of revenue for governments rather than as an aid in reducing tobacco consumption. Taxes on cigarettes since the 1950s lagged behind income growth and inflation, thus making cigarettes ever more affordable. Only since the 1980s has a higher excise tax on tobacco products became a widely accepted policy instrument to control the use and spread of tobacco in developed and developing countries (Lewit and Coate, 1982; Jha and Chaloupka, 1999, 2000). Most higher-income countries have increased their cigarette taxes substantially since the 1980s, and the European Union has even attempted to harmonise taxation at a high level among its members (Cnossen and Smart, 2006). This has resulted in a tax incidence of 60–80% of the retail purchase price in these countries. Since the mid-1980s advanced industrial countries also have made an effort to maintain the value of cigarette taxes in line with inflation, and more justify it on health grounds. In contrast, in many developing countries the tax rate remains too low to make any significant impact on consumption (WHO, 2008, 2011b).

Until 2009 the US was an exception to this pattern. It has lagged for a long time, even if one considers the financial costs imposed on the tobacco companies under the 1998 Master Settlement Agreement (MSA) between 46 US states and the tobacco industry as a form of taxation (it is, in effect, a country-wide policy, even if not mandated by the federal government). In 2002 the overall average tax rate in the US was 40%, with wide variation among the states. Subsequently several US states have increased cigarette taxes and the federal government levied its largest-ever tax increase in 2009, doubling it. That brought the overall average US tax rate (state and federal) to 45% of the total price. With MSA costs, it is approximately 55%, still below the norm for advanced industrial countries, Japan excepted.

Since research findings became publicised in the early 1980s, concern has been focused on the regulation of SHS (to reduce passive smoking). Over the past three decades, countries first instituted limited restrictions on SHS in public places, then outright bans in an increasing number of locations. In the US in particular, the evidence on the health effects of secondhand tobacco smoke was a catalyst for civil society mobilisation against tobacco use (Nathanson, 1999). Other measures also have grown in popularity. Cessation through media advocacy and the availability of government-supported services have become more prevalent. Australia has led the way in substituting tobacco sponsorship with public health funds through health promotion foundations. The United States devoted considerable resources to 'capacity-building' efforts, using federal funds to assist states and communities in their local tobacco control efforts. Some countries began to focus on youth access prevention, including establishing or raising the age at which cigarettes could be purchased legally. Private litigation for health damages caused by smoking became established in the US, Canada, and Australia. The unusual approach in the US of governments suing for healthcare cost recovery has also received significant international attention, although government litigation is still restricted to a small number of countries, principally Canada (Blanke, 2002; Studlar, 2007). In 2010, Australia became the first country to announce a policy of plain packing for all tobacco products after earlier suggestions for its adoption in Canada in the mid-1990s (Cunningham, 1996; Mamudu et al, 2011a). Tobacco control has also increasingly become the subject of international initiatives and agreements, including air travel treaties, European Union directives, and, most recently, the Tobacco-Free Initiative (TFI) of the WHO and the negotiations for the FCTC (Chapter 9).

How much change?

In comparing the present with the early post-war period, we can identify an emergent paradigmatic change, both domestically in industrialised democracies and even internationally. Countries are increasingly using a similar repertoire of policy instruments for tobacco control. More jurisdictions have moved toward broadly inclusive 'comprehensive' tobacco control policies. The most significant changes in tobacco policy have occurred in the past three decades. Before the mid-1980s, there were only a handful of countries in which tobacco control policy was the subject of government legislation and regulation rather than the voluntary agreements favoured by the tobacco industry. Furthermore, tobacco-growing countries often had various subsidies, in the form of tariff barriers, export promotion, research assistance, and loans, in order to encourage domestic production of leaf tobacco and manufactured cigarettes. This situation has changed dramatically, especially in advanced industrial democracies. Governments have been more willing to take strong regulatory action to limit tobacco consumption and to raise excise taxes on tobacco products.

However, there is also some evidence of incremental change, such as governments increasing taxes, strengthening restrictions on advertising, and better communicating the links between smoking and illness, rather than policies introduced from a blank slate. In other words, we may not find evidence of the rather dramatic process we associated, in Chapter 2, with Hall's (1993) paradigm change (we revisit this issue in Chapter 10). Further, there remains considerable variation in the strength of specific instruments, the level of comprehensiveness, and the commitment to enforcement (Corrao et al, 2000; WHO, 2002). While there has been a clear shift in the agenda and a qualitative difference in the policy instruments now selected, policy change also requires policy implementation. This is particularly important in a policy area with a long history of voluntary and ineffective policies.

Institutions: Who has responsibility for tobacco policy?

In some chapters we describe a shift in policy responsibility to new levels or types of government (such as in Chapter 5 where the EU and devolved governments supplemented UK government action). However, in all chapters the common theme is a shift of policy responsibility across government *departments*. The evolution of tobacco policy has gone hand-in-hand with the evolution of government institutional involvement. In the days of tobacco promotion, the ministries concerned were Treasury, Agriculture, and Trade since the product was seen as a revenue raiser and a jobs producer. Since pure competition in tobacco agriculture would lead to lower prices, many governments limited production and arranged for it to be sold to tobacco companies manufacturing cigarettes in their countries. As more developing countries became active in tobacco growing, however, the international competition became more intense and these domestic protection schemes worked less well.

Although the older ministries remained involved, the rise of scientific information about the physically damaging effects of tobacco consumption brought health ministries to the fore. Few were well-prepared for this, however, since tobacco harm was an unprecedented problem. Public health was only a minor part of health policy and was focused on contagious diseases rather than socially-transmitted ones. It is difficult to assess bureaucratic strength, especially on a comparative basis, although numbers and experience of personnel as well as financial support are relevant factors (Rose, 1984). Until the 1980s, the number of civil servants working on tobacco control was tiny. Further, health was usually a less politically powerful ministry than the others involved in tobacco. Therefore, its initial role in combating the tobacco epidemic was limited. Early tobacco control measures were achieved with minimal financial and personnel resources in health ministries, and sometimes despite opposition from powerful finance ministries who were reluctant to disturb cigarette consumption since they viewed tobacco taxation as a 'cash cow'. Health ministries have increased their policy research on tobacco issues through an infusion of personnel and financial resources over the years and are no longer as easily dominated by revenue-raising concerns in inter-departmental decisionmaking on tobacco.

The rising importance of the role of health ministries was a consequence of three key developments. The first was a general commitment in a growing number of countries to pursue tobacco control, which led to a rise in resources and influence for health ministries from the 1980s. The second was a hardening of attitudes within these ministries against tobacco use. For example, the Lalonde Report (Health and Welfare Canada, 1974) in Canada popularised the idea of preventive health (Healthy Public Policy) and tobacco use reduction quickly became the main target of HPP goals (Leichter, 1991). The third was a change in Treasury attitudes, from a department resisting tobacco control in the interests of protecting a significant source of revenue, to one that increasingly recognised the relative inelasticity of cigarette taxation due to addiction (USDHHS, 1988) and therefore agreed that higher taxes would not harm state revenues in a major way. This shift followed an increased focus on tobacco as a source of ill-health and therefore economic inefficiency (Abedian, 1999; Barnum, 1994; Jha, 1999, 2000). The economic, healthcare, and life expectancy costs of tobacco use became increasingly stark in economic analyses in the 1990s. A significant increase in taxes became useful for both ministries: it could raise more revenue, at least in the short term, and reduce smoking at the same time. This brought treasury departments into greater cooperation with health interests in some countries, notably Canada and the UK (see Chapter 5 on the agreement between the Treasury and Department of Health to tackle smoking as the key cause of health inequalities).

There is similar potential for health and treasury department alliances in developing countries and at the international level. For example, the World Bank and WHO collaborated in 1999 on the *Curbing the Epidemic*, which concluded that tobacco control is good for health and the economy (except in Malawi and Zimbabwe), while subsequent country-level economic analyses of tobacco control reinforced this message within increasingly receptive governments (Mamudu and Glantz, 2009; Mamudu and Novotny, 2008).

The WHO also collaborated with the WTO in 2002 to examine the relationship between international trade and health. They produced a report arguing that World Trade Organisation agreements should support the ability of countries to promulgate policies to 'protect human, animal or plant life or health,' including tobacco control as long as they are 'necessary', 'least restrictive' do not constitute 'disguised restriction on international trade' or 'arbitrary or unjustifiable discrimination' (Mamudu et al, 2011a; WHO and WTO, 2002). Although the goal of this report was to facilitate the FCTC negotiations on the relationship between trade and health, the final

FCTC document did not include any explicit provision on the issue (Mamudu et al, 2011a).

Agendas: How important is tobacco control as a policy issue? How is tobacco framed?

In asking how the tobacco problem is framed, we seek to identify the dominant policy image within government as a means to explain the impetus behind policy choices. However, there are many images to draw on, and policy may be linked to a complex combination of several features promoted by different actors in and out of government at different times. Much also depends on the levels of attention to the issue. As Baumgartner and Jones (2009: 92–3) note, for a long time in Western countries tobacco enjoyed a glamorous image, prevalence was high, smoking was a normal part of life and government, media and public attention was minimal and largely positive. From World War I until at least the 1950s, tobacco policy was discussed mainly in terms of political economy – production, trade, jobs, and tax revenue. Further, when the image of tobacco as an economic good came under threat, it was often supplemented by defensive arguments concerning freedom of choice and the threat of the 'nanny state'.

To some extent, arguments about the rights of the individual have been challenged by public health campaigns based on the immorality of smoking, non-smokers' rights to clean air and, in some countries, such as Japan and Australia, a focus on the effect of smoking on the environment (or at least the avoidance of litter). Morality was a major concern of early anti-tobacco advocates in the late 19th and early 20th centuries and has returned as a mobilising force in conjunction with public health arguments. In fact, many of its most ardent advocates are public health professionals (Larsen, 2008), who are adamant that the evidence of tobacco damage is clear and that corrective public policy measures should be implemented immediately; to do otherwise is a moral wrong as well as physically damaging, particularly since smoking addiction is increasingly a lower-class disease in developed countries. This zealotry has energised the anti-tobacco movement politically (although it has also often been divisive concerning strategies, the tone of campaigns and ultimate goals, especially harm regulation/minimisation versus elimination of smoking – Nathanson, 1999; Pertschuk, 2001). While some religious groups continue to oppose smoking on principle, most of the moral zeal of the anti-tobacco movement is based on a 'secular morality' valuing physical health rather than religious precepts (Brandt and Rozin, 1997; Studlar, 2008).

More importantly, public health has become increasingly important as a way for governments to define the tobacco policy problem. The economic and political benefits of cultivating and manufacturing tobacco have been challenged by the evidence on the economic costs of smoking (relating not only to the cost of healthcare but also workdays lost due to illness). The 'right to smoke' has been challenged by the 'right to health' or 'right to clean air' as evidence on the effects of SHS has been accepted increasingly across the globe (Mamudu et al, 2011b). We can also identify in the US a focus on protection of the young through groups, such as the Campaign for Tobacco-Free Kids and claims by prominent actors, such as former US Food and Drug Administration Commissioner David Kessler, that tobacco use is a 'pediatric disease' (Kessler, 2001). Such claims provide further ammunition against arguments about civil liberties and individual adult choice. Further, anti-tobacco groups in the US have gone the furthest in developing the 'denormalisation' argument against tobacco, describing the industry as an illegitimate business engaged in deception and knowingly propagating a pandemic across the world, and arguing that it should not be rewarded by having a legitimate role in deliberations over tobacco control policy. This strategy is increasingly apparent in global health debates.

However, as our discussion of the adoption of policy instruments across the globe demonstrates, the success of such challenges has varied markedly over time and from country to country. There is a particular disparity between the rate and tempo of policy innovation between developed and developing countries. In most of the developed world the dominant image of tobacco within government is now clearly related to public health. Indeed, the health image is so dominant in most developed countries that the policy agenda now relates primarily to *how* to reduce tobacco use – what policies, instruments, and calibrations are desirable to prevent mass disease and death while still preserving individual choice – rather than if the effort should be made (Cairney, 2009a: 473). However, this shift took place over several decades, often in fits and starts. Further, the issue only reaches the top of the political agenda sporadically.

The previous political economy framing of tobacco policy was based on the power of its intense minority of economically-based supporters to keep the issue off the political agenda. When health questions arose, they produced remedies that addressed these concerns in ways that suited the industry and growers (Cairney, 2007a: 57). Even with growing scientific evidence and public endorsement of the dangers of tobacco use, the issue was often suppressed until the dramatic evidence was better known and political entrepreneurs in and out of government were able to mobilise a countermovement backed by substantial finance, organisation, and enthusiasm. The general public has become more sceptical of tobacco promotion claims as well as more aware of the dangers of tobacco use but is rarely willing to make this a critical voting issue. Thus, interest groups in most countries have been faced with a 'permissive consensus', a public that is increasingly supportive of tobacco control measures but largely willing to allow the debate to proceed at the level of elites. Government officials are willing to give tobacco only limited and sporadic attention, as the issues perceived to be critical to public support and election lie elsewhere. In most countries, tobacco issues are not openly partisan, and success in developing policy may not lead to further advancement for politicians or even re-election for their governments (Studlar, 2002; Studlar et al, 2011).

This long term, and often low key, process of agenda-setting means that changes are usually incremental. Tobacco promotion was supplemented gradually by small initiatives on public education and advertising, followed by more regulation and taxation as the scientific evidence accumulated and anti-tobacco groups became more organised (see below). But these choices were slow to be faced, and tobacco control only gradually became more important than tobacco promotion. Education and regulation worked slowly to reduce the tobacco toll, and anti-tobacco groups, including public health professionals, physicians, and scientists in some countries, clamoured for more dramatic, far-reaching, and uniform governmental responses. Over time this moved from restrictions using a few instruments, to increasingly tougher calibrations of these instruments, ending in some cases at full bans. At the turn of the 21st century, 'comprehensive' tobacco control policy became the goal in some countries, but the relative contributions of different policy instruments toward improving public health results remains a contested subject.

This lack of sustained, directed attention to tobacco is a problem for public health efforts in developing countries. The FCTC (Chapter 9) is designed to provide a stimulus to policy movement in the developing world and thus to avoid their need to experience the entire cycle of the Tobacco Epidemic Model before taking action. In effect, policy transfer can act as a 'short circuit' to the long-term process of attention and problem definition shifts in developed countries over the past 50 years.

Networks: Has there been a shift in power between pressure participants?

The balance of power between tobacco and public health interests within developed countries has changed markedly since the early post-war period. Tobacco company and agriculture dominance in the first half of the 20th century has been replaced by public health dominance in the 21st century. The shift was caused partly by a change within government towards health ministry centrality, a development which itself can be linked to the transformed policy image of tobacco. Previously tobacco companies enjoyed privileged access to policymaking through other ministries, and they could use not only their value to the economy, but also their wider political support, as a resource to influence policy. Tobacco manufacturers were joined by employees, growers and their local communities, as well as those who benefited from tobacco sales, including vendors, hospitality providers, advertisers, media outlets, and even the charities and sports activities that benefited from tobacco company donations. At the same time, public health advocates were few in number and less well organised. Aside from a few crusading journalists, there was no organised anti-tobacco movement even as the scientific evidence against tobacco mounted. The most likely candidates for such a campaign, medical charities and physicians' groups, were relatively timid and compromised by the donations of cigarette companies and its recruitment of medical personnel into the army of tobacco users.

This position became transformed over several decades, the last 20 years in particular, as public health advocates have become more organised and powerful both outside of and within governments. Anti-tobacco groups have grown substantially over the years, first organising in the 1950s and 1960s, growing in the 1970s, and proliferating in the 1980s (Mamudu, 2008). The pattern of domestic growth and the number of groups operating in each country varies somewhat. The core anti-tobacco groups in most developed countries were founded by, or related to, medical organisations. They are usually volunteer charities organised against tobacco-related diseases (such as heart, respiratory, and cancer), professional public health organisations, non-smokers' rights groups, and various country-specific and independent organisations in the English-speaking world (Canada and the US excepted) called ASH (Action on Smoking and Health). They are also often organised into overarching coalitions for lobbying purposes. What they lack in finance and organisation in comparison to industry-affiliated groups, they counter with greater moral zeal and capacity to mobilise those with ideal commitments toward public health rather than mainly material goals. The more successful groups, especially in English-speaking countries, have also benefited from some degree of government sponsorship under the aegis of 'capacity-building' for public interest groups. The model was founded by the US Inter-agency Task Force on Smoking in the 1960s (consisting of public and private organisations) and subsequently adopted over the next 30 years by Canada, the United Kingdom, Australia, New Zealand and the European Union (Studlar, 2006; Mamudu and Studlar, 2009).

Over time these groups have become more powerful and have managed to gain the upper hand over tobacco promotion groups in most developed countries. They have done so by pursuing a long-term strategy: building up organisational capacity, gathering and disseminating scientific evidence, promoting smoking reduction measures controlled by health ministries (such as smoking cessation services and health education), lobbying legislatures and forming domestic and international networks to share best practice and coordinate their efforts. Consequently, cigarettes and smoking have become denormalised in society, and the prospect for further tobacco control has increased over time.

At the same time, the tobacco manufacturing industry has lost influence within government; it has been subject to increasingly vociferous criticism from the media and politicians (following the public health lead) and its credibility has been undermined. In particular, it has never fully recovered from the negative publicity which followed the release of thousands of company documents that reveal the extent of their knowledge of the harmful and addictive effects of smoking, particularly since that knowledge was denied by the CEOs of major US companies in televised US Congressional hearings in 1994. The term 'Big Tobacco' now has negative connotations. Overall, a shift in policy emphasis, driven by health ministries with closer links to public health groups, has combined with a reduction in the economic value of tobacco, and a general loss of respect for the tobacco industry, to further a change in fortunes within tobacco policy networks.

However, the effect should not be exaggerated, for three main reasons. First, the initial position of tobacco companies allowed them to slow down the change in policy that contributed to their eventual displacement. Most of the post-war period is characterised by successful attempts by tobacco interests to address health concerns with policies more suitable to producers than public health groups – such as introducing filters for cigarettes, funding medical research and providing ventilation rather than smoking bans in public places (Cairney, 2007b: 57). In particular, governments in many countries were willing to allow cigarette manufacturers to police themselves with voluntary codes to regulate issues, such as advertising and then smoking in public places. This made the problem of regulation much simpler, especially when it was not clear in what direction – control or promotion – the debate was going to go. Second, tobacco companies may still have behind-the-scenes influence in many developed countries, especially Germany, Japan, and parts of the US. The tobacco manufacturers, led by Philip Morris, British American Tobacco Company, and Japan Tobacco International, are multinational corporations based in developed countries with immense financial resources to hire publicists, lobbyists, attorneys, and other personnel as needed (the tobacco industry is estimated to worth more than US$400bn). Even smokers' rights organisations, such as FOREST in the UK, receive financing by tobacco companies.

Third, tobacco is now a global and still highly profitable industry; the major companies have maintained their economic power and extended their political influence by exploiting new markets in developing countries (Yach and Bettcher, 2000; Mamudu, 2008). Through acquisition and mergers, four transnational tobacco companies dominate the world tobacco market (see Figure 1.2). Much of their operations in terms of buying leaf and finding consumers have shifted to the developing world, where political economy still remains an important frame for tobacco control policymaking and the vast majority of people are still not conversant on the health effects of tobacco use. The lack of an equivalent shift in policy networks in developed countries is a further reason for developed countries and NGOs to pursue the issue through a combination of the FCTC and capacity-building initiatives to ensure that there is enough domestic pressure to ensure FCTC implementation. In some countries we can identify an arrangement that is similar to the early post-war period in developed countries: tobacco companies with strong economic power enjoying close links to government and remaining relatively immune from threat by public health advocates. Further, in China, tobacco production is state-controlled, and the Chinese government supports a large part of the farming sector. There are also few domestic sources for tobacco control pressure; less than half of Chinese physicians have a comprehensive knowledge of the links between smoking and illness, while more than one-third admitted to smoking in front of their patients (Wu, 2008; Cairney, 2009b: 1106–7).

Anti-tobacco groups began developing as a global movement and part of the tobacco control epistemic community following the First World Conference on Tobacco or Health (WCTOH) in 1967 in New York (Mamudu, 2008). A group of mostly developed countries began the process of diffusing scientific knowledge among themselves and eventually to developing countries, as well as nurturing the emergence of public health groups in developing countries through logistic and financial support and capacity-building activities. Until the mid-1990s, large domestic charities in tobacco control in developed countries, such as the American Cancer Society, and international counterparts, such as the International Union Against Cancer (UICC), the International Union Against Tuberculosis and Lung Diseases (IUATLD), and the International Organisation of Consumer Unions (IOCU) were at the forefront of encouraging anti-tobacco groups in developing countries. These anti-tobacco groups allied with the WHO in the worldwide promotion of tobacco control. Thus, to ensure the successful development of the FCTC, the WHO mobilised the support of these groups, who became the Framework Convention Alliance (FCA), an independent actor in the entire process (Mamudu and Glantz, 2009). Since the mid-2000s, these anti-tobacco groups have allied with philanthropists in developed countries, such as the Bloomberg Foundation and the Bill and Melinda Gates Foundation to promote tobacco control policy and advocacy and to nurture nascent tobacco control civil society in developing countries.

Socioeconomic factors

The relationship between socioeconomic factors and the processes we describe (shifts in institutions, problem definition and networks) are symbiotic. For example, tobacco policy strategies rely to a large extent on their socioeconomic context: falling smoking prevalence makes it easier to introduce further tobacco control policies, which help reduce smoking prevalence further and, in many cases, reduce opposition to additional measures. As a general relationship, we would expect the willingness of policymakers to introduce tobacco control to be relatively high when smoking prevalence is low, tobacco provides a dwindling source of tax revenue and jobs, and when opinion polls highlight a reduction in public opposition to (or increase in support for) policy innovation. Again, we can identify a contrast between developed countries. In the former, prevalence, economic value, and opposition are generally dropping. In the latter, economic value may be relatively high, prevalence levels are often rising (sometimes from low levels), and opposition remains strong. Overall, the socioeconomic context facilitates tobacco control in developed countries but constrains the process in developing countries – a further rationale for developed countries and NGOs to pursue policy transfer.

Smoking prevalence and behaviour

In the 1950s smoking prevalence was around half the population in most developed countries. It was considerably higher among men (up to 70%), and it spread across society after starting among the economically better off. After the 'health scare' of the early 1950s, smoking rates dropped briefly, at least in the US and Canada, but then returned to even higher levels. Public warnings by medically-related groups and eventually governments helped raise the issue of tobacco as a health issue in the 1960s, but public attention was erratic. Once again smoking prevalence dropped for a time in some countries but later rose again. To a large extent, the early health warnings struggled to compete with tobacco advertising, particularly when it appealed to the women's liberation movement of the time, attracting an increasing proportion of younger women as smokers even as smoking declined in other demographic groups. Further, in the 1970s, the development of the 'light', 'mild', and 'ultra light' cigarettes, which were supposedly less harmful than regular cigarettes, helped retain and recruit smokers. Educational measures alone seemed to have minimal effect, and even bans on television advertising were counteracted with other forms of promotion, such as the sponsorship of televised sports and arts events. Overall, the decline of cigarette smoking in developed countries was slow and erratic. It also fell more slowly among some social groups; upper and middle-class groups gave it up at greater rates, leaving mass cigarette consumption more class-based.

Rates and amounts of smoking vary markedly across regions and levels of wealth account for much of this variation. Laugesen and Meads (1991) examine total tobacco products consumption per adult. In 1965 the range in 14 developed countries was from 1,649 grams per adult in Italy to 4,672 in the US. Some poorer, more agrarian countries, such as Italy and Ireland, saw consumption grow as their economic prosperity increased, a familiar relationship that is still apparent in developing countries elsewhere (Nellen et al, 1995; FAO, 2003). From 1965–1991 there was a mean reduction of 20% over these 14 countries, especially pronounced in later years. The range was considerable, however, from an *increase* of 35% in Japan to a 53% reduction in New Zealand. Nine countries had declines, but three countries had increases. By the first decade of the 21st century, some developed countries had achieved overall adult smoking rates of around 20%, but others still had rates of 30–40%. Smoking rates among (especially younger) women in a few Northern European countries exceeded those of men. This is a historical reversal not yet apparent in several Asian countries, notably China, Japan, and Indonesia, where male smokers outnumber female smokers sometimes by 50–60 percentage points (Shafey et al, 2009; WHO, 2008).

Overall, there are more people smoking than ever before as the numbers grow in populous developing countries, with the exception of countries with strong tobacco control programmes, such as Singapore, South Africa, Thailand, Uruguay, and Venezuela (FAO, 2003). There also is a considerable incubation period between high rates of smoking and later high rates of consequential diseases, suggesting the potential for lurches of attention. In turn, governmental attention to tobacco control will not produce an immediate reduction in morbidity and mortality rates.

Economic benefits of tobacco

The economic and social benefits of tobacco cultivation and manufacture were once unquestioned. Not only did governments view tobacco crops as a regular, desirable source of income for their rural populations, but they also subsidised their production. In addition, organisations, such as the World Bank and the UN Food and Agricultural Organisation (FAO) once promoted tobacco as part of developmental programmes in the developing world (Ramin, 2006; Mamudu et al, 2008b). Domestic subsidies have been phased out in most developed countries. This, combined with competition from developing countries, has produced a steep decline in tobacco agriculture in the industrialised world. Total employment related to the manufacture of cigarettes has never been very large and has shrunk further in developed countries as technology became more important. As tobacco companies have bought more leaf from developing countries, the economic and political importance of tobacco was reduced in developed countries. The more significant measure of the companies' value to governments was the proportion of a country's GDP raised in excise taxes, as well as the amount lost through smuggling and counterfeit tobacco. Tax revenue in the developed countries has been reduced as smoking prevalence has fallen.

In contrast, there are still many cases in developing countries where governments regulate tobacco lightly, promote tobacco cultivation, and/or rely more heavily on tobacco-related taxes. The relative decline in smoking prevalence and the increase in regulation in developed countries (particularly since the 1980s) has encouraged tobacco companies to shift their operations to developing countries in Latin America, Asia, and Africa. In some of these countries, the companies provided a tax base and jobs that were not easily replaced. The tobacco industry also wields economic and political influence through activities, such as the development of economic impact studies to demonstrate the importance of tobacco (Mamudu et al,

2008b). International trade rules negotiated through the General Agreement on Tariffs and Trade Uruguay Round of Trade Talks, 1986–1994, treated tobacco as any other commercial product and, in the 1980s, the US Trade Representative (USTR) was especially aggressive in helping open foreign markets for companies in Asian countries previously under the exclusive domain of the state tobacco monopolies (Japan, South Korea, Taiwan, and Thailand). Furthermore, the end of planned economies in Central and Eastern Europe and the collapse of the Soviet Union led multinational tobacco companies to compete for the markets and the residue of state monopolies in these countries (Gilmore et al, 2004; Gilmore and Zatoński, 2002), although they later came under the aegis of EU tobacco control policy (see Chapter 4). Meanwhile, the state-owned Chinese National Tobacco Company has a virtual monopoly of supply for one-third of the world's smokers. Tobacco production has contributed 8–11% of total government revenue in China in the past 15 years and supports a large part of the farming sector (Wu, 2008; Cairney, 2009b: 1106–7).

Social attitudes

We identify in both developed and developing countries a 'permissive consensus' in public opinion, where the public appears not to demand government action but is increasingly willing to support it. Or, at least, the majority of the general public may be willing to allow the political battle over tobacco to be conducted by organised elites without close attention. It is relatively difficult to present a precise picture of social attitudes to tobacco control because comprehensive polls on the subject have not been taken until recently and the results vary according to the measure used. Nevertheless, most surveys show that a majority of the public across developed and developing countries support tobacco control, particularly smoke-free policies. As we discuss in Chapter 5, there are at least three different ways in which social attitudes to tobacco control can be used in the policy process. First, policy participants interpret and publicise public opinion data according to their own purposes. A classic example is the choice between arguing that the vast majority of the public want restrictions on smoking in public places versus arguing that most do not want a complete ban. Second, governments may rely more on responses to their official consultations, which may result in higher levels of support for tobacco control from an active minority encouraged by organised anti-tobacco groups. Third, policymakers act on less precise perceptions of the public mood. Significantly, all three rely on the interpretation and use of public opinion data by interest groups and policymakers; the facts do not necessarily speak for themselves.

On that basis, we provide a broad picture here and present more detailed analysis in individual chapters. The available evidence indicates that the publicised dangers of smoking cigarettes have been absorbed, at least on a general level, by members of the public. Public opinion has gradually shifted toward greater willingness to have the government legislate tobacco control measures. Perhaps because of the lack of open partisan and ideological confrontation over the issue, there are relatively few electoral benefits in tobacco control legislation. However, governments have acted on public opinion information in different ways. For example, in the UK many policymakers have expressed (and acted on) a perception that tobacco control has become a more pressing issue recently and that there has been a surge of support for measures, such as a ban on smoking in public places (Chapter 5). This contrasts with a sense in many developing countries that policymakers do not feel the same pressure to act. Perhaps public health advocates in these countries are not as able to translate the evidence on public opinion into a pressing reason for governments to act (Chapter 8).

The role of ideas: Scientific knowledge

To a large extent the major change in problem definition, from tobacco as an economic to a health issue, reflects the rising importance of cumulative scientific evidence (Mamudu et al, 2011b). It is now widely accepted that the damaging health effects of primary and secondary exposure to tobacco smoke include almost a dozen cancers and chronic diseases, and that tobacco use is not only a major cause of death worldwide but also a preventable one (see Chapter 1). Moreover, the situation is complicated by the issue of information asymmetry, whereby smokers are not informed about the full consequences of their choice and many of them begin smoking as minors. This knowledge has been used to reframe the policy image of tobacco and to advocate and justify tobacco control. In particular, this made it more difficult for tobacco promoters to argue for individual choice as the evidence on addiction grew and studies established that the effects of these choices had negative health consequences for others (non-smokers). However, the progression from evidence to policy was by no means immediate or inevitable. It took a long time for cumulative research to make any inroads on public policy, and even today the public health/morality regime's dominance is uneven across (and within) countries. In some countries in continental Europe, such as Germany, there is resistance to accepting the evidence on secondhand smoke (Schneider and Glantz, 2008). More generally, the tobacco industry has used its immense financial power to fund studies which cast doubt on the links between smoking, passive smoking and illness (a strategy that has been adopted by many companies in other sectors – Oreskes and Conway, 2010).

The scientific evidence began to become significant in the post-World War II period. There was some earlier work produced in Germany, but this was considered to be too closely related to the Nazi regime (and Hitler in particular) to have a longer-term positive impact (Proctor, 1999; Duina and Kurzer, 2004). Initially, the major source of research on tobacco and health came from the UK and the US; indeed, most countries with smaller research capacities were content to leave the research to a few larger countries, led by these two. The publication of the first large-scale, English-language studies of the effects of cigarette smoking in the early 1950s (see, for example, Doll and Hill, 1950) began a slow process of changing the terms of the political debate on smoking. The causal links between smoking and health were definitively established within the policy process by the reports of the UK Royal College of Physicians (1962) and the US Department of Health, Education and Welfare (1964). However, tobacco control policies did not begin to proliferate in developed countries until the mid-1980s after a sustained period of 'policy hesitancy' (at a time when smoking prevalence remained above 40% in some countries) (Studlar, 2004).

A similar process can be identified in relation to passive smoking. The link between SHS and illness, first established in Japan by Hirayama (1981) was authoritatively endorsed in the US by official reports from the US Surgeon General (USDHHS, 1986), the National Academy of Sciences (in 1986), and the Environmental Protection Agency (in 1992) (see also Ong and Glantz, 2000; Mamudu et al, 2011b), and an increasing number of country-specific investigatory agency reports elsewhere (European Commission, 2004; note the irony that its impact was less significant in Japan). Over recent years many countries have moved from limited restrictions on SHS to outright bans in an increasing number of public locations. In the US in particular, the evidence on the health effects of secondhand tobacco smoke was a catalyst for civil society mobilisation against tobacco use and cessation advocacy through the media and the provision of government services (Nathanson, 1999; Pertschuk, 2001; Wolfson, 2001; Glantz and Balbach, 2000). However, this process has taken over two decades, with some developed countries having only partial smoking bans 20 years after the first US Surgeon General's report.

Scientific knowledge therefore represents a set of powerful ideas that have been used to stimulate profound change in the way that tobacco is framed and solved as a policy problem. However, the lag between the production of that knowledge and policy change is significant, and the variation in policy across the globe demonstrates that change is not inevitable. In particular, the translation of ideas to policy faced several obstacles. First, the tobacco industry often played a critical role in the funding, direction and dissemination of the medical research (Ong and Glantz, 2001). Second, it was often able to address medical concerns with non-threatening policies, such as the introduction of filter tips and 'mild' varieties of cigarettes to make smoking look safer, and some concessions, such as voluntary regulations, to make it look like the problem had been solved. Third, governments which had hitherto favoured cigarette smoking as a predictable source of revenue were loath to give it up. While it may *now* seem inevitable that the evidence would lead to tobacco control, this is a relatively novel perspective. For example, in the 1960s the less cumulatively established evidence was competing in the minds of policymakers with the following facts: (1) smoking prevalence was high; (2) regulations may have been greeted with intense opposition; (3) key finance and trade ministries had close links with the tobacco industry; (4) there were few sources of public health advocacy, and they competed with tobacco advertising and a relatively innocuous media presence; and (5) there were other, more pressing social and political problems on the agenda.

The transfer of ideas

We can identify two distinct processes of tobacco policy transfer. First, leading developed countries have produced a 'comprehensive' package of tobacco control measures (see Chapter 2). Second, this allows other developed countries to learn and adapt policy lessons, drawing on the experience of predecessor countries through direct visits or indirect links via domestic medical and public health networks (which are themselves part of strong transnational policy networks). This process has produced an impressive degree of policy convergence across multiple countries (Studlar, 2004; Cairney, 2009a: 473; Studlar et al, 2011). However, it has only occurred in countries that (in most cases) exhibit particular trends: the shift towards health ministry centrality; public health influence at the expense of tobacco companies; from political economy to public health as the dominant frame; and, favourable socio-economic conditions which include a reduction in smoking prevalence. The relevant networks have also taken decades to develop.

Since tobacco control policy was initially a new and unfamiliar issue, countries had little experience dealing with such non-contagious public health issues and were willing to look for usable lessons from abroad. From the 1960s many governments and NGOs have referred to foreign sources for scientific information and policy feasibility. Combinations of science and advocacy, such as the Report of the Royal College of Physicians in the UK (1962, 1971) or, more frequently, US Surgeon General's reports, are convenient sources of this information. When new policies are under consideration, so-called international 'super-experts', government officials or NGO advocates, are often solicited to give personal testimony (Thomson and Wilson, 2001). US litigation activity has also received broad international attention, but so far little emulation (Studlar, 2002). Not all countries are equally attentive to lessons from abroad. Smaller countries with limited research and policy bureaucracies are especially likely to look for evidence elsewhere. However, even these countries can be information and policy lenders as well as borrowers. Countries identified as leaders in tobacco control have spread their messages through bilateral contacts and NGOs, institutions, such as the EU, WHO, the UN, and World Bank, conferences, such as the periodic World Conference on Tobacco Or Health since 1967, international networks, such as GLOBALink, research/advocacy institutions, such as the Research for International Tobacco Control of the Canadian International Development Research Center and US Centers for Disease

Control and Prevention (CDC), and publications, such as the journal *Tobacco Control* since 1992 (Mamudu, 2008). Much of this learning can now take place electronically (Wipfli et al, 2010; Mamudu, 2008; Mamudu et al, 2011b).

Second, the widening gap between tobacco control policy in different regimes, coupled with the global spread of the tobacco industry, has prompted leading developed countries, international organisations and NGOs to foster policy learning through initiatives, such as the FCTC. The country-to-country learning and emulation process began to metamorphose into global collective action on tobacco control in the early 1990s. The idea of an international health treaty to control tobacco was first broached in the 1990s by academics and researchers (Mackay, 2003; Roemer et al, 2005; Mamudu and Glantz, 2009). It was embraced by the WHO in 1995, which initiated the negotiation of the FCTC through a World Health Assembly resolution. The pace of the entire FCTC process was slow until Gro Harlem Brundtland became Secretary-General of the WHO in 1998; she made tobacco control one of her top two priorities and elevated it to a cabinet-level issue. The idea of an international treaty for tobacco control came to fruition with the adoption of the FCTC in 2003. The process of negotiating the FCTC made governments, especially health ministry officials from developing countries, aware of instruments and developments elsewhere. Much of what is in the FCTC has already been adopted by many developed countries (Laugessen et al, 2000; Shibuya et al, 2003). Thus, much like the EU, the FCTC can be considered as a major policy transfer platform to help countries (mostly developing) learn from these experiences (see Chapters 4 and 9).

Conclusion

In many (if not most) developed countries, tobacco policy is radically different now in comparison to the early post-World War II period. An era in which the tobacco industry was encouraged by governments to grow and sell tobacco has been replaced by an era of increasingly restrictive tobacco control. Indeed, it has changed markedly since the 1980s. In most cases, the pre-1980s picture is one of limited tobacco control: taxes were relatively low, bans in smoking in public places were thin on the ground, measures to discourage tobacco advertising beyond television were based on ineffective voluntary agreements, health warnings were low key, health education struggled to compete with tobacco advertising, and few smoking cessation services were available. In contrast, many countries have now introduced punitive tax regimes, legislation to ban advertising and smoking in public places, graphic health warnings, extensive and hard hitting health education, and cessation services. There is therefore no doubt that we have witnessed major policy change over the long term.

We can explain such policy change with reference to the five factors introduced in Chapter 2: health ministries have replaced other government departments as the focal point for tobacco policy (institutions); policy choices are based on the framing of tobacco as a health problem rather than an economic benefit (choices); public health groups have replaced tobacco companies at the centre of government (networks); smoking prevalence, opposition to tobacco control, and the economic benefits of tobacco have fallen (socioeconomic factors); and, the scientific evidence on the links between smoking, SHS and health have been accepted within, and shared between, governments (ideas). While each factor is insufficient on its own to explain change, all five combine to reinforce each other. For example, health ministry centrality ensures greater access and influence for public health groups, while those groups (often funded by health departments) helped secure the shift in problem definition that facilitated institutional change by disseminating the scientific evidence. Similarly, tobacco controls contribute to a drop in smoking prevalence, while reduced levels of smoking often facilitate the introduction of further controls.

By extension, we can explain why tobacco policy has *not* changed as quickly in developing countries with reference to the absence of many of these processes: while health ministries are more central than they once were, the political economy frame is still important; public health groups are less organised, active and strong; tobacco companies are more influential within government; and, smoking prevalence and/or the economic value of tobacco is high. Consequently, there are fewer sources of domestic pressure to change tobacco policy in most developing countries. This lack of tobacco policy capacity, combined with the widening gap between tobacco control policies in different regimes, has prompted government actors, international organisations and NGOs to promote tobacco policy transfer through mechanisms, such as the FCTC.

4
European Countries and the EU

This chapter outlines the main policy developments within the European Union (EU), individual member states, and other European countries. In the past half century both the EU and several member states (and their substate governments) have taken action on tobacco policy. The EU has had a formal role in tobacco control since 1987 when it assumed shared responsibility for public health policy with its member countries. The EU's public health authority has expanded since then to cover most of Europe as it has grown from 12 member states in 1987 to 27 in 2011. More generally, European tobacco policy has changed markedly in the post-war era. We identify a broad trend towards more restrictive tobacco control, with the number, range, and strength of tobacco policy instruments increasing markedly in the last 25 years. However, the effect is by no means uniform. There is considerable variation in the timing and substance of tobacco control within the EU and, in some cases, within member states. In particular, until recently, tobacco control has been generally less well developed in the 12 recent 'accession' states (mostly from Central and Eastern Europe). As a result, the effect of the EU as a source of policy diffusion has varied. Its role is relatively limited with 'leader' states that have demonstrated a willingness to go beyond the EU agenda. In contrast, its role is significant for 'laggard' states that are obliged to implement EU regulations beyond their current requirements, as well as accession states mandated to engage in tobacco control as a condition of EU membership.

The aim of this chapter is to identify and explain policy change in Europe (largely west of Russia and the remaining East European states where Russia still exerts some influence). The chapter charts the adoption of tobacco policy instruments across European countries, identifying leaders and laggards over time. It also displays some differences from the global picture we outline in Chapter 3. In most instances we identify the same causal factors: institutional change, with departments of health becoming more central to the policy process; agenda-setting, with tobacco increasingly seen as a health problem rather than a source of economic benefit; networks, with anti-smoking groups becoming more organised and better represented within government; socio-economic factors, with levels of smoking and opposition to tobacco control decreasing; and the role and transfer of ideas, with the evidence on the health effects of tobacco becoming more accepted within government and policy solutions increasingly shared and adopted across the EU. There is also value in comparing the experience of developed and developing countries in Europe.

However, the EU also provides an added element of institutional change and policy transfer. The EU has taken increasing responsibility for tobacco control, supplementing the role of member states and providing a new venue of influence for interest groups. The EU acts increasingly as the hub for policy diffusion – setting a policy framework, passing regulations that member states are often obliged to adopt, and encouraging the wider process of voluntary transfer when member states and interest groups share ideas.

What is tobacco policy in Europe?

Sustained political action against tobacco did not occur in most jurisdictions, including the EU, until the 1980s (Studlar, 2004). Figure 4.1 presents a picture of the extent of change, since the mid-1980s, in 15 EU member states (12 further members joined from 2004–7). The tobacco policy 'scores' are based on the extent to which each country adopted a particular policy instrument. A score of 2 is assigned to a relevant policy ban and a score of 1 to

Figure 4.1 Comprehensive Tobacco Control Policy in the Older European Union

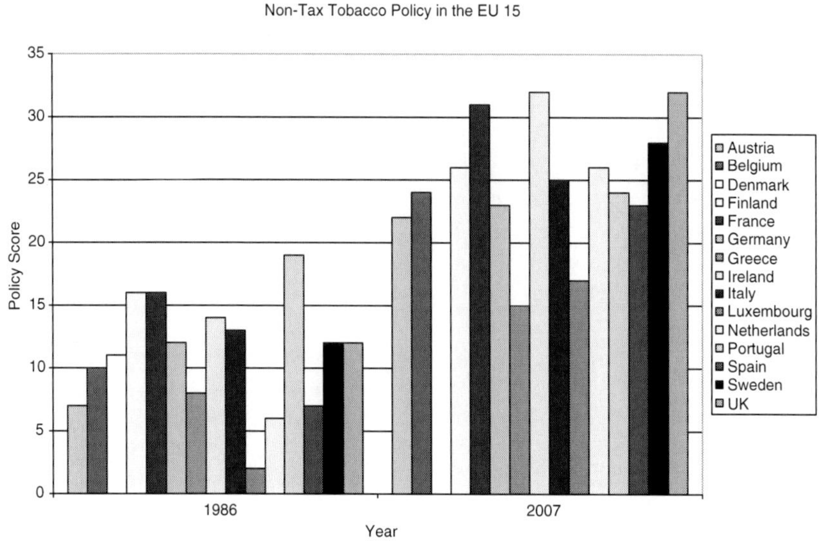

Source: Adapted from Studlar et al (2011)

a more limited policy restriction. The maximum possible score is 34, based on the availability of 17 policy instruments (see Studlar et al, 2011 for a full account). The scores are significantly higher in 2007 in all cases, suggesting that tobacco policy within the EU has become more restrictive over time. Both the scale and speed of government responses have increased substantially. Existing policy instruments have been strengthened and some countries with voluntary agreements with tobacco companies have found self-enforcement to be inadequate and replaced these with governmental legislation and executive orders. Overall, there has been significant policy convergence in the use of regulatory, financial and educational instruments.

Regulation

Calls for governments to restrict the direct advertising of tobacco products, and indirect advertising through sponsorship of sports and cultural activities and other promotions of its corporate name and products, were met first with restrictions and later bans. The new focus on the effects of second-hand smoke (SHS) made a *prima facie* case for restrictions on where people could smoke, especially in public, enclosed areas, such as airplanes, auditoriums, public transport, and government buildings. Restrictions in these venues were extended to others, including restaurants, bars, and gaming premises. Bans replaced restrictions in the former venues and, although they were more difficult to impose, comprehensive bans diffused after 2000. By 2008 12 European countries (ten in the EU) had such comprehensive bans (Scoggins et al, 2009). Other instruments have also developed in a less consistent way: age restrictions for purchase; sales restrictions, including vending machines and minimum size packages, and limitations on point-of-sale advertising.

Economic

Another re-prioritisation of instruments concerned the influential view that cigarette taxation could be increased for punitive purposes, to discourage smoking rather than only to raise revenue. Reliance on revenue from tobacco taxation at the central government level has long varied considerably across Europe, without any evident relationship to the general strength of tobacco control restrictions (Wilensky, 2002: 567; Studlar et al, 2011). In the longer term, EU governments have reduced their reliance on tobacco taxes for revenue and focused more on reducing consumption (European Commission, 2004: 85–6). In the 1970s a few governments increased taxation for health purposes, but more did so in the 1980s, and by the early 1990s the EU had decided to harmonise cigarette taxation at a high level, over half the purchase price. However, price differentials still occurred among countries, leading to sometimes severe smuggling problems (see Chapter 5 for UK examples). The entry of ten new members from Central and Eastern Europe in 2004 and 2007 has complicated the taxation issue, with some countries receiving temporary derogations from EU harmonisation requirements, as well as provided opportunities for the extension of tobacco regulation into an area that had little of it during the Communist era (Frisbee et al, 2009).

Education

Health warnings on packages became more universal, direct, and varied (a policy pioneered by Sweden in 1975). By the mid-2000s, the EU had endorsed graphic health warnings. The EU was also proactive in ingredient disclosure and product regulation; since the early 2000s it has required information on the major toxic contents of cigarettes and the volume of ingredients on many packages. Anti-smoking media campaigns were more frequent and more direct.

Other measures

Although more erratically developed, eventually other instruments were employed more broadly as well, sometimes at levels below the state: capacity-building, mainly government aid to tobacco control organisations; and periodic government reports and goals for a strategic tobacco control policy. One difference from the US has been that litigation has only rarely been pursued in European countries since their legal systems are less conducive to this approach. Nevertheless, the EU has taken legal action against tobacco companies for smuggling activities (European Commission, 2004).

As Figure 4.1 suggests, the basic trend is towards further tobacco control. The repertoire of instruments utilised to combat tobacco use has broadened and deepened. Government concern about the increasing burden on the public healthcare system of death and disease from tobacco consumption has been a stimulus for increased activity, even in tobacco control laggards. Governments became more willing to oppose tobacco industry and grower interests (including the International Union of Tobacco Growers, UNITAB) in the face of mounting evidence of health harm and a declining domestic tobacco economy. Both leaf growing and the market for manufactured cigarettes were moving to developing countries. In Europe there were calls for governments to restrict not only direct advertising of tobacco products, but also indirect advertising through tobacco industry sponsorship of sports and cultural activities and other promotions of its corporate name and products. Such pressure eventually produced moves to ban these activities.

However, while there is considerable convergence and a clear direction of response, there is also a high degree of variation from one country to another. The uneven progress of policy across European countries has created space for the EU to act as a facilitator and coordinator. This was made possible by the *Single European Act* of 1987, which provided for measures, such as the harmonisation of health and safety standards for products, to create a single market among the then 12 member states. Over the past two decades there has been shared responsibility between the EU and member states for certain public health policies, including tobacco control.

While member states retain most authority, the EU has the capacity to coordinate, complement, and support public health efforts.

The first EU involvement in tobacco policy involved subsidies to agricultural producers (see Table 4.1). Until recently tobacco was the most heavily subsidised product in the EU. Direct agricultural production subsidies for tobacco, amounting to 2% of the EU's Common Agricultural Policy (CAP), were phased out in 2010 (Elinder et al, 2003; European Commission, 2004). They represented far more money than is spent on tobacco control efforts (European Commission, 2004: 70). The first tobacco agricultural subsidies were followed in 1972 by the EU's first attempt to harmonise taxation policy. However, the modern pursuit of tobacco control really began with the 'Europe Against Cancer' programme, starting in 1987. Through directives, binding on member states, the EU has attempted to shape major instruments, such as taxation, advertising, health warnings, and product content while using recommendations to urge member states to action on other instruments, most recently non-smoking areas (Scoggins et al, 2009). But the EU has also engaged in media campaigns, capacity-building through aid to 'public interest' anti-tobacco non-governmental organisations, and a limited amount of litigation against tobacco companies. These developments, supplemented by its active participation in the Framework Convention on Tobacco Control (FCTC), have made the EU a leading international tobacco control jurisdiction (Asare, 2007) and provide a new institutional setting for struggle over policy (Princen, 2008; Mamudu and Studlar, 2009).

The European position is therefore a combination of member state initiatives and increasing EU involvement, producing a mixed picture of policy convergence and variation. For example, some states have recently introduced a policy that appears to represent the pinnacle of tobacco control – comprehensive indoor smoking bans – while others only meet basic EU standards for tobacco control (Joossens and Raw, 2006, 2007; Studlar et al, 2011; Scoggins et al, 2009). EU influence is especially evident in the case of the 12 recent accession members (Gilmore et al, 2004; McKee et al, 2004). Eight of the accession countries had no tobacco control instruments in place before they shed Communism; by the time of their accession, all of these countries had a full array. Recent EU application for membership and later accession was associated with a swift and significant policy downloading and convergence in tobacco control with older countries (Frisbee et al, 2009). EU influence also extends to countries, such as Germany, that often resist tobacco control measures. The most significant case regarded the first *Tobacco Advertising Directive*, which banned advertising and sponsorship in numerous venues beyond television, including radio, billboards, magazines, newspapers and the internet. This was challenged successfully in the ECJ by Germany in 2000. In response, the European Commission introduced a second, more limited *Tobacco Advertising Directive*, covering only trans-border, direct advertising (Duina and Kurzer, 2004; Gilmore and McKee, 2004).

Table 4.1 Chronology of Tobacco Control in the EU

1970	Tobacco growing subsidised in Common Agricultural Policy (CAP)
1972	First attempts at harmonisation of cigarette taxes
1985	First European anti-tobacco campaign announced (implemented 1987)
1987	*Single European Act*
1989	First EU health warnings; Television ad ban; Limits on product labelling; First EU non-binding resolution on tobacco control, second hand smoke
1990	First limits on toxic ingredients
1992	Tax harmonisation for cigarettes becomes renegotiated every few years
1993	Maastricht Treaty expands EU role in health, also emphasizes markets and subsidiarity; EU-level tobacco industry became more organized
1994	First EU financing of NGO capacity-building projects
1995	First advisory body on tobacco control, BASP, ends, eventually replaced by ENSP (1997)
1996	First general EU statement on tobacco control policy (others 1999, 2002)
1997	First EU general ad ban approved (TAD1)
1999	Amsterdam Treaty, Article 129, 'A high level of human health level protection shall be assured in the definition and implementation of all Community policies and activities.' EU recommended policies for member states
2000	ECJ strikes down TAD1; Lisbon Process
2001	Tobacco Products Directive, including larger health warnings, ban on 'light and mild' descriptors
2002	EU sues tobacco companies for smuggling in the US; Council recommendation on improving tobacco control
2003	Revised EU print, telecast, and internet ad and sponsorship ban (TAD2): Graphic warning labels approved
2004	EU signs FCTC; Ten new accession countries join EU

Table 4.1 Chronology of Tobacco Control in the EU – *continued*

2005	Agricultural price support for tobacco reduced, to end by 2010; Ten accession countries given delays for *acquis* on tobacco tax; Ratification of FCTC
2006	Commission refers Germany to the ECJ for lack of advertising ban transposition; Finnish Presidency emphasises health in all policies, including tobacco
2007	Green Paper on second-hand smoke restrictions; Two new accession members
2009	Council Recommendation on Smoke-Free Environments
2010	Revised EU tax harmonisation policy; EU signed an anti-smuggling agreement with British American Tobacco
2011	Fire-safe cigarettes approved as mandatory safety standard; Revision of Tobacco Products Act under discussion; Tobacco Products Directive replaces Act in its current form

Source: Adapted and updated from Asare et al (2009)

Policy change and policy convergence in Europe

We can gauge tobacco policy trends in three main ways, by: identifying the scope, or number of policy instruments adopted; measuring the tempo, or speed at which policy instruments were adopted; and, measuring the strength, or degree of restrictiveness, of those policy instruments. We can also make useful comparisons, over time and space, between the older EU countries (15) and new accession members (12), plus three of the four European countries which are outside the EU but still accept the same EU tobacco control policies as members in order to give them access to the Single Market, mainly through the European Economic Area (EEA).

Table 4.2 identifies scope and tempo. The scope of policy is assessed through how many different types of instruments are adopted by a jurisdiction, with an index of 1.00 meaning that a country has adopted all of the indicated instruments. Tempo is assessed through an analysis of how quickly

Table 4.2 Scope and Tempo of Policy Adoptions in Western Europe, to 2007

	N	Scope	Range	Years	Tempo	N*
1. Ireland	23	0.96	1971–2004	34	1985	21
2. UK	22	0.92	1908–2006	99	1981	21
3. Norway	22	0.92	1965–1996	32	1981	20
4. Iceland	24	1	1969–1984	16	1981	21
5. Sweden	23	0.96	1964–1996	33	1986	19
6. Finland	22	0.92	1965–1999	35	1980	19
7. Italy	23	0.96	1934–2005	72	1979	17
8. France	24	1	1976–2003	28	1984	21
9. Netherlands	21	0.88	1981–2002	22	1994	19
10. Belgium	23	0.96	1975–2002	28	1985	20
11. Denmark	20	0.83	1972–2007	36	1989	19
12. Portugal	20	0.83	1981–2004	24	1989	16
13. Greece	17	0.75	1952–2002	51	1987	12
14. Germany	20	0.83	1965–2004	40	1989	20
15. Switzerland	20	0.83	1975–2004	30	1991	13
16. Spain	22	0.92	1982–2005	24	1993	18
17. Austria	23	0.96	1973–2005	33	1996	20
18. Luxembourg	16	0.67	1977–2006	30	1991	16
Overall Average	21	0.9	1908–2007	100	1987	18

Sources: WHO Regional Office for Europe 2007, http://data.euro.who.int/tobacco; Roemer, 1982, 1993; European Commission. 1982; Sasco et al, 1989, 1992.
Note: N* refers to the number of cases for which exact dates of adoption can be found. The number of measures differ in each table according to the availability of data.

countries adopt various tobacco control instruments. This is measured through the mean year of adoption, with lower scores meaning earlier adoptions, either of individual or multiple instruments. It shows the pattern across 18 West European countries (15 EU members plus Norway, Iceland, Switzerland) in terms of the first introduction of policy instruments and the mean year of adoption for all of these 24 instruments. The instruments are largely regulatory and educational, with taxation excluded (see Studlar, 2009, for a full list). The countries are listed according to their positions on the Joossens and Raw (2006, 2007, 2008) tobacco control strength scale (Table 4.3). While individual countries may have slight adjustments to their Joossens-Raw rankings, the same group of countries tops each measure.

The top-ranked countries on the Joossens-Raw scale (Table 4.3) are also those that tend to have the widest scope of policy instruments as well as

Table 4.3 Western Europe, Tobacco Control Scores, 2004, 2005, 2007, 2010

Country	Scale Position 2004, 2005, 2007, 2010	Total Score (100)
UK	2, 2, 1, 1	72, 73, 93, 77
Ireland	4, 1, 2 =, 2	62, 74, 74, 69
*Norway	3, 3, 4, 3	67, 71, 66, 62
*Iceland	1, 4, 2 =, 4 =	76, 70, 74, 61
France	6, 8, 7, 6	54, 56, 59, 55
Finland	8, 6, 8 =, 7 =	53, 58, 58, 52
Sweden	5, 5, 6, 9	55, 60, 61, 51
Belgium	11, 12, 8 =, 10	38, 50, 58, 50
*Switzerland	13, 15, 18, 11	35, 35, 47, 48
Italy	9, 7, 10, 12	41, 57, 57, 47
Denmark	9, 13, 20, 13 =	41, 45, 45, 46
Netherlands	6, 10, 14 =, 13 =	54, 52, 50, 46
Spain	15, 16, 12, 13 =	32, 31, 55, 46
Portugal	12, 12, 23, 19 =	37, 39, 42, 43
Germany	13, 14, 27, 26	35, 36, 37, 37
Luxembourg	18, 18, 28 =, 29	23, 26, 36, 33
Austria	17, 16, 30, 30 =	31, 31, 35, 32
Greece	10, 13, 28, 30 =	40, 38, 36, 32
Average 15 countries		45, 48, 50, 48
Average 18 countries		47, 50, 51, 49

Source: European Commission, 2004: Joossens, 2004; Joossens and Raw, 2006, 2007, 2008, 2011 (*non-EU)

having a more rapid tempo (Table 4.2). In other words, they started early and accelerated their efforts rapidly across a broad range of instruments. Those at the bottom of the strength scale tend to have fewer total instruments and, for the most part, started later. Insofar as members of this group have been broadening their scope, it has been in recent years, even among the few that had early starts. Some countries have bursts of activity concentrated in a few years (Switzerland, Spain, Romania), while others return to the tobacco control agenda persistently or periodically to add instruments. Table 4.2 therefore shows a discernible pattern of tobacco control leaders, fence-sitters, and laggards (Börzel, 2002). Although some countries leap forward over a few years, most leaders, fence-sitters, and laggards establish early patterns that they continue with incremental or periodic changes. Once there is an institutional infrastructure for a restrictive tobacco control policy, with commitments in money and personnel as well as laws, then it can be built upon (although plateau effects may occur occasionally, as with early leaders Sweden and Finland in the 1980s) (European Commission, 2004).

However, there has also been clear convergence in the number and types of tobacco control policies across Europe: most countries have now adopted the majority of relevant policy instruments. This picture of upward convergence is reinforced by the studies led by Joossens and Raw and outlined in Tables 4.3 and 4.4. The rankings are based on a score derived from the six main instruments promoted by the World Bank: price increases, bans on smoking in public places, funded public information, advertising bans, health warnings and smoking cessation treatment – with each measure receiving points based on an estimate regarding the extent to which it influences smoking prevalence (see Chapter 1). Following the findings of much tobacco control research, price receives the largest score, but the relative importance of the other factors is more debatable. There was considerable change in the measurement of instruments and therefore scores assigned between the 2007 and 2010 studies, including attempting better assessment of implementation. This accounts for some of the variations and even reductions in scores for some countries between the two time periods.

Tables 4.3 and 4.4 present two main findings. First, there are clear leaders and laggards within Europe, and they are pretty consistent over this short term. The UK, Ireland, Norway, and Iceland contrast markedly with Germany, Luxembourg, and Austria. Overall, the leading countries in Western Europe are English-speaking and Nordic ones, with German-influenced and lower income countries trailing. Among Accession countries, Malta, with its history of British rule, is the most restrictive and is among the leaders of all EU countries. The German-influenced Czech Republic and other Central and Eastern Europe (CEE) countries are at the bottom. Second, although there is now more policy uniformity, the Accession countries, especially the CEE ones, are still lower as a group. The 18 West European countries rated

Table 4.4 EU Accession and Candidate Countries, Tobacco Control Scores, 2004, 2005, 2007, 2010

Country	Scale Position 2004, 2005, 2007, 2010	Total (100)
*Turkey	–, –, –, 4 =	–, –, –, 61
Malta	5, 5, 5, 7 =	58, 62, 62, 52
Romania	–, 29, 14 =, 16 =	–, 27, 50, 45
Latvia	25, 28, 24, 17 =	31, 29, 41, 44
Slovenia	13, 22, 25 =, 17 =	47, 36, 40, 44
Estonia	12, 17, 11, 19 =	47, 45, 56, 43
Poland	10, 12, 14 =, 19 =	52, 50, 50, 43
Lithuania	22, 25, 21, 22 =	35, 34, 44, 41
Slovakia	15, 14, 17, 22 =	43, 49, 48, 41
Bulgaria	–.16, 13, 24 =	–, 46, 54, 40
Cyprus	14, 11, 19, 24 =	44, 51, 46, 40
Czech Rep	27, 20, 25 =, 27 =	27, 38, 40, 34
Hungary	11, 15, 22, 27 =	49, 47, 43, 34
Average		43, 43, 48, 43

Source: European Commission, 2004; Joossens, 2004; Joossens and Raw, 2006, 2007, 2008, 2011 (*non-EU)

somewhat higher than the twelve others (now 13, with Turkey, a candidate member and a significant tobacco controller, being included in 2010) in all four years, in comparing the means of the two groups for each year: 47/43, 50/43 51/48 and 49/43. On the one hand, it is remarkable that Accession countries have made such progress in tobacco control (mainly in order to meet EU admission requirements); on the other, the new scoring scheme for 2010 showed the gap between old and new EU members to be widening, perhaps because of implementation problems in the latter group.

The situation in the CEE countries can be contrasted with that in Russia and other non-EU states formerly part of the Soviet Union. In those countries, especially Russia and the Ukraine, tobacco industry investment after the collapse of Communism has not been effectively countered by either the state or NGOs. The result is that smoking, already at high levels among men, has increased among both men and women, in line with what one might expect from middle income countries under the Tobacco Epidemic Model (Gilmore and McKee, 2005; Pomerleau et al, 2004; Lopez et al, 1994). The emergent international tobacco control regime has yet to have an impact, despite these countries signing the FCTC.

Institutions: Who has responsibility for tobacco control?

There are at least three institutional dimensions that could be relevant to the direction of tobacco policy in Europe. First, there are now more venues in which policy can be addressed. Tobacco control policy involves multi-level governance in the EU (Hooghe and Marks, 2001; Bache and Flinders, 2004; Mamudu and Studlar, 2009). In other words, over the past two decades the member states' monopoly on all tobacco control policy has been replaced by shared authority among different levels of government. The central state now shares responsibility with the EU for policies on taxation, health warnings, advertising and tobacco product regulation. In some cases it has allowed regional or local authorities to have authority for health education, smoking cessation strategies, and indoor non-smoking regulation. Several jurisdictions are involved, ranging from the local level to the EU (Princen, 2008; Princen and Rhinard, 2006; Strünck, 2005). This institutional arrangement increasingly resembles that in the US, in which there is often no exclusive jurisdiction for policy problems and no 'iron clad logic' for an issue to be considered at a particular level, producing the potential for a shift of responsibility across venues (Baumgartner and Jones, 1993: 43).

The 'Europeanisation' of policy refers to the mediating role of the EU in changing institutions, networks, political views, and public policy across member and associate countries. Sometimes this may be through the formulation and implementation of EU policies, but it may also occur through other processes of policy learning and diffusion. In fact, this pattern of multi-level governance in tobacco control has now been extended to the international level in the form of the FCTC as a guideline for EU and member state policy (see Chapters 9 and 10; Mamudu and Studlar, 2009; Council Recommendation, 2009).

In the EU system, the institutional responsibility for tobacco control policy is complex. The executive branch of the EU is the European Commission, a group of 27 members (one for each state but representing EU interests, not the member states), led by a President chosen by the member states and approved by the European Parliament. The 27 Commissioners are the effective cabinet for EU affairs. While the Commission is the main EU body for proposing tobacco control measures, others are also involved. The Council of Ministers, representatives of member state governments, must approve all directives, and are also subject to approval by the European Parliament, composed of directly-elected legislators from all member countries. While the former body represents the political executives of the states, Members of the European Parliament (MEPs) are less bound by party loyalty. The European Council, the meeting of member state heads of government, can also play a role by setting the long-term agenda. In tobacco control this occurred through the Council's initiation of the Europe Against Cancer programme that launched EU responsibility for tobacco control. The ECJ also becomes involved in the process if there is litigation over the legality of legislation or persistent implementation failures by states after warnings by the EU Commission.

Second, health departments may play an increasing role in tobacco policy. On the EU level, the Directorate of Health and Consumer Affairs (DG Sanco), is the main ministry responsible for tobacco matters, with some involvement by the ministries of Agriculture, Competition, Trade, Occupational Safety, Justice, and Finance (although the EU does not benefit directly from tax harmonisation, which flows through member state coffers). Within individual governments, the major ministries with an impact on tobacco control are health, treasury, agriculture, and sometimes commerce, industry, and occupational safety (see Chapter 5 on the UK). The balance among departmental responsibilities, and the level of institutional capacity for tobacco control policy, varies among the members of the EU. In the first decade of the 2000s, of the 15 older member countries, eight had a government agency specifically devoted to tobacco control (Shafey et al, 2009). Twelve countries had earmarked some taxes for tobacco control expenditures. Thirteen had government-funded tobacco control research (European Commission, 2004). Ten had tobacco control goals, but only one (Ireland) had a central research institute (Shafey et al, 2009). The lack of tobacco-specific institutional capacity in some member states makes the role of the EU more significant although its resources are also limited. In particular, regulatory and research personnel are in short supply, and the EU's influence in policy implementation is often weak (European Commission, 2004). Nevertheless, a Regulatory Committee of the Commission, established under the TPD, is composed of representatives of member states as well as DG Sanco civil servants. This committee meets twice per year to consider all dimensions of tobacco control, especially those concerning implementation issues and future possible proposals.

Third, member states have different constitutional arrangements (although we do not have evidence that they make a systematic difference to tobacco policy). Most European countries have parliamentary government, with an executive chosen by and responsible to the directly-elected lower house of the legislature. Party loyalty, especially if one's party helps form the government, is important and assures that backbench legislators have limited policy independence. However, most European countries also have multi-party systems, proportional representation electoral systems, and coalition governments; these institutions demand political compromise on the part of governing parties. The major exception is the UK, with a single member plurality electoral system and usually single-party government (although a coalition government was formed in 2010). France is the only clearly semi-presidential system although other regimes have elected presidents with some power in foreign policy. Most countries in Europe have a largely unitary form of rule, with the central government broadly responsible for all health issues, including public health. Aside from some federal systems (Germany and Switzerland but not Belgium and Austria) and a few that have developed asymmetrical forms of devolution (Spain, UK) or have more decentralised healthcare systems (Denmark, Portugal, Italy), full responsibility for tobacco control is lodged at the central level of the state (WHO Regional Office for Europe, 2007). The effects of decentralisation on tobacco control policy outcomes are unclear, particularly since most policy is made within the central executive (Studlar et al, 2011).

Broadly speaking, parties in the centre and left of the political spectrum are more favourable toward greater tobacco control, but only rarely has tobacco policy been the subject of major partisan controversy. Normally there has been a moving consensus on policy, with few policy reversals except in some formerly Communist regimes in the early years of democracy (Hungary) when transnational tobacco companies (TTCs) entered the country (Szilágyi, 2006). In countries, such as Germany and Denmark that consider tobacco control policy to be largely an issue of individual choice (morality), free votes on bills have occurred (Albæk, 2004; Frankenberg, 2004).

Agendas: How important is tobacco control as a policy issue? How is tobacco framed?

The major change in tobacco policy in the past half century reflects the way that the problem is now framed and its heightened status on the political agenda. Tobacco problem definition in Europe has changed in line with our broad findings in Chapter 3. In the 1950s tobacco smoking was considered an unobjectionable part of normal social life. The industry was viewed relatively positively and its status was often supported by its ability to sponsor many of the most popular arts and sporting events. At the beginning of the 1960s, some governments were aware, but had yet to address the implications, of the previous decade's scientific reports of the dangers of cigarette smoking. No governments had policies regulating tobacco consumption other than a few specific provisions, which, other than broadly cautionary admonitions to beware of possible health effects of smoking, were often relics from an earlier era and poorly enforced. As we discuss in Chapter 5, policy reflected the 'political economy' frame, with a focus on jobs, exports, and taxes. In some countries, such as France, Spain, and Italy, tobacco companies were government-owned.

In a period of less than 50 years, however, tobacco dimensions, such as smoking behaviour, the product, and even the industry have become controversial and even, in some respects, denormalised (Studlar, 2002; Mamudu and Studlar, 2009). Tobacco policy has moved, however hesitantly, away from a political economy model and toward a public health model, based on a new frame, with smoking now considered to be a major health problem that needs to be solved or at least managed (Cairney, 2007a). While cigarettes are still legally manufactured and sold in all countries, the driver of tobacco control policy clearly has changed. There may also be overtones of the morality policy that we identify in the US (Chapter 6), but this frame is less prominent in Europe (Leichter, 1991) and it competes with the idea of civil liberties in some countries (Chapter 5). There has also been uneven progress across Europe, reflecting partly the importance of idiosyncratic narratives in some countries, such as the strong association in Germany between public health measures and the former Nazi government, as well as the continuing influence of the tobacco industry (Proctor, 1999; Cooper and Kurzer, 2003; Grüning et al, 2006, 2008).

Networks: Has there been a shift in power between pressure participants?

Groups can be divided into pro-tobacco consumption interests (the tobacco manufacturing industry and its allies – see Chapter 3) and anti-tobacco groups (medical and public health professionals, organised health charities, non-profit anti-tobacco organisations). The balance of power within European countries has changed markedly, shifting from the former to the latter since the early post-war period, although the extent of change varies somewhat by country and should not be overstated. It sits between the profound shift in the UK identified in Chapter 5 and the more qualified global change outlined in Chapter 3. We may argue that public health groups now dominate in many countries, but this process is still ongoing; it is a struggle that has not ended.

The power transition may have been influenced by the various policy styles of each government which, in turn, may be a product of political systems (although we express concerns about this interpretation in Chapter 2). Domestic interest group structures in older European countries range from pluralist (UK, Ireland, France, and Southern Europe) to corporatist (all Nordic countries, Germany, Austria, Benelux countries), while those in new Central and Eastern European democracies are generally pluralist. We might expect that established pro-tobacco interests would have longer-lasting influence in corporatist than in pluralist systems since the former are less open to new groups than the latter. Comparative empirical studies have demonstrated that, in general, corporatism hinders tobacco control (Wilensky, 2002; Studlar et al, 2011). Yet, there are variations. For example, the pluralist UK had a corporatist-style relationship with tobacco companies for much of the post-war period, while corporatist countries, such as Norway were quicker to incorporate public health interests. Such cases suggest that the size of the tobacco industry was more of a predictor of group-government relations (Baggott, 1988). The role of the EU has also complicated matters by providing alternative venues for groups dissatisfied with policy in central government (or perhaps keen to reinforce policy in multiple venues). With a relatively new interest group structure developing, competition for influence in the EU is relatively open, hence-pluralist, even for groups accustomed to corporatist domestic arrangements. EU pluralist group competition is also likely to affect group-government relationships in the new accession states and, in particular, the former communist states once having strong central control.

The tobacco industry network

As an entrenched economic interest on both the domestic and transnational levels, the tobacco industry has traditionally had a supportive network in many countries. Where finance laws allowed, they often sponsored party political events. Tobacco influence on governments has persisted longer in German-speaking and German-influenced countries (principally Germany, Switzerland, Austria, and the Czech Republic) than elsewhere. Its influence has also become apparent in CEE countries that moved from tobacco production controlled by the state towards increasing provision from the Western-based TTCs (most notably Philip Morris). TTCs improved their position by fostering relationships with policymakers at various levels of government and lobbying to keep tobacco prices (including taxes) low and ward off advertising bans and content standards.

This new influence from TTCs has been offset to some degree by the EU demands for policy harmonisation (with its *acquis communautaire*) before these states were admitted (Frisbee et al, 2009). However, the tobacco industry and its allies have also worked to influence the EU from within (European Commission, 2004; Neuman et al, 2002). The tobacco companies have used sympathetic states (principally Germany) and front groups to affect EU tobacco policy (European Commission, 2004). For example, they have sought to alter the EU's excise tax policy on tobacco (Bingham, 1988; Bishop, 1998), opposed the Tobacco Advertising and Tobacco Products directives, tried individually (and collaboratively through the Tobacco Manufacturing associations) to weaken EU influence during the FCTC negotiations (Mamudu and Studlar, 2009), and tried to block further EU tobacco control measures under the rubric of 'better, less burdensome regulation'. The tobacco companies used the farmers' group in the EU (UNITAB), which is an affiliate of International Tobacco Growers' Association (ITGA), to lobby the EU on tobacco control and the FCTC. Tobacco companies have also received grants from the EU regional development programme to help equip cigarette factories and fund training projects, which contradicts the EU commitment to reduce its citizens' economic dependence on tobacco (Barr, 2010).

Anti-tobacco groups

The role and influence of anti-tobacco groups became significant from the 1980s in most Western European countries. Their positions were strengthened by the scientific evidence, such as reports on the damaging effects of SHS and evidence that tobacco use is addictive rather than a free choice, which allowed them to coalesce around a common reference point. Anti-tobacco non-governmental organisations seized on the evidence of health hazards to buttress their long-standing 'discomfort' arguments about cigarette smoke. Further, more groups were formed or took political stands against tobacco in the 1980s. The latter includes the politicisation of health charities, such as Cancer, Heart, and Lung/Respiratory societies, which may have already enjoyed close links to government in relation to the science and treatment of illnesses but had yet to exploit those links to lobby for tobacco control. Public health practitioners, academics, medical associations, and independent 'cause' groups also played an increasing role as they became better organised and better funded. In some countries these anti-tobacco groups were aided by grants from their central government (and departments of health in particular) for research or as 'public interest' advocates. Nevertheless, there has been an uneven process of social and group mobilisation across countries. While anti-tobacco groups have begun to dominate policy networks in the UK and in some surprising places, such as France, this shift in power is not matched in all countries.

Princen (2008) argues that the establishment of a new venue for tobacco control policy through the EU has been an advantage for anti-tobacco civil society groups, especially those in member states that lacked the influential connections to government agencies in their own countries that tobacco companies often had. Furthermore, those countries that had corporatist interest-group structures, often with tobacco industry involvement, were faced with a new, more pluralist structure in the EU and had to adapt their strategies accordingly. Since 1997, anti-tobacco groups in EU Member States have coalesced under a common umbrella organisation, the ENSP, set up under EU initiative and partial financing. ENSP was a replacement for the disbanded European Bureau of Action on Smoking Prevention (BASP), the first EU-level non-state advisory body on tobacco control, whose EU funding had been withdrawn (Gilmore and McKee, 2004). It is made up of 28 member state-level coalitions, with hundreds of member organisations and international networks active in tobacco control in Europe, including the European Federation of Allergy and Airways Diseases Patients Associations, National Survey of Families and Households, International Network of Women Against Tobacco, and European Union of Non-smokers. With its secretariat in Brussels, ENSP's mission is to develop a strategy for coordinated action among tobacco control organisations to promote comprehensive tobacco-control policies. More recently, ENSP's influence has been rivalled by the more independent Smoke Free Partnership, an alliance of the European Heart Network, the European Respiratory Society, Cancer Research UK, and until 2010 the French National Cancer Institute. Other networks, such as Association of European Cancer Leagues have also become actively involved in EU tobacco control policymaking processes and programmes, showing how pluralistic the EU interest-group structure has become.

Recently, harm regulation issues have created new alliances in tobacco control. All smokeless tobacco is banned in the EU except for Sweden, plus European Economic Area member Norway. Major tobacco companies have lobbied the EU to lift this ban, based on the favourable results for lower risks of some types of cancer for snus users. This move has been endorsed by some anti-smoking groups and the UK Royal College of Physicians, but remains controversial. A division in anti-tobacco ranks on the issue of harm reduction may be developing in Europe.

Socioeconomic factors

Economic benefits of tobacco

In the early post-war period, many governments viewed tobacco crops as a desirable source of income for their rural populations. Some European countries, such as France had government-owned tobacco companies, which were interested in maintaining semi-protected domestic markets. While EU single market competition rules led to governments selling these companies, until 2010 the EU subsidised tobacco agriculture directly *and* encouraged tobacco control. The EU and EEA countries constitute the fifth-largest unit of tobacco growers and the second-largest producers of manufactured cigarettes (25%) in the world. The tobacco industry varies by country, usually a mixture of domestic producers and branches of transnational corporations. Twelve older EU countries have significant domestic producers and all have a tobacco industry presence (European Commission, 2004). Together, Greece and Italy produce almost three quarters of the leaf. However, European tobacco leaf is low quality and has been losing market share to foreign growers (European Commission, 2004: 70). The three centres of tobacco manufacturing and export in the EU, and among the largest in the world, are Germany, the Netherlands, and the UK, with approximately two-thirds of the cigarette output in the EU (European Commission, 2004: 71; Shafey et al, 2009). Increasingly automated production processes reduced direct employment in tobacco manufacture to 0.13% of total EU-15 employment in 2000 (European Commission, 2004: 72).

Perhaps more important from a socioeconomic perspective is that most governments were accustomed to treating the tobacco industry as a key source of tax revenue. For example, tobacco taxation represented a staggering 16% of UK government income in 1950, falling to 3.6% by 1996 (Chapter 5). The lower figure is now similar to that in most EU countries, with tax revenue generally accounting for 1–5% of total government revenue. The exceptions are Greece (9%) and the Czech Republic and Poland (6–7%) (European Commission, 2004: 85). Governments are also increasingly aware of the economic costs of smoking. The health costs of smoking are estimated at about €100 billion ($146 billion), or around 1% of the EU's Gross Domestic Product (GDP). This is not much less than the €127 billion EU budget for 2011.

In the face of mounting evidence of health harm and a declining domestic tobacco economy, governments in developed countries became more willing to oppose tobacco industry and grower interests. Pressured by shrinking markets in the West, TTCs sought new markets in CEE countries where acceptance of, and dependence on, the product were high (Gilmore et al, 2004). In pre-collapse CEE countries, the tobacco market could typically be characterised as being a monopoly of one domestic producer controlled by the state. Advertising for tobacco products was superfluous. The government controlled the price of cigarettes, and the revenue stream from these products was significant. In the vacuum left in all aspects of society by the departure of the communist regimes in Central and Eastern Europe, Western-based TTCs saw tremendous market potential and seized the opportunities presented, until checked by the desire of these countries to join the EU (Lipand, 2007; Szilágyi, 2006).

Smoking prevalence

Smoking prevalence rates vary considerably across Europe, but have generally been converging downward. In the 1960s about half of the European population smoked, with even higher rates among males. In the mid-1980s smoking prevalence remained at approximately 40% across Europe, including Communist countries, with male rates usually above that figure. Generally, smoking is higher in CEE countries than in Western ones, especially among men (WHO, 2008). By 2010, these rates were reduced by about 25% almost everywhere (to around 30% overall), but more for men than for women and for those in the older EU than in the accession countries (Frisbee, 2010; European Commission, 2004: 146–7). Countries that were stronger on tobacco control restrictions generally had lower prevalence rates and greater reductions in smoking over time (Wilensky, 2002: 566; Studlar, 2004; European Commission, 2004; Frisbee, 2010). Nevertheless, these rates are still relatively high compared to other parts of the industrialised world, such as Canada, Australia, the US, and New Zealand, where the rates are near 20%. Only a few European countries, mainly Nordic ones, had comparably low rates to these non-European leaders, with others displaying higher prevalence.[3]

Public opinion on tobacco control policy

Governments operate within a climate of public opinion on tobacco control policy that they also help shape by, for example, reducing smoking prevalence. Even though public opinion data on tobacco issues in Western Europe is limited, there are some data available through the periodic Eurobarometer series conducted for the EU. Recent tobacco-related questions in these surveys exist for 2005, 2006, and 2009 (Table 4.5) and we can compare some of the results with less regular surveys in 1987 and 1995 (not in the table – see Europe Against Cancer, 1987; Eurobarometer 43, 1995). Three of these surveys have one common question, banning smoking in public places.

Table 4.5 % Favouring Smoking Bans, Europe

	2005	2006	2005	2006	2009	2005	2006	2009	2005	2006	2009
	Public Places		Work			Restaurants			Bars		
Ireland	88	86	90	88	79	93	88	78	82	84	70
UK	85	72	86	76	77	84	74	76	67	48	56
Sweden	93	90	95		90	89	86	81	82	75	70
Finland	93	91	92		87	89	50	65	82	41	52
Italy	91	77	91	77	88	90	74	88	88	73	87
France	88	69	91	77	73	78	49	60	59	29	41
Netherlands	82	67	88	88	63	68	37	53	46	19	31
Belgium	79	68	86	59	76	79	57	72	56	29	41
Denmark	79	61	83	66	63	69	36	49	48	19	34
Portugal	82	76	83	75	82	81	65	76	69	53	56
Greece	81	63	80	73	74	70	39	59	56	30	47
Germany	84	75	87		67	69	51	54	46	32	28
Spain	80		79			70			62		
Austria	65	47	71	46	66	62	31	38	42	21	24
Luxembourg	85	69	89	77	77	77	67	73	53	32	39
Whole EU	84	88	86	88	73	76	77	63	61	62	47

Source: Special Eurobarometer 239, 2006; Special Eurobarometer 272, 2007; Special Eurobarometer 332, 2010.

Public opinion has become progressively more supportive of tobacco control, and bans on smoking in 'public places' in particular. The largest increase in 'public places' occurred between 1987 and 1995, followed by an even more restrictive stance in 2005. These positive attitudes to smoking bans at work, in restaurants and in bars continue to 2007 before dropping somewhat in 2009. The general relationship between the strength of a government's tobacco control measures and public opinion is apparent. The most anti-tobacco opinion can be found in countries at the top half of the Joossens-Raw scale. The evidence is less clear when one examines opinion on particular instruments (in the 1987 and 1995 surveys). In general, there are substantial differences in the percentages of those favouring more restrictive policies on 'easy' issues, such as age limits and public place bans compared to more controversial issues, such as duty-free sales and banning smoking in restaurants and pubs. For example, some countries lower on the scale, such as Germany and Luxembourg, have developed strongly restrictive opinions on smoking in 'public places' that rival the level of the policy leaders, Ireland and the United Kingdom, but the differences are more marked when asked about restaurants and bars.

While one cannot infer from these data that public opinion was driving the adoption of more restrictive tobacco control policies, opinion has moved broadly in tandem with restrictive measures in the leading countries and is ahead of political elites in others. Over the past quarter century, opinion towards tobacco has remained highly negative in some countries and has become more uniformly unfavourable across EU members. Public opinion on tobacco control tends towards the 'permissive consensus' we identify in Chapter 3. Thus, governments have had considerable leeway in which to take action, and the direction of policy influence is more from governments to the public rather than the reverse.

The role of ideas: Scientific knowledge

Chapter 3 paints a global picture in which there is a significant time lag between the acceptance of the scientific evidence on smoking and ill-health and tobacco control policy. Public health may now be the dominant frame, but this shift in problem definition took decades to achieve. The same picture is apparent in the EU and in individual countries. Government attention to tobacco control trailed considerably behind the scientific evidence of harm (which began to gain attention from 1950). Since many of the respiratory, cardiovascular, and oncology diseases resulting from smoking normally take time to develop, the long-term effects of tobacco use were only being discovered decades later – and tobacco control generally was also slow. The exceptions were Nordic countries (excluding Denmark) which legislated on advertising and health warning labels relatively quickly (Baggott, 1988; Wilensky, 2002; Albaek, 2004; Roemer, 1993). Most other countries did not go beyond education, televised advertising bans, and reliance on voluntary agreements with the tobacco industry. In the 1980s, further scientific research (on smoking and SHS) combined with better-organised anti-tobacco advocacy groups and more responsive governments to promote tobacco control through a broader array of instruments. SHS had, in effect, 'socialised' the issue into one which was not simply a matter of choice for individuals, but one that had broader harmful consequences for the affected populations. Gradually these findings became incorporated into official government reports, although sometimes this did not occur until a decade or two later. Indeed, the European Commission (2004: 34) highlights the time it took for significant reports to perform a cumulative effect; a report on passive smoking in Germany was produced in 1986, to be followed by a report by 'Europe Against Cancer' in 1997 and the UK Government's scientific committee in 1998 – but smoking bans generally took place from the mid-2000s.

The transfer of ideas

As Chapter 2 suggests, diffusion can occur in three ways – top-down, horizontal (between similar jurisdictions), and bottom-up. Most analyses of horizontal diffusion postulate a regional (territorial) effect (Berry and Berry, 1999), but European countries are more likely to learn tobacco control horizontally through 'families of nations' with shared language, culture, and/or history (Castles, 1993, 1998; Obinger and Wagschal, 2001; Goetz, 2006; Castles and Wagschal, 2008). Although the groupings differ slightly, the most empirically-supported one is for an English-speaking family, a Nordic family, a Continental family (sometimes divided into French and German-speaking branches), and a Southern family. Horizontal diffusion is based on whether patterns of clustered convergence exist that can be attributed to communication among non-governmental organisations and/or governments (although in practice many studies identify policy similarities rather than evidence of direct learning).

Table 4.6 Families of Nations and Tobacco Control, European Countries

	Strength			Scope	Tempo
	2004	2005	2007		
English-speaking: UK, Ireland	67	74	84	0.94	1983
Nordic: Iceland, Sweden, Finland, Norway, Denmark	58	61	61	0.93	1983
Total 'Periphery' (7)	*61*	*65*	*67*	*0.93*	*1983*
Continental:France, Germany, Austria, Switzerland, Netherlands, Belgium, Luxembourg	39	41	46	0.88	1990
Southern: Italy, Spain, Portugal, Greece	38	41	48	0.87	1987
Total 'Core' (11)	*39*	*41*	*47*	*0.87*	*1989*

Table 4.6 shows that such a pattern of clustered convergence does exist in tobacco control for three major measures: strength, scope, and tempo. However, countries cluster more in the form of two groups (Core and Periphery) rather than four. The Core group is composed of the Continental and Southern families, usually with strong commitments to the EU, including all six original members. The Periphery (English-speaking and Nordic) countries largely consist of later-entry, less enthusiastic, and/or affiliated members of the EU. The Periphery group has consistently stronger, broader, and faster anti-tobacco policies than the Core (although we do not relate this to the date of EU membership in the way the figures might suggest). The Periphery group lacks a consistent leader although it does have a persistent laggard, Denmark. Among the others, a process of leapfrogging has occurred as different countries surge to the fore, depending on the introduction of different, sometimes reinvented, instruments. Only recently has the UK become a clear leader (Chapter 5). Although initially strong on broad advertising bans and package health warnings, the Nordic countries were late on SHS. Recently touted as a tobacco control leader because of its ban on smoking in restaurants and bars, Ireland actually has had a persistent if incremental tobacco control policy. Among Core countries, there is a more erratic pattern of adoption. France and Italy are the most consistent forerunners, as shown by their relatively high rankings on the recent strength measures. Other Core countries have tended toward sudden outbursts of activity, sometimes after long periods of dormancy (Belgium and Spain are recent examples).

A key mechanism for policy learning in Europe, either voluntarily or coercively, is through the EU, which represents 'a giant policy transfer platform' (Bulmer and Padgett, 2005). EU policies themselves are products of the experiences of the member countries and their interactions within EU institutions. In short, there is 'uploading' of policies from one or more member countries to the EU as well as 'downloading' of policies from the EU to individual members. In addition to policy formulation, there are also questions of how well member states implement agreed EU policies. Directives and regulations to control tobacco consumption are binding on member states. Directives have to be adopted into state laws within a limited time period, allowing for adjustments to member states' specific circumstances, while regulations have to be adopted immediately and uniformly by member countries (Asare et al, 2009: 85; Gilmore and McKee, 2004: 233). However, the resources of the European Commission to monitor and ensure implementation of policies are limited. For applicants, the EU can impose convergence criteria, requiring that they adopt certain policies before they are granted entry. The EU can also recommend action when its powers are more ambiguous or there is insufficient consensus for a directive. Since 2000, the Lisbon Process has been an additional tool to encourage member states to adopt new policies through 'benchmarking' (league tables of outcomes for similar policies in different jurisdictions) and 'best practices' (the highest-ranked policies).

Coercive harmonisation is the most studied form of 'Europeanisation' of policy (Featherstone and Raedelli, 2003) although 'soft law', referring to non-binding EU policies with no explicit sanctions, is beginning to be analysed as well (Falkner et al, 2005; Borrás and Jacobbsson, 2004). Periodically, since 1989, the Council of Ministers has passed non-binding resolutions and recommendations on tobacco control, especially concerning indoor non-smoking restrictions (see Table 4.1). The EU has also initiated and funded media campaigns and capacity-building projects, especially through subsidising European-wide NGOs (Khanna, 2001). Some of these revenues formerly came from a small portion of the cost of the now-ended support for tobacco growing in the Common Agricultural Policy.

There is now an established literature arguing that the EU influences member states' tobacco control policies (perhaps even when some member states adopt some policies before they are definitively included in EU directives) (e.g. Gilmore and McKee, 2002; Dagfinn Haybråten, 2003; Yach, 2000; Read, 2005; Nielsen, 2003). The independent report to the European Commission (2004) on tobacco control in European countries also gives examples of EU influence on member and non-member states, particularly through directives ('hard law'). To explore the effect of top-down diffusion we focus on eight indicators of EU actions, five involving the first directives on a television ban (1989), general advertising ban (1998), health warnings

Table 4.7 EU and Family Influences on EU Directives and Recommendations

		Countries, Mean Year of Adoption					
	EU	Overall	N	Periphery	N	Core	N
Directives							
Advertising ban	1998	1993	16	1990	7	1995	9
Television ban	1989	1978	18	1976	7	1979	11
Health warning	1989	1980	18	1976	7	1983	11
Rotating health warning	1989	1987	18	1981	7	1991	11
Cigarette content restrictions	1990	1988	18	1990	7	1987	11
Recommendations							
Ban in government offices	1989	1998	13	1995	5	2000	8
Ban in work places	1989	1999	12	1998	5	1999	7
Ban on public transport	1989	1991	12	1996	5	1987	7

Sources: European Commission, 2004; WHO Regional Office for Europe, 2007; Roemer, 1982, 1993; European Commission, 1982; Sasco et al, 1989, 1992.

(1989), rotating health warnings (frequently changing the health message on packs) (1989), and restrictions on cigarette contents (1990) while three others concern the first resolution for a ban on smoking in public places (1989), which can be interpreted as including indoor workplaces, government offices, and public transportation. Which European countries had these policies in place before the EU action and which after? Those who acted first may have acted as a stimulus for uploading of such policies to the EU while those who acted after may have been downloading them from the EU.

Table 4.7 indicates the mean tempo for instruments endorsed by the EU. In the case of directives, the mean years occurred before the EU took action. This is a reflection of some countries acting early, as far back as the 1960s. On the advertising ban, debate within the EU was initiated by the European Parliament in 1990 and continued until passage of the first directive in 1998, annulled by the European Court of Justice (ECJ) in 2000. The process of EU consideration may have encouraged individual countries to take action on this issue, both before and after the ECJ decision (European Commission, 2004). A second EU Advertising Directive took effect in 2003. What other data (available from the authors) indicate is that 16 of the 18 states had telecast bans prior to the 1989 EU directive, eight had advertising bans before 1998, 17 had health warning labels before 1989, seven had rotating warning labels before 1989, and ten had contents restrictions before 1990. Thus, it appears that EU hard law has acted as a force for tobacco control policy adoptions, but more on some instruments than others. EU directives influence states on instruments where they are lagging. The Nordic states (Denmark excepted) were not EU or even EEA members in 1989 and yet, in 16 cases out of a total of 20, were among those states that adopted measures before the EU did. On the other hand, Austria, which joined the EU in 1995 along with Sweden and Finland, had few tobacco control instruments in place before 1992. Thus, for both existing and some prospective EU members, the EU was an important source of policy, even before the adoption of the Copenhagen Criteria for convergence of new members in 1993. The results are somewhat different for EU soft law through the 1989 resolutions on non-smoking areas (data available from authors). While more states developed such laws subsequent to the 1989 resolutions, they were often slow, and the process is not yet complete. This has resulted in further resolutions on the same topic, the most recent being in 2009. The EU also has used accession negotiations for candidate members to impose its tobacco control policies through the *acquis communautaire* on former Communist states in CEE. For these laggard countries, the incentive of joining the EU has stimulated rapid, coercive policy development in a short period of time (Gilmore and Zatoński, 2002; Bozicevic et al, 2004; Gilmore et al, 2004; Frisbee et al, 2009).

In summary, both generally and by individual instruments, there has been a marked convergence of tobacco control policy across European countries. While countries have proceeded at different paces, the process of convergence in policy has been accelerated by the EU's advocacy of tobacco control policies since the mid-1980s as well as by more countries joining the EU or adopting EU policies through European Economic Area (EEA) agreements. In some instances, directives from the EU may have accelerated the adoption of instruments. Thus, we have significant evidence of Europeanisation of tobacco policy although the exact processes of policy learning or transfer are not always clear.

Conclusion

Tobacco control has changed profoundly in European countries since the early post-war period. Both the scale and speed of government responses have increased substantially. Existing policy instruments have been strengthened and new measures introduced. While policy change has taken place at a different tempo in different countries, policy has become more uniform in coverage, and significant convergence has occurred.

We can explain such policy change with reference to the five factors introduced in Chapter 2. First, there has been major institutional change. The European picture has an added element to the global picture we outline in Chapter 3. Health ministries may have replaced other departments as the main focus for tobacco policy, but the main institutional change for most countries has been the shift in power from member state to the EU (and, in some cases, to sub-state institutions). Over the past two decades the member states' monopoly on tobacco control policy has been replaced by shared control among different levels of government. The central state now shares authority with the EU for policies on taxation, health warnings, advertising and tobacco contents. In some cases it has also allowed regional or local authorities to have authority for health education, smoking cessation strategies, and indoor non-smoking regulation. While decisions made at the EU level are left to individual countries to implement (through the framework approach), the European Commission and the ECJ exercise considerable executive oversight and judicial powers. The Europeanisation of tobacco policy has occurred in both older and accession members, but more rapidly in the latter. The EU has clearly influenced policy in its recent accession members through its membership requirements, and its influence also extends to EEA members through their adherence to the provisions of the Single Market. This shared authority between the EU and member states also extends to the international arena (see Chapter 9).

Second, the agenda-setting context for policy has changed. Policy choices are now based on the framing of tobacco as a health problem rather than an economic benefit. Over the past 25 years the EU and its member and affiliated states have moved, at varying rates of speed, toward a public health view of tobacco control while reducing the political economy orientation. The EU role as a 'regulatory state' (Majone, 1997) in tobacco has given it the tools to accelerate this movement, especially among its more laggard and new members.

Third, anti-tobacco groups, some funded by public money, have become increasingly capable of challenging the governmental influence of tobacco companies. Industry dominance began to be questioned politically only in the 1960s and seriously challenged in the 1980s. Now public health seems to be superior, but the economic importance of tobacco manufacturing, especially TTCs, retains residual power to contest further actions designed to reduce tobacco consumption in Europe.

Fourth, smoking prevalence, opposition to tobacco control, and the perceived economic benefits of tobacco production have fallen almost everywhere, albeit in an uneven pattern (particularly in the CEE countries where tobacco use initially rose when the TTCs entered their markets in the 1990s). All three factors suggest that the obstacles to tobacco control have also declined and that a stable permissive consensus of opinion favourable towards tobacco control has developed.

Finally, the scientific evidence on the links between smoking, SHS, and health have been accepted within, and shared among, governments. There is a significant time lapse between the production and acceptance of scientific evidence. However, the absorption of the evidence has now reached a critical level, allowing most governments to move from older discussions about whether to act, to new discussions about the best way to reduce smoking. This effect is particularly marked in the English-speaking and Nordic countries (except Denmark), those that may be most likely to push the EU agenda and oblige others to follow suit.

The report commissioned by the EU Health Directorate (European Commission, 2004), written by anti-tobacco experts in the global tobacco control epistemic community (Mamudu et al, 2011b), contained a set of recommendations for further EU action. These included full implementation of the FCTC, greater financial investment in tobacco control, dedicated tobacco agencies in all member states, a strong EU role in coordination and support, greater EU capacity through a regulatory agency, greater research capacity and coordinated data collection among EU countries, and more comprehensive tobacco control policies.

While only some of these recommendations have been adopted, the EU continues to move forward. Following a Green paper (DG Sanco, 2007), and a European Parliament resolution, the EU passed a Council Recommendation (2009) advocating not only smoke-free environments, but also improved advertising regulations, an investigation of the legal basis for plain packaging, and a synergistic approach to tobacco control. Furthermore, the EU has undertaken new tax harmonisation regulations in 2010, fire-safe cigarettes to be introduced in 2011, and a reconsideration of the Tobacco Products Directive, including possibly stronger bans on vending machines, point-of-sale advertising, and sales to young people. In summary, the EU has emerged as a major venue of tobacco control policymaking and will continue to consider and possibly advocate or even mandate further restrictions on tobacco.

5
The UK: A Case Study

Tobacco policy in the UK demonstrates a period of rapid legislative change following decades of policy continuity. Tobacco advertising was banned in the UK in 2002 and bans on smoking in public places in the UK and devolved territories were introduced from 2005–6. These measures, combined with others already in place, such as smoking cessation services and health education, make the UK the most active tobacco control member state in the EU. It now ranks number one in the *Tobacco Control Scale* discussed in Chapter 4. Yet, for most of the post-war period, tobacco policy was marked by a relative lack of regulation. Tobacco control measures were often voluntary rather than legislative, while public health arguments often came second-best to those based on individual choice and the economic benefits of tobacco (Cairney, 2007a). Indeed, it is little over 20 years ago that Baggott's (1988) study of UK and Norwegian policy sought to explain why the former was such a laggard compared to the former. The UK therefore represents one of most fruitful case-studies of tobacco policy change because it seems to have engaged in radical policy change in a relatively short period of time. Our aim is to explain this shift in policy direction. A complementary aim is to consider the issues in relative depth (compared to the broader comparative chapters), identifying the substance and nature of policy (considering, for example, the nature of voluntary agreements), and considering the forces for change, in greater detail.

The first section explores what we mean by 'rapid change'. As we suggest in Chapter 1, tobacco policy can be subdivided into at least 14 different policy instruments. While legislation is most likely to be publicised, the UK had already initiated a range of measures to reduce smoking prevalence and was second on the *Tobacco Control Scale* in the year before it banned smoking in public places (Table 4.3). UK tobacco policy is marked by continuity and change, prompting us to consider more than one interpretation of events. Recent tobacco regulation may suggest radical change, as ineffective voluntary agreements are replaced by statutory measures, or incremental change, as new legislation builds on and accelerates existing policy.

It also informs our other key narratives of tobacco policy. For example, the extent to which recent UK legislation was enforced or prompted from elsewhere, such as the EU and the UK's devolved governments, depends on how we characterise its policy trajectory (was change incremental or radical?).

The second section seeks to explain tobacco policy change in terms of the five factors outlined in Chapter 2. It outlines who has responsibility for the main tobacco policy instruments and charts the extent to which changes in that responsibility have been associated with policy change. This can relate to domestic changes, such as a change in the institutional responsibility from treasury, trade, and agriculture to the health department. It can also relate to a rise in multi-level governance and the new opportunities, provided by Europeanisation and devolution, for public health interests to pursue tobacco control. The MLG effect can be divided into two related processes. First, it increases the scope for venue shopping (Baumgartner and Jones, 1993); pressure participants seek new audiences if they are dissatisfied with progress in their initial focus of pressure. Second, the introduction of new venues influences the policy image of tobacco as policy is made by new participants with a different understanding of the problem and/or their involvement puts pressure on existing participants to emulate their behaviour. The chapter charts the extent to which the dominant policy image of tobacco has changed within government over the post-war period and also considers the extent to which this change is reflected in media and public opinion.

Multi-level governance also refers to the blurry boundaries between formal and informal action, related to the regular consultations between those who make policy and those with whom they communicate; policy is the 'joint product of their interaction' (Rose, 1987: 267–8). This process has been apparent in tobacco policy long before the identification of MLG. In particular, the post-war period was marked by a very close relationship between tobacco companies and key members of the UK Government. It has been replaced by a more open policy network influenced most strongly by public health interests, with tobacco companies increasingly marginalised in the policy process. This shift of influence within government over five decades has gone hand-in-hand with changes in socioeconomic conditions as smoking prevalence, public opposition to tobacco control, and the economic value of tobacco to government have all fallen. It also reflects the importance of the role of ideas, such as the promotion of new scientific evidence and its acceptance within government, and the influence of the experience of other governments which has encouraged policy learning and transfer. These five factors – policy responsibility, agenda-setting, group-government relations, socioeconomic conditions, and the role and transfer of ideas – can be separated analytically, but they all combine to explain UK tobacco policy change.

What is UK tobacco policy?

We can assess the trajectory of UK policy with reference to the 14 policy instruments outlined in Chapter 1 (although not all instruments are relevant to the UK) and a table (Table 5.1) of major events in chronological order (see Cairney, 2007a: 49–50; ASH, 2005a, 2005b; Read, 1996; Baggott, 1988; Taylor, 1984; Berridge and Loughlin, 2005; CRUK, 2010; ASH, 2010c).

I. Regulation

1. *Tobacco advertising and promotion*. Cigarette advertising on TV was banned in 1965. The first voluntary agreement with the tobacco industry on advertising (adverts contained the words 'Every pack carries a Government health warning') and health warnings on cigarette packs ('Warning by HM Government: Smoking can damage your health') was introduced in 1971. It was amended in 1972 (including health warnings on brand advertisements and providing further health advice on packs), 1977 (banning the advertising of high tar cigarettes), 1980 (a commitment to increase the health warning and reduce advertising spending), March 1982 (regarding an increase in prize money for sporting events but with related advertising carrying a health warning), October 1982 (adding health warnings to point-of-sale advertising plus a ban on advertising on video cassettes), 1986 (banning advertising in cinemas and introducing more health warnings, reducing advertising spending and banning advertising in women's magazines aimed at a 16–24 audience), 1987 (banning sports sponsorship), 1991 (reducing the amount of point of sale advertising), and 1994 (increasing the size of health warning on adverts and stipulating that advertising billboards should be at least 200m from schools). Westminster passed legislation to ban tobacco advertising in 2002.
2. *The sale of tobacco*. Bans on the sale of tobacco to children under 16 were introduced in 1908 (one of the earliest in the world) but have always been dogged by ineffective implementation. In 1933 a new bill banned the sale of cigarettes to children under 16 and in 1986 this prohibition was extended to all tobacco products. The British legal minimum age to buy tobacco rose to 18 in 2007. Cigarettes may not be sold in packs smaller than 10, on the assumption that children are more likely to buy singles. Bills passed by Westminster in 2009 (covering, England, Wales and Northern Ireland) and the Scottish Parliament in 2010 banned cigarette vending machines and advertising at point of sale.
3. *Smoking in public places*. Smoking on public transport and in cinemas began to be phased out from the 1970s. A voluntary code of practice on smoking in public places was introduced by the UK government in 1991, suggesting that non-smoking should be the norm if a member of the public was in a building (e.g. post office) through necessity. A government-backed code of practice by the hospitality industry to reduce

exposure to SHS was introduced in 1999. Westminster passed legislation to ban smoking comprehensively in public places in 2006 (for England and Wales; the Scottish Parliament legislated in 2005 and a separate decision was made for Northern Ireland in 2005). The Department of Health provided £29.5m (US$47.2m) for English local authorities to implement the ban (ASH, 2010c: 7).[4] Many NHS hospitals have introduced bans on smoking in NHS property and many local authorities have introduced restrictions on the ability of smokers to foster children (due to concerns about passive smoking in the home).

4. *Ingredients, such as the levels of tar in cigarettes.* The EU Tobacco Products Directive limits the amount of tar, nicotine and carbon monoxide in cigarettes (Table 4.1). The UK had previously relied on voluntary agreements.
5. *Customs enforcement on smuggling and counterfeit cigarettes.* The UK government announced in 2000 a £200m ($320m) project to reduce smuggling, reducing the illicit market share from 21% in 2000–1 to 15% in 2003–4.[5] It then announced in 2006 a plan to reduce this market by 1,200 tonnes by 2007/8. It estimates that it employs 2,150 staff at a cost of £96.5m (US$154.4m) per year and has spent £1.5m (US$2.4m) over five years (2003–8) on advertising its new initiative (ASH, 2010c: 3).

II. Finance

6. *Taxation and other levies.* Tax increases on tobacco were used extensively from the 1970s and promoted as a way to discourage smoking from the 1980s. By 1990 the tax (including duty and value added tax) was 73% on a packet of 20 cigarettes, rising to 80% in 2001 and falling to 77% by 2010 (TMA, 2010b). The decrease followed an abandoned commitment to increasing tax by 5% per year. Instead, duty has risen slightly above inflation (ASH, 2010c: 3). While this move has been criticised by Action on Smoking and Health (ASH) (Press Association, 2010), the UK government position is that 'levels of tax on tobacco have peaked, given the threat of smuggling' (Cairney, 2007a: 50).
7. *Spending on directed health services.* The first smoking withdrawal clinic was established in 1958. The National Health Service Stop Smoking Service was established in 1999. It treats approximately 250,000 people per six months (CRUK, 2010). Spending in England rose from £21.5m (£27m, or US$47.2m in 2008 prices) in 2000 to £74m in 2008 (ASH, 2010c: 5).
8. *Economic incentives.* The UK contributed indirectly to the subsidisation of tobacco growing (from 1973 to 2010) as subsidies to tobacco farmers in other countries were included in the Common Agricultural Policy. It has also given tax breaks to tobacco companies sponsoring the arts and sports. Both practices have now ceased.

9. *Litigation against tobacco companies*. This is a practice much more apparent in the US than the UK where the courts have played a minimal role in tobacco control (and class action suits have proved unsuccessful). Indeed, one of the most significant court interventions initially granted (in 1999) a tobacco industry injunction to stop UK government regulations to ban tobacco advertising.

III. Capacity-building

10. *Funding for community development programs and organisations to combat tobacco use*. The most relevant group is ASH, set up by the Royal College of Physicians in 1971 to campaign on smoking issues. The UK government has traditionally been ASH's largest contributor. In 1988 it provided £170,000 (£351,900, or US$ 563,040 at 2008 prices) per annum – almost all of ASH's income (Baggott, 1988: 10; Taylor, 1984: 43). In 2009 it provided £142,000 (US$227,000) in project funding (19% of total income), but ASH's core funding is now met by Cancer Research UK and the British Heart Foundation (ASH, 2009).

IV. Education

11. *Health warning labels on cigarette and tobacco packs*. Packs of cigarettes in the UK now contain health warnings with pictures, under EU authorisation rules (Chapter 4). The UK Government signalled its intention to consult on plain packaging by the end of 2011.
12. *Health education campaigns combating tobacco usage*. The nature of health education shifted from 'stating the facts' and letting individuals decide in the 1950s, to harm reduction (promoting 'low tar' cigarettes) in the 1960s, and to 'absolutism' (there is no safe level of tobacco smoking) in the 1970s. Spending on health education concerning tobacco increased from £414,000 in 1973 (£4m or US$6.4m in 2008) to £24m (US$38.4m) in 2008 (ASH, 2010c: 8). The rise is reinforced by the cessation of tobacco advertising since 2002 (it was £17m (£53m, US$84.8m) in 1981 – Taylor, 1984: 49).

V. Learning and information tools

13. *Legislative hearings and executive reports*. This element is more important in the US, where Congressional hearings and reports are often used to challenge legislative stalemates and set the policy agenda. However, there have been some notable reports in the UK, from the Chief Medical Officer's annual reports calling for stricter tobacco control (Cairney, 2007a: 62), to the UK Government's White Paper (Cm 4177, 1998) setting out a new tobacco control strategy.
14. *Funding scientific research*. The UK government-funded Medical Research Council (MRC) has a long history of tobacco research, including support for the work of Richard Doll and Bradford Hill (who produced

one of the earliest studies on tobacco and health – MRC, 2007a, 2007b).

The UK government has also set targets to reduce smoking prevalence. The significance of such measures is unclear. While the enforcement of some UK government targets (on, for example, waiting times in hospitals) have a strong effect on organisational behaviour, population targets may be meaningless unless linked to particular policy instruments. That said, there is a reasonable link between smoking prevalence and broad targets. The Conservative government aim to reduce smoking prevalence from 30% to 20% from 2000 to 2010 (see Townsend, 1996: 135) was unsuccessful, but the Labour aim to reduce prevalence to 21% by 2010 was met by 2007 (ASH, 2010b: 1; note that the Scottish government has separate targets). The 2020 target for England is 10% (Department of Health, 2010).

Narratives of UK tobacco policy change

A comparison of the immediate post-World War II period to the present day demonstrates that policy has changed radically, with government support for tobacco as an economic product replaced by a comprehensive set of tobacco control policies designed to minimise smoking prevalence. Most tobacco control measures were absent before the 1970s. Until then, statutory measures focused on the sale of tobacco to children and a ban on televised advertising, the main role for taxation was to raise revenue, and public education focused on a reduction in smoking or a shift to safer methods (the so-called 'harm reduction' or 'harm regulation approach' more likely to be found in drugs treatment and not used in relation to tobacco in many countries – see Berridge, 2004). The 1970s were notable for the rise in tobacco control based on voluntary agreements with the tobacco industry (health warnings on cigarettes) and a shift in health education towards abstention over harm reduction, coupled with the first funding for ASH. This approach continued into the 1980s, with voluntary agreements on tobacco advertising supplemented by an increase in health education funding and the use of taxation to discourage smoking. The late 1990s were marked by the beginnings of much stronger tobacco control, with a sharp rise in tobacco taxation, coupled with measures to reduce the unintended consequences related to illegal tobacco, an increase in smoking cessation provision, a rise in health education messages through the media and cigarette packets and, in the 2000s, legislation to ban, comprehensively, tobacco advertising and smoking in public places.

Incremental versus sudden or radical change? This chronology informs our characterisation of change. It demonstrates that, although there has been a broad move in the direction of tobacco control in the post-war era, most change appears to have taken place in a concentrated period of time, accel-

Table 5.1 Major Tobacco Control Events and Decisions in the UK, 1908–2010

1908	Ban on the sale of tobacco to under 16
1950	Publication of Richard Doll and Bradford Hill's initial research
1950s	Limited health education campaigns begin
1958	Introduction of the first smoking cessation clinic
1962	First Royal College of Physicians report *Smoking and Health*
1960s	Health education focus on harm reduction
1965	Ban on cigarette advertising on TV
1970s	Beginning of new health education strategy
1971	Royal College of Physicians report *Smoking and Health Now*
1971	Phase-out of smoking in cinemas and on public transport begins
1971	First voluntary agreement on advertising cigarettes
1971	Action on Smoking and Health established
1977	Royal College of Physicians report *Smoking or Health*
1980s	Taxes on cigarettes begin to be used to discourage smoking
1983	Launch of 'National No Smoking Day'
1984	Ban on smoking in London Underground following fire
1986	Launch of European Commission's 'Europe Against Cancer'
1990	London Regional Transport bans smoking on all of its buses
1991	Voluntary code on smoking in public places
1991	UK Government Green Paper sets targets on smoking prevalence
1991	New health warnings on tobacco packaging (based on EU directive, size of warning opposed by tobacco companies)
1992	Nicotine patches available on prescription
1993	EU Workplace Directive requires smoke-free rest areas
1993	UK Government commitment to increase tobacco taxation by 3% per year
1997	Labour government elected
1998	Scientific Committee on Tobacco and Health report on passive smoking
1998	White Paper on tobacco control includes new targets on prevalence, the NHS smoking cessation programme and proposed voluntary agreement on smoking in the workplace
1999	Voluntary code on smoking in public places, hospitality sector
1999	National Health Service *Stop Smoking Service* established
1999	Class action against tobacco companies by lung cancer sufferers fails
2000	European Court of Justice rejects Tobacco Advertising Directive 1
2000	UK Government initiates major project on cigarette smuggling
2002	Ban on tobacco advertising
2003	Framework Convention on Tobacco Control adopted by 171 countries
2005	Ban on smoking in public places – Scotland
2006	Ban on smoking in public places – rest of the UK
2007	Legal age to purchase cigarettes rises to 18
2009	Legislation banning cigarette vending machines and advertising at point of sale (2010 in Scotland)
2010	Department of Health publishes *A Smokefree Future – A Comprehensive Tobacco Control Strategy for England*
	UK Government public health White Paper signals a commitment to consult on plain packaging of tobacco products
2011	UK Government Tobacco Plan for England sets target to reduce adult smoking rates from 21.2% to 18.5% by the end of 2015
	Tobacco duty raised by 2% above inflation
	UK Government reduces amount of tobacco that holidaymakers can bring back from EU

erating from the mid-1980s (under a Conservative party often considered to be pro-tobacco) and again from 1997 (when the New Labour government was first elected). However, our focus on a wide range of policy instruments suggests that flagship legislation to ban tobacco advertising and smoking in public places may have marked a sea change in those particular dimensions but not for tobacco control altogether. Rather, it reflects a much wider or 'comprehensive' package of measures that now marks the UK's tobacco regime out as the most restrictive in the EU and one of the most restrictive in the world.

A key unresolved issue relates to the status of voluntary agreements, since this determines how rapid policy change has been in key areas. A public-health-oriented narrative suggests that these agreements were ineffective and that they were often produced to maintain a close negotiating relationship between tobacco companies and the government, to provide the appearance of tobacco control, and bolster a positive image for the industry (for a similar argument in the US, see Pollay, 1994). For example, the ban on advertising high tar cigarettes only occurred when their share of the market was dwindling; a limit on advertising expenditure favoured the companies with the most established market shares; the health warnings on packs were traded for the ability to name brands when advertising; and, most recently, the voluntary agreement on smoking in public places only required pubs to put up stickers declaring that they were not smoke-free (Cairney, 2007a: 52). This perspective indicates that legislation on these topics marks a sea change in policy in a relatively short period of time. The alternative is to view the agreements as tools adopted regularly by the UK government in many policy areas outside tobacco (Berridge, 2004: 136; Baggott, 1988). They represent statements of intent, to be followed by stronger measures if they are not as effective as hoped. It suggests that policy change took place over a much longer period, with a degree of initial success followed by stronger statutory measures (Cairney, 2007a: 50–1).

Voluntary versus enforced change? The status of voluntary agreements also affects our view about the role of the EU. If we treat them as ineffective, then we can trace many significant developments in tobacco policy change, including regulating tar, introducing health warnings on cigarette packs, and banning tobacco advertising (as well as raising taxes), to developments in the EU. Yet, the idea of EU-led coercion does not correspond to the UK's position at the top of the tobacco control league tables. Nor does it explain why the UK has introduced most tobacco control policies before it has been obliged to by the EU.

Leaders or laggards? Finally, the status of the agreements affects the evaluation of UK policy overall. If we view them as ineffective, then we argue that the UK has been a policy laggard for a significant part of the post-war period – at least when compared to countries, such as Norway (Baggott, 1988). We may also say that the UK only became a leader when it replaced voluntary with statutory measures. The overall point is that policy as a whole is difficult to characterise. As Berridge (2004: 136) asks, how do we compare the UK's high taxation and voluntary regime with countries that introduced more formal measures in some areas but did not emulate the wider adoption of policy instruments that we find in the UK?

A combination of narratives presents us with a very mixed picture of change. On the one hand, we can point to evidence from the post-war period to suggest that the UK government was a policy laggard that relied on voluntary agreements favoured by a powerful domestic tobacco companies before being obliged to legislate to ban tobacco advertising and smoking in public places following direct coercion from the EU and indirect coercion from the devolved governments. On the other hand, we can identify a tendency to lead the rest of Europe on most other measures of tobacco control, a decision to control advertising beyond the minimum requirements of the EU, and a decision within the UK's Department of Health to support devolved legislation as a means of pursuing a smoking ban in England. Thus, it is possible to defend two competing views of UK policy development – as a laggard forced by others to catch up and change policy dramatically, or as a leader introducing legislative controls as a logical consequence of its overall incremental strategy (Cairney, 2007a, 2009a). This argument is crucial to the remainder of the chapter (and to the broader discussions of change throughout the book) because we need to be clear about what we are trying to explain – is it incremental change over a long period of time or a concentrated period of change? We explain the broad shift towards tobacco control in the post-war era in the following section before returning to this issue of explanation in the conclusion (and Chapter 10).

Institutions: Who has responsibility for UK tobacco policy?

The Department of Health

In the early post-war period tobacco-related issues were addressed primarily by the Treasury, which, as the hub for tax raising and spending, has always been the key department within government, as well as the Department for Trade and Industry (DTI), which was the key actor responsible for promoting tobacco as an exported good and for lobbying the World Bank and IMF on tobacco (Mamudu, 2008b; although see Berridge, 2004: 119 on exceptional anti-tobacco ministers, such as Dell at the DTI). The Department of Employment was also involved. As a whole, central government activity was related primarily to the economic advantages of tobacco – as a source of tax revenue, a contributor to the balance of payments (between imports and exports), and a significant provider of jobs (Cairney, 2007a: 47; Taylor, 1984: 69).

The only department with a strong incentive to treat tobacco consumption as a problem to be solved was the Department of Health, but it was often a relatively low status department marginalised from the centre of tobacco policy discussions. Unlike in Norway, there was no coordinating body to give the Department of Health regular access to other policymaking departments (Baggott, 1988: 14 argues that the Norwegian National Council for Smoking and Health was set up following, and represented a focal point for, anti-smoking pressure). The closest equivalent was an advisory body, the Independent Scientific Committee on Smoking (ISCS, and later the ISCSH then SCOTH). Instead, major policy decisions were taken by cabinet committees led by other departments, such as the Home Office and dominated by departments, such as the Treasury (Baggott, 1988: 38). The Department of Health was part of the larger Department of Health and Social Security (DHSS) from 1968–88, a situation that reduced the status of health ministers and often presented it with contradictory incentives (e.g. healthier people would live longer and collect more social security benefits) (1988: 39). It was also staffed by ministers who were reluctant to innovate or short of time or political support when they tried (Cairney, 2007a: 52). Indeed, as recently as the mid-1980s, a junior Conservative health minister was removed from his post for pursuing a ban on advertising and sports sponsorship (Taylor, 1984: 94). In other words, although we identify the significance of this shift of responsibility towards the Department of Health, we also show that the change was relatively recent and by no means inevitable.

To some extent the new emphasis was furthered by a change of party in government; the Labour party elected in 1997 expressed a stronger commitment to tobacco control than its Conservative predecessor (and previous Labour governments). Policy change was also encouraged by shifting priorities within the Treasury. When a Treasury report identified smoking as 'the single most significant causal factor for the socioeconomic differences in the incidence of cancer and heart disease' (HM Treasury and Department of Health, 2002: 5), it signalled a reduced willingness to support the tobacco industry as a source of tax revenue. Finally, the change was augmented by John Reid's appointment as Health Secretary in 2003. Reid was a strong Secretary, supported by Prime Minister Tony Blair, who ensured that any decision on issues, such as the smoking ban would be made by the Department of Health. This also gave greater prominence to its Chief Medical Officer, who in the past had been marginalised in tobacco discussions (Cairney, 2007a: 62).

The EU

The EU has become a key player in tobacco policy (Chapter 4), but tracking its effect on UK policy is difficult for two reasons: (1) the strength of EU policy varies from compulsory regulation to the promotion of best practice; and (2) the UK had adopted some policies before the EU made them compulsory for member states. Key EU requirements include: cigarette packs to carry a health warning of 4% (1989) and then 30% at the front and 40% on the back (2001) of cigarette packs; a ban on TV advertising (1989), replaced by an advertising ban on cross-border print media, the internet, and sponsorship (2003); attempts to harmonise taxes (from 1972 and 1992); and, recommendations about bans on smoking in public places (Table 4.1; Asare et al, 2009: 86). In most cases UK policy on these issues occurred earlier and/or went further than required by the EU: taxation on tobacco aimed at reducing smoking dates back to the 1980s; the UK committed itself to health warnings on cigarette packs (via voluntary agreements) before the first EU directive; and, it banned smoking in public places well in advance of any EU requirement (Asare et al, 2009: 91). Tobacco advertising presents a mixed picture because the UK government opposed both Tobacco Advertising Directives before introducing legislation to ban tobacco advertising in a way that went beyond EU requirements before the latest EU ban went into force (Duina and Kurzer, 2004: 58; Cairney, 2007a: 55).

Devolved governments

Devolution in 1999 to Scotland, Wales and Northern Ireland included health and education policy and therefore some tobacco policy instruments, such as smoking cessation services, health education and the ability to fund or commission services from organisations, such as ASH. Issues of taxation, customs enforcement, health warnings on cigarette packs and regulations on the product itself remain reserved to the UK government (or Europeanised), while the funding of scientific research is largely a UK responsibility (via the Medical Research Council), with scope for additional devolved funds. In most cases the new devolved responsibilities have not prompted significant policy innovation or divergence because each devolved health department has similar ideas to the Department of Health. The exceptions come from tobacco advertising and the ban on smoking in public places. When it became clear that the bill, introduced in 2000, to ban tobacco advertising in the UK would be delayed (following the dissolution of Parliament in 2001), a separate bill covering Scotland was introduced in 2002 by an opposition MSP (Nicola Sturgeon, who became Scottish Health Secretary from 2007 to the present day), largely to set the agenda and put pressure on the UK government to reintroduce UK-wide legislation (Cairney, 2007b: 55; 2007c).

The issue of smoking bans initially followed a similar path, with the first bill introduced by an opposition MSP in 2003 subject to the same uncertainty about the legislative competence of the Scottish Parliament. The difference in this case is that the bill received significant parliamentary support. It also became clear that prominent public health advocates, such as ASH Scotland and the British Medical Association (BMA) Scotland were prepared to back this bill and criticise the lack of Scottish Executive action (the BMA is the main trade union of the medical profession and has a significant campaigning role in health policy; the BMA Scotland is a devolved branch of the UK body; ASH Scotland is a separate organisation from ASH UK, reflecting separate Royal Colleges in Scotland). This prompted the Scottish Executive, which had previously relied on a voluntary agreement with the Scottish hospitality industry, to introduce its own comprehensive bill in 2005 (see ASH Scotland, 2005; Cairney, 2006).

As with the EU, the influence of devolved policy activity is often difficult to gauge. While the advertising bill was significant to the Scottish Parliament, it had much less of an impact on the debate in Westminster (Cairney, 2007a: 55). While the decision of the Scottish Executive to ban smoking in public places (combined with similar commitments in Wales and Northern Ireland) raised the issue on the UK agenda, the UK's health secretary John Reid remained committed to a partial smoking ban which exempted bars (pubs) and private clubs.

The UK Parliament (Westminster)

The history of the role of Parliament in tobacco is one of constant post-war involvement but limited influence – until it played a key role in the smoking ban. Its limited influence on tobacco control reflects not only the peripheral role of Parliament to the policy process (Richardson and Jordan, 1979) but also the role of pro-tobacco Members of Parliament (MPs), who ensured that a succession of private members' bills introduced in Parliament to control tobacco were defeated. Parliamentary influence was used in the 1970s as a resource by ministers when negotiating voluntary agreements with the tobacco industry (Berridge, 2004: 123; Baggott, 1988: 30), but the effect of pro- and anti-control advocates ensured that the issue 'tended to float on and off the agenda' (Baggott, 1988: 32). This position changed dramatically in 2006 when Westminster voted for legislation to ban smoking comprehensively in public places despite attempts by ministers in the Department of Health for more limited bans (see Cairney, 2007a: 63).

Overall, the evidence points to policy change caused partly by a combination of institutional changes. The significance of influence from the EU and devolved territories is marked when we consider its combined effect with UK institutional change. As Cairney (2009a: 477) argues, there is a 'long tradition of campaigning "clientelism" in the UK's Department of Health'. In the past, the marginalisation of the Department of Health and health ministers prompted them to seek new ways to influence tobacco policy. Its main route was to fund groups, such as ASH to raise issues and criticise policy on its behalf. Now, this influence extends to the EU and devolved territories. EU regulations can be used as a benchmark or minimum point from which to build, and devolved policy can be used to put pressure on the UK government as a whole.

Agendas: How important is tobacco control as a policy issue? How is tobacco framed?

There was a time in the UK when tobacco enjoyed a glamorous image, smoking was a normal part of life and media attention was minimal and largely positive. Much early post-war policy centred on supporting tobacco as an industry. This economic image became increasingly challenged by public health groups promoting new scientific evidence on the links between smoking and serious illness. It was also challenged increasingly within the media. In particular, the position of the print media changed when newspapers and magazines no longer relied on significant tobacco advertising revenue (following restrictions and then the ban on advertising). However, the effect of this new image was not uniform within government. The case for tobacco control was increasingly accepted within the Department of Health but not in other departments more likely to focus on employment, export and taxation.

For most of the post-war period the economic image of tobacco was reinforced by an image related to the importance of civil liberties and public opinion. Governments were reluctant to restrict the advertising of a product that was not illegal to sell and people were free to consume. The Labour government rejected calls in 1968 to legislate to ban tobacco advertising and sponsorship primarily because it would be unpopular among Labour's working class base (Taylor, 1984, Cairney, 2007a: 52; note that the successful ban on TV advertising was ensured without recourse to further legislation). This attitude was reinforced from 1979 by a Conservative government ideology stressing a minimal role for the state in regulating behaviour, and therefore placing unusual emphasis on the role of civil liberties compared to most other countries addressing tobacco (see Studlar, 2002). The proposal by a junior minister to legislate to ban tobacco advertising was decried by many Conservative MPs and ministers (including the Prime Minister) as 'an attack on "freedom not cigarettes"' (Cairney, 2007a: 52; Taylor, 1984: 145). Instead, governments sought voluntary agreements with the tobacco industry.

The election of Labour in 1997 marked a significant shift in the willingness of government to accept public health as the dominant tobacco policy image (suggesting, considering Labour's past attitudes, a highly-qualified party effect). This reinforced the rising status of the scientific evidence on the significance of links between exposure to SHS and illness. A developing policy image linked to passive smoking not only reinforced attention to tobacco as a health issue, but also undermined an image based on civil liberties, with the right to smoke now competing with the right to enjoy clean air and attention to the voluntary act of smoking competing with 'involuntary smoking' (Berridge, 2004: 124). The argument that tobacco taxation had a disproportionate effect on poor and older smokers gave way, first, to the argument that taxation would reduce tobacco consumption among those groups and, second, that smoking was a 'waste of working class life' (Berridge, 2004: 131). The argument that a reduction in smoking would allow people to live longer and therefore increase the government's social security bill gave way to health economist arguments highlighting an overall economic cost of tobacco consumption.[6]

The Labour government was more willing to legislate to ban tobacco advertising and accelerate measures to reduce smoking prevalence, such as higher taxation combined with an expansion of cessation services (Asare et al, 2009: 93). Yet, the images related to popularity and civil liberties remained an important reference point. Legislation to ban smoking in public places was passed eventually, 10 years after Labour's election. In the meantime, it promoted voluntary codes of practice with employers and the hospitality industry. Therefore, the idea of a changing policy image or a new dominant image related to tobacco is important, but we should not assume that this reframing alone led inevitably to policy change.

Networks: Has there been a shift in power between pressure participants?

The balance of power between tobacco and public health interests within government has shifted profoundly since the early post-war period. As Read (1992) (see also Taylor, 1984: 69–71) argues, earlier tobacco policy represented one of the clearest examples of a producer-dominated 'policy community' (or 'cozy network'). Representatives of tobacco companies commanded privileged access to senior ministers and civil servants and their relationship was insulated from most other actors. The relationship was institutionalised during World War II when the Tobacco Advisory Council (TAC, effectively replaced as the political arm of tobacco by the Tobacco Manufacturers' Association, TMA), consisting of representatives of tobacco companies and the UK government, was established to ensure the supply of cigarettes to civilians and members of the armed forces. Its importance as a venue for group-government relations continued because the tobacco industry provided clear economic benefits (taxation, employment, exports). Links with senior government actors in the DTI were maintained to monitor and promote tobacco exports, while other factors, such as tobacco sponsorship in arts and sports and the role of tobacco employment in marginal constituencies influenced the support of several ministers and MPs (Baggott, 1988: 20). Notably, the reliance by government on voluntary agreements with the industry gave the latter a legitimate reason to maintain close contacts and negotiate with the Department for Health and Social Security on a basis that no other organisation rivalled (Baggott, 1988: 16). Indeed, Baggott (1988: 40) argues that the tobacco industry 'enjoyed almost a veto power over policy'.

Read (1992, 1996) suggests that this closed policy community was surrounded by a wider 'issue network' of participants who sought to influence government but had more limited scope for access and influence. This includes affiliates of the tobacco industry who could be called on for support, including representatives of tobacco workers, retailers and consumers (such as Freedom Organisation for the Right to Enjoy Smoking Tobacco, FOREST), and organisations, such as the Advertising Association, which opposed any tobacco advertising ban that would cause a reduction in revenue (Baggott, 1988: 21).

The issue network also included their opponents within public health. Advocates of stronger tobacco control were not well funded or organised in the early post-war period. The Royal College of Physicians was the main voice in the 1950s and 1960s, but its role was restricted primarily to the dissemination of new scientific information. It established ASH in 1971 (ASH Scotland was established by the Royal College of Physicians Edinburgh in 1973), and ASH anti-tobacco advocacy was joined increasingly by the British Medical Association (BMA). However, a concerted anti-smoking campaign was still in its infancy (Cairney, 2007a: 48). The BMA was not nearly as active or organised on this issue compared to the present day (Baggott, 1988: 11). ASH received almost all of its money from government and so had to be careful about the tone of its criticism (Baggott, 1988: 10). There was also minimal lobbying activity by cancer charities (Baggott, 1988: 15). Further, each group was most likely to form its most effective links with the Department of Health, which, at the time, operated at the margins of the tobacco policy community. Therefore, public health groups were effectively obliged to pursue a long-term strategy: building up organisational capacity, gathering and disseminating scientific evidence (the RCP was a key actor in this regard), promoting measures (such as smoking cessation and health education) more readily controlled by the Department of Health, lobbying Parliament, and forming domestic and international networks to share best practice and coordinate their efforts.

The effect of this strategy was long-term success, in terms of the policy effect and the status of public health advocates within government, although change took decades and public health advocates may have not felt successful at the time. The early post-war period contrasts starkly with the 21st century. The influence of tobacco companies has diminished, not only because the economic benefit of tobacco has diminished, but also because the changing policy image of tobacco has resulted in its main avenues of influence being either less receptive (the Treasury) or less central to tobacco policy (the DTI). In contrast, public health groups have close links to the Department of Health as the central government department responsible for policy innovation. The BMA is more organised and has a better developed campaigning role. Although ASH still receives income from government, the proportion has fallen (perhaps making it more independent, even though the Department of Health generally supports its aims). There are more actors involved on a regular basis, including Cancer Research UK which, as a large and independent charity funding scientific work on a large scale, has always had close links to the Department of Health (and, unusually, it used them to promote tobacco control).

The effect of this shift within policy networks is not inevitable policy change. In this section we have identified privileged access to ministers and civil servants, not dominance of policymaking itself. Rather, this new institutional arrangement represents a new locus of information and the main source of feedback during consultation. It reinforces the newly dominant policy image (health, not economy) that determines the context within which policy decisions are made.

Socioeconomic factors

Economic benefits of tobacco

Most indicators suggest that the importance of tobacco to the economy fell at a time when attention to the economic ill-effects of smoking rose. However, exact figures are elusive partly because the competition between public health groups and tobacco companies to set the agenda on tobacco extends to basic measurements, such as the number of jobs that the tobacco industry provides. The TAC estimated that tobacco provided 300,000 jobs (many of which were in economically depressed and/or marginal constituencies) in 1979 (Cairney, 2007a: 47; Taylor, 1984: 69), based on the argument that 'suppliers and in wholesale, distribution and retailing were dependent on the UK tobacco industry' (TMA, 2010a). This fell to 5,000 direct and 80,000 indirect jobs by 2004. ASH suggests a figure of 40,000 in 1979 which fell to 11,000 by 2003 (Cairney, 2007a: 47; Taylor, 1984: 69). The tax raised on tobacco products has also declined because an increase in the tax price per cigarette[7] has been offset by a reduction in smoking. In 1950, tobacco taxation accounted for a staggering 16% of government revenue, prompting Minister of Health Ian MacLeod to state in 1954 that, 'We all know that the Welfare State and much else is based on tobacco smoking' (Berridge, 2004: 117). It fell to 8% in the 1960s and 3.6% by 1996, remaining at about 4% (Townsend, 1996: 140; Aspect, 2004: 86).

The UK does not grow tobacco, but it is the home country for some of the largest tobacco companies in the world. In 1988 the top four British tobacco companies made £1.89bn (£3.91bn, or approximately US$6.3bn, at 2010 prices) in pre-tax profits and the UK was home for three of the top seven tobacco multinationals (excluding the state owned Chinese tobacco company which dominates the Chinese market) – British American Tobacco, Imperial Tobacco, and Gallaher (Baggott, 1988: 17). These companies dominated the UK market, which meant that any tobacco control policies would primarily affect the domestic industry (1988: 24). This position has changed somewhat following alterations in the market and the rise of cheap imported cigarettes and illegal smuggling. The UK still is home for the second (British American Tobacco) and fourth (Imperial Tobacco) largest companies, but Gallaher (commanding 38.7% of the UK market share) has been owned by Japan Tobacco International (JTI) since 2007 (ASH, 2007). In 1988 cheap imports accounted for 10% of the UK market share (Baggott, 1988: 25). While this has not risen significantly, the UK government estimates that £2.4–4bn (US$3.84–6.4bn) of tobacco taxation was lost from smuggling and cross-border shopping, compared to £10bn (US$16bn) raised in excise and VAT (sales) taxes in 2007/8, suggesting that 19–28% of the market is not taxed (TMA, 2010c).[8]

Smoking prevalence and behaviour

ASH (2010b: 1) states that the highest recorded level of smoking among men (including pipes, cigars and cigarettes) was a staggering 82% in 1948 (the highest smoking rate in the world at that time, no doubt influenced by wartime tension), while prevalence among women was 41% in 1948, rising to 45% in the mid-1960s. By 2008 the figures had fallen to 22% and 21% (Table 5.2). In 2008, the 22% who smoked compared to 32% who had quit smoking and 46% who had never tried (ONS, 2009: 8). The proportion of people who say they want to give up, primarily for health reasons, has remained constant, at approximately 70%, since the late 1990s (2009: 17; 20), while the daily consumption of cigarettes has fallen from 21.6 in men and 16.6 in women in 1979 to 14 and 13 by 2008 (ASH, 2010b: 3). The proportion of people who say they would not smoke in the presence of children rose from 54% in 1997 to 78% in 2008 (ONS, 2009: 70).

Table 5.2 Smoking Prevalence in the UK, 1948–2008

Year	1948	1974	1986	1998	2008
Men	82%	51%	35%	30%	22%
Women	41%	41%	31%	26%	21%

Source: ASH (2010b)

The long-term trend is therefore clear, and it suggests that a smaller proportion of the population will oppose increased tobacco control. There are also trends within the overall figures that may influence government policy in more detail. For example, the identification of a strong relationship between class and smoking prevalence prompted the Department of Health (2002: 61) to target a specific reduction in prevalence among manual workers, with a particular emphasis on smoking cessation services and tailored education in prisons, hospitals and factories (Department of Health, 2008: 9).

Social attitudes

There is a broad trend in the UK towards a permissive consensus on tobacco control (Chapter 3). Berridge (2004: 119) suggests that Richard Crossman's (Secretary of State, DHSS) opposition to legislation banning advertising in 1967 was based primarily on 'electoral considerations, rather than industry influence', while Baggott (1988: 32) reports that only a small majority of the public favoured an advertising ban in the 1970s. However, the ONS (2009: 90) suggests that, since 1996, approximately one-third of the population has supported an increase in tobacco tax representing 'A lot more than inflation', while approximately half have supported 'A lot more than inflation' or 'Just above inflation'.

We suggest in Chapter 3 that it is relatively difficult to present a precise picture of social attitudes to tobacco control because comprehensive polls on the subject have not been taken until recently and the results vary according to the measures employed. Fortunately, there is a wealth of data on the UK that can be used to inform the wider comparative picture. Cairney (2009a: 478) identifies three relevant factors to analyse attitudes to the smoking ban:

1. The use of different opinion polls or the selective use of the same data.
2. The use of consultation documents rather than opinion polls to demonstrate support.
3. The less precise feeling among decisionmakers about changing levels of public opinion and the scope for change.

Few policymakers would find a clear message from opinion polls because the results are subject to manipulation regarding the way the question is asked and the results are publicised: while ASH Scotland used the ONS Omnibus Survey to show over 80% support for restrictions in most public places and growing support for restrictions in bars (to 54% by 2002), the TMA suggested that, according to a Scottish Executive commissioned poll, Scottish opinion was 50:50 on the same issue, with 77% against a total ban; in Northern Ireland, the Health Promotion Agency stated that 61% of respondents supported a law to make all workplaces smoke-free but not that only 34% wanted a complete ban in pubs; while Alun Pugh AM (Assembly Member) argued that 80% supported controls, the Welsh Assembly's Committee on Smoking in Public Places reported that attitudes varied, with 91% in favour of restrictions in schools but 50% in bars (Cairney, 2009a: 478–9).

The solution in Scotland and Northern Ireland was to use consultation documents to supplement opinion polls, perhaps partly because those in favour of a smoking ban were more likely to respond (2009a: 479). In Scotland, the 80% support in consultations for a smoking ban and the 56% support for a comprehensive ban was used by the Scottish Executive to justify change, while the figure of 91% support was promoted by pressure participants via the media and used by the (UK Government's) Northern Ireland minister to justify action. There is also evidence in Scotland that a comprehensive ban was pursued only when the initial media opposition in 1999 dissipated and the Scottish Executive sensed a shifting public mood from the early 2000s (2009a: 480).

The process was significantly different and rather more convoluted in England (and therefore in Wales which depended on Westminster legislation). A key difference is that the John Reid-led Department of Health was less likely to use consultations and opinion to justify a complete ban. Rather, it downplayed the importance of its consultation results (2009a: 480) and instead sought to follow public opinion to the letter:

> Surveys ... show 86% of people in favour of workplace restrictions, and a similarly substantial majority of people supporting restrictions in restau-

> rants. But when people are asked whether smoking should be restricted in pubs the figures fall substantially – to around 56% – and when people are asked which sort of restrictions they would prefer in pubs only 20% of people choose 'no smoking allowed anywhere' and the majority tend to be opposed to a complete ban. (Cm 6374, 2004: 98)

This was the government position when its legislation was introduced in Westminster. Yet, Labour MPs were influenced by the argument that attitudes to smoking bans were changing rapidly and that the ban itself would increase support (based on the experience in Ireland and Scotland) (Cairney, 2009a: 480). This proved to be the case in England, with (qualified) support for a smoking ban in pubs rising from 48% in 1998 to 56% in 2003, 65% in 2004 and 75% in 2007 and 2008 (2009a: 480; ONS, 2009: 84). Support for the comprehensive smoking ban itself was also high at 80% in 2007 and 81% in 2008 (2009: 88).

The role of ideas: Scientific knowledge

For our purposes the role of ideas has two key aspects: the development of scientific evidence used to reframe the tobacco problem, and the extent to which the UK government has imported ideas from other governments. At first glance it appears that the acceptance within government of the scientific evidence, and therefore a reframing of the tobacco problem, was almost inevitable. Policymakers no longer question whether or not smoking causes ill-health, while few question the connection between exposure to SHS and illness. Instead, the policy agenda is concerned with how far to go with tobacco control as a result of the problem.

Yet, the strong connection between ideas and policy only seems inevitable in retrospect. The public health-driven anti-smoking agenda did not begin in the 1950s. Although the association between smoking and lung carcinoma was highlighted by Doll and Hill in 1950, there was considerable uncertainty within the Ministry of Health about how to assess this evidence (Berridge, 2004: 118). It also took time for adjustments within the public health field to take place, which involved movement from a focus on coal pollution and epidemics associated with infectious diseases (Berridge, 2004: 118). Notably, the Royal College of Physicians' *Smoking and Health* report in 1962 was undertaken to educate *doctors* (Berridge, 2004: 118), suggesting that the smoking-illness link was by no means taken for granted and therefore that its effect on some policymakers from the 1960s was impressive. It is also significant that the 1962 and 1971 reports recommended a form of harm reduction (from cigarettes to cigars or pipes) rather than the contemporary all-or-nothing push to smoking cessation (Berridge, 2004: 121). In other words, the evidence itself did not cause any policy change, particularly since considerable resources were devoted by tobacco companies to challenge the smoking-illness association. Rather, this was prompted by a different approach to its dissemination and a reinterpretation of the policy consequences. Berridge (2004: 123) suggests that the new focus, which involved encouraging abstention through health education, tobacco taxation, and a ban on advertising, only developed from the 1970s, while the acceptance of this approach within government took much longer to establish.

The same can be said about the scientific evidence on exposure to SHS, with studies linking SHS to serious illness published in medical journals from the early 1980s but only causing legislative action to ban smoking in enclosed public places from the mid-2000s. While the ISCSH accepted a degree of increased risk to health from passive smoking in 1988, the link did not become a 'scientific fact' within government until its successor, the Scientific Committee on Tobacco and Health (SCOTH), highlighted the risks to lung cancer, heart disease and other illnesses and called for smoking in public places to be restricted (2004: 125). This accords with the Department of Health argument (in interviews in 2006, recounted in Cairney, 2007a: 50–1) that the connection was not 'set in stone' until the SCOTH report (compare with Aspect Consortium, 2004: 34). Even then, the acceptance of evidence within government does not cause an inevitable comprehensive ban on smoking in public places. Many other options to accommodate the wishes of smokers and non-smokers could have been found (Berridge, 2004: 125) and were tried initially, including the UK government's initial agreement with employers and the hospitality industry to restrict smoking to particular areas or discourage non-smokers from entering certain premises, and the tobacco company plan to introduce air filtration systems.

The transfer of ideas

There are similar issues regarding the transfer of ideas from other governments. The post-war debate on the scientific evidence appears to have been won in developed countries, prompting them to share ideas on further tobacco control and produce an impressive degree of international policy diffusion (see Chapters 8 and 9). The UK is very much part of this picture. However, we identify two key phases which qualify the role of transfer to some extent. First, when the UK was a post-war laggard it was resistant to the importation of measures, such as a ban on tobacco advertising (Baggott, 1988). Second, when the Labour government was elected in 1997 it had already committed itself to a degree of tobacco control that went beyond the international agenda (although this was based on advice from members of key epistemic communities).

The main exception to this picture relates to the smoking ban introduced by the Scottish and UK Governments. In this case there were at least two important sources of learning. The first was the accepted international model (developed from the experiences of California and New York) of incremental change in which smoking restrictions were steadily increased to denormalise smoking in public places, influence public opinion and isolate bars and clubs before a complete ban (Cairney, 2009a: 481–2). The second, based on more recent experience in Ireland (which is closest in size to the devolved territories and shares a border with Northern Ireland), was an immediate and comprehensive ban. The UK as a whole adopted the Irish model and there is clear evidence of learning (Asare and Studlar, 2009), albeit at different times and in different ways (see Cairney, 2009a on four separate 'windows of opportunity' for policy change).

Conclusion

The clearest outcome from this study of the UK is that tobacco policy is radically different when compared to the early post-war regime. It has also changed markedly since the mid-1980s, with tobacco control accelerating particularly since 1997. This general post-war conclusion holds regardless of one's view on the status of voluntary agreements. These agreements have demonstrated at best a partial degree of success in each case (health warnings, advertising, smoking in public places). Yet, while a shift from voluntary to statutory action may have produced a lurch in policy in certain areas, in each case they represent incremental changes when viewed alongside the wider range of policy instruments pursued by the UK government. We return to this issue, of incremental changes leading to radical change over the long term, in Chapter 10.

We explain this shift in policy by focusing on the five core processes identified in Chapter 2. Institutional change has been important, with the Treasury and DTI replaced by the Department of Health as the central actor and the EU and devolved territories (and, occasionally, Westminster) providing new sources of policy impetus. The policy image of tobacco has been reframed, from a focus on its economic benefits and the right to sell and smoke tobacco replaced by a focus on health, the tobacco epidemic, and the right to clean air. The fortunes of pressure participants has shifted dramatically, with the tobacco companies that were once at the heart of policy-making now increasingly marginalised in favour of medical and public health interests. The economic benefits of tobacco, public attitudes against tobacco control, and smoking prevalence have all fallen significantly. The status of scientific knowledge demonstrating the connections between smoking, exposure to SHS, and ill-health have been 'set in stone' within the UK government now seeking, often with the help of international experience, to know which restrictive measures are the most effective rather than if tobacco control is necessary.

The five factors combined and reinforced each other to produce significant change over a long period. For example, the increased promotion of tobacco control by the EU and devolved governments (and, latterly, Westminster) helped change policy, but perhaps more importantly provided the Department of Health with more avenues for influence. The rise in the evidence regarding exposure to SHS and the receptivity in multiple levels of government to scientific argument, promoted by public health groups, helped transform the policy image of tobacco – from an economic image bolstered with reference to civil liberties and the voluntary nature of smoking (and a tendency towards voluntary agreements with the industry) to an image based on ill-health and the involuntary inhalation of SHS. The funding of ASH by the Department of Health, combined with the rise in lobbying activities by the BMA (and, more recently, cancer charities), helped disseminate the evidence on smoking (domestically and internationally – see Chapter 9), influence smoking prevalence, and provide a platform for further tobacco control. The reduction in the economic benefits of tobacco undermined the policy influence of the industry. The reduction in smoking prevalence influenced public attitudes to tobacco, which in turn furthered a 'permissive consensus' to tobacco control which was exploited in different ways by different governments. The experience of the Irish and devolved governments put pressure on the UK government to emulate its comprehensive ban and, when this pressure was resisted, helped public health groups put pressure on MPs to vote against the government line. The key point is that no single factor explains this change. Rather, they are all necessary but insufficient conditions for major policy change.

6
The United States

The United States (US) deserves special consideration because of its leading economic and political position in the world, its scientific research, its generally high rating on overall tobacco control, and its capacity to influence others. It is also an interesting case because policy has not changed as much or as quickly as expected. There was not a shift from minimal to relatively comprehensive tobacco control that we find in other leading, developed, English-speaking countries (Chapters 5 and 7). Some elements of tobacco policy in the US are surprising, such as its leading position in scientific and biomedical research on tobacco, but also its often slow development of policy, especially on the central (federal) level. This limited progress, almost a half century after the US Surgeon General's report of 1964 on the hazards of tobacco use, represents a paradox since the US has possessed significant anti-tobacco group mobilisation since the 1960s, some of the largest reductions in smoking among industrialised countries, and innovative tobacco control policies and programmes at the state and local government levels in spite of entrenched tobacco interests. In other words, civil society appeared more committed to tobacco control than some political institutions.

This chapter describes US policy development on tobacco, considering how far policy has travelled and the issues remaining to be addressed. It links policy progress to the five factors that we identified in Chapter 2. First, it highlights the role of institutions as a source of both continuity and change in public policy. The US political system is rather fragmented and strong central control is unusual. It provides multiple venues for change, and the role of states, local government jurisdictions, and courts provide a distinctive path to change. However, it also provides multiple points of inertia and ways for tobacco interests to block policy change – by, for example, funding the campaigns of pro-business and anti-regulatory US politicians, highlighting the concerns of major tobacco-growing districts and the hospitality industry, exploiting the super-majority rules of the US Senate, and challenging major tobacco control policies in the courts. Second, the chapter highlights a broad shift in the framing of tobacco, from political economy to public health but also suggests that a distinctive US frame based on morality developed and may have been necessary to further the debate in such a fragmented system where tobacco only rose to the top of the central policy agenda sporadically. Third, it charts a change in the balance of power between pro- and anti-tobacco groups, but notes that this occurred relatively recently and that, while the tobacco network is becoming fragmented, the anti-tobacco network is, to some extent, internally divided, reflecting the pluralist group-government system. It outlines a reduction in smoking prevalence, the value of tobacco to the economy, and opposition to tobacco control, but notes that tobacco companies are still profitable and powerful. Finally, it identifies the US' position as scientific leader and the leading global role of states, such as California, Massachusetts, and New York but contrasts this picture, to some extent, with limited policy diffusion *within* the US. Overall, these five factors help explain why the US remains one of the leading countries in global tobacco control but lags behind some other English-speaking countries in some respects.

What is US tobacco policy?

While US tobacco policy largely follows the six phases outlined in Table 3.1, there has always been a degree of variation, reflecting the fact that states and local governments have traditionally taken the policy lead. The 50 US states, plus the federal District of Columbia, vary widely in terms of tobacco-related characteristics, including social and economic context and tobacco control laws. Adoption of many policy instruments varies considerably, although over time more states are adopting more stringent laws.

Policy at the turn of the 20th century was rather limited. By 1890, 26 states had prohibited sales to minors (Troyer and Markle, 1983). Until the early 1920s, 15 states prohibited cigarette sales and/or smoking and 22 others considered such measures (Tate, 1999). However, these laws were erratically enforced and sometimes rapidly repealed despite the US Supreme Court upholding state sales bans laws as a constitutional regulatory practice. Unlike alcohol prohibition, there was never a serious attempt at a US constitutional amendment or central legislation against tobacco. Nicotine was excluded from the *Food and Drugs Act* of 1906. The federal government only became involved when the Supreme Court ruled, on the basis of a lawsuit initiated by a state, that the Tobacco Trust led by James B. Duke constituted a restraint of trade in violation of the Sherman Anti-trust Act and had to be dissolved. As in many countries (see Chapters 5 and 7 in particular), most anti-cigarette policy was swept away by the patriotic role that manufactured cigarettes played in the morale of soldiers at the front in World War I. Instead, the US government aided the production and consumption of cigarettes through such programmes as the Agricultural Adjustment Act of 1933 providing price supports for leaf growing, below-market prices for cigarettes on military bases and Native American reservations, and their inclusion in international trade negotiations. The context for policy changed in the early postwar era as the scientific evidence on the hazards of tobacco consumption began to be published (below). However, a comprehensive set of tobacco control measures took five decades to produce and policy only really began to accelerate in the 1980s and 1990s.

Regulation

Regulation and education were intertwined in the earliest US central intervention after the 1964 Surgeon General's report. An industry voluntary code was rejected in favour of legislation to mandate package warnings (education) although also forbidding further regulation of advertising until the Federal Trade Commission (FTC) could determine the effects of these warnings. Thus, the US was among the earliest countries to legislate warning labels. The 1970 renewal changed the warning and banned cigarette advertising in broadcasting. A warning appeared on advertisements in 1972. Nevertheless, all of these health warnings were weaker than those proposed in 1964 by the Federal Trade Commission (FTC), and they pre-empted state action on this issue (Studlar, 2004; Kluger, 1996). Some states and local governments were active in regulatory legislation limiting tobacco sales venues and smoking areas, especially from the 1970s (Warner, 1981; Fishman et al, 1999; Studlar, 2002; Bailey, 2004). Beginning with Arizona and Minnesota in the mid-1970s, some states passed laws for non-smoking areas in public buildings and enclosed transportation, but these proceeded slowly in the absence of persuasive evidence that second-hand smoke (SHS) harmed others (Bayer and Colgrove, 2002).

Analysts have come to view early Congressional measures as largely a victory for the tobacco industry against the potential of more stringent measures (Drew, 1965; Doron, 1979; Kluger, 1996). Through Congressional inaction, several opportunities were missed to put tobacco into a regulatory framework in the 1970s. There were few restrictive government policies, especially on the central level, until the 1980s when concerns about the health effects of SHS and addiction precipitated wider concern. Otherwise, economic concerns trumped public health (Troyer and Markle, 1983, cf. Bailey, 2004).

A reluctant Congress eventually did authorise some specific tobacco control measures starting in the mid-1980s, including rotating health warnings (Pertschuk, 1986) and bans on smoking in airplanes (Studlar, 2003). Various Executive agencies banned smoking in public buildings (Fritschler and Rudder, 2006). Nevertheless, in 1994 an anti-tobacco NGO 'report card' on federal institutions gave most of them low marks on tobacco control policy (Leary, 1994). Protection of children as a vulnerable group of the population has been emphasised, especially in federal policy, since the early 1990s. The Synar Amendment to the Comprehensive Drug Education Act of 1992 required states to monitor and reduce sales of cigarettes to minors at the peril of loss of federal drug enforcement funds, with variable results in implementation (Jacobson and Wasserman, 1997).

With the dissemination of findings on the dangers of SHS, state and local non-smoking laws began to accelerate in the 1980s (USDHHS, 1992). The pro-tobacco network fought back by influencing some 31 states to pass preemption laws, which meant that localities could not have stronger laws on various dimensions of tobacco control, often SHS, than those of the state (CDC, 1999). Further, despite extensive public hearings, the Occupational Health and Safety Administration (OSHA) failed to pass a general workplace smoking restriction in the 1990s (Givel, 2006a). An increasing number of states and other jurisdictions have now passed laws prohibiting smoking in cars with children present. By 2011 some 36 states, including tobacco-growing Tennessee and North Carolina, had general indoor smoking bans in workplaces and/or restaurants and/or bars (ANRF, 2011a).

The 2009 *Family Smoking Prevention and Tobacco Control Act* (FSPTCA) was heralded as the most important public event for central tobacco control since the 1964 Surgeon General's Advisory Committee report. It centralised (limited) regulation of tobacco in the Food and Drug Administration (FDA) and provided for stronger warning labels, regulation of cigarette ingredients, approval of new products, and limitations on marketing, advertising, and sales, with the tobacco companies paying the costs. Much of the authority was similar to what the FDA tried to claim in 1996 (see below).

Finance

Once states gave up the attempt to limit smoking through regulation in the early 20th century, they quickly discovered the revenue benefits of cigarettes as a 'sin tax.' Between 1921 and 1969 all 50 states imposed such taxes (Warner, 1981). There is considerable variability among the US states (plus the federal District of Columbia), reflecting their social and economic contexts. Six states are major tobacco growers, and tobacco manufacturing is similarly concentrated, mainly in the same states. However, states have been willing to raise taxes, especially in times of fiscal stress and as the evidence of harm through smoking grew (Tax Burden on Tobacco, 2006). Nevertheless, the affordability of cigarettes still rose dramatically because excise tax increases have not kept up with consumer purchasing power. There was no federal tax increase between 1950 and 1982. Wide variations in state cigarette taxation in the 1970s led to smuggling problems requiring the intervention of a federal law-enforcement agency, the Bureau of Alcohol, Tobacco and Firearms (BATF) (Advisory Commission on Intergovernmental Relations, 1977, 1985). This lack of tax harmonisation among US jurisdictions has been eased somewhat recently as both federal and state taxes have risen (Table 6.1), although not yet to levels comparable with similar countries (see Chapter 3). The largest central tax increase on cigarettes occurred to finance the *Children's Health Insurance Act* of

Figure 6.1 Cigarette Sales Taxes in US, 2011

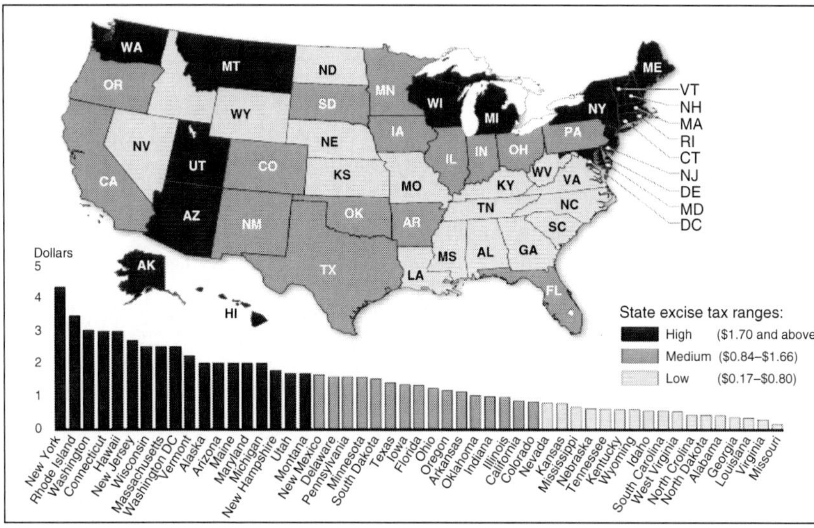

Source: US Government and Accountability Office (2011)

2009. However, there continues to be wide variation, with taxes generally highest in the states in the Northeastern region of the country and lowest among Southeast tobacco producers.

There is also variability in tobacco control spending (CDC, 1999, 2007). States spending more on tobacco control, especially those implementing a multi-dimensional comprehensive tobacco control policy according to CDC standards, have performed better in public health goals for reducing tobacco use. However, most states spend relatively little on tobacco control, and fiscal stress tends to reduce spending.

There has been a decline in tobacco agriculture in the US, although this is mostly due to tobacco companies shifting their leaf purchases to foreign growers. As an extension of the Master Settlement Agreement (below), in 1999 an agreement was reached between tobacco companies and 14 states representing tobacco leaf property owners and growers, compensating them $5.15bn for loss of production and sales. In 2004 the US Congress legislated a phased buyout of federal tobacco price support programmes.

In the 1980s the US Special Trade Representative insisted that countries with state tobacco companies, such as Thailand, Japan, and China, open their markets to US competition under the free trade agreements of the World Trade Organization. In 1997, however, the 'Doggett Amendment' prohibited this practice (Yang and Novotny, 2009).

The US has a reputation as the global leader in the pursuit of tobacco companies through the courts. Indeed, from 1998 until 2009 the MSA was the closest existing US equivalent to a general tobacco control policy. The MSA between states and the industry, described in more detail below, directs the industry to provide compensatory financial payments (originally set at $206bn, but depending on sales) to states as compensation for the costs of healthcare for smokers, as well as limiting its marketing and political activity. However, the 'big bang' expectation that litigation would do serious economic damage to tobacco companies has not been realised. The MSA was a signal victory for the litigation approach, but its impact was limited, especially since the money transferred from the tobacco industry to the states mostly has been used for general spending rather than specifically for tobacco control. Limitations on advertising did not prevent an increase in the tobacco industry promotional expenditures (Slade, 2001). Perhaps the most important impact of the MSA was that the price of cigarettes increased – a de facto tax increase. In return, the industry received relief from further state litigation and a decline of tobacco control on the public agenda until 2009.

Education, learning, information and capacity building

In education, the central government has played a more active role. As previously noted, health warnings have been centrally legislated since 1965. Also included in this category are regular reports by the Surgeon General, the 1992 declaration of the US Environmental Protection Agency (EPA) that SHS was a health danger, the informational activities of the Centres for Disease Control and Prevention (CDC) (see below), Congressional funding to the National Institutes of Health for research on tobacco effects and to the National Cancer Institute (NCI) and CDC for the formation of grassroots citizen anti-tobacco organisations, and periodic Congressional hearings, most famously the one in 1994 in which tobacco company executives denied the harmful properties of cigarettes (Studlar, 2002, 2003).

From a longer term perspective, tobacco as a product and smoking as a behaviour began to be denormalised, beginning in the 1950s and accelerating in the 1960s, largely as a result of educational instruments (Troyer and Markle, 1983; Studlar, 2002). Some observers consider the Federal Communications Commission's (FCC) 'fairness doctrine' televised anti-smoking public information notices of the late 1960s to be a key ingredient in this process because they gave graphic testimony about the health consequences of smoking cigarettes at a time when industry advertising was emphasising rugged individualism and women's rights (Bailey, 2004). These ended, however, when cigarette advertising was removed from the airwaves. More quietly, various federal agencies and programmes aided research and policy development in tobacco control. The CDC made tobacco use reduction a central goal of its *Healthy People* ten-year plans for health promotion conducted research, published findings on smoking prevalence and tobacco-related morbidity and mortality, and offered 'best practice' recommendations. Eventually the Office of Smoking and Health at the CDC assumed direction for all federal capacity-building funds directed through the states to local tobacco control coalitions, a programme initiated in the mid-1980s by the NCI (Studlar, 2002). Some states have developed long-term tobacco control strategies based on the CDC recommendations for Comprehensive Tobacco Control, including prevention (of smoking initiation), cessation (of current smoking), and protection (against SHS).

There was also increasing dissemination of major Surgeon General's reports, which covered SHS in 1986, the addictive properties of cigarettes in 1988, a focus on youth in 1993, and a comprehensive report in 2000 (Bayer and Colgrove, 2004). Other reports by the California EPA and the private Institute of Medicine of the National Academies of Science have been influential.

Institutions: Who has responsibility for tobacco control?

In most chapters we identify at least three important institutional dimensions – the role of the health department, the scope for venue shift and the (highly variable) role of the courts – and the US is distinctive in each case. First, it is more difficult to identify an era-defining shift from finance and industry departments towards a central role for the US Department of Health and Human Services (DHHS); the US political system is relatively fragmented and the role of central government in relation to tobacco control policy has traditionally not been as strong as in other countries. This is obviously true for the vertical (central/state/local) level in the US federal system, but it is also true for the horizontal institutions at the same level – executive, legislative, and judicial. Even within the executive branch, the President (or Governor for states) has difficulty in controlling executive departments and agencies. Thus, no institution can claim to be the key one for tobacco control policy. Instead, at the central level there are several regulatory agencies, some of them officially semi-independent of presidential control, that can assume roles in various dimensions of tobacco policy. We can at least identify a shift in the centre from tobacco promotion to control, but this has taken longer and in more incremental fashion than in most countries. For most of modern history, the central level has either resisted tobacco control or become disengaged from it; some states and localities have been more willing to address the issue.

A tobacco promotion network (subsystem) composed of Congressional committees primarily concerned with agriculture, interest groups, and executive agencies resisted tobacco control, largely successfully, for almost all of the 20th century. It was left to independent regulatory agencies to propose specific tobacco regulations, many of which were overruled by Congress (Fritschler and Rudder, 2006). When Health Secretary Joseph Califano (1981) attempted to establish a stronger, more coordinated central anti-smoking role in the late 1970s, he was ostracised by President Jimmy Carter and his fellow cabinet members. Profound policy and organisational change only occurred in 2009 with the passage of the *Family Protection and Tobacco Control Act* giving the FDA some limited central control over tobacco ingredients, sales, and marketing (although this was presaged by the short-term FDA Rule in 1996).

Because of fragmented central authority over tobacco policy, the DHHS never has played a strong coordinating role over tobacco control policy despite the presence of the National Interagency Committee on Smoking and Health as an advisory body (Studlar, 2002). The Surgeon General heads the Public Health Service and has research, educational, and lobbying power, but no direct policy authority. The role of the Office of Smoking and Health (OSH) in the CDC is similar. After the frustrated attempts at greater central authority through the FDA in the 1990s, OSH become the closest to a policy coordinator in US, although its authority encompasses the production of information and distribution of capacity-building grants to state tobacco control coalitions, not regulation. Congress, the FTC, and the FCC have power over health warnings and advertisements, the departments of Commerce and Agriculture over the business aspects of tobacco production, the Interstate Commerce Commission (ICC) and Federal Aviation Administration (FAA) over public transportation, and the EPA in the SHS debate. The new (2009) FDA role over tobacco promises a more coordinated central government policy response in such areas as product labelling, contents, marketing, and sales, but its legislated authority is still limited and most jurisdiction over sales is possessed by the states.

Second, some analysts have attributed strong US tobacco control to the opportunity for 'venue shopping', that is, being able to persuade different institutions at the federal, state and local levels to address the issue (Baumgartner and Jones, 1993, 2009). Although there is some lack of coordination of competing constituencies and institutions in all countries, the US case is notable for its fragmentation. In the US, public health is a shared responsibility among different levels of government. Although Watts (2008) claims that public health is mainly a state/provincial responsibility in federal systems, the powers in this domain, varying somewhat by instrument, are shared among central, state/provincial, and local jurisdictions, with considerable influence by affected private organisations. Thus, there are multiple potential venues for making policy on most instruments, especially if one considers the pervasive role of the judiciary. For example states and local governments can enact policies on sales, taxes and smoke-free environments (but not on health warnings), while the federal government can intervene on any instrument unless overruled by the federal judiciary.

However, for tobacco control advocates, venue shopping success has varied. For example, the first US President to oppose tobacco promotion directly was Bill Clinton, some 30 years after the 1964 Surgeon General's report. These multiple venues also provide an improved capacity for tobacco promotion interests to block control measures. A federal second chamber that responds to regional considerations more than partisan ones has resulted in tobacco-defending interests frequently blocking central legislation in the Senate (Studlar, 2003). However, if an executive agency or Congress attempts to control tobacco, there is always the possibility of litigation and an adverse decision (as, for example, by the Supreme Court in 2000 over FDA authority). There is also unusual scope in the US for direct action. Within the 24 US states that allow them (particularly California and Massachusetts), ballot initiatives and referenda have been employed by both anti-tobacco and pro-tobacco groups, usually to the advantage of the former group (Tung et al, 2009).

Many regulatory powers co-exist between the central and state levels, and even between the state and local. The higher level in each instance has sometimes enacted legislation to pre-empt actions by the lower level. The federal government did this on cigarette advertising in 1965, renewed in 1970 (Fritschler and Rudder, 2006), rejecting attempts by some states to regulate. Subsequently, the US Supreme Court overturned Massachusetts' attempt to regulate advertising venues (Derthick, 2005). The 2009 FSPTCA selectively reduced the federal pre-emptive authority over advertising. The continued, albeit declining, existence of a number of state pre-emption laws led to a *Healthy People* goal of eliminating such clauses because they stifle local innovation (CDC, 2010).

The states have played the most active role in tobacco control policy (despite some limits on what they can do because of pre-emptive federal legislation concerning regulation of advertising). For over a century the US has had a decentralised process of tobacco control led by the state and local government level, with only occasional bursts of federal activity, notably in 1964 and 2009. The states have led on instruments, such as taxation, regulation of SHS, cessation programmes, such as quitlines, anti-smoking education campaigns, and litigation against tobacco manufacturers for healthcare costs, creating a mosaic of tobacco control in the country. Even though states lack uniformity of policy, they do engage in considerable policy innovation, re-invention, and lesson drawing.

The same is true for local government jurisdictions, whose authority is mainly limited to SHS or smoke-free laws. Indeed, among some advocacy organisations, the model for developing smoke-free laws amidst institutional inertia at higher levels of government is 'bottom-up', which is to start working for policy change at the local levels (Glantz and Balbach, 2000). This strategy is usually couched in the US ideal of local community values that is perceived to be antagonistic to 'outside' tobacco companies trying to influence local policies. Consequently, as of January 2011, there were over 450 local laws and ordinances on smoke-free environments (ANRF, 2011b).

Third, the role of litigation and the courts has been particularly significant. A strong, politically active judiciary provides unusual scope for venue shopping in the US although, again, it is by no means the sole preserve of anti-tobacco advocates. Several judgements finding tobacco companies liable have been overturned or reduced on appeal (Jacobson and Warner, 1999). Most of the policy initiation has come from states. The first attempted 'Global Settlement' (renamed the 'National Settlement') for tobacco control, came from a legal initiative of state attorneys general and private tort lawyers against tobacco companies, with some involvement from the President of the US (Derthick, 2001; Mollenkamp et al, 1998; Spill et al, 2001). The National Settlement included provisions for 25-year payments from the tobacco companies to the state to cover the cost of cigarette-related illnesses of Medicaid patients (poorer people whose healthcare costs are paid by state governments), limits on tobacco company advertising, marketing, and political activity, protection for the companies against further legal liability, and agreement that the FDA would be authorised to regulate tobacco. This was effectively a bottom-up initiative, presented to Congress for its approval because certain legal provisions of the agreement required it. It was defeated by filibuster in the US Senate in 1998.

When the Senate refused to ratify the agreement, a substitute legal arrangement was enacted between 46 states and the tobacco companies, with no central government imprimatur. The MSA concerned compensatory financial payments from the industry as well as marketing and political activity limits. Since the process was a judicial one rather than executive-legislative decisionmaking, separately-elected attorneys general could act independently of the wishes of their governors, and no group of states could veto the process. The litigation took place in state courts, generally less sympathetic to tobacco companies than federal ones. Thus, tobacco-growing states eventually gave up their reservations in favour of sharing in the financial spoils of the MSA. Further, individual lawsuits by four other states, principally Minnesota, resulted in further legal settlements, including making tobacco industry documents available for public inspection (available online at the Legacy Tobacco Documents Library, University of California, San Francisco). The US central government then followed with a lawsuit against the tobacco companies for conspiracy, which resulted in no punitive damages although it did mandate changes in marketing behaviour, including the banning of 'light and mild' cigarettes, and included Judge Gladys Kessler's ruling in 2006 that tobacco companies violated the Racketeer Influenced and Corrupt Organizations (RICO) Act, which makes the companies subject to more lawsuits.

Agendas: How important is tobacco control as a policy issue? How is tobacco framed?

Even though tobacco regulation has become an important issue for the public health of the population of the US, it has been on the political agenda only sporadically, first around the turn of the 20th century and then again erratically after the rise of concern in mid-century. The landmark report of the US Surgeon General's Advisory Committee in 1964 on the health hazards of cigarettes gave tobacco control a higher agenda status, and prompted new ways to consider it. The framing of tobacco policy broadly follows the phases outlined in Table 3.1.

From 1885 to 1950 the dominant frame was political economy. Public, media and governmental attitudes to tobacco were largely favourable and promoted the economic growth of this new, popular product. The mass media of newspapers, magazines, radio, film, and eventually television created a 'smoking culture' that became an accepted part of everyday life in the US (Brandt, 2007). Tobacco production and consumption benefited large sectors of society, including growers, investors, retailers, and advertisers. While there were some early attempts to control tobacco on both health and morality grounds, they were swept away by the association of cigarette manufacturing with patriotic efforts to keep the troops satisfied during both world wars. Restrictions on tobacco consumption were off the public political agenda for almost a half century during the 'era of good feeling' toward cigarettes, when governments aided production. The few remaining outposts of anti-tobacco opinion, such as the widely read *Reader's Digest* (Kluger, 1996), presented arguments mainly on public health grounds but were unable to mobilise a response from either the attentive or mass public, much less government officials.

Health-based arguments became more prominent when claims that tobacco consumption caused ill health began to cumulate after 1950 (especially after the Surgeon General's 1964 report). Public health arguments often combine morality and science to advocate certain population-based policies. 'Secular morality' describes the attitudinal and behavioural goals of public health policies stemming from epidemiological studies, grassroots health promotion advocacy, and the Healthy Public Policy goals of governments (Brandt and Rozin, 1997; Katz, 1997). The focus is on improving and extending lives through good long-term health practices, including exercise, diet, and avoidance of risky behaviour. As the population ages in the US, preventive health has become more integral to healthcare reform (as, for example, in the Patient Protection and Affordable Care Act of 2010).

Cigarette smoking is the chief source of risk to people's healthy longevity. Katz (1997) argues that this is a crucial test case for morality applied to disease (not to be confused with the pre-World War II arguments concerning tobacco as a 'gateway' for other anti-social behaviour, such as gambling, alcoholism, prostitution, and criminality). Scientific evidence mobilises public health and anti-tobacco advocates, who disseminate it for wider public consumption. Making this a morality concern as well as an issue of science and health increases its appeal to the mass public, the target audience. This is particularly likely to be the case in a country, such as the US, which has a strong tradition of moral appeals on public policy issues (Morone, 2003), used partly to overcome institutional inertia, where many issues reach the political agenda only to stay in a convenient distributive or regulatory subsystem with producer interests dominant for decades (Baumgartner and Jones, 1993). Exercising self-discipline, protecting children, and associating unhealthy behaviour with marginalised groups have been characteristics of a moralised tobacco control policy of 'sin' throughout the 20th century (Brandt and Rozin, 1997). For example, Dr. C. Everett Koop moved from being US Surgeon General in the 1980s into a new career as a moral crusader against smoking (Koop, 1998; Katz, 1997).

One aim related to this agenda is the denormalisation of smoking in terms of the behaviour, product, and industry (Studlar, 2002). Smokers have become increasingly socially isolated, treated, in effect, as 'second class citizens' because of their continued adherence to a harmful habit (see also Troyer and Markle, 1983). Often smokers themselves agree with this stigmatisation and cite it as a motivation to quit. The disproportionate contribution of smokers to healthcare costs has led to differential insurance rates and in some instances a refusal by organisations to employ smokers. Morone (2003) and Kersh and Morone (2002) demonstrate how the politicisation of issues of personal health behaviour in the US is often couched not only in ideological terms but also through demonisation of the opposition; 'the politics of moralisation'. They find a similar pattern for such familiar issues as drink, drugs, sexuality/family planning, tobacco and obesity (see also Engs, 2000 on cycles of health reform).

Included in this process is a shift from 'the demon user' to 'the demon industry,' such as the Legacy Foundation 'Truth Campaign' that sought not only to educate people about the hazards of tobacco use and SHS but also to illuminate how tobacco companies manipulate people (Farrelly et al, 2005, 2009). Moral objections toward cigarette manufacturers as 'disease vectors,' 'drug dealers,' 'racketeers,' and 'murderers' responsible for a 'pandemic' became more frequently employed (Studlar, 2002). 'Big Tobacco' became a pejorative term, especially after the televised public denials of addiction and harmful health effects by tobacco company chief executive officers in 1994 Congressional testimony reinforced the issue of their lack of credibility (Mamudu et al, 2011).

The scientific evidence on SHS prompted public health advocates to focus their campaigns around young people and other vulnerable groups. Until the 1980s, cigarette consumption was still dominantly framed as an individual choice. The two major Surgeon General's reports on SHS in 1986 and on the addictive properties of cigarettes in 1988 undermined this frame, which was largely replaced by attention to the damage to innocent victims – non-smokers, families, children, and fetuses. The image of the cigarette smoker changed from one of rugged independence into one of an addicted person whose activity was socially irresponsible, legitimating government action (Nathanson, 1999).

In line with this reframing of the issue, protection of children as a vulnerable group of the population has been emphasised, especially in federal policy, since the early 1990s. The 1993 report of the Surgeon General was the first to focus on youth, followed by other authoritative reports (Bayer and Colgrove, 2004). Most smoking begins in the teenage years, and the appeal of Joe Camel as a cartoon advertisement for cigarettes provoked interest in how tobacco companies were trying to entice youth into smoking. When the FDA attempted to exert jurisdiction over tobacco in 1996, its two main arguments were that tobacco companies manipulated the levels of nicotine in cigarettes to keep smokers addicted and that smoking was a 'pediatric disease' (Bayer and Colgrove, 2004; Bailey, 2004). One of the major anti-tobacco lobbies in Washington, DC, over the past decade has been the Campaign for Tobacco-Free Kids. Protection of youth from an addictive drug has been a position on which most US anti-tobacco campaigners have agreed to frame tobacco control policy despite some prominent dissent (Glantz, 1996; Nathanson, 1999). Even proposed tax increases are sometimes justified on the basis that raising prices discourages youth purchases (Bailey, 2004). Anti-tobacco campaigners have proposed that any commercial film in which smoking is featured automatically be given an 'R' rating to limit youth admissions.

Countering the industry contention that tobacco was an economic benefit for society, anti-tobacco advocates developed an argument in the 1990s that the economic costs of consumption were a drain on the public purse, especially through increased healthcare costs borne by governments through the Medicaid (central and state shared programme for low-income people) and Medicare (central programme for the aged and disabled) (Bayer and Colgrove, 2004). This economic analysis underpinned lawsuits for healthcare costs by state attorneys general and the federal Department of Justice. Tobacco companies contending that smokers dying younger actually saved expenses for taxpayers were sometimes compelled to apologise.

Finally, moral arguments have been used to counter the idea of harm reduction through less damaging delivery devices to satisfy nicotine addiction. Harm reduction encompasses the tolerance of reduced risk forms of nicotine delivery through product redesign, substitute nicotine products, limited marketing and sales outlets, and/or plain packaging. This poses a challenge to those aiming for a nicotine-free future through demand reduction. The principle of harm reduction for tobacco has engendered ferocious, moralistic debate among anti-tobacco advocates, the majority of whom remain neo-prohibitionist (Mamudu et al, 2011).

Networks: Has there been a shift in power between pressure participants?

The major contenders in policy are, on the one hand, the tobacco network composed of manufacturers, growers, and affiliated economic beneficiaries from production and consumption, such as retailers, advertisers, mass media and the hospitality industry and, on the other, anti-tobacco campaigners from citizen advocate and public health organisations. The political struggle is mainly one between an economic interest on one side and a public health/morality group on the other, and this has been waged for over a century. While those advocating a more restrictive tobacco control policy have recently become the dominant coalition, the tobacco industry remains a highly profitable business and it would be going too far to describe tobacco companies as political outsiders (particularly since they remain some of the top contributors to political campaigns in the country).

The interest group system in the US is generally considered to be pluralist, with many groups competing for influence. However, as soon as subsystems hosting certain interest groups and governmental institutions within a jurisdiction become established, they may dominate a system for an extended period of time until disrupted by actors with different policy framing (Baumgartner and Jones, 2009). This was the case with pro-tobacco interests for most of the 20th century. Until at least the 1980s, a pro-tobacco interest group-executive agency-legislative subsystem of decisionmaking constituted a classic, stable 'cozy triangle' of pro-tobacco policy. It operated largely out of public view and focused on bargaining for promotion and distribution of benefits from tobacco production in domestic and foreign markets through the Agriculture and Commerce departments (Troyer and Markle, 1983; Baumgartner and Jones, 2009). Tobacco growers, concentrated in a few Southeastern states, were an integral part of this network. Traditionally, US manufacturers bought tobacco leaf exclusively from domestic producers, solidifying 'tobacco state' economic and political loyalty to a remunerative product, especially in rural communities. Although some 20 states grew tobacco, six states were eventually responsible for approximately 90% of it, with manufacturing facilities also concentrated there: North Carolina, Kentucky, Tennessee, South Carolina, Georgia, and Virginia. This gave the tobacco states considerable political influence in Congress, especially through the one-party Democratic party South at the time (it wielded considerable political clout during the long period of Democratic dominance in Congress from the 1930s to the 1980s). With powerful legislative committee chairs chosen on the basis of seniority, the tobacco-growing states were well placed to advance their economic interests. Even the US military and Native American reservations became part of the network by distributing free or reduced price cigarettes (Wagner, 1971).

From 1958 to 1997, the industry primarily advanced its cause politically through the Tobacco Institute (disbanded as part of the MSA). For the first 20 of those years it had an unusual ally in the American Medical Association (AMA), which was more concerned about issues, such as publicly-financed healthcare legislation than tobacco, accepted tobacco company finance for its research, and delayed its endorsement of the 1964 US Surgeon General report until 1978 (Studlar, 2002: 56). Indeed, Wolinsky and Brune (1994) suggest that they effectively brokered a deal: the tobacco companies would oppose Medicare and, in return, were able to buy further research to keep the scientific question open even after the 1964 report. On some advertising restriction issues, the industry has been supported by the American Civil Liberties Union. On the state and local levels, pro-tobacco forces were supported by other economic development interests, including vendors and the hospitality industry of hotels, bars, restaurants, gaming, and other entertainment venues.

Since the formation in the 1960s of the National Interagency Council on Smoking and Health, public and private anti-tobacco groups have worked closely together (Hall, 1969; Kluger, 1996; Studlar, 2002, 2011). Organisations critical of tobacco usage were the US Public Health Service, plus heart, respiratory, and cancer charities. In the early 1980s, the three major anti-tobacco private organisations – the American Heart Association (AHA), American Lung Association (ALA), and American Cancer Society (ACS) – assumed a more political role by joining forces under the Coalition on Smoking OR Health (COSH). Others important in the anti-tobacco forces at varying times included the American Public Health Association, John Banzhaf's Action on Smoking and Health (ASH), Ralph Nader's Public Citizen, the California-based Americans for Nonsmokers' Rights, the American Dental Association, the American Legacy Foundation, the Robert Wood Johnson Foundation, eventually the AMA (especially through its journal, *JAMA*), and state and local tobacco control coalitions, the latter financed by federal money since the 1980s. With tobacco control possible at several levels of government, multiple policy entrepreneurs have emerged, sometimes unexpectedly. Tort lawyers and state attorneys general became prominent in the 1990s when litigation became a promising strategy for forcing changes in tobacco company behaviour as well as for financial rewards. In line with the new focus on protection of children, in 1995 a new umbrella anti-tobacco organisation, the Campaign for Tobacco-Free Kids, was formed.

Changing frames of reference began to shift the debate in favour of such tobacco control interests, particularly from the 1980s and 1990s. The 1964 Surgeon General's report made tobacco a more contested political issue between the established pro-tobacco network and anti-tobacco health groups. Fearing the potentially financially disastrous consequences, the tobacco in-dustry publicly denied that there was persuasive evidence of harm from cigarettes for many years and funded surrogates to support its claim. However, the effectiveness of this strategy has diminished and tobacco has been seen increasingly as a social menace. Legislation limiting advertising, the decline of domestic tobacco agriculture, limits on smoking venues, and dissemination of unfavourable information has eroded the pro-tobacco network. Smokers' rights organisations rely heavily on tobacco industry funding to support them and have been notably unsuccessful, especially on the central level. The pro-industry network was able to use mass advertising, divisions in the anti-tobacco lobby, and the need for an extraordinary majority in the US Senate to defeat the National Settlement in 1998 when amendments to the legislation became unacceptable to them. However, it was not able to prevent its successor, the MSA. Revelations from tobacco industry documents during litigation, and subsequent public access to this information, have harmed the industry's credibility by revealing its early awareness of harmful health consequences (Glantz et al, 1995; Slade et al, 1995; Hanauer et al, 1995). As more tobacco control has been legislated, the peripheral members of the network have become less important and it has become more fragmented. The core members, growers and manufacturers, became increasingly alienated as the purchase of foreign leaf increased, and subsequently the central price support system has ended.

Nevertheless, there are two factors that qualify the idea that the balance of power has shifted irrevocably. First, the industry's wealth and political connections have allowed it to maintain influence, shifting more toward the Republican Party because of its pro-market ideology and rise in the South since the 1970s. Increasingly, this influence varies by company rather than industry and often has to be pursued outside the public view. The companies have had to respond to the changing frames of the tobacco issue. Philip Morris (PM), the market leader (see Figure 6.2) has been the most adept, changing its name to Altria Group (in 2008, Philip Morris International became independent of Altria), publicising its corporate social responsibility and philanthropic projects, acknowledging addiction 'as the term is currently used' on its website, engaging in its own youth smoking prevention programme, complaining that high taxes only encourage smuggling, and even supporting FDA authority over tobacco as the basis for greater stability and predictability in the market. Other tobacco companies referred to the 2009 central legislation as the 'Marlboro Monopoly Act,' arguing that FDA regulatory authority would allow PM, with its greater resources, to meet the requirements more readily and thus enhance its dominant market position.

Figure 6.2 The Market Shares for Tobacco Companies in the United States, 2011

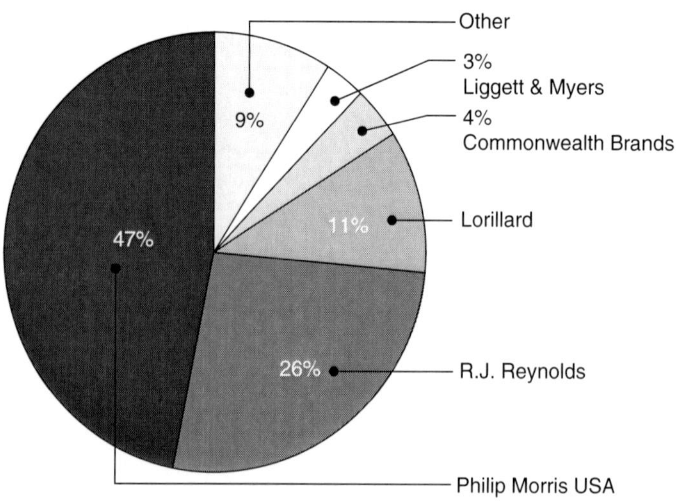

Source: US Government Accountability Office (2011)

The exemption for menthol in the ban on candy-flavoured cigarettes in the 2009 legislation was a victory for industry influence.

Second, as Pertschuk (2001; see also Glantz and Balbach, 2000) describes, the anti-tobacco movement has suffered divisions, especially over 'industry denormalisation' and 'harm reduction' proposals. Some in the anti-tobacco movement condemned the National Settlement and the FDA legislation as a compromised 'deal with the devil.' Tobacco control as morality policy has these dangers.

Socioeconomic factors

Economic benefits of tobacco

Over the long term, there has been a major decline in domestic tobacco agriculture as companies sought cheaper leaf abroad. The US share of leaf production is still fourth in the world, with the third largest share of exports behind Brazil and China (USDA National Agricultural Statistics Service, 2010). However, the major profits in tobacco are in cigarette manufacturing (GAO, 2011). In the words of famed US investor Warren Buffet: 'I'll tell you why I like the cigarette business. It costs a penny to make. Sell it for a dollar. It's addictive and there's fantastic brand loyalty' (Marotte, 1997). Tobacco sales are a $90 billion per year business in the US, and tobacco companies remain highly profitable (CDC, 2010). The decline in smoking rates in the US has not damaged tobacco companies' profits to an appreciable extent. US companies are part of multinational conglomerates, with some companies owning shares in others and having more wealth than many medium-income countries. In some years PM has been the largest taxpayer in the United States (Rosenblatt, 1994).

Smoking prevalence

Daily adult smoking prevalence has dropped by over 50% and the amount of cigarettes smoked by 33% since the 1960s. Smoking has declined substantially in the upper and middle income groups but less among lower income groups. This trend has been aided by the production of discount brands in recent years and selective tobacco company price reductions (Kluger, 1996). Smoking prevalence began a slow decline among men from its high of 60% in 1959. Women's rates, traditionally lower, increased to 35% in the mid-1970s as more joined the labour force and advertising appealed to younger women's independence. As women's prevalence rates slowly declined as well, overall smoking rates were reduced to approximately 20% among daily smokers in the 21st century. The number of cigarettes smoked began a similar descent in the early 1970s. Trends in consumption have decreased very slowly in recent years, however, and smoking rates among youth have been more volatile. Increasingly smoking has become concentrated in the less-educated working class. Smoking rates do not vary greatly across US states, ranging from less than 15 to around 25%. Rural, poor, and tobacco-growing states, such as Kentucky and West Virginia tend to have the highest smoking prevalence rates. The lowest rates are in Utah (for religious reasons), California, and Massachusetts (State Healthstats, 2011). The most recent CDC *Healthy People* goal is to reduce the mean adult smoking rate to 12%, but meeting CDC projected goals have proven to be elusive in the past (Healthy People, 2011).

Public opinion

Public opinion largely was a passive actor in the policy debate, but one that moved toward endorsing greater restrictions on tobacco usage. As the share of smokers, tobacco farmers, and industry workers declined, sympathy for tobacco promotion was reduced. A 'permissive consensus' developed (Key, 1961; Viscusi, 1992; Studlar, 2002). While smokers might be considered to be favourable toward tobacco promoting interests, many want to quit, blame the tobacco industry for their habit, and may even sue the companies. Still, overcoming the entrenched lobbying power of pro-tobacco interests, especially when they were concentrated in Congressional tobacco-growing districts, constituted a formidable challenge.

The role of ideas: Scientific knowledge

The US has been on the cutting edge of scientific research on the relationship between tobacco and health. The Era of Public Health began in the 1950s with published scientific research in the US and Britain about the serious health consequences of smoking cigarettes, which led to a 'cancer scare', popularised in 1952 by the *Reader's Digest* article, 'Cancer by the Carton'. The most persuasive evidence of the dangers of cigarette smoking were based on the new science of epidemiology, first retrospective and later prospective comparative studies of morbidity and mortality rates between matched groups of smokers and non-smokers. Research published in 1954 by the ACS established that smoking was associated with lung cancer. Nevertheless smoking rates remained high, advertising went on relatively unabated, and cigarettes remained a normal part of social behaviour.

The political implications of the findings from smoking and health research were disputed by powerful vested interests in tobacco promotion, and they utilised the variety of veto points in the US system to block rapid policy changes from the science, especially on the central level. The public was confused. Although the US Surgeon General gave Congressional testimony against smoking in 1957 (Kluger, 1996) and the FTC issued regulations to eliminate extravagant claims by cigarette advertisers (Friedman, 1975), there was no major policy debate until publication of the landmark report of the US Surgeon General's Advisory Committee in 1964. There were few restrictive government policies, especially on the central level, until the 1980s, when concerns about the health effects of SHS and addiction precipitated wider concern. The early post-war period therefore contrasts with the current situation in which policymakers take the scientific evidence almost for granted. Both private and public scientific research on tobacco control topics, and their implications for political action, have increased, to greater receptivity in specialist and more general public health journals.

The transfer of ideas

Whether or not the US is a leader or a laggard in particular policy instruments at a certain time, its influence is too great to be ignored. The multiple institutional venues, common language, and professional connections within the country facilitate lesson drawing and policy borrowing among groups and institutions. Furthermore, the CDC has actively worked to spread ideas, data, and '*Best Practices*' in tobacco control (CDC, 1999, 2007). After the CDC specified tobacco reduction targets as part of its *Healthy People* goals, several states developed their own goals. Individual policy entrepreneurs and leading state tobacco control jurisdictions, such as California, Massachusetts, and New York City (indoor non-smoking policies) are important internationally as well as domestically. In terms of overall tobacco control restrictions, California is usually considered the leading state, especially since 1988 when a referendum passed a state tax increase specifically to fund tobacco control. California has become a beacon of restrictive tobacco control measures for other jurisdictions in the US and abroad (Glantz and Balbach, 2000).

There is evidence of limited tobacco policy diffusion across US states, both in the earlier era of tobacco control as well as recently (Studlar, 2002). Shipan and Volden (2006) examine US tobacco control policy across various levels of government. They find that the path of policy diffusion depends on the issue at stake. Restrictions on smoking in government buildings are likely to be bottom-up from localities within a state; a snowball effect. Restrictions on restaurant smoking areas, however, spread state-to-state. Out-of-package sales restrictions, designed to inhibit youth consumption, also diffuse laterally among states. State-to-state diffusions were more likely on controversial policies and those with significant economic effects, restaurants and out-of-package sales, rather than SHS in government buildings.

Litigation strategies as public policy, especially healthcare cost recovery lawsuits, proceeded from the private to the public state sectors, spread uniformly across the 50 states (a rare instance), and then were adopted by the central government as well. They have also diffused to foreign countries, especially Canadian jurisdictions (Chapter 7; Studlar, 2002, 2009). Similarly, the US Surgeon General's reports and other authoritative research on the health hazards of tobacco use have had widespread foreign influence. The US bottom-up model of local efforts at limiting smoking venues also has been exported.

This is an example of what Mossberger (2000) terms intergovernmental polydiffusion networks. With its multiple jurisdictions, fragmented institutions, and sometimes slow development of policy, the US has often been an unacknowledged borrower of policy from abroad as well. Examples include rotating and graphic health warning labels, advertising limits, and vending machine restrictions, listed in the 1997 National Settlement and eventually adopted in the 2009 FDA legislation; almost all of these originated in Canada (Mollenkamp et al, 1998). In fact, over the past quarter century there has been an abundance of both intergovernmental and intergroup interaction between the US and Canada, leading to cross-border diffusion of policy in both directions (Studlar, 2002). The idea of using tax policy for health as well as revenue purposes originated with US researchers (Lewit and Coate, 1982) but was first utilised in Canada, which in turn generated interest in similar policies in the US (Studlar, 2002). Policy borrowing might be expected for Canada, a less populous country with fewer research resources, but it is unusual for the US to do this. This reflects the tendency for US institutions to trail in tobacco control policy behind their 'Family of Nations' neighbour. Thus, US groups and governments had Canada as a nearby policy laboratory in which to observe, adapt, and in some cases advocate and emulate policy. There was especially close coordination between US and Canadian central governments, state/provincial governments, and anti-tobacco groups during the middle 1990s when tobacco control was high on the policy agenda in both countries.

Conclusion

The US has moved from an era in which it promoted tobacco as an economic product to an era in which tobacco control is now the norm. Economic incentives and subsidies (and minimal taxation) have been replaced by multiple tobacco control instruments, from regulation and education to higher taxes, financial sanctions on companies through litigation and legislation, incentives to leave tobacco growing, and restrictions on official support for tobacco company expansion abroad. Since education is less expensive, less confrontational, and more diffuse in implementation than regulation, the former instrument was favoured in the initial days of the modern Era of Public Health. As the years have passed, stricter regulation has become the norm. The 2009 FDA legislation, along with the large cigarette tax increase for the State Health Insurance Program (S-CHIP) has the potential to create a more comprehensive, centrally controlled and effective tobacco control policy. However, several public policy issues remained unresolved. The 2009 legislation allowing the FDA to regulate cigarettes is designed to deal with some of them, but in tobacco control the design and effects of implementation are important factors; for example, some parts of the FDA legislation are the subject of litigation. Further, given the size of the health problems resulting from tobacco consumption, the resources spent on tobacco control are relatively sparse, especially in comparison to the costs of treatment in the health-care system (although the US spends more per capita on tobacco control than any other developed or developing country – European Commission, 2004).

There are several lessons from this analysis of tobacco control policy in the US. First, the fragmentation of the US political system makes it a source of both continuity and change (Marmor and Lieberman, 2004). It provides multiple venues in which to contest issues: federalism, the courts, and ballot initiatives (at the state level) can provide opportunities for groups advocating innovations in public policy to bypass the difficulties of getting central-level legislation passed. It also provides constraints: veto groups exist in many state/local governments as well as at the central level. Policy innovations may diffuse only with difficulty to other jurisdictions within the same country, or may even be overruled by the central executive, legislature, or courts. US states and localities have taken the lead in many areas of tobacco control policy, and there has been a discernible trend toward more restrictive regulation of tobacco (even in tobacco-growing states), but there has been a lack of uniformity, producing a mosaic of tobacco control policies in the country. Attempts to regulate tobacco at the central level have often resulted in fragmented, combative policy battles among institutions, settled by Congress or the courts. Many issues, including advertising regulations by the states, FDA assumption of authority over cigarettes, the EPA report on the dangers of SHS, the characterisation of tobacco companies in anti-tobacco advertising, and financial compensation for the health costs of smokers to government programmes, have been contested in state and/or federal courts. The earliest struggle was between the FTC and Congress over the content of warning labels to be placed on cigarette packages. Later Congress altered FTC proposals for new, rotating warning labels as well as other cigarette regulations (Pertschuk, 1986). Congress attempted to establish a strong but limited central role with the 1965 and 1970 pre-emptive legislation on warning labels and television advertising, but then it largely left policy to other central agencies and levels of government. The culmination of this process was the National Settlement and eventually the MSA, a private-public effort at creating a more uniform countrywide policy over a range of instruments. The MSA was the most comprehensive US tobacco control policy until the 2009 act giving the FDA authority over tobacco. Overall, policy has developed in a piecemeal fashion, with central government devolving much responsibility (there is no US equivalent to a shift to Department of Health centrality in the UK) and states taking the policy lead in part by exploiting the unusually prominent role of the courts.

Second, the dominant framing of tobacco control policy has changed over the long term. Morality, political economy, and public health perspectives have competed for dominance in tobacco policy over the past 125 years in the US. Elements of all three frames remain, making this a blended policy area.

Morality framing operates in concert with public health, acting as a simplifying and mobilising force by demonising the opposition. The appeal of political economy, on the other hand, is more practical, focusing on the benefits and costs of tobacco production and consumption. As cigarettes became established as the major means of smoking in the early 20th century, public health and moral objections were overridden by economic benefits. This strongly pro-tobacco era lasted until mid-20th century, when public health evidence slowly began to influence public policy. The public health perspective did not become dominant, however, until it was reinforced with the mobilisational arguments of morality in the 1980s. The agenda definitively shifted in 1964 with publication of the US Surgeon General's Advisory Committee Report, a focusing event but one with incremental, multi-level responses. Despite the potentially enormous benefits for life expectancy and healthcare costs, public attention to restrictive tobacco regulation is sporadic.

Third, there has been a shift in the balance of power from pro- to anti-tobacco groups. However, tobacco companies remain powerful (and may still enjoy relationships with government outside the public spotlight) and anti-tobacco groups are not as united as their counterparts in other leading tobacco control countries. Traditionally the pro-tobacco network largely has been unified in its economic interests and political positions while anti-tobacco advocates have been divided, mainly over whether morality and strategic concerns should prevent compromises with the industry in the interests of achieving a smoke-free society. This is reflected in debates over industry denormalisation and harm reduction. But recently, pro-tobacco groups have suffered strains between industry and growers as well as among the companies themselves, which may leave them less unified than the anti-tobacco groups. The US has a long history of pursuing policy through networks of governmental and non-governmental organisations. The leading actors in tobacco control in the 1950s were private organisations, pro- and anti-tobacco, while governments at all levels were passive. Once the central government became involved, it worked with non-governmental groups. This took the form of public-private partnerships in the 1960s (Hall, 1969). Furthermore, private litigation has sometimes been a trigger for government action. The television advertising ban in 1970 was the legislative response to a private legal petition and FCC ruling that 'fair time' be offered to anti-tobacco groups to respond to cigarette advertising. The federal government has continued to support private efforts, mainly through funded scientific research, education, and financial support for anti-tobacco coalitions.

Fourth, the socioeconomic conditions in the US are now more conducive to tobacco control, but the effect should be qualified in most cases. The value of tobacco to the economy has fallen, but tobacco companies are still major taxpayers and lobbyists. Smoking prevalence has fallen, and so too has opposition to tobacco control but, then again, it is rare for there to be a clamour for comprehensive measures to restrict tobacco. In the US, political change usually follows social change. Thus, tobacco control through public policies may accelerate, but it remains to be seen whether this will be in a more 'neo-prohibitionist' or 'harm regulation' direction.

Finally, the US is a leader in scientific research on tobacco, and the central government has been active in sponsoring research and information diffusion. Further, US states, such as California are known globally as tobacco control leaders, and the US central government is a key player in global tobacco control policy. Nevertheless, the lack of a central, comprehensive policy in the US, even in the wake of FDA legislation in 2009, is perhaps surprising. Many of the provisions of the FCTC have been adopted by states and localities in the US, but the US central government has not yet ratified the treaty (see Chapter 9). The US is *a*, but not *the*, worldwide leader in tobacco control policy.

7
Other Advanced Industrial Countries

In addition to the European Union and United States, there are four advanced industrial democracies whose tobacco control regimes have attracted extensive attention and analysis: Australia, Canada, New Zealand, and Japan (Feldman and Bayer, 2004; Wilensky, 2002; Studlar, 2005, 2007). The first three stand out as world tobacco control leaders while Japan is considered to be a laggard, based on the proportion of people who smoke as well as the number and variety of tobacco control measures. Indeed, the indicators are strongly related, with tobacco control policy now considered a key contributor to recent reductions in smoking prevalence. The three leaders have long been treated as part of a wider, transoceanic English-speaking 'family of nations' in public policy, linked through culture and diffusion to the UK (Castles, 1993; Obinger and Wagschal, 2001) and tobacco control policy can be seen within that context. In contrast, although Japan is famous for its policy borrowing proclivities from Western countries since the 19th century, it is generally considered to be a foot-dragger in the growing worldwide movement for greater tobacco regulation.

Chapter 7 considers the extent of tobacco control policy in these four countries, identifying the differences in approach between the three leaders and Japan and also comparisons among Australia, Canada, and New Zealand. It seeks to explain the differences in relation to the five main explanatory factors that we identify in Chapter 2. With regard to institutions, it explores variations in governance arrangements in countries less subject to coordination from a supra-national body and with no equivalent to the EU's role in policy transfer. It also highlights country-level differences, such as the ability of Australian states (provinces) to take the policy lead and the scope for actors to pursue litigation in different countries. It considers differences in the way that tobacco is framed, comparing a public health emphasis in three countries to Japan where, until recently, the emphasis has tended to be on public cleanliness and politeness. It charts differences in the balance of power between pro-tobacco and anti-tobacco interests and the socioeconomic context in each country. Both factors are linked closely in the case of Japan, with networks based on the strong economic position of the Japanese tobacco industry. Japan has a state interest in tobacco production, with close links between tobacco companies and civil servants. Finally, it explores the role of ideas, including the significance of the scientific knowledge on tobacco control policy and varying levels of policy learning.

What is tobacco policy?

The post-war context

The broad history of tobacco control is similar in the three English-speaking countries. The oldest measures were economic, beginning with taxation for revenue purposes. In the late 19th and early 20th centuries a small wave of anti-cigarette legislation occurred at the central level in Canada, New Zealand (and in more limited fashion in Japan) and at the state level in Australia (Walker, 1984; Tyrrell, 1999; Thomson, 1992a, 1992b; Cunningham, 1996). These were mainly prohibitions on sales to underage purchasers, passed to maintain the physical and moral health of male youth. This was to prevent their indulging in the 'cigarette fiend,' considered a gateway drug to anti-social behaviour. Even though some of these laws remained on the statute books, enforcement was weak (Tyrrell, 1999; Reynolds and Woodward, 1993; Thomson, 1992a). Anti-tobacco activity was then swept away by the patriotic role that manufactured cigarettes played in the morale of soldiers at the front in World War I. Tobacco became cultivated and the industry subsidised, policies that were rarely questioned until the last two decades of the 20th century. Each country subsequently had high cigarette consumption in the post-World War II period, as well as a government-supported tobacco-growing sector and domestic manufacturing capacity (owned by transnational corporations, such as Philip Morris, British American Tobacco, Imperial Tobacco, and Japan Tobacco International). Taxes were the most significant tobacco control measure (Warner, 1981) but were still seen primarily as revenue producers rather than as a means of discouraging cigarette consumption. Further, tax rates often lagged behind wage increases, making cigarettes more affordable, until the 1970s and 1980s.

Australia and New Zealand

Australia and New Zealand have tended to move in tandem towards comprehensive tobacco control, but the shift from tobacco support took several decades to develop. Beginning in the 1920s, Australia provided government subsidies for tobacco leaf growing and manufacturing at both the federal and state levels (Tyrrell, 1999) through market stabilisation plans, including protection against foreign imports, required domestic leaf purchase, and research (Walker, 1984).

In the 1960s and 1970s some restrictions were passed on broadcasting. Bans on some forms of advertising and health warnings on cigarette packages were based on voluntary agreements in New Zealand and intergovernmentally-agreed legislation in Australia. These limited measures were followed in the 1980s by broader print advertising restrictions and bans and sponsorship replacement, government-endorsed stronger health warnings (with multiple messages being rotated), educational campaigns through the mass media, and some limited restrictions on SHS. More recently, advertising regulations have been extended to include product displays at point of sale, and both governments have introduced more comprehensive and restrictive measures on SHS in indoor and even some outdoor public venues. Not only have graphic warnings been introduced, but Australia is the first country in the world to introduce plain packaging (Cancer Council of Victoria, 2008).

Taxation became a major tobacco control instrument, and increased cigarette taxes were designated specifically for this purpose (Smith, 2004). For example, government-funded health promotion foundations, based on dedicated tobacco tax revenues, took over the sponsorship of sport and cultural events from tobacco companies, an unusual policy innovation. Until the 1980s, tobacco leaf growing remained the most heavily government subsidised economic sector in Australia, but this changed with greater economic liberalisation. This process was accelerated in the 1990s by two government reports that began the phasing out of tobacco stabilisation policies (Ballard, 2004; Industries Assistance Commission, 1987; Industry Commission, 1994). Australia eliminated leaf production subsidies and domestic content rules for manufacturers while lowering tariffs and initiating buy-outs of tobacco quotas through the central Commonwealth and state governments (Jha and Chaloupka, 2000). Similar practices of protection and subsidy applied in New Zealand from 1926 until 1980. Once government sponsorship was withdrawn and replaced by financial encouragement to leave the sector, tobacco growing became uneconomical and largely ended in 1997 (O'Shea, 1997), a process that also was implemented in Australia (Ballard, 2004; Cancer Council of Victoria, 2008).

Government-initiated litigation against tobacco companies has not featured prominently in New Zealand, but in Australia there have been some important court judgements and out-of-court legal settlements, discussed below (Cancer Council of Victoria, 2008). Overall, strategic plans have been developed to attack tobacco consumption in these two countries under the rubric of anti-drug strategies. Targeted capacity-building and education programmes have become a mainstay of population-level tobacco control interventions. Adult cessation has been a persistent theme of Australian campaigns but has been emphasised only recently in New Zealand. Campaigns in both countries have been designed to target groups especially susceptible to cigarette use – youth, women, and eventually indigenous Australians and Maori – although some of these have received only minimal funding (Ballard, 2004; Thomson and Wilson, 1997).

Canada

Canada's current status, of having some of the most comprehensive tobacco control legislation in the world, contrasts with the pre-1980s picture in which tobacco farming was subsidised indirectly (through research and marketing boards), there was little attempt to regulate cigarettes except through taxation (considered mainly as a revenue source), and voluntary agreements with the tobacco industry were the norm. The Canadian central government made its first domestic voluntary agreement in 1971. The tobacco industry controlled itself through warning labels, advertising limits, and other measures as a substitute for threatened federal legislation. Unlike the US or Australia, only the province of British Columbia passed its own legislation on advertising, quickly rescinded. The first restrictive legislation since the turn of the century, the broadly-based *Tobacco Products Control Act* covering advertising package health warnings, youth access and cigarette contents, as well as the *Nonsmokers' Rights Act* regulating smoking in government buildings, was passed in 1988. The first was overturned by the Supreme Court of Canada in 1995, but its only-slightly revised successor, the *Tobacco Act*, replaced it in 1997. Canada introduced the first rotating graphic health warnings in 2000.

The shift to a comprehensive tobacco taxation regime in Canada was protracted. The federal government lowered its taxes in 1952 and 1953 because of smuggling pressures across the US border (Cunningham, 1996). Provinces and territories also were slow to establish cigarette taxation; it took from 1941 until the early 1970s for all of the provinces to have such taxes (Friedman, 1975; Studlar, 2002). From the 1970s, however, there was a rapid move toward coordinated increases in provincial/territorial taxation as well as a federal tax spiral until the early 1990s. Then another cross-border smuggling crisis with the US, especially through the Awaknasne reservation spanning the Ontario and New York border, resulted in reductions in both central and some provincial taxation. Taxes have increased in these jurisdictions, but there remains a serious international cross-border smuggling problem in this region, which exerts downward pressure on cigarette taxes in Ontario and Quebec, the two most populous Canadian provinces (Benzie and Brennan, 2009).

The Canadian central government announced its first Tobacco Diversification Plan in 1987 to provide financial compensation to farmers exiting tobacco production and to aid in developing alternatives to tobacco agriculture. Periodic infusions of federal money have followed. Some provinces have also followed suit. Aided by international market pressures, these programmes have had some success in reducing the number of farmers dependent on tobacco. Unlike Australia and New Zealand, Canada has not attempted to end tobacco farming completely, and loopholes in the most recent central aid have generated accusations that it amounts to support for continued tobacco growing (Cunningham, 1996; Global Tobacco Control Forum, 2008, 2010).

There were also various central government research publications, anti-smoking campaigns, tobacco control strategies, and capacity-building grants issued through Health Canada, the lead agency for tobacco control. These began in earnest in the mid-1980s. After two earlier federal strategies, the National Tobacco Strategy (1999) was designed to encompass both levels of government. Subsequently, the federal government developed its own supplementary Federal Tobacco Strategy (2001). Canada also has a long history of learning and information provision, beginning with the Royal Commission report on the American Tobacco Company's anti-competitive practices in Canada (1903), followed by the Agriculture Department's establishment of a tobacco research facility (1906) and House of Commons hearings by the Select Committee on Cigarette Evils (1914).

Japan

Japan has lagged in tobacco control initiatives, especially those that are countrywide in scope and other than educational/voluntary measures. Since 1900 it has been illegal for those under 20 years of age to smoke, but there is no mechanism for enforcing this law, a distinction that perhaps typifies the status of tobacco control in Japan. In response to more cigarette imports in the 1980s, advertising actually expanded rather than shrank. (Winder et al, 1993). Until recently there were few central-level laws except for health warnings on cigarette packages, some limitations on smoking in public transportation, and limited hours for advertising cigarettes on television. Voluntary limits on advertising were advanced by the manufacturers' association, the Tobacco Institute of Japan (TIOJ), in 1998. Although cigarette taxes were relatively high for government revenue purposes, prices remained among the lowest in the industrialised world. Almost all costs of production, including purchase of tobacco leaf, were contained within a geographically small country, assisted by the government (Vogel et al, 1993; Feldman, 2004, 2006). In 2010, the government increased tobacco taxes substantially, with further rises possibly to follow (McCurry, 2010).

Japanese tobacco control restrictions have been relatively haphazard and largely local. Since 1964 the Ministry of Health and Welfare has issued various statements on tobacco control, including a vaguely-worded document called Healthy Japan 21 in 2000. The Japanese Diet (legislature) subsequently passed a Health Promotion Law. As a result, more non-smoking areas, including heavily traveled public outdoor venues, were introduced in Japanese cities. On the central level, age restrictions on purchases were passed, including for vending machine sales. Stronger, multiple-rotating warning labels on packages began to appear in 2005, replacing the formerly weak ones (Sato, 1999; Feldman, 2004). Although indoor non-smoking restrictions are rare, by 2010 Kanagawa became the first of Japan's 47 prefectures to prohibit smoking in schools, hospitals and other public buildings (McCurry, 2010). After passing a countrywide voluntary non-smoking measure in early 2010, there were indications that a more stringent one may follow (Inamura and Koizumi, 2010).

Comparison

Table 7.1 gives an overall picture of the scope and tempo of tobacco policy in the four countries. It summarises 25 different policy instruments that have been utilised in each country, with dates of their initial adoption. This encompasses the central governments of Japan and New Zealand and any state, territory, or central government in Australia and Canada.

The table shows that the three English-speaking countries usually introduce similar tobacco control instruments within the same period of time.

Table 7.1 Patterns of First Policy Adoption

Instrument	Aus	Can	NZ	Japan
Regulation				
Broadcast Ads Banned	1972	1971V	1963V	1998V
Billboard Ads Banned	1992	1988	1973V	2004
Point-of-sale Ads Restricted or Banned	1990	1996	1990	–
Promotions Restricted or Banned	1990	1988	1990	–
Minimum Sales Age of 18	1916	1892	1997	(1900)
Penalties for Underage Sales	1900	1891	1903	–
Minimum Pack Size	1986	1993	1997	–
Vending Machines Restricted or Banned	1984	1993	1998	1989
Government Facilities Restricted or Banned	1988	1989	1990	2003
Enclosed Workplaces Restricted or Banned	1984	1997	1990	2010V
Restaurants Restricted or Banned	1994	1990	1990	2003
Bars Restricted or Banned	1994	1990	1990	2010V
Public Transport Restricted or Banned	1959	1988	1990	2004
Airline Ban	1987	1988	1988V	1999
Broad Executive Authority over Tobacco	1988	1997	1979	–
Finance				
First Major Tax Increase on Cigarettes	1973	1981	1931	2003
Support for Leaving Tobacco Growing	1990	1987	1980	–
Sponsorship Substitution (Health Promotion Funds)	1987	1998	1990	–
Court Judgment Against Passive Smoking	1991	1980	N.A.	–
Education				
Mass Media Campaign	1957	1960	1962	1979
Cessation Services	1983	1977	1999	–
Health Warnings on Cigarettes	1972	1971V	1973V	1972
Rotating Health Warnings on Cigarettes	1985	1989	1988	2004
Public Report	1977	1963	1985	1987
Comprehensive Government Strategy	1995	1986	1990	–
Overall Average	1974	1978	1980	2003
Number of instruments	25	25	24	15

Notes: V = Voluntary Code; adoption refers to first adoption by central or devolved government

Japan has a considerably smaller repertoire of legislated instruments. The average for the years that instruments were introduced finds Australia coming out ahead, then Canada, followed closely by New Zealand, but all became more active across instruments in the late 20th century. All Japanese policies have been adopted since 1972 and its mean year of adoption is over 15 years later than the others. Even if one included the 1900 declaratory ban on youth smoking, the Japanese mean would be over ten years later than the three other countries. Australian jurisdictions took earlier action on ten instruments, Canadian on seven, and New Zealand on five (with three ties). Japan acted quickly to introduce health warnings, but has not come first at any time.

The table also indicates that little was done in any of these countries until the 1970s, and then only on selected issues, such as taxation, health warnings on packages, mass media campaigns and advertising bans on broadcasting and billboards. As in most other industrialised democracies, the mid-1980s saw a surge in the variety and frequency of adoption of policy measures against tobacco use (Studlar, 2004). There also has been a considerable amount of recalibration in tobacco control. Not only have new policy instruments been introduced, but there has been a tightening of coverage for previously established regulations. In Canada there were two such central measures, in 1988 and 1997. In New Zealand there were three consolidating pieces of legislation in 1990, 1997, and 2003. Court decisions in Canada and on state/territorial taxation in Australia have led to reinventions as well. In the budgeting systems of these countries, cigarette taxes can be recalibrated every year. Since the 1980s, the general trend has been toward more stringent controls on tobacco, sometimes with a major increase, although in Canada the smuggling crisis of the early 1990s led to a temporary move in the opposite direction (Harrison, 2005).

In addition, some provinces adopted comprehensive policies. In the Australian federal system, as well as for most Canadian provinces, the process was more piecemeal. This led to a process of emulation, whereby lagging jurisdictions either caught up or moved ahead by leapfrogging existing regulations, such as restrictions in more venues or moving from restriction to prohibition in some cases. By the late 1990s, all three countries had adopted the whole range of instruments, although some Australian and Canadian jurisdictions lagged into the early 2000s. As Table 7.1 indicates, the 2000s witnessed more comprehensive advertising and smoking bans being passed rather than targeted restrictions. Overall the process is one of significant change and policy convergence among the three English-speaking countries, with Japan trailing.

Institutions: Who has responsibility for tobacco control?

There are multiple venues for making tobacco control policy in each of these countries, and there are at least four institutional dimensions that could be relevant to the direction of tobacco control policy. First, the strength of tobacco control may be linked to the power of the health department and the extent to which it takes the lead within government. In Australia, matters are complicated by the strong decentralist tendencies in tobacco control. Despite this, the Department of Health and Aged Care has coordinated central-provincial responses to produce relatively uniform policies across the country. For the past three decades the Canadian Health Ministry has been the lead central agency for tobacco control information and regulation, assisted by the Finance Ministry and not often publicly opposed by the Agriculture and Trade ministries. We can also identify instances in which strong health ministers became associated with advances in tobacco control, such as Helen Clark in New Zealand and Jake Epp in Canada. However, the role of individuals, compared to institutions or wider political factors, such as the role and rise of supportive interest groups, should not be overstated, particularly since we could also identify cases where individual initiatives proved unsuccessful (Smith, 1993). In Japan, the shift toward health department dominance may only now be occurring. Heretofore policy has been controlled by the ministries related to industry and finance (Feldman, 2006; Mochizuki-Kobayashi et al, 2003; McCurry, 2010).

Second, the role of the judiciary may vary, with policy change through legal decisions more likely in some systems than in others. Lijphart's (1999: 226) rankings of the power of judicial review, strongly correlated to policy-making capacity, finds Canada to have strong, Australia medium, Japan weak, and New Zealand no judicial review. Despite the presence of judicial review in Australia and Canada, the 'creative ambiguity' of the sometimes tedious but ongoing negotiation processes through ministerial committees under executive federalism is preferred to litigation by government jurisdictions (Painter, 1991; Bakvis and Brown, 2010; Baier, 2008). According to the *Tobacco Atlas* (Shafey et al, 2009), all four of these countries have pending litigation against tobacco companies but thus far only in Australia and Canada have the courts been a venue for major policy-changing decisions on tobacco. Despite legal limitations in Australia, some decisions and agreements adverse to tobacco companies have resulted from lawsuits concerning legal liability for harm from SHS as well as tobacco company behaviour, notably concerning 'light and mild' cigarettes in 2005. These have been instigated through action undertaken by individuals or governments. Tobacco companies themselves have litigated as well, with relatively little success (Cancer Council of Victoria, 2008).

Canada has been a late convert to the politics of adversarial legalism in tobacco politics. There have been a few successful individual suits against tobacco companies for damages from SHS and more recently governments have pursued cases against tobacco companies for complicity in smuggling (successfully) and cost recovery for medical expenses of smokers (currently in the courts). The judiciary in Canada has usually become involved in tobacco politics through lawsuits by tobacco companies challenging federal and provincial legislation. The industry has lost more of these than it has won although even delay can be financially beneficial to them (Global Tobacco Forum, 2008). There has been less tobacco-related judicial activity in New Zealand. In Japan the few cases of litigation have been lost by anti-tobacco forces although they may have had some impact politically (Feldman, 2001, 2006).

Third, power in relation to tobacco is largely shared among central, state/provincial, local and even private organisations. Although both Australia and Canada have increased the intergovernmental nature of their programmes in the past decade, on a scale of centralisation of tobacco control policies these countries rank as (1) New Zealand, (2) Japan, (3) Canada, and (4) Australia. Under federalism (Australia, Canada), new policies in tobacco control may arise sooner because they need to be adopted by only one jurisdiction, but they can be slow to spread. In unitary systems (New Zealand, Japan) there may be fewer sources of policy innovation but, when a unitary government decides to act, there are also fewer problems related to policy uniformity (fewer veto points), at least at the policy formulation stage. Thus, there may be trade-offs between innovation and uniformity in the two federal systems; Australia has six states (provinces) and two territories; Canada has ten and three.

Is policy more likely to be top-down, bottom-up, lateral, or some combination in each country? Tobacco control is something of an anomaly in the two federal systems under consideration. While Australia is the more centralised by most measures (especially fiscal), it has had a relatively decentralised tobacco control process in which lower-level jurisdictions collaborate with each other (Ballard, 2004) and the central government. The Commonwealth government has resources for vertical and horizontal policy coordination but has only reluctantly invoked its considerable authority, except when prioritising the provision of a more uniform business and public health environment. The National Tobacco Strategy (1999) was developed in concert by the Commonwealth and states/territories. Central-level mandates have only been enacted in areas where the Commonwealth has clear authority, as on advertising, and as a last resort when coordination is impossible, such as on warning labels in 1992. However, even with states and territories protective of their own authority and the lack of major central financial support, tobacco control in Australia has resulted in relatively uniform legislation over time. Perhaps this is due to the similar urban domination of most Australian jurisdictions. At times different jurisdictions have become tobacco control leaders; this has allowed others to justify similar measures and even to leapfrog them with new ones. Even the longtime laggards in tobacco control in Australia (Queensland and Northern Territory) have converged recently with others (Studlar, 2007).

In Canada, a country containing strong regional sentiments, the provinces are very jealous of their policy authority and often resent central attempts at control through fiscal and other means. The provinces also have most of the authority over commerce, education, and public health. Nevertheless, cooperative federalism has been an important factor in tobacco control (Friedman, 1975; Studlar, 2002, 2010). In fact, the usual process for tobacco control has effectively been top-down. The federal government (through Health Canada) relied on a tobacco company 'voluntary agreement' as *de facto* public policy until 1988 when the *Tobacco Products Control Act* was passed, but provinces did not fill the gap in central policy, unlike in the US and Australia. Central legislative acts were permissive, allowing provinces and territories authority to pass stronger legislation. But in all of these instances (with the exception of a ban on sales to minors in 1890), ranging over a century, the central government took the lead and the provinces either did nothing or followed hesitantly, in piecemeal fashion, and with less than uniform policies (Studlar, 2007). Even provincial tobacco taxes were slow in being adopted. However, the permissive policy of the federal government (the opposite of central pre-emption in the US) has, within the past decade, allowed provinces to move beyond central policies in several respects.

It was only in the 1990s that the provinces began to take more action against tobacco use, operating through horizontal diffusion. They have progressively increased the scope and restrictiveness of regulation in advertising, sales, and SHS as well as suing tobacco companies for medical expenses. However, overall tobacco control policies in Canada have been surprisingly varied, with provinces proceeding at different paces and sometimes taking their own initiatives rather than following others' leads (Studlar, 2007). Over time, the provinces became more active in coordination efforts with the central government as well. There has been ad hoc central/provincial/territorial consultation, led by Health Canada, since at least the 1970s. This increased after the smuggling crisis of the early 1990s. Coordinated tax reductions between the federal government and five provinces were offset to a limited degree by capacity-building grants from the federal government to provinces, territories, and local governments for tobacco control programmes. Since 1999 this has been formalised into an interlocking series of committees and meetings, in line with the usual negotiated 'executive federalism' in Canada.

Local governments/municipalities in all four countries have some regulatory powers over tobacco, especially concerning health and safety regulation, such as non-smoking areas in public places. While local government in the three English-speaking countries is comparatively weak, local prefectures in Japan have considerable authority over public health (Feldman, 2006). In Australia, local governments have deferred to the states and central government on tobacco control. Over the past two decades Canadian local governments, especially municipalities, have become less deferential. Like the provinces, they began to initiate policy (especially on SHS) largely in the 1990s, providing models for later provincial legislation (Cunningham, 1996; Lachance et al, 1990; Asbridge, 2004; Nykiforuk et al, 2008). In New Zealand, there were local initiatives in tobacco control before the centre began to dominate policy from the *1990 Smoke-Free Environments Act* (Beaglehole, 1991). While most policy on tobacco in Japan is centrally determined, a few local governments, in the form of prefectures, have taken policy initiatives on SHS although these have had only limited diffusion (Feldman, 2006; McCurry, 2010).

Fourth, political parties and electoral systems combine with different institutional arrangements to produce policy change. Tobacco control rarely prompts high-level partisan controversy and internal divisions have often been notable, particularly in parties with strong bases in tobacco-growing regions (Ballard, 2004; Smith, 1993; Studlar, 2003). Nevertheless, left-wing parties are generally more closely associated with tobacco control, especially in initiating policy. In Australia and New Zealand, left wing parties have introduced most legislation on the central level although it was the Conservatives in Canada, prodded by a private member's bill from an NDP (leftist party) backbencher, who took the first steps at the central level in 1987. In Australia provincial/territorial governments controlled by the left often have innovated in tobacco control instruments although rightist governments usually have been willing to follow, except in pro-tobacco Queensland and the Northern Territory. Similarly, Canadian provinces under left-wing rule have been more innovative in tobacco-control policies while those under right-wing governments often move later (Studlar, 2002).

In Japan, the centre-right Liberal Democratic Party (LDP), in power almost continuously from 1955 to 2009, was generally sympathetic to the tobacco industry. Greater change in the direction of SHS and tax policies common in the rest of the industrialised world arrived when a government led by the centre-left Democratic Party of Japan came to power (McCurry, 2010). Speed of policy change in New Zealand is associated with how likely the electoral system is to produce a single-party executive with a majority in parliament, which is better able to act swiftly. Under a single member plurality electoral system, in 1990 a single-party Labour government enacted legislation in less than a year, ahead of a forthcoming election (Smith, 1993). Since 1996 a mixed electoral system has resulted in more parties being represented, with a need for interparty consensus to pass legislation. In contrast, to 1990, it took four years to pass the *Smoke-free Environments Amendment Act 2003* under a Labour-led coalition government, even through the committed anti-tobacco activist Helen Clark was serving as Prime Minister, having risen from a position as Health Minister in the earlier government.

Agendas: How important is tobacco control as a policy issue? How is tobacco framed?

Chapter 3 suggests that political economy has been replaced by public health as the dominant policy image within government. Governments have shifted their focus to the negative health effects of smoking. The issue of tobacco control has also risen on the policy agenda, and many governments have introduced comprehensive tobacco control in that context. The three English-speaking countries appear to be a manifestation of 'secular morality' (see Chapter 6) related to more prevention in public health, which began to have a wider appeal in the mid-1970s. Secular morality, based on individual and collective preventive health, became incorporated into government policy through 'health promotion' and 'healthy public policy' documents, such as the Canadian Health Ministry's Lalonde Report (Health and Welfare Canada, 1974) and the Ottawa Charter for Health Promotion (1986). This approach has spread via international conferences and other routes of policy transfer. This may also help explain why some groups, such as trade unions, have shifted their attitudes toward support of non-smoking in enclosed public places. In Japan, it has been argued that the major influence in limiting smoking has been the cultural norms of politeness and social conformity, recently encouraged by governments at different levels (Feldman, 2006). In addition, promoting tobacco control is also framed in terms of cleanliness (avoidance of litter) and the protection of youth.

Networks: Has there been a shift in power between pressure participants?

While the three English-speaking countries are considered to have 'pluralist' interest group systems, there can also be subsystem dominance by a particular policy community. In Australia and New Zealand, such tobacco policy communities developed during war efforts when governments and tobacco companies worked together to ensure an adequate supply of cigarettes to troops and civilians. The relationships were then maintained and exploited by large, profitable transnational companies who built networks of affiliated organisations (Walker, 1984; Tyrrell, 1999; Deeks, 1992; Thomson and Wilson, 2002). As in other countries, the tobacco industry utilised its multi-pronged network to resist, delay and weaken efforts to restrict tobacco consumption. This was done through an international network of tobacco companies and industry associations alert to the implications of restrictive tobacco control measures anywhere (McLoughlin, 1990; Deeks, 1992; Thomson and Wilson, 2002; Tofler and Chapman, 2003; Chapman and Carter, 2003; Chapman, 2003; Chapman et al, 2003; Carter, 2003).

Canada is another country dominated for most of the 20th century by a pro-tobacco network led by producer interests in the form of three transnational tobacco manufacturers and a substantial, government-aided group of tobacco growing interests. As in Australia and New Zealand, tobacco growing was concentrated in certain regions. In Canada, however, the companies had their headquarters in Quebec while the major growing region was in Ontario. This economic foothold in the two most populous provinces gave them substantial political clout (Cunningham, 1996). While the Australian and New Zealand companies looked toward the headquarters of their companies in the UK, in Canada the largely British-based industry also was close to developments in the US.

This pro-tobacco dominance has been successfully challenged in all three countries. In Australia, from the mid-1950s, professional groups, such as the National Health and Medical Research Council (NHMRC) – an advisory body representing the medical profession and government health departments – and the Australian Medical Association recommended action against tobacco. In the 1960s the Australian Council on Smoking and Health (ACOSH) and various professional organisations, including the Victorian Anti-Cancer Council, began to lobby for Australian government action after the early 1960s reports on tobacco and illness (Table 3.2) (Ballard, 2004). By 1979, with central and state governments still hesitant to act, the Non-Smokers Movement of Australia (NSMA), Movement Opposed to Promotion of Unhealthy Products (MOP UP) and Billboard Utilising Graffitists Against Unhealthy Promotions (BUGA UP) brought the distinctive style of Australian civil disobedience to protest against tobacco sales (Chapman, 1996). Throughout the 1980s, more organised and vociferous anti-tobacco interest groups orchestrated a campaign for specific tobacco control measures throughout the jurisdictions of Australia, with varying impact. In 1984 Action on Smoking and Health (ASH Australia) was formed as a federation to coordinate these efforts, with financial support from the central government (Ballard, 2004; Chapman and Wakefield, 2001). More recently ASH, ACOSH, the Heart Foundation, and the Cancer Council combined to form the Tobacco Control Coalition (Ballard, 2004). These groups, together with the institutions noted previously, have managed to shift the tobacco agenda into one emphasising public health.

In Canada, from the 1970s (and accelerating in the 1980s), anti-tobacco interest groups were formed, sometimes with financial support from the Canadian government as 'public interest groups' offering a perspective not adequately funded by other sources. The major Canadian central government-oriented groups, sometimes operating under the umbrella of the government-financed Canadian Council on Smoking and Health, included the Heart and Stroke Foundation, the Canadian Cancer Society, Physicians for a Smoke-Free Canada, la Coalition québecoise pour le contrôle du tabac, and the Non-Smokers' Rights Association. These groups first became important in lobbying for federal legislation in the 1980s (Cunningham, 1996). Research organisations enjoying government financial support, prominently the International Development Research Corporation (IDRC), have also played a role. There were fewer such anti-tobacco groups on the provincial/territorial level before the 1990s.

Anti-tobacco groups in New Zealand, many of them formed especially to combat tobacco use, have similarly contributed to a shift in power. The most persistent has been the New Zealand version of ASH, founded in 1982 after the British precedent. Offshoots of MOP UP and BUGA-UP also were formed in New Zealand (Deeks, 1992). In 1989 ASH was considered 'too radical', leading to the creation of two other groups to lobby for the Smoke-Free Environments Bill (McLoughlin, 1990). Reflecting the two major dimensions of the legislation, these were (1) the Coalition Against Tobacco Advertising and Promotion (CATAP) and (2) the Smoke-free Coalition. They were supported by various professional groups, such as Heart, Cancer, and medical associations, which wanted to maintain a distance from political lobbying (Smith, 1993). Aided by government agencies, such as the Toxic Substances Board and the Department of Health, they helped rally anti-tobacco opinion in New Zealand (McLoughlin, 1990; Beaglehole, 1991; Carr-Gregg, 1993; Deeks, 1992). The leader of CATAP, Michael Carr-Gregg, wrote the first draft of what became the 1990 legislation (McLoughlin, 1990; Smith, 1993). Although both CATAP and the Smoke-free Coalition were disbanded following passage of the 1990 legislation, the latter was reconstituted in 1995 when tobacco control stalled (Thomson and Wilson, 2001).

The balance of power between pro-tobacco and anti-tobacco interests has shifted the least in Japan, but this may be changing. The group-government structure in Japan is corporatist, with close relations between the tobacco manufacturing industry in the form of the government-owned Japan Tobacco International (JTI), tobacco growers, and the Ministry for Industry, which traditionally has dominated tobacco control policy (Lijphart, 1999: 177; Feldman, 2006). Japan Tobacco Inc., which owns the domestic Japan Tobacco as well as JTI, was formerly a directly-controlled government company. JTI has worked closely with the Ministry for Finance, and the latter has dominated government policy on both economic production and health policy on tobacco (Feldman, 2006; Mochizuki-Kobayashi et al, 2003).

Tobacco control groups in Japan have been relatively ineffective against the entrenched status of the political economy of tobacco since the 1970s, at least in formal terms. The Group to Establish Non-Smokers Rights formed in 1978 to combat SHS and undertook a lawsuit trying to force the government to establish non-smoking carriages on Japan's many trains. Although it was unsuccessful in litigation, Feldman (2001) argues that, informally, anti-tobacco groups and foreign examples have stimulated Japan's slow movement towards tobacco control. Recently the Japan Medical Association took an anti-tobacco stance and was a key critic of activities of the Japanese delegation during the FCTC negotiation (see Chapter 9). With the demise of LDP dominance, however, there are now signs that the Health, Labour and Welfare Ministry is becoming increasingly influential, which may bring some of the anti-tobacco groups into more favourable positions.

A 'transnational advocacy network' of groups inside and outside government has also influenced tobacco policy in Australia, Canada, and New Zealand, although less so in Japan. Tobacco companies led in international coordination for many years. Anti-tobacco advocacy groups became more numerous, organised, and vociferous in the 1980s in all countries, and they developed international linkages. These groups orchestrated campaigns for specific tobacco control measures, with varying impact. Anti-tobacco groups, medical associations, and public charities representing cancer, heart, and respiratory organisations sometimes banded together into coalitions (except in Japan), and became more politically active, advocating for tobacco regulation. More recently, both businesses and trade unions have taken lessons from overseas court decisions on passive smoking and been willing to have stronger regulations on SHS.

Socioeconomic factors

Economic benefits of tobacco

Tobacco control has had some effect on the domestic tobacco industry in all four countries. The influence of the pro-tobacco network has declined in the three English-speaking countries. Although it remains politically significant in Japan, even there its role may be declining. As in other advanced industrial countries, tobacco manufacturing has slowly shrunk as a share of the domestic economy. Its overall contribution to tax coffers has been reduced, with the proportion of the population smoking decreasing as taxation levels have increased substantially. This is offset somewhat, however, by population increases and the general affordability of cigarettes (Mackay et al, 2006: 104–5).

In each country, a few transnational producers dominate the market. Tobacco manufacturers in Australia, Canada, and New Zealand are branches of larger transnational companies with headquarters in Britain, the US or, more recently, Japan. This includes PM and BAT. JTI is the third largest private tobacco manufacturer in the world and controls approximately 65% of its domestic market as well as having extensive operations abroad, principally in China. Formerly it was a directly-controlled government company; eventually the government's share is supposed to shrink to 50% of the stock, allowing it to be more competitive internationally (Feldman, 2004). Only under US trade pressure in the mid-1980s did Japan agree to allow foreign companies into its cigarette market. Other companies now control approximately 35% of the Japanese market. JTI expanded its international operations in the first decade of the 21st century, acquiring Gallaher of the UK in 2006 and part of Imperial Tobacco in 2007.

Tobacco agriculture plays a similar and declining role in the economies of all four of these countries. In Canada, 90% of tobacco agriculture is concentrated in the province of Ontario (the fourth largest state/provincial grower in North America), with small amounts grown in other parts of Eastern Canada. Even in Ontario, tobacco recently has been only the eighth-ranked cash crop in an agricultural economy that is less than 2% of the total provincial Gross Domestic Product. International market forces and government aid for diversifying agriculture have reduced the number of farmers dependent on tobacco.

In Australia and New Zealand, economic dependence on tobacco growing and the manufacture of tobacco products in specific regions of both countries created demands for government assistance and support for tobacco consumption. This entrenched economic interest in tobacco later led to political resistance to restrictive government measures even as evidence of public health damage accumulated. Tobacco growing constituted a greater share of the agricultural economy in Australia than in New Zealand although both have shrunk dramatically in recent years (Corrao et al, 2000: 378, 410). In Australia, a majority of tobacco leaf was raised in Queensland, with lesser amounts grown in northeastern Victoria and New South Wales (Tyrrell, 1999: 163; Walker, 1984: 81). In New Zealand, the chief growing region was near Motueka (O'Shea, 1997).

In Japan, tobacco remains second only to rice as an important domestic agriculture crop. Because of limited available arable acreage and higher costs than in developing countries, however, domestic leaf growing has seen its purchase by manufacturers decline (Feldman, 2006). The amount of acreage devoted to leaf production has shrunk by 75% over the past half century, the number of tobacco farmers has declined by 90%, and government support for tobacco farming has been reduced (Feldman, 2001). Unlike the other three countries, in Japan tobacco has been grown throughout the country on small plots although this is more concentrated in the southern part (Feldman, 2001). Although tobacco agriculture has had electoral clout in each country, this can be attenuated by party discipline in the legislature. As domestic leaf growing has declined, so has its political influence. Nevertheless, the close ties between organised agriculture through the National Political League of Tobacco Cultivators and the long-reigning LDP in Japan has facilitated tobacco farmers' continuing influence (Feldman, 2006).

Smoking prevalence

Cigarette smoking spread in the early and mid-20th century in all four countries, but later in Australia, New Zealand, and Japan because of their lower per capita incomes at the time. In all four countries, the smoking prevalence rates amounted to approximately half of the population at its post-World War II peak, with men more heavily represented, and then declined slowly thereafter. The decline was accelerated in the three English-speaking countries after the major US and UK reports on the link between smoking and disease in the early 1960s (Table 3.2). In Japan, overall smoking rates continued to rise until the mid-1970s (Studlar, 2002; Hay, 1993; Easton, 1995; Tyrrell, 1999: 187–8; Sato, 1999b). By 2010 the three English-speaking countries had similar, same comparatively low smoking prevalence rates, around 20% (Shafey et al, 2009). Smoking rates are relatively uniform across states/provinces in Australia and Canada.

Japan's prevalence rate has been about 50% higher, but recently it has declined as well (McCurry, 2010). Unlike other industrialised democracies, Japan has Asian smoking patterns, with high smoking prevalence among men but much lower among women. Prevalence rates for men are among the highest in developed countries (over 30%), even though they have been halved over the past half century. Women are around 15% although rising from even lower levels, dating to the opening of the Japanese market to foreign competition in the mid-1980s (Sugarman, 2001; Sato, 1999b; Mochizuki-Kobayashi et al, 2003; Winder et al, 1993; McCurry, 2010). In contrast to other advanced industrial countries, in Japan smoking remains solidly entrenched in the professional classes, including healthcare workers.

Public opinion

Large-scale change in public opinion about tobacco consumption has been considered a necessary, even if not sufficient, basis for policy change (Troyer and Markle, 1983). Gradually over the years, especially since the mid-1960s, public opinion in all of these countries began to view tobacco consumption as a public health problem deserving of government intervention rather than an individual life-style choice. This trend has been more pronounced, however, in the English-speaking countries than in Japan (Walker, 1984; Tyrrell, 1999; Carter and Chapman, 2003; Ministry of Health, 1999; de Zwart and Stellman, 2002; Sato, 1999b; Studlar 2002). Although the evidence is spotty, there appears to have been a continuous growth in negative attitudes toward smoking and the tobacco industry, leaving only the hard-core smokers resistant to stronger tobacco control measures.

The role of ideas: Scientific knowledge

While Australia, Canada, and New Zealand are small population countries that do not have large scientific research establishments, they are alert to developments elsewhere, particularly in the US and UK (Carr-Gregg, 1993). Thus, their anti-tobacco networks, medical establishments and governments were well aware of the growing research and reports on the health hazards of cigarettes emanating from those two countries since the 1950s. As in Chapter 3, we can identify in each country a significant time lag from the acceptance of the evidence to the adoption of comprehensive tobacco control. The early, widely publicised scientific findings about the damaging health effects of tobacco use had minimal immediate policy impact. After the Canadian government rejected a call to establish a special committee to investigate the cigarette issue in the early 1950s, the Department of Health and Welfare did initiate a major study on the health effects of smoking. As previously noted, the English-speaking democracies paid close attention to the authoritative reports from the UK (1962) and the US (1964), which were followed by declines in smoking prevalence. There were few restrictive government policies, however, until the 1980s, when concerns about the health effects of SHS and addiction precipitated wider concern and anti-tobacco groups had been formed to combat tobacco consumption. The importance of policy transfer may be in its increasing ability to reduce the time lag between the production of the scientific evidence, organised advocacy and a government response. Japan, like Germany, is a somewhat deviant case, with scientific research not necessarily having a major domestic impact. Some of the pioneering scientific studies on the toxic effects of SHS appeared in Japan in the early 1980s (Hirayama, 1981). Nevertheless, Japan still lags in government policy.

The transfer of ideas

In addition to the scientific work, all four countries have paid attention to tobacco policy developments abroad. Again, the three English-speaking countries have been willing to incorporate these into their own policies, sometimes through interest groups, epistemic communities, and policy entrepreneurs, while Japan has been more resistant despite its knowledge of foreign developments. While the three English-speaking countries may have taken their policy leads in early 20th century tobacco control measures from their imperial homeland, the UK (Thomson, 1992a; Walker, 1984), this influence has declined over the years. The voluntary agreements for tobacco control instituted by New Zealand and Canada in the wake of the alarming reports about tobacco consumption in the 1960s were some of the last vestiges of British influence on their policies. Much of Canada's policy subsequently has resulted from close interaction with its near neighbour, the US (Studlar, 2002). Australia has taken some ideas from Canada, notably graphic cigarette warning labels. New Zealand has looked to Australia and Canada for its policy inspirations.

Canadian interactions with the US have occurred through multiple political jurisdictions in both countries as well as through both tobacco companies and anti-tobacco NGOs, such as the NSRA in Canada and cancer societies in both countries (Studlar, 2002). There is a long-established pattern of Canada and the US mutually recognising the scientific and policy initiatives concerning tobacco in the other country and deciding to emulate, modify, or reject the policy approach of the other. For instance, when the US central government took legislative action for health warnings and limiting tobacco advertising in the 1960s, a select committee in the Canadian House of Commons and also the cabinet considered going even further, but then drew back in favour of the voluntary code offered by the industry. After Canada's *Tobacco Products Control Act* became a worldwide touchstone for comprehensive tobacco control in 1988, similar proposals in the US, such as the FDA Rule, the National Settlement, and the MSA incorporated elements of it; this also extended to the 2009 US federal legislation empowering the FDA to regulate cigarettes. For their part, Canadian provinces have adopted several policies from US states, notably the 'litigation' approach of suing tobacco companies for healthcare costs incurred by government programmes. The path-breaking legislation changing the law to enable the government of British Columbia to file a civil suit against tobacco companies was based on the success of such litigation in US states (Studlar, 2002; Hausegger et al, 2009). Interest groups on both sides of these issues have relied on information and sometimes public testimony from their counterparts in the other country.

Bilateral lesson drawing has occurred particularly in New Zealand, a borrower of policies from Australia and Canada through both governments and NGOs, including: use of the Canadian *Tobacco Products Control Act* as an exemplar for its own 1990 legislation, the Tran-Tasmanian Mutual Recognition Arrangement (1996) for tobacco product standards and observer status at many intergovernmental meetings in Australia, including the Tobacco Policy Officers Group (Studlar, 2005). There has also been 'bottom-up' diffusion (see Chapter 6), mainly in the Australian federal system from the states but also in New Zealand from early municipal legislation on SHS. Multilateral diffusion from abroad has occurred, especially within the English-speaking world and through international bodies, such as the WHO, the WCTOH, and the UICC (Studlar, 2002, 2005; Thomson, 1992b). Awareness of developments in other countries and advocacy of similar measures domestically began in the 1960s, but the lag time between scientific evidence, advocacy and legislation has been progressively reduced.

As Farquharson (2003) points out, an international epistemic community may be a necessary but not a sufficient condition to get tobacco control legislation adopted. A transnational advocacy network of tobacco control groups inside and outside government helped get legislation enacted in both Australia and New Zealand. Tobacco companies were ahead in international coordination for many years. Anti-tobacco advocacy groups became more numerous, organised, and prominent in the early 1980s in Australia, slightly later in New Zealand, and both developed international linkages. Over time governments in both countries became more committed to restrictive tobacco control measures. The dominant pattern in all three countries, therefore, is a variation of intergovernmental 'polydiffusion' networks (Mossberger, 2000). In Australia, the states and territories usually lead, but the federal government controls large-scale financial resources and on occasion has acted as a coordinator and enforcer. In Canada, the provinces/territories have increasingly taken active responsibility for tobacco control policies that they can assume under the permissive federal regime. Even in areas, such as the regulation of SHS, various central agencies have taken the lead for their own buildings although this is an issue on which localities in Canada and New Zealand have played a large role (Cunningham, 1996; Kent, 1989). Overall, these three countries have been a laboratory of policy innovation for the rest of the world. Examples include Australia on advocacy campaigns and plain packaging, Canada on media campaigns, graphic health warnings, and comprehensive legislation, and New Zealand on central-level smoke-free policies. Australia, Canada, and New Zealand all played positive roles in the FCTC negotiations and quickly ratified the treaty (Sparks, 2010; Mamudu and Glantz, 2009; Mamudu et al, 2011a).

Japan has a long history of paying attention to, and borrowing policies from, Western countries in Europe and North America. There is also considerable population contact among these countries through travel, media, and other forms of communication. Japanese changes in law and behaviour in the early 2000s have been attributed to several factors, but among them are the attention paid to international developments, such as participation in the FCTC. There has been extensive Japanese media coverage of tobacco control activities in other industrialised countries. Anti-tobacco MPs in Japan have invoked Europe as a standard for cigarette tax rises. Japan was a sometimes-reluctant and troublesome participant in the FCTC negotiations (Assunta and Chapman, 2006; Mamudu and Glantz, 2009) but signed and ratified it, becoming a member of the FCTC Conference of the Parties. Also, JTI is now a major international company, having to compete with other transnationals, even in Japan. Thus, both the informed public and government officials are aware of Japan's deviant status in emerging global tobacco control norms. After a decade of slow economic growth in the early 2000s, Japan is more willing to countenance political and cultural change. Nevertheless, by most measures Japan remains a laggard among industrialised democracies in its tobacco control policy (Feldman, 2006; Sugarman, 2001; Mochizuki-Kobayashi et al, 2003).

Conclusion

In Australia, Canada, and New Zealand, tobacco policy change has been profound in the post World War II period. Minimal tobacco restrictions have been replaced by comprehensive control, with the modern tobacco control regime beginning in the 1980s and accelerating in the 1990s. Initially, legislation against tobacco developed slowly and policy change was often piecemeal and protracted. The entrenched economic and political power of tobacco interests in these countries made the process of getting agreement on tobacco control measures prolonged and difficult. Further, in Australia, public health matters were largely a state and territorial concern, and the central government was reluctant to challenge tobacco-friendly governments in Queensland and New South Wales. By the early 21st century, Australia, Canada, and New Zealand were widely recognised as among the leading tobacco control regimes in the world. In fact, across almost all indicators of strength of tobacco control, these countries rank highly. Unlike the US, there is now less internal variation in Canada and especially Australia. This picture contrasts with tobacco control policy in Japan, which has been much slower to develop.

To a large extent, we can explain the differences in policy trajectory with reference to institutions, agendas, networks, socioeconomic factors and the role of ideas. First, the common institutional theme is that health departments have increasingly taken the policy lead on tobacco in the three English-speaking countries, while in Japan tobacco has largely remained within the domain of departments responsible for industry and finance. We have a more mixed picture regarding the structures of political systems. There is some evidence that tobacco control policy has progressed in Australia and Canada because they are federal systems with multiple venues and sources for anti-tobacco advocacy and policy innovation. This helps explain the distinction with Japan but not New Zealand (we return to the role of multiple venues, federal and unitary states in Chapter 10). The role of the judiciary is also not uniformly strong enough to explain the overall direction of policy change. Second, the agenda-setting context may be different, with the three English-speaking countries adopting the view that tobacco use is a problem that must be solved (indeed, in Australia and New Zealand, tobacco is now classified as a toxic, albeit legal, substance), while Japan has remained more committed to the importance of tobacco as an economic product.

Third, a shift in the balance of power between tobacco and anti-tobacco interests is clearer in the three English-speaking countries. Larger, more unified, and aggressive anti-tobacco coalitions arose in all three of these countries at approximately the same time (the early 1980s), which suggests that they were collective manifestations of underlying shifts in values and/or the opportunity structure of institutions in these countries (Deeks, 1992; Pross and Stewart, 1994; Chapman and Wakefield, 2001). More recently trade unions have becoming increasingly sensitive to the protection of their members from the effects of SHS. On the other hand, Japan is a classic case of the powers of resistance to tobacco control through corporatism, with companies and growers involved with a long-ruling dominant party in government, the LDP. These patterns of tobacco promotion have proven difficult to change, even in the face of domestic as well as foreign scientific evidence, shifting public opinion, and an appreciation of policy change elsewhere in the world. It remains to be seen whether the new ruling party, the Japanese Democratic Party, can stay in power long enough and be purposeful enough to change this tobacco subsystem in a significant way.

Fourth, the economic value of tobacco and smoking prevalence is lower in the three English-speaking countries. Tobacco growing was once a significant source of economic activity in some regions, but its importance has fallen and farmers have been encouraged to diversify. Tobacco taxation has declined as a source of government revenue, allowing finance departments to relax their defence of tobacco as an economic benefit. While tobacco manufacturing is important in certain regions, its economic importance has diminished, and decisions are made abroad for branch plants. While there were once regions with relatively high smoking prevalence and resistance to tobacco control policy, regional differences have diminished, and prevalence is now around 20%. Even without a concerted government policy against smoking in Japan, smoking prevalence has been falling, to less than 30% by 2010, although there remain substantial gaps between men and women. Furthermore, tobacco manufacturing is still a significant source of revenue, and the power of the tobacco lobby has not been substantially diminished.

Finally, the role and transfer of ideas has helped transform policy in the three English-speaking countries and may yet influence Japan as well. Some policies are centrally adopted, such as the graphic health warnings on cigarette packages introduced by Canada and later by Australia and New Zealand, and plain packaging in Australia. But innovations in state/provincial jurisdictions also can spread across international borders to other countries through the efforts of both governmental and non-governmental actors. Victoria in Australia and Ontario and British Columbia in Canada are leaders in this process. Thus, federalism may be an asset in international as well as domestic policy transfer because there are more jurisdictions both to send and to receive policies. Tobacco control in Australia was led by the states, with the federal government only assuming prominence later. On the other hand, Canada followed its earlier tendencies to have the central government lead on this issue, and that government paid attention to what was being done elsewhere. Only after the federal government had established a comprehensive policy did the provinces and territories begin to act; they looked to each other and to similar jurisdictions in the US. New Zealand tended to follow policies first developed abroad, especially in Australia and Canada, but then leaped ahead in some policies, particularly central secondhand smoke policies in the late 1990s.

All five factors combine to inform our explanations of relatively large policy change in Australia, Canada and New Zealand, but policy lethargy in Japan. Japan is an unusual case indeed: a developed country with a relatively low level of tobacco control and, unlike Germany within the EU, relatively free from coercive international influence. But even Japan shows signs of abandoning its holdout position among industrialised democracies in favour of joining the international consensus through the FCTC and changing its central-level domestic policies towards more punitive economic and regulatory ones.

8
Tobacco Control Policymaking in Developing Regions

In this chapter we focus on the developing regions: Asia Pacific (AP), Latin America and the Caribbean (LAC), Middle East and North Africa (MENA), and Sub-Sahara Africa (SSA). Tobacco policy in these regions generally exhibits two distinctive tendencies. First, in most cases, tobacco control policies and programmes were virtually non-existent as recently as the 1970s. Second, few developing countries have developed policy exclusively from domestic sources. Rather, it has developed mostly through policy transfer from developed countries; this process has culminated in the production of the 2003 WHO Framework Convention on Tobacco Control (FCTC) (Chapter 9). These points influence how we analyse tobacco control policy change in developing regions. We still focus on the five key explanatory factors, but in two different ways: as a means to explain *limited* policy change during most of the 20th century and then to demonstrate how policy has changed more recently through transfer.

With regard to institutions, we identify a historical tendency for departments of health to be lone voices within government, drowned out by other departments, such as agriculture, finance and trade. In developed countries, we can often help explain change with reference to a shift in the institutional framework, with the Department of Health taking a central role. In developing countries we identify the more significant role of the Department of Health as a link to international policymaking; as an avenue of global policy diffusion. Further, we identify an unusually prominent role for international governmental organisations, such as the WHO and non-governmental organisations (NGOs), such as the International Union Against Cancer and the International Union Against Tuberculosis and Lung Disease. The agenda-setting context for policy choices is also distinctive. Tobacco consumption is a major problem for developing countries, where over 80% of world tobacco users live and the rate of use continues to increase (WHO, 2008, 2011b). However, it is a problem that rises rarely to the top of the domestic policy agenda. Instead, tobacco control became a global issue in the 1990s (Mamudu, 2008) and, as a result, it has become part of the policy agenda of almost all countries around the world, including developing ones (Mamudu, 2008;

Mamudu and Glantz, 2009). There is no evidence of a major shift in the balance of power from pro- to anti-tobacco interests in developing countries. Rather, this shift has taken place at the international level, with a limited domestic group infrastructure supplemented by international NGO efforts.

The socioeconomic context is also less conducive to tobacco control: smoking prevalence and rates of consumption are particularly high among men in many countries and tobacco companies are highly profitable and appear to be economically valuable actors within developing countries (if governments ignore the economic costs of ill-health related to tobacco use). Tobacco is indigenous to countries in Latin America and the Caribbean (LAC) and arrived in Asian Pacific (AP), Middle East and North Africa (MENA), and Sub-Saharan Africa (SSA) between the 16th and 18th centuries through European merchants. Then, transnational tobacco companies (TTCs) moved into these countries after World War II and have a significant presence in most cases (with the notable exception of China which has a state controlled monopoly, Figure 1.2). Finally, the role of ideas is distinctive. The gap between the production of the scientific knowledge on smoking and the policy response is relatively wide and the role of policy transfer is particularly significant. Based on the experience of developed countries, the expansion of TTCs generated concerns about an impending tobacco-induced epidemic, prompting individuals and organisations to, first, engage in activities in the 1980s and 1990s that diffused and transferred knowledge and ideas on tobacco use and control and, second, to pursue a global tobacco policy agreement. As of September 2011, 36 of 37 countries in AP, 28 of 33 countries in LAC, 16 of 18 countries in MENA, and 42 of 48 countries in SSA have ratified the FCTC (becoming 'parties' to the agreement).[9]

The developing countries' experience provides a new dimension to policy. While the trajectory of the tobacco epidemic in developing countries seems similar to developed ones (Lopez et al, 1994), the policy process is different because of the strong linkages with international dynamics. The change in behaviour of developing countries in tobacco control generally emanated from international effects, but was mediated by domestic political and societal dynamics. These developments occurred amidst tobacco industry expansion in the 1970s and 1980s (linked to a drop in cigarette demand in developed countries), turning these countries into battle grounds between the companies and transnational actors seeking tobacco control. Policy is effectively an outcome of the interplay between transnational and domestic factors at multiple levels of government (Inter Matrix Group, 1981; Keohane and Nye, 1971; Risse-Kappen, 1994, 1995).

What is tobacco policy?

Tobacco control instruments were virtually non-existent before the 1970s in most developing regions (US National Clearinghouse For Smoking, 1973;

US Public Health Service, 1970; WHO, 1976). There are some exceptions: research on the health effects of tobacco consumption started in India (Muller, 1978; Sanghvi, 1974) and South Africa (Dean, 1959) in the 1960s and countries, such as Argentina and Thailand had a tobacco control policy by 1970. However, only four developing countries had tobacco control legislation by the mid-1970s (US Public Health Service, 1970: 282; WHO, 1976: 33; Roemer, 1993: 31; Roemer, 1982: 12). In the 1980s, tobacco industry voluntary codes began to proliferate throughout the developing world. Evidence from tobacco industry documents suggests that, since the 1980s TTCs: developed these voluntary codes to demonstrate the industry's ability to regulate itself; proposed legislation that would be considered by public health advocates to be weak or watered-down; and, sued to overturn tobacco control legislation (Global Smokefree Partnership, 2009; Hirschhorn, 2006). These activities have contributed to the low number of countries with significant tobacco control legislation (Shafey et al, 2009; WHO, 2008, 2011b).

Since the 1970s the cumulative number of countries with a tobacco control policy or programme has increased to the extent that by the late 2000s one can hardly find a developing country with absolutely nothing on tobacco control (US Public Health Service, 1970; WHO, 1976; WHO, 2008, 2011b). Some developing countries have also become innovators in pictorial health warnings (Fong et al, 2006), plain packaging (Mamudu et al, 2011a), the regulation of characters smoking in the movies (WHO, 2009), and smoke-free environments (Global Smokefree Partnership, 2009). There is also a degree of variation within some countries (such as Argentina and Mexico) where local governments have stronger policies than central government (Griffith et al, 2008). However, most developing countries still lag behind developed ones in terms of the *density* of policies and programmes (in other words, *strength*, or the number of policies, their coverage and the levels of punishment involved).

As Table 8.1 outlines, tobacco control in developing countries now consists of a combination of regulatory actions and programmes that basically replicate those in developed countries. Comparison of the number of countries and density of policies in developing regions by 1997, the period of the initiation of the FCTC from 1999, and by 2009, shows an overall increase in number (Griffith et al, 2008; Global Smokefree Partnership, 2009; The ITC Project). In particular, the number of countries with policies on ingredient disclosure, spending on programmes to help people to quit, funding for community programmes and organisations to combat tobacco use, and scientific research has increased. As such, there seem to be some FCTC effects, although it is too early to make any definitive inference.

Several things are worth noting about tobacco control policy in developing countries. First, throughout developing countries, the existence of such policies does not imply an existence of a national legislation; most policies are administrative orders or decrees covering specific regions, institutions or populations. For example, in SSA, of the 23 countries that have smoke-free policies covering at least one place by 2009, only two, Kenya and

Table 8.1 Tobacco Control Policies and Programmes in Developing Regions of the World

	1997				2009			
	AP	LAC	MENA	SSA	AP	LAC	MENA	SSA
I. **Regulation (through legislation or voluntary agreements)**								
Tobacco advertising and promotion	19	16	11	10	21	10	16	27
The sale of tobacco	8	9	2	3	26	21	10	11
Smoking in public places	28	17	12	16	14	8	13	23
Ingredients regulation	4	–	4	2	13	3	11	3
Customs enforcement on smuggling and counterfeit cigarettes	–	–	–	–	–	2	–	–
II. **Finance**								
Taxation and other levies	15	20	5	5	20	27	14	44
Spending on directed health services	1	–	1	1	17	34	16	33
Economic incentives	–	–	–	–	–	–	–	–
Sponsorship substitution	–	–	–	–	–	–	–	–
Litigation against tobacco companies	–	–	–	–	8	7	2	4
III. **Capacity building**								
Funding for community development programs and organisations	–	–	–	–	23	27	16	34
IV. **Education**								
Health warning labels on cigarette and tobacco packs	17	17	10	8	13	15	12	13
Health education campaigns	18	11	3	8	14	22	4	6
V. **Learning and information tools**								
Legislative hearings, executive reports	–	–	–	–	–	–	–	–
Funding scientific research	–	4	–	–	4	4	–	2

Sources: Carrao et al, 2000; Shafey et al, 2003; WHO, 1997, 2008, 2009; Shafey et al, 2009
Note: The figures refer to the numbers of countries with a relevant tobacco control programme. The maximum number in each case is: AP 36; LAC 33; MENA 18; SSA 48.

South Africa, have passed comprehensive smoke-free legislation (Griffith et al, 2008). In March 2011, Nigeria became the third country in SSA to pass a similar policy. Second, the most prevalent tobacco policies in developing countries are bans on advertising and promotions, policies on the sales of tobacco, smoke-free policies, excise tax, health warnings, and health education. Third, the change in the number of countries with tobacco policies by 1997 and by 2009 appears to be most dramatic in SSA, where the number increased in almost all policies. Fourth, there appears to be an association between income level and prevalence of certain policies in developing regions, which is why there are more countries in LAC and MENA (relatively middle- to upper-middle-income countries) with programmes that require resources, such as Nicotine Replacement Therapies and cessation services. Fifth, while litigation is not very prevalent in developing countries, it has emerged as part of tobacco control. Finally, even though illicit trade in tobacco products is prevalent throughout developing countries (Holden et al, 2010; Collin et al, 2004; LeGresley et al, 2008) it is yet to be taken seriously by governments, at least in terms of policies to confront the problem. In sum, there is broad awareness of policies needed to combat tobacco use, but there is still a limited number of comprehensive legislative programmes in existence across developing countries.

Institutions: Who has responsibility for tobacco control?

Domestic institutions

There are four institutional dimensions that might affect the substance of tobacco control. First, the use and type of policy instruments varies by political system for several reasons. The political structure for tobacco control in developing countries differs widely, from stable democracies, such as India, to stable autocracies, such as China, Cuba, and North Korea, to kingships in MENA and in places, such as Bhutan, Brunei, and Swaziland. In 2008, Freedom House (www.freedomhouse.org) data suggest that a majority of the countries in these four regions were either 'partly free' (democratising) or 'not free' (autocracy). Additionally, the data show that, over the past four decades, many countries in these four regions experienced high levels of political instability, some in LAC and SSA alternating between democratic governance, military dictatorships, and civil and political conflicts. For these reasons, the political structures or venues for policymaking in general are not only different but have also been unstable. The result is that instruments, such as parliamentary legislation (democracies), executive and administrative orders and decrees (democracies, autocracies, and kingships), and to some extent judicial decisions and religious rulings, are used for tobacco control. This instability in the political systems in many developing countries over the past 50 years likely contributed to the low level of tobacco control on the policy agenda (in other words, armed conflict and political instability drive down other policy concerns).

In many cases, the role of religion is particularly distinctive in developing countries (Islam, 1998; Jabbour and Fouad, 2004; Yong et al, 2009). The sociocultural influence of monks in places, such as Bhutan (Ugen, 2003),

Cambodia (Smith and Umenai, 2000), and Thailand (Swaddiwudhipong et al, 1993; Yong et al, 2009) and Imams and Mullahs in MENA (El-Awa, 2003; Hameed et al, 2002) and Malaysia (Yong et al, 2009) allow them to issue religious rulings that aim to control the use and spread of tobacco. In the late 1970s, Gulf Cooperation Council countries banned tobacco advertising based on religion (Verkerk and INFOTAB, 1985) and, since then, religious leaders in countries, such as Egypt and Iran have issued Fatwa (Islamic rulings) against tobacco use (El-Awa, 2003, 2008). Also in AP and LAC, religious organisations, such as the Seventh Day Adventist Church, conducted education programmes to raise awareness about the harmful effects of smoking based on religion, especially in the 1980s and 1990s when domestic tobacco control NGOs were virtually non-existent (Chapman and Wong, 1990; WHO, 1997). The WHO has urged that religion should be integrated in tobacco control in these areas because societies comply with these religious rulings on tobacco control (Jabbour and Fouad, 2004).

Tobacco control in developing countries has also been influenced by political leadership in isolated cases, such as the Gulf Cooperation Council in the 1970s, South Africa (Asare, 2007; Yach, 1996: 36), Pacific Island states (WHO, 1997) and Syria in the 1990s and Uruguay in the 2000s. In certain authoritarian and paternalistic states, political leaders usually make proclamations or issue decrees for tobacco control, which was the case in countries in the Gulf Cooperation Council in the 1970s (Verkerk and INFOTAB, 1985) and Syria in 1996 and 2009 (BBC, 2009). In democracies, presidential leadership was critical in the enactment of South Africa's 1993 Tobacco Control Act and Uruguay's 2008 Tobacco Control Act that was preceded by a presidential decree in 2006. At the same time, the political leadership in places, such as Argentina (Sebrie et al, 2006) and Malawi (Otanez et al, 2006, 2007) has had adverse effects on policy development at the central level.

Second, the scope for venue shopping varies by country (Griffith et al, 2008). A few countries, particularly those in LAC, have federal and decentralised administrative systems with more scope for policy variation and innovation. For example, in Argentina, Brazil, and Mexico, provincial and municipal governments play important roles in policymaking, resulting in a situation where local governments have stronger policies than the central government. However, most countries have unitary systems of government; power is concentrated in the central government and policy choices are fairly uniform throughout the countries. Because of this general concentration of policymaking authority at the centre, the national government and parliament are the main arenas for policymaking in democracies and during periods of democratisation. The diverse interests, but strong tobacco influence in government and parliaments, have impeded policy developments in many countries, likely accounting for why almost all developing countries have ratified the FCTC, but few parliaments have produced legislation for it (Table 8.1) (Shafey et al, 2009; WHO, 2008).

Third, the Ministry of Health has been the most active political institution for tobacco control over the past four decades. However, its influence has varied. On the one hand, it has been undermined rarely by partisan disputes because there is generally no clear-cut ideological and partisan division on tobacco control. Even in Latin American countries where there is an ideological fault-line between the left and right on many socio-economic issues, there is a consensus on tobacco control, as it is considered to belong to the public health realm (suggesting a redefinition of the policy image – see below). On the other hand, pro-tobacco interests still have a strong role in government policy. In the 1980s and the 1990s, the Ministry of Health was often a lone voice in government advocating for tobacco control, sometimes in conflict with the Agriculture and Trade ministries, who were more supportive of tobacco as an economic product.

In effect, the influence of health departments is an empirical question. We can identify some relatively active states, where the government led the development and promotion of tobacco control and the Ministry of Health spearheaded such efforts (Figure 8.1). Across these four regions, countries with a strong and influential Ministry of Health, such as Brazil, India, South Africa, and Thailand have more comprehensive tobacco control policies and programmes (Shafey et al, 2009; WHO, 2008; Griffith et al, 2008). In less active states (the majority), the role of the ministry has been to provide a focal point for transnational networks or links between domestic and international anti-tobacco interests, with less direct effect on policy.

In general, we can identify an embryonic process of tobacco control promotion in which the Ministry of Health often collaborates with other agencies, including the Ministry of Education and Sport and NGOs. In countries in Latin America, the Middle East, and South Asia, a national tobacco control committee or commission made up of government agencies, academic institutions, and NGOs became an important institution for tobacco control (Shafey et al, 2003). Even in autocracies in MENA, this institution mediates the development of tobacco control policies and programmes, likely mitigating the impact of differences in the system of governance on the policy process (although such an institution is generally absent in SSA, the Caribbean, and Pacific Island states). Additionally, the Ministry of Health collaborated with international governmental and non-governmental organisations and counterparts in mostly developed countries to promote tobacco control. For this reason, the Ministry of Health in developing countries is usually the focal point not only for liaising domestic tobacco control efforts but also for collaborating with their counterparts and international organisations. As the main governmental agency for health, the Ministry of Health has, since the 1970s, led the country to participate in governance in global tobacco control.

Fourth, the involvement of the judiciary as a venue for tobacco control is a recent phenomenon in policymaking in developing countries. So far, only a handful of tobacco lawsuits have appeared (Shafey et al, 2009). In the 2000s, based on the experience of developed countries, advocates and advocacy organisations began to sue the TTCs to desist from promoting tobacco use and also the government to enact laws to halt tobacco promotion and protect non-smokers from exposure to second-hand smoke (SHS). In a place, such as Uganda, where cases were adjudicated in favour of tobacco control interests, litigation has become an integral part of tobacco control. However, unlike developed countries, such as the US, the use of the judiciary as a venue for tobacco control policymaking through litigation is primarily by organisations rather than individuals or personally affected groups. In a few cases, the government is involved as a defendant or co-defendant. Moreover, litigation as a strategy for tobacco control in developing countries faces two major challenges: cultural norms and lack of resources. Tobacco control litigation in Asian countries has not garnered much interest because of the cultural aversion to litigation in general (personal communication, Mary Assunta, leading tobacco control advocate in Malaysia, 2008). Also, the resources needed to engage in costly and lengthy litigation with wealthy TTCs undermine the appeal of litigation for many advocates. As a result, even as individuals and organisations have become conversant with the idea of litigation for tobacco control, the use of the judiciary as venue for tobacco control is yet to gain any momentum.

Intergovernmental organisations

Policies and programmes led by institutions, such as the WHO, World Bank, and the UN have contributed to tobacco control in developing countries; they provide channels for policy diffusion and venues for developing countries to participate in the global tobacco control agenda. In this regard, the most important institution is the WHO. The World Health Assembly became interested in tobacco control in 1970 and, by 1976, tobacco control in developing countries often rose to the top of its agenda. Its involvement culminated in the 1983 WHO Expert Committee on Smoking Control Strategies in Developing Countries (WHO Expert Committee, 1983). Drawing on the experiences of the Nordic countries and others, such as UK and the US, the expert committee recommended that developing countries should learn and borrow ideas on tobacco control from developed countries.

Between the late 1970s and early 1990s, the WHO promoted tobacco control in developing countries through its Tobacco or Health programme, which was transformed into the WHO Tobacco Free Initiative (TFI) in 1998 when Gro Harlem Brundtland became the Director General. The WHO engaged in activities which ranged from ordinary advice to technical cooperation through its six regional offices and country representatives. It then developed a global tobacco control framework under its Action Plan for the Tobacco or Health programme in the 1990s, which the regional offices used to develop their own Action Plans for tobacco control (No Author, 1994; APACT, 1995;

WPRO, 1994). An integral part of these efforts has been the annual World No Tobacco Day to raise awareness about tobacco use and control (WHO, 1997). These activities have been conducted usually in collaboration with other UN agencies, particularly the UN Food and Agricultural Organization in crop diversification and the World Bank in economics of tobacco use and control (Jha and Chaloupka, 1999; Mamudu and Glantz, 2009) and international NGOs in education and advocacy campaigns (Mamudu, 2008; WHO, 1997; WHO Expert Committee, 1979, 1983).

Agendas: How important is tobacco control as a policy issue? How is tobacco framed?

There is a yawning gap between the size of the tobacco problem and levels of attention to it. The idea of a tobacco epidemic has existed since the 1970s, but it was not until the 1990s that significant levels of attention could be identified. Generally, tobacco control only becomes part of the policy agenda of developing countries when it is a global issue. We can identify a similar distinctiveness in problem definition. Chapter 3 outlines a broad global shift in the framing of tobacco, from positive to negative; from tobacco as an economic product to be encouraged (the political economy frame) to smoking behaviour as a health problem to be solved or minimised (the public health frame). Yet, this shift is least marked in developing countries.

For many years, political economy concerns guided policy choice and developing countries sought assistance from the World Bank and others to fund tobacco projects. In fact, as part of the efforts towards industrialisation and development, some developing countries courted the TTCs and many established state monopolies. Tobacco companies fostered this political economy frame for policy choice by demonstrating the economic benefits of tobacco manufacturing and growing (Philip Morris, 1981a; INFOTAB, 1990; B. Simpson and INFOTAB, 1985). Even as this frame became increasingly challenged, it has been bolstered by other tobacco company-led images. Since the 1980s, the TTCs' activities have evolved to include: promoting the social acceptability of tobacco; framing tobacco control as a developed countries issue (i.e. suggesting that the smoking-illness link is more prevalent in developed countries); promoting 'courtesy of choice' or 'accommodation' programmes that allow both smokers and non-smokers to share facilities; undertaking corporate social responsibility programmes to demonstrate that the industry does good works; promoting tobacco industry youth smoking prevention programmes to make tobacco use an 'adult choice'; and, diverting attention to other health issues to maintain a relatively positive image of smoking and the tobacco industry (Global Smokefree Partnership, 2009; Hirschhorn, 2006).

In this light, the role of international organisations, such as the WHO is to raise awareness of tobacco use, promote tobacco control and make public health a frame for policy choices. Indeed, problem definition has taken a distinctive path, with anti-smoking groups focusing not only on the public health frame, but also distinctive issues, such as the shift of tobacco-induced morbidity and mortality from developed to developing countries, the socio-economic costs of tobacco use, and the strategy of the tobacco industry to target developing countries. The latter frames encouraged developing countries to play the leading role in the adoption of the FCTC as a global policy response, in contrast to most developed countries where a shift in problem definition was linked to shifts in the balance of power within government and policy networks.

Three main factors prompted increased policy attention to tobacco in developing countries. First, attention shifted to the prospect that developing countries will be the main victims of continuous tobacco use in the 21st century (FAO, 1990; WHO, 2008, 2011b). Over 70% of tobacco-attributable mortality by the 2020s will occur in developing countries (Jha and Chaloupka, 1999, 2000), reaching over 80% by the 2030s (WHO, 2011b). Second, tobacco control advocates have used the increasing evidence that tobacco control does not harm the economy, and that tobacco use has direct economic consequences in terms of healthcare and indirect costs in terms of lost productivity and other social dislocations, to challenge the political economy frame (Barnum, 1994; Panos Institute, 1994; Jha and Chaloupka, 1999). In 1995, for example, 22 individuals and international organisations issued the Bellagio Statement on Tobacco and Sustainable Development, pointing out that 'the net economic costs of tobacco are profoundly negative' (Bellagio Conference, 1995), and thereby linking tobacco use to faltering economic development in developing countries. This economic-cost frame has been particularly useful in challenging the key tobacco industry arguments and allaying governmental concerns over lost revenue and tobacco generated employment. Third, litigation in the US helped expose the marketing strategies of tobacco companies. The idea of tobacco industry targeting developing countries as source of new markets is nothing new and anecdotes have existed since the 1970s. However, the evidence became apparent from the late 1990s when litigation forced the TTCs to release their previously secret internal documents (Glantz et al, 1995; Slade et al, 1995; Hanauer et al, 1995).

Accordingly, attention to the shift of tobacco-induced morbidity and mortality has prompted developing countries' attention to collective actions, such as the FCTC negotiations (Mamudu and Glantz, 2009). African countries stated this point in their declarations to support tobacco control and the FCTC (Mamudu and Glantz, 2009). Mamudu et al (2008, 2009) found in their study on the FCTC that socioeconomic reports, particularly the World Bank's *Curbing the Epidemic* have been very useful for advocating for policies and programmes in developing countries. These ideas about socioeconomic influences of tobacco use have emerged as an alternative and challenging frame for policy choice in tobacco control in developing countries. Further, evidence about how the TTCs entered the economies of these countries, marketed tobacco to their populations, and influenced the policymaking process helped mobilise action for tobacco control (Aguinaga and Shatenstein, 2002; Global Smokefree Partnership, 2009; Hammond and White, 2001; WHO, 2000; Mamudu and Glantz, 2009).

Networks: Has there been a shift in power between pressure participants?

Domestic networks

Chapter 3 identifies a shift in the balance of power between pro- and anti-tobacco interests within developed, but not developing, countries. Indeed, one consequence of the shift in developed countries is that tobacco companies have moved their attention to larger markets in developing countries. Domestic tobacco policy networks are generally dominated by the tobacco industry. Tobacco control interests are generally weak in developing countries, with limited (but increasing) influence in the policy process (Chapman and Wong, 1990). Indeed, the number of groups devoted to tobacco control is small, despite the work international NGOs have been doing since the 1980s to mobilise and nurture them (Ashton, 1993; Chapman and Wong, 1990; Wipfli et al, 2010; note that we use GLOBALink and Framework Convention Alliance membership as proxy indicators of group numbers). For example, in China, a major effort to develop a tobacco control advocacy workforce was only launched in 2009 (Yang et al, 2009). Generally, domestic tobacco control networks appear to be strongest in LAC (Albuja and Daynard, 2009; Crosbie et al, 2011: 20, 64–72; Sebrie, 2006) and weakest in MENA (El-Awa, 2003).

Until the 2000s, voluntary, medical and health professional associations engaged in tobacco control intermittently (Chapman and Wong, 1990; WHO, 1997). We can link, in a very broad way, their status within government to the structure of each political system. For example, it is less apparent in democratising or autocratic societies where the civil liberties and political rights of citizens are circumscribed, but more apparent in democracies, such as India, where civil liberties and political rights are respected. We can also identify a growing number of these organisations since the 2000s and the existence of national tobacco control committees or commissions in some countries, particularly in LAC and MENA (Shafey et al, 2003). However, there is little evidence available regarding their impact on the domestic policy process. Further, their modest rise can largely be linked to the agenda set by international tobacco control networks. Effectively, developing countries represent venues for the interplay between 'transnational networks' (Sikkink, 1998; Stone, 2000).

International tobacco industry networks

An industry network for developing countries began to emerge from the late 1970s amid concerns over increasing tobacco control activities of the WHO, individuals, and international NGOs (BAT, 1980). Spearheaded by the

International Tobacco Information Center (INFOTAB, replaced by the Tobacco Documentation Center after it was disbanded by the 1998 US Master Settlement Agreement), an industry network consisting of the TTCs and manufacturers' associations emerged in the 1980s and subsequently expanded to include others, such as leaf growers and dealers and the advertising and hospitality industries (INFOTAB and Advisory Group, 1983; B. Simpson and INFOTAB, 1985; Verkerk and INFOTAB, 1985). This network has played three roles across developing countries: (1) penetrating and consolidating markets; (2) marketing and promoting tobacco use; and, (3) undermining tobacco control policies and programmes (WHO, 2000).

Since the early 1980s, TTCs have worked collaboratively and individually to undermine tobacco control at all levels. Globally, by 1983/84, INFOTAB had created the 'Developing Countries Project', used to counter tobacco control activities of the WHO and NGOs, monitor the World Bank and UN Development Programme in developing countries, assist manufacturers' associations in their political efforts, and organise regional workshops aimed at undermining tobacco control (Philip Morris, 1981a; Hargrove and INFOTAB, 1981; INFOTAB, 1984; B. C. Simpson and INFOTAB, 1983). A multi-dimensional approach was a potent way of influencing the behaviour of developing countries in tobacco control. Numerous activities, ranging from the subtle influence of public opinion to active lobbying against policies and programmes development and covert and overt threat of international trade litigation (for example, in March 2010 Philip Morris International sued Uruguay in the World Bank's Center for the Settlement of Investment Disputes for its policies pertaining to health warnings and brand switching), have contributed to the low number of countries with tobacco control legislation (Shafey et al, 2009; WHO, 2008) even as their policymakers have increasingly become conversant with knowledge and ideas on tobacco use and control.

Figure 8.1 Tobacco Control in Developing Countries

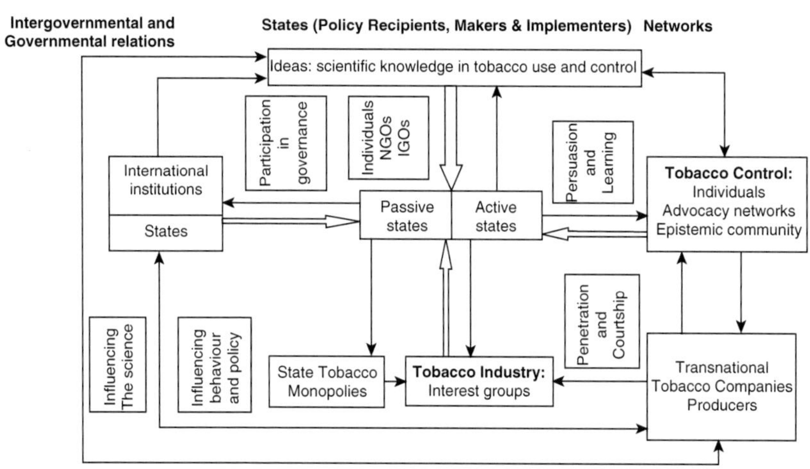

The International Tobacco Control Network (ITCN)

The international tobacco control network emerged to challenge the influence and dominance of the tobacco industry. This network has grown worldwide and members communicate, interact, and spread knowledge on tobacco use and control through channels, such as conferences and the internet, and directly influence policy through procedures, such as legislative testimony and technical support. In the 1970s and 1980s actors in this network led the efforts to promote tobacco control in developing countries in a 'bottom-up' manner, focusing on raising public awareness on tobacco use and control, mobilisation of societal forces, and policy development (Figure 8.1). These activities were organised through the International Union Against Cancer tobacco control programme (No Author, 1994; The Observer, 1985) and the International Liaison Committee on Smoking Control (Leonard Zahn and Associates, 1981). As a result, the tobacco companies regarded these kinds of collaborations as an 'international "conspiracy" against tobacco' (Philip Morris, 1981b). In the 1990s, these activities became organised under the American Cancer Society, 'The Trade for Life Global Plan', which was launched during the 7th World Conference on Tobacco or Health in Perth, Australia (BAT, 1995). Under this plan, the NGOs agreed to coordinate activities at the regional level and worked to highlight the problem of tobacco use and tobacco industry activities in developing countries, establishing tobacco control regional networks and presenting the case for policy and programme development.

The international tobacco control network has expanded since the 1990s to include NGO alliances and coalitions, such as the International Non-governmental Coalition Against Tobacco and specialised networks, such as the International Network of Women Against Tobacco as well as regional networks, such as the Latin America Coordinating Committee of Smoking Control and the Asia Pacific Association for Control of Tobacco (Philip Morris, 1993). During the FCTC negotiations in the early 2000s, these NGOs and coalitions worked successfully to influence the development of the FCTC while consolidating their presence in developing countries (Mamudu and Glantz, 2009). Additionally, the efforts to implement the FCTC in developing countries have attracted Western philanthropists into the international tobacco control network. In 2006, the communications magnate and Mayor of New York, Michael Bloomberg, partnered with the WHO and organisations in Europe and North America to create the Global Tobacco Control Initiative, which has been funding tobacco control activities in 15 countries, 12 of which are in these four regions. Similarly, in 2007, the Bill and Melinda Gates Foundation in the US sponsored the Canadian-based Research for International Tobacco Control to assess tobacco control in SSA, and subsequently funded a consortium led by the American Cancer Society in 2009 to promote tobacco control in SSA (although it withdrew funding in 2010 when it became clear that the Chair of the International Development Research Center had been a director of Imperial Tobacco in Canada). These activities have increased ties between the international tobacco control network and the private sector in the developed countries to promote tobacco control in developing countries, and to contribute to the proliferation of domestic and regional tobacco control networks. Consequently, regional networks have emerged and expanded in all developing regions but MENA.

The activities of this network since the 1970s contributed to change (modestly) the behaviour of developing countries in tobacco control, mainly through learning and persuasion. Actors and NGOs from developed countries engaged in activities to diffuse knowledge about tobacco use and control and mobilise domestic and regional actors. In the 1980s and 1990s, these actors fought against the TTCs' efforts to penetrate markets in the developing world (for example, see Chitanondh, 2001 on Thailand) and have continued to campaign for the 'denormalisation' of the tobacco industry. The activities of the international tobacco control network have intensified since the 1990s, elevating awareness of tobacco use and control, and promoting an increase in the number of countries with a policy or programme on tobacco control (Shafey et al, 2009; WHO, 2008). While it is difficult to measure the policy impact of the international tobacco control network in developing countries as a whole, it certainly played an important role in the development of national tobacco laws in countries, such as Argentina and Nigeria.

Overall, the nature of domestic tobacco policy networks is relatively difficult to determine. We can say with relative certainty that there is no equivalent to the shift of power from pro- to anti-tobacco interests in developing countries as observed in developed countries. Rather, anti-tobacco groups fare well on the international stage, fostering the FCTC and encouraging developing countries to sign up to its agenda. The next stage is for those countries to translate a broad commitment into concrete domestic policies. It is too soon to tell if the tobacco control agenda in developing countries will be reflected in a more prominent role for public health groups.

Socioeconomic factors

Economic benefits of tobacco

The economic value of tobacco relates to tobacco leaf production, the value of TTCs to government, and the value of tobacco taxation and employment. Although we do not have reliable data for the latter, we can certainly say that the most tobacco dependent countries in the developing world are Malawi and Zimbabwe (Jha, 1999; FAO, 2003). Developing countries have emerged rapidly as major tobacco leaf producers in the world and, since the 1960s, global tobacco leaf production has become concentrated in the developing world (Chapman and Fahey, 1989; FAO, 2003; WHO, 2004; World Bank, 2003). Their share of world tobacco production increased from 53% in 1962–1964 to 69% in 1985–1987, mainly due to increased production in places, such as Bangladesh, Brazil, China, India, Indonesia, South Korea, and Thailand (WHO, 1991). Between 1971 and 1997 China's share of global production increased from 17% to 47% (FAO, 2003), emerging as the second largest tobacco exporter behind Brazil. In spite of this growing concentration of tobacco production in developing countries, it generally contributes to less than 5% of export revenues of most countries in the developing world (except Malawi and Zimbabwe) (Jha, 1999). For example, although Brazil and India are among the top five tobacco leaf exporters in the world, such exports constituted 2.55% and 0.44% respectively in 1995 (Jha, 1999).

The resources of the TTCs have often represented a source of attraction for many governments seeking development, especially in the 1960s and 1970s. This value has allowed TTCs to penetrate developing countries through legitimate means, such as the establishment of new manufacturing plants, acquisition of state monopolies, and joint ventures. However, a widespread allegation in the tobacco control literature is that they are also linked strongly to the illicit trade (counterfeiting and smuggling) of tobacco (Aguinaga and Shatenstein, 2002; Collin et al, 2004; Gilmore and McKee, 2004; LeGresley et al, 2008; O'Sullivan and Chapman, 2000; Shafey et al, 2009; WHO-EMRO, 2004; Chitanondh, 2001; US Department of Health and Human Services, 1992; Holden, 2010).

Usually referred to as 'Duty Not Paid (DNP)' or 'in transit' goods, the illicit trade in tobacco products makes international cigarette brands available to local populations at cheaper prices. In 2005, the estimated volume of cigarettes smuggled in Asia was 275 billion (9% of market share), in Africa and the Middle East it was 62 billion (15% of market share), and in LAC it was 59 billion (20% of market share) (Shafey et al, 2009). In 2007, six of the top ten countries with the greatest illicit trade in cigarettes in the world were from these developing regions (Joossens et al, 2009). In low- and middle-income countries, the market share of illicit cigarettes has been estimated to be 16.8% and 11.8% respectively; representing an estimated 657 billion cigarettes and US$40.5 billion in lost government revenue annually (Joossens et al, 2009). This illicit tobacco trade undermines tobacco control and is linked to criminal organisations and money laundering (Guevara, 2008; International Consortium of Investigative Journalists, 2001; WHO-EMRO, 2004). It is also a trade that single countries struggle to control, prompting the FCTC Intergovernmental Negotiating Body to begin negotiation of a protocol in 2008.

Smoking prevalence

Total smoking prevalence in developing countries (Tables 8.2; 1.1) could be deceptive due to the gender gap and paucity of data, particularly on the use of other tobacco products (not cigarettes). The existing data, however, suggest that whereas total and per capita consumption decreased in developed countries between 1970 and 2000, it generally increased in developing ones (except in few countries, such as South Africa, Thailand, Uruguay,

Table 8.2 Prevalence of Tobacco Use for Adults (15+)

WHO Region	Male	Female
Africa	7.3	2.8
Americas	30.1	18.7
Eastern Mediterranean	32.7	4.5
Europe	44.4	23.2
South East Asia	39.1	4.6
Western Pacific	55.7	5.0
Income Group		
Low income	30.1	4.0
Lower middle income	51.7	4.6
Upper middle income	44.4	18.3
High income	33.3	21.4
Global	**38.7**	**17.4**

Source: WHO, 2008

Venezuela, and others in LAC in 1980s) (Guindon and Boisclair, 2003; USDHHS, 1992). The total volume of tobacco consumption worldwide increased from 4.2 to 7.4 million tons within the period, 70% of which was in developing countries (FAO, 2003; Guindon and Boisclair, 2003). The largest increase occurred in China, where the volume increased from 100 billion in the early 1950s to 1,800 billion by the late 1990s (Liu et al, 1998; Niu et al, 1998). Per capita adult cigarette consumption in China also increased by 46% (Guindon and Boisclair, 2003). The general annual rate of increase was 3.1%, but 4.4% and 3.3% in the fast-growing economies of China and India respectively (FAO, 2003). As a result, the UN Food and Agricultural Organisation (FAO) projected in 2003 that this trend would continue through 2010 due to factors including population growth, urbanisation, and increasing incomes (FAO, 2003). Consistent with this projection, the total volume of cigarettes exported to developing countries (excluding China and duty-free cigarettes) increased from 2,017 in 2004 to 2,172 billion units in 2008, but those to developed countries (excluding the US and duty-free) declined from 1,297 to 1,170 billion units (Camilleri and Morgan Stanley, 2009). As a result, tobacco-induced morbidities, such as cancer (previously a developed world phenomenon) have emerged across developing countries (Guindon and Boisclair, 2003).

To some extent, this rise can be linked to the marketing and promotional activities of the TTCs. Upon entering markets in developing countries, TTCs use sophisticated marketing, advertising, and promotional strategies to encourage tobacco use (White, 1997). As a result, unlike the mostly inefficient state monopolies, tobacco consumption increases whenever the TTCs enter any developing country, which was certainly the case when the TTCs entered Asian countries in the 1980s (Chaloupka and Laixuthai, 1996; Mendelowitz, 1990).

Public opinion

Chapter 3 suggests that comprehensive polls on tobacco control have not been taken until recently and that the results vary according to the measures used. Public opinion is also difficult to gauge in some parts of developing regions because levels of education and the literacy rate vary. However, people with some form of education are aware of the health effects of tobacco use and exposure to SHS, and the majority of smokers and non-smokers support tobacco control (CDC, 2009; Environics Research Group Limited, 2001; Laforge et al, 1998; RTI International and Harris Interactive, 2009; Warren et al, 2009). For example, to gauge the support for the FCTC, the WHO and Environics conducted a survey between November 2000 and January 2001 in Argentina, India, and Nigeria, and the results show an overwhelming support for tobacco control (Table 8.3).

Table 8.3 Public Support for Tobacco Control (%), 2001

Policy Instruments	Argentina	India	Nigeria
Ban on Advertising and promotion of tobacco products	89	97	83
Health Warning messages on tobacco products	93	98	88
Control of Smuggling	92	99	88
Monitor and regulate ingredients in tobacco products	96	98	82
Restrictions on smoking	94	98	79
The Framework Convention on Tobacco Control	93	99	81

Source: Environics Research Group Limited, Toronto, Ontario, Canada

Additionally, in the Global Youth Tobacco Survey conducted between 1999 and 2007, the weighted average of support for a ban on smoking in public places was 72% in AP (84 survey sites, 24 countries); 82% in LAC (127, 31); 79% in MENA (33, 17); and 59% in SSA (47, 29) (CDC, 2011). In 2006, over 80% of the Uruguayan public supported its 100% smoke-free law, the first in the LAC (WHO, 2008). Even in China where a (poorly enforced) smoke-free policy has only just been introduced (2011), over 90% of people living in large cities support a ban on smoking in public transport, schools and hospitals (WHO, 2008; Ministry of Health, People's Republic of China, 2007).

This popular support for tobacco control has not been translated into policies and programmes (Shafey et al, 2009; WHO, 2008; Burstein, 2003;

Lau and Schlesinger, 2005). Rather, policy still represents an unsettled battleground: the tobacco control network has used educational awareness and campaign programmes to help people quit tobacco use and support control measures, while the tobacco network has used strategies, including challenging scientific evidence and social acceptability programmes, to keep people smoking and influence non-smokers to accept smoking as part of the fabric of society (BAT, 1980; Global Smokefree Partnership, 2009). Earlier, of course, these strategies had been successful in developed countries, such as the US (Brandt, 2007). The increasing favourability of support for tobacco control in developing countries suggests that the tobacco control network has had some success in this contest but has been unable to close the gap between the generally favourable opinion on tobacco control and the development of policies and programmes. As in our discussion of a 'permissive consensus' in other countries, public opinion alone is not enough to ensure tobacco control policy development.

The role of ideas: Scientific knowledge

As Chapter 3 suggests, although the direct links between tobacco use and illness are now widely accepted, the gap between knowledge and policy action is widest in developing regions. To some extent this is because TTCs still have some success in challenging the evidence, prompting developed and developing countries to collaborate to ensure the effective dissemination of scientific knowledge. Governmental institutions and agencies in developed countries have collaborated with governments in developing countries to promote tobacco control through different procedures, beginning with workshops and seminars in the 1980s (WHO Expert Committee, 1983), a process that has intensified since the 1990s. In this respect, the US Center for Diseases Control and Prevention (CDC), through region-wide programmes, has been a major force in LAC (USDHHS, 1992).

The most relevant part of these collaborations is research. The general paucity of data in developing countries has prompted government agencies, NGOs, and foundations to provide support for tobacco control research. Government agencies, such as the CDC, the Canadian International Development and Research Center and the Swedish International Development Agency have been helping developing countries to build a domestic knowledge-base for tobacco control. In 1999 the CDC collaborated with the WHO and other governmental and non-governmental organisations in Canada, UK, and the US to launch the Global Tobacco Surveillance System in order to systematise tobacco use and control data. As a result, tobacco control research, which was virtually non-existent in the 1970s, has proliferated throughout these developing regions over the past decade. Between 1999 and 2008, the Global Youth Tobacco Survey, for example, was conducted in 162 sites throughout these four regions – AP (44), LAC (58), MENA (22) and SSA (38) (Warren et al,

2009). In 2006, a total of 165 tobacco control research projects funded by developed country-based organisations were carried out throughout countries in these four regions (Mackay et al, 2006; Shafey et al, 2009). They supplement the research evidence which demonstrates that tobacco use has a negative impact on economic development, the standard of living and the environment.

The intensification of these research efforts over the past decade has made local evidence on tobacco use and control increasingly available to policymakers, contributing to the rise of public health as the frame for policy choice. While this research continues to arm individuals, organisations and policymakers with the necessary evidence for policy development, it is still hard to gauge its impact on policy.

The transfer of ideas

Consequently, organisations have also sought more direct action: the transfer of policy solutions and ideas. During the 1970s, individuals (Horn and Fletcher, 1970; Muller, 1978; Wickstrom, 1979) and NGOs (World Development Movement, 1981) in developed countries became increasingly concerned with the expansion of activities of the TTCs in developing countries and began to write, campaign and mobilise domestic and international forces against it. Daniel Horn, Director of the National Clearinghouse on Smoking in the US, and Charles Fletcher, Secretary of the Royal College of Physicians in the UK, wrote in 1970, 'In developing countries, where cigarette smoking is rapidly taking hold, measures are needed to arrest the growth of the habit and thus to prevent the increasing premature deaths and disablement it would inevitably cause' (Horn and Fletcher, 1970). This assertion is consistent with the World Development Movement's (1981) briefing document, written to persuade UK policymakers to oppose the expansion of the TTCs (World Development Movement, 1981).

The World Health Assembly adopted its first resolution relating to tobacco control in developing countries in 1978, because it was 'seriously concerned at the alarming increase in production and consumption of cigarettes during the last two decades in some of the countries, particularly developing countries, in which it was previously not widespread' (WHO, 1978). This culminated in the 1983 WHO Expert Committee on Smoking Controls in Developing Countries (WHO Expert Committee, 1983). However, the process of diffusion through transfer and learning to developing countries was not uniform; domestic political and societal dynamics mediated the influence of these transnational effects on the policy process, accounting for the wide variations in tobacco control (Mitchell, 1991; Shafey et al, 2009; WHO, 2008). Whereas the vast majority of developing countries were passive policy recipients, others, including Brazil, India, Singapore, South Africa, and Thailand, were active in receiving, seeking, and developing policies.

Prior to the FCTC, transfer and learning took place through the resolutions of the World Health Assembly and the UN Economic and Social Council (ECOSOC). Since 1970 the World Health Assembly has adopted resolutions on tobacco use and control, as did ECOSOC from 1993, when the UN created the Focal Point, a system-wide tobacco control programme that became the Ad Hoc Interagency Task Force on Tobacco Control in 1999. Although these resolutions were mainly 'soft laws' (i.e. not backed up with a way to oblige implementation – Abbott and Snidal, 2000; Taylor and Roemer, 1996), developing countries' involvement in these processes made them familiar with the underlying scientific evidence and arguments. As these resolutions accumulated over the decades, developing countries became more interested in tobacco control, particularly in areas of health education and warning labels (Shafey et al, 2003, 2009; WHO, 1997, 2008).

As Chapter 9 discusses, the ultimate source of policy transfer is now the FCTC (Albuja and Daynard, 2009; Eriksen and Cerak, 2008; Fong et al, 2006; Mamudu and Glantz, 2009; Sussman et al, 2007; Wipfli et al, 2010) which places specific obligations on parties in a manner that *may* constitute 'hard law' (Abbott and Snidal, 2000; Taylor and Roemer, 1996). All parties are under obligation to translate the FCTC into domestic laws. The FCTC processes have had a significant impact on developing countries because the country delegates became more informed about tobacco use and control. Moreover, the FCTC ratification processes at the country level elevated the profile of tobacco control through the involvement of both governmental and non-governmental actors as well as the media and international attention. However, the issue now is the translation of the FCTC into specific policies. As of September 2011, only a handful of countries, including Argentina and Uruguay (LAC), Lebanon (MENA) and Kenya and Nigeria (SSA) have enacted specific domestic tobacco control laws since the FCTC became international law in 2005 even though almost all developing countries have ratified it (Shafey et al, 2009; WHO, 2008; Griffith et al, 2008). This lag in the translation of the FCTC into specific domestic policies is, in large part, due to the influence of the tobacco industry and the persistence of the political economy frame of policy choice throughout the developing world.

Conclusion

Tobacco control policy was almost non-existent in developing regions until the 1970s, with only a small number of countries, such as Brazil, India, South Africa and Thailand displaying a serious commitment to tobacco control (Assunta, 2004; Feldman and Bayer, 2004). This picture began to change from the 1990s, and by 2009 there was a range of policy instruments in place in each region, with a few becoming policy innovators in areas, such as health warnings and smoke-free policies. As of September 2011, almost all developing countries have signed and ratified the FCTC. However, the future remains relatively uncertain because most developing countries do not have an established domestic structure and capacity within which to promote and sustain tobacco control. Rather, tobacco control has become globalised, with most developing countries importing policy instruments associated with the FCTC. In this regard, while there is general awareness of policies to control the use and spread of tobacco, domestic legislation is yet to be produced (WHO, 2008; Griffith et al, 2008). Indeed, tobacco control in developing countries has generally become a proxy contest between the tobacco industry and transnational actors seeking to thwart the use and spread of tobacco.

These developments can be analysed in the same way as in other chapters, with a focus on the five main factors to explain why policy has been slow to develop and how it has changed as the global agenda has developed. Over the past 50 years, while the institutions for policy development in many developing countries have varied and been unstable, the Ministry of Health has generally been a key player in tobacco control within most countries. Although its voice is often crowded out domestically by other departments, such as agriculture, finance and trade, it has proved to be a key link to international institutions, particularly when backed up by strong political leadership. International organisations, such as the WHO have also supplemented its power. Particularly since the 1980s, the WHO worked through its regional offices and country representatives to promote tobacco control, often in collaboration with other intergovernmental organisation, the Ministry of Health, and international NGOs.

Central to the proxy contest between transnational actors over the past 50 years has been the frame for policy choice: political economy promoted by the TTCs versus public health promoted by international governmental and non-governmental organisations. The TTCs have tried to focus attention on tobacco's economic benefits, but international health groups have focused attention on the ill-health produced by tobacco use. International efforts, spearheaded by the WHO, helped to diffuse knowledge on tobacco use and control, and to contribute to changing frames. At the non-governmental level, the international tobacco control network led the spread of knowledge and ideas on tobacco use and control to developing countries, particularly in the 1970s and 1980s using seminars and workshops, informational and awareness campaigns, and mobilisation of domestic groups. These activities incrementally shaped the behavior of developing countries in tobacco control through persuasion and learning, and contributed to the continuous shift to public health as frame for policy choices.

Unlike in developed countries, this change in problem definition has not gone hand in hand with a shift in the balance of power from pro- to anti-tobacco groups. TTCs have cultivated allies at multiple levels of government to protect their main activities in developing countries – penetration and consolidation of markets, marketing and promoting tobacco use, and undermining tobacco control policy development. There is also a relatively small number of domestic groups devoted to tobacco control and they rely on the efforts (and financing) of international NGOs to supplement their power. However, the group-government system may be becoming more open and competitive in many countries, with TTCs challenged increasingly by public health, and anti-smoking groups disseminating knowledge on the negative effects of tobacco. The international tobacco control network has liaised with emerging domestic NGOs and regional NGO coalitions and alliances to promote tobacco control. The unresolved issue is that these NGOs are mostly dependent on international support, which raises concerns over their long-term viability.

The socioeconomic context is less conducive to tobacco control: while the majority of the population may support tobacco control, there are still low levels of awareness of the health effects of tobacco use and SHS. Smoking prevalence is still high among men and increasing among women, reflecting the movement of TTCs into new markets and their successful promotion of smoking. The tobacco industry is still often considered to be an asset in many countries. This situation is compounded by the continuous efforts of the TTCs to make tobacco use appealing to segments of the population in developing countries and shaping the image of the tobacco industry as socially responsible. On the contrary, domestic and international NGOs have sought to 'denormalise' both tobacco use and the industry. In this regard, another transnational proxy contest in developing countries has been about shaping the public image of tobacco use and the image of the tobacco industry.

Finally, the role of ideas is distinctive. Developing country governments are increasingly armed with scientific knowledge on the negative health and economic effects of smoking, but this has not led to equivalent policy change. Indeed, policy movement is largely based on the perceived need to transfer policy; to supplement developing country efforts with an international response to counter the power of the tobacco industry. In this respect, scientific knowledge for tobacco control policy development across developing countries generally has international origins. Since the early 2000s, governmental and private sector support from developed countries started to generate domestic research on tobacco use and control, gradually supplementing international information. These domestic efforts are still relatively insignificant as sources of policy change.

In sum, international effects have been salient in tobacco control policy development in developing countries, but their impacts are mediated by domestic political and societal dynamics. The ultimate influence on tobacco control in developing countries was the development of the FCTC and the subsequent Intergovernmental Negotiating Body and the Conference of the Parties processes that has put tobacco control high on their institutional agenda. However, more research is required to gauge the long-term effects (building on country-specific case studies such as those on China (Hu, 2008) and Ecuador (Albuja and Daynard, 2009)). While we can say with increasing confidence that the tobacco problem is on its way to being 'solved' in many developed countries (i.e. governments are now committed to comprehensive tobacco control), there is still a pressing and growing problem in developing countries. Of particular concern is that there is still generally a low number and density of policies and programmes that could prevent these countries from progressing to higher levels of the tobacco epidemic. This situation persists despite developing countries' participation in the FCTC, increasing awareness of the effects of tobacco use and control, and public support for tobacco control. Closing this gap will require translation of the FCTC into specific domestic policies and increased and sustained tobacco control activities domestically and regionally.

9

The WHO Framework Convention on Tobacco Control (FCTC)

In May 2003, the 192 members of the World Health Assembly, the decision-making body of the World Health Organisation, unanimously adopted the Framework Convention on Tobacco Control (FCTC) (WHO, 2003). The WHO (2010) describes it as a 'milestone for the promotion of public health' and 'one of the most widely embraced treaties in UN history'. It marks the first time that the WHO has used its powers under Article 19 of its Constitution to develop an international public health treaty (WHO, 2006). As of September 2011, it had 174 'parties' (see note 9).

The FCTC effectively represents global tobacco control (GTC) policy and, if implemented, provides the potential to mark a radical shift of policy in many (mostly developing) countries. It contains provisions regarding smoke-free environments, package labelling, bans on sales to minors, advertising bans, tax increases, and finding alternatives sources of livelihood for people dependent on tobacco production. These provisions represent a combination of best practices based on current evidence, largely from developed countries (Shibuya et al, 2003), and negotiations to determine what could be agreed among the participants. In other words, it may not match the strength of some of the most comprehensive tobacco control programmes that we identify in some chapters, but it goes well beyond the provisions in most developing countries (and many developed countries).

We can describe and explain this movement towards global tobacco control policy using a modified discussion of the five main explanatory factors in public policy. Our discussion of institutions refers not only to the role of international organisations, such as the WHO, but also the 'institutionalisation' of global tobacco control using the FCTC as a template for a new form of 'global governance'. The processes resemble domestic shifts towards the centrality of the Department of Health. First, the WHO replaced the UN and World Bank as the main tobacco policy actor. Then, its role expanded as the issue rose on the international agenda. When we discuss the agenda-setting context for policy choices we highlight, first, the time it took for the tobacco problem to rise on the international agenda and, second, the role of the FCTC as the provider of a new frame of reference – particularly for countries that have traditionally paid little attention to tobacco and have limited tobacco controls.

Our discussion of policy networks highlights a profound imbalance of power at the WHO level (where public health interests are almost exclusively represented, at the expense of tobacco interests) which acts as a means to redress the lack of public health influence in the domestic policy networks of many countries. Our discussion of the socioeconomic context highlights the WHO's increasing role in highlighting and addressing the costs of tobacco, as well as the evidence of international public opinion on tobacco control. Finally, we discuss two aspects of the role of ideas. First, the FCTC process lagged behind the production of the evidence on smoking and second-hand smoke (SHS). Second, however, its initiation has marked the beginning of one of the most significant global tobacco control policy diffusion projects ever. Its role is to bridge that gap between the identification of the problem and the policy response.

What is FCTC policy?

The FCTC is driven by a 'comprehensive' approach to tobacco control. It is based on two main ideas: (1) that tobacco use and control is a multifaceted issue and transnational in scope; and, (2) that controlling the use and spread of tobacco requires a combination of certain policies and programmes. For example, the 1986 World Health Assembly resolution outlined a nine-point strategy, including smoke-free environments, protection of children from smoking, health warnings, and public education for states to implement (WHO, 1986b). By the time the FCTC negotiations started in 1999, the WHO had gathered extensive evidence on the effectiveness of elements of this comprehensive approach, particularly taxes, smoke-free environments, advertising bans, health warnings, public education, bans on sale to minors, and cessation programmes (WHO, 1997; Laugesen, 2000; Shibuya et al, 2003; WHO, 2003). The four-year production of the FCTC by governments was based on this agenda, with negotiations to determine the strength of the policy instruments that signatories would be expected to introduce.

The FCTC is a composite of demand- and supply-side measures to reduce the use and spread of tobacco (WHO, 2003). The core demand reduction provisions are contained in Articles 6–14 which outline price and tax measures and non-price measures, while Articles 15–17 set out the core supply reduction provisions. Overall, the strategy addresses:

- Price and tax measures to reduce demand
- Demand reduction measures concerning tobacco dependence and cessation

- Protection from exposure to tobacco smoke
- Regulation of the contents of tobacco products
- Regulation of tobacco product disclosures (regarding ingredients)
- Packaging and labelling of tobacco products
- Education, communication, training and public awareness
- Tobacco advertising, promotion and sponsorship
- Illicit trade in tobacco products
- Sales to and by minors
- Provision of support for economically viable alternative activities.

A novel feature of the Convention is the inclusion of a provision that addresses liability, encouraging countries to cooperate in their efforts to take legal action against tobacco companies and other actors. Further, mechanisms for scientific and technical cooperation and exchange of information are set out in Articles 20–22. These provisions are supplemented with protocols and guidelines negotiated by the parties. Thus, as of September 2011, there were ongoing negotiations on illicit trade protocols and seven guidelines have been developed (Articles 5.3: Protection of public health policies with respect to tobacco control from commercial and other vested interests of the tobacco industry; 8: Protection from exposure to tobacco smoke; 9 and 10: Regulations of the contents of tobacco product and tobacco products disclosures; 11: Packaging and labelling of tobacco products; 12: Education, communication, training and public awareness; 13: Tobacco advertising, promotion and sponsorship; and 14: Demand reduction measures concerning tobacco dependence and cessation).

Overall, the FCTC seems to represent a major transformation in global tobacco control policy, at least in terms of policy *choices*, particularly for (mostly developing) countries with lagged tobacco control. Between 1970, when the WHO first became involved in tobacco control, and 2003, when the FCTC was adopted, the World Health Assembly used resolutions to encourage member states to adopt and implement recommended tobacco control policies – but they were mostly ignored. Similarly, the UN, under the focal point arrangement, used relatively ineffective resolutions through the Economic and Social Council to encourage tobacco control in member states. In comparison, the FCTC seems relatively strong. It contains obligatory provisions, such as Article 11 that place specific requirements on parties, as well as other voluntary measures that parties are effectively obliged to adopt when they sign the treaty. The FCTC, for the first time, institutionalises global tobacco control through bodies, such as the Convention Secretariat, located in WHO, and the Conference of the Parties (Figure 9.1). It there-fore seems to represent a policy backed up by greater levers to ensure implementation. That said, the FCTC does not entail any enforcement mechanism beyond shaming, and compliance is still up to the goodwill of parties. In effect, the long-term evidence will tell us how strong the FCTC is.

Table 9.1 Timeline for the Framework Convention on Tobacco Control (FCTC)

Year	Activities
1992	Allyn Taylor, a professor at University of Maryland in the US, published a paper on WHO constitutional powers to use legal instruments to achieve tobacco control (Taylor, 1992)
1994	World Conference on Tobacco or Health adopted a resolution to global tobacco control, an International Strategy for Tobacco Control, engineered by academic researchers
1995	Resolution WHA48.11, An International Strategy for Tobacco Control. The World Health Assembly adopted a resolution for FCTC feasibility studies
1996	Resolution EB97.R8, An International Framework for Tobacco Control
	Resolution WHA49.16, Tobacco or Health Program; Resolution WHA49.17, an International Strategy for Tobacco Control
1997	In June, representatives of Canada, Finland, France, Switzerland, Thailand and the United States met in Halifax, Novo Scotia, Canada to begin making preparation for the development of the FCTC
1998	Gro Harlem Brundtland elected the Director-General of WHO, and she made FCTC a priority of the organization
	The WHO Tobacco or Health programme was reconstituted as the Tobacco Free Initiative
	In December, public health experts met in Vancouver, British Colombia, Canada, and developed a plan for the FCTC
1999	Resolution EB103.R11 – Towards a WHO Framework Convention on Tobacco Control WHO collaborated with World Bank to publish *Curbing the Epidemic: Governments and Economics of Tobacco Control*, which was used as economic justification for the FCTC The first meeting of the Intergovernmental Working Group began drafting the elements of the FCTC Resolution WHA52.18, Towards a WHO Framework Convention on Tobacco Control. WHA approved negotiation of the FCTC
1999	International Policy Conference on Children and Tobacco, Washington, D.C., USA International meeting on economic, social and health issues in tobacco control, Kobe, Japan

Table 9.1 Timeline for the Framework Convention on Tobacco Control (FCTC) – *continued*

Year	Activities
2000	WHO's Tobacco Free Initiative (TFI) and the Norwegian Ministry of Health organized International Conference on Advancing Knowledge on Regulating Tobacco Products The New Delhi, India, conference on Global Tobacco Control Law: Towards a WHO Framework Convention on Tobacco Control The Intergovernmental Working Group completed the draft FCTC First meeting of the Intergovernmental Negotiating Body started the negotiation of the text for the FCTC Framework Convention Alliance formed
2001	Amman, Jordan, Consultation on litigation and public inquiries as tools for tobacco control Geneva, Switzerland, WHO Consultation on Potential Liability and Compensation Provision for the WHO FCTC
2002	Illicit Trade on Tobacco Conference was held in New York, USA
2003	The final and 6th meeting of the Intergovernmental Negotiating Body completed the FCTC text The WHO Member States unanimously adopted FCTC
2005	FCTC became international law after 40 countries signed
2006	First meeting of the FCTC Conference of Parties in Geneva, Switzerland
2008	First and second sessions of the Intergovernmental Negotiating Body on a Protocol on Illicit Trade in Tobacco Products

Institutions: Who has responsibility for tobacco control?

(1) International organisations

International organisations often develop autonomous identities, independent of the constituent parts or the membership (Cook, 1996; March and Olson, 1984) which, in turn, help to shape the interests and identities of the parts (Wendt, 1987). In this section, we discuss the changes within the WHO, and the general UN system, that facilitated collective action among states. The most significant point to note is that, while the WHO (the UN's public health arm) has always been driven by public health concerns, many parts of the UN were more closely aligned to pro-tobacco interests and often adhered to a political economy understanding of tobacco.

The World Health Organisation

The WHO was created by states in 1947 and made responsible for global health issues (WHO, 2006). As such, the underlying frame for all WHO activities is public health. Its role has changed from a producer of scientific information in the 1970s, to an agent for tobacco control from the 1980s to the mid-1990s, and a facilitator for collective action in tobacco control between the mid-1990s and 2003 when the FCTC was adopted.

The WHO has been concerned with cancer-related issues at least since the 1960s, but its role in tobacco control was formalised by the 1970 World Health Assembly resolution (WHO, 1970b). The two key policy concerns of this resolution were youth smoking and the need to find crop substitution for tobacco producing countries. The World Health Assembly passed three additional tobacco control resolutions in the 1970s, the essence of which were to encourage states to develop policies and programmes and for other UN agencies to conduct more investigations and to collaborate on tobacco-related issues. The WHO role was to gather evidence. It created an expert committee to examine the scientific evidence on tobacco use in 1974, conducted a survey on legislative actions on tobacco around the world in 1976, and created a further expert committee to study tobacco control in 1978 (WHO, 1975, 1976, 1979).

The WHO's role expanded throughout the 1970s, reflecting the accumulating scientific evidence on tobacco use and control, and increasing concern about the spread of tobacco worldwide, especially to developing countries where tobacco use had been minimal. These activities became formalised in 1980 under the Tobacco or Health programme (WHO, 1980b, 1985, 1988c, 1992b). The most marked change in the WHO's role occurred in 1986 when the World Health Assembly, while outlining nine specific policy recommendations for member states, mandated the WHO to take the 'global public health approach and action to combat the tobacco pandemic' because 'the use of tobacco in all its forms is incompatible with the attainment of [the 1978 Alma Alta Declaration of] health for all by the year 2000' (WHO, 1986b). The WHO subsequently established an Advisory Group on the WHO Global Action Plan on Tobacco or Health in March 1988 (WHO, 1988b, 1988d). The work of this group led to a 1988–1995 Plan, which the World Health Assembly adopted in 1989 (WHO, 1988e, 1989). The WHO had three broad roles under this plan: promote the development of national policies and programmes; advocate for tobacco-free societies and the non-use of tobacco; and serve as a clearinghouse for the scientific information on tobacco use and control (WHO, 1988e). The 1986 resolution, together with four others in the 1980s, helped the WHO to develop a unique identity in tobacco control. It became a key conduit for the dissemination of knowledge and ideas on tobacco use and control, and an advocate for states' actions instead of a passive policy broker (WHO, 1985, 1988c, 1996a, 1996b).

The WHO's role was enhanced further by the World Health Assembly resolution of 1990 that called on member states to implement the multi-sectoral comprehensive tobacco control strategies contained in the 1986 resolution (WHO, 1986b, 1990b). In 1992, the World Health Assembly adopted a resolution to reinforce the shift from actions by individual member states to this multi-sectoral collaboration among governments, UN agencies, and NGOs (WHO, 1992a). In effect, the idea to develop an international treaty on tobacco control emerged in the early 1990s, and the WHO had already evolved to a point where member states were more receptive to it (Mackay, 2003; Mamudu, 2008; Roemer et al, 2005). As such, there was little contention over the WHA48.11 resolution of 1995 that initiated the development of the FCTC (WHO, 1995b). It made the WHO, as the body responsible for the development of the FCTC, a facilitator of global collective action.

The United Nations

The UN inter-agency collaboration on tobacco use and control can be traced to the first UN inter-agency consultation on tobacco control in 1981, when the agencies within the UN system approved the WHO work in tobacco control (WHO, 1981, 1983). Until the early 1990s, the UN was not directly involved in global tobacco control even though several agencies had been collaborating with the WHO on tobacco-related issues since the 1970s (WHO, 1985, 1996a). Before the early 1990s, inter-agency collaboration within the UN focused particularly on collaboration with the Food and Agricultural Organisation (FAO) on issues of crop diversification by tobacco-dependent countries instead of tobacco control, suggesting that the UN was more concerned with the political economy impact of tobacco control than public health. However, in the WHO's effort to implement the idea of multi-sectoral collaboration on tobacco-related issues among UN agencies in the early 1990s, the Director-General requested that the UN Secretary-General put the issue on the Economic and Social Council (ECOSOC) 1993 meeting agenda, which he did (WHO, 1992a, 1992b). Subsequently, based on the 1992 World Health

Assembly resolution (WHO, 1992a), the ECOSOC adopted resolution E/1993/79 in 1993, requesting the Secretary-General to seek full collaboration of UN agencies in the implementation of effective comprehensive strategies for tobacco control (ECOSOC, 1993a, 1993b). This made tobacco control part of the UN agenda. The resolution created a UN Focal Point (a UN tobacco control programme located within the UN Conference on Trade and Development), to coordinate tobacco-related activities and requested the Secretary-General to periodically report to ECOSOC on its progress. The creation of the Focal Point institutionalised the UN's direct role in global tobacco control.

Between 1993 and 1999, political economy concerns remained a dominant frame of policy choice within the UN; thus very little contribution was made to the Focal Point. Indeed, tobacco interests within the UN dominated the Focal Point and drove its activities on tobacco use and control. This situation changed when WHO Director-General, Gro Harlem Brundtland (below), worked with the UN Secretary-General Kofi Annan, to transfer the UN tobacco control programme under the Focal Point to the WHO. This move was fiercely resisted by tobacco interests within the UN, including countries, such as Malawi (Otanez et al, 2009), mainly due to concerns that public health would eventually dominate the UN decision making processes on tobacco-related issues. After the transfer of the UN tobacco control programme to the WHO in 1999, it was reconstituted as the Ad Hoc Interagency Task Force for Tobacco Control, making public health concerns the drivers of its decisions. Since the late 1990s, this Task Force has become an organisation devoted to global tobacco control, facilitating cooperation and collaboration among UN agencies on tobacco-related issues, including the FCTC (Figure 9.1).

Figure 9.1 Structure of Global Governance in Tobacco Control

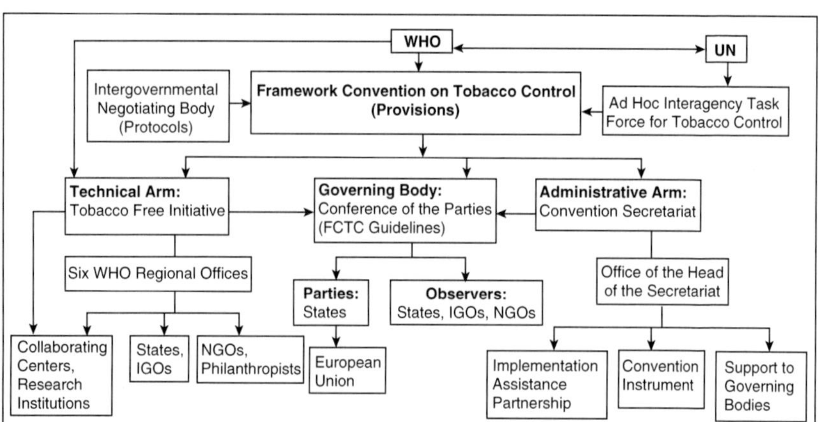

The IARC and World Bank

The WHO has also worked closely with intergovernmental organisations, including the International Agency for Research in Cancer (IARC) and World Bank, particularly on the production of knowledge (see Table 9.2). From the 1980s, the WHO collaborated with IARC on research into tobacco use and produced monographs on tobacco smoking in 1986 (IARC, 1986) and SHS in 2002 (IARC, 2002). The World Bank is another organisation that once supported the tobacco industry but reversed its position in 1991/92 (Mamudu et al, 2008b; Ramin, 2006). The WHO has been collaborating with the World Bank on tobacco-related issues, such as crop substitution since the 1970s. However, their most notable partnership relates to their work on the economics of tobacco and tobacco control in the 1990s that culminated in the 1999 World Bank publication *Curbing the Epidemic* (Jha and Chaloupka, 1999). The WHO used the 1986 IARC to help develop its 1988–1995 Action Plan for the Tobacco or Health programme (WHO, 1988e), then used *Curbing the Epidemic* to mobilise support for the FCTC (Mamudu and Studlar, 2009; Yach, 1999; Mamudu and Glantz, 2009).

(2) The institutionalisation of global tobacco control

While the FCTC does not constitute a 'global government', it has institutionalised norms on tobacco control and fostered collaboration and cooperation among governmental and non-governmental actors who seek to encourage common practices and goals (Commission on Global Governance, 1995; Gordenker and Weiss, 1996; Krahman, 2003). For this reason, the FCTC can usefully be described as a form of 'global governance'; a collection of rules, norms, policies and regulations that structure public and private behaviour across national boundaries (Krahman, 2003). It represents the institutionalisation of efforts to regulate the worldwide use and spread of tobacco and discourage the export of the tobacco epidemic to low- and medium-income countries that in many cases still have a low smoking prevalence rate (WHO, 2008). Over time, the relationship between the WHO and member states has changed, with the former increasingly taking centre stage and exhorting individual countries to follow its agenda.

Between the 1970s and 1995 (when the World Health Assembly initiated the development of the FCTC) states (countries) were at the centre of governance in global tobacco control even as the WHO became expansively involved in it. Major decisions occurred primarily at the national level and, to some extent, the regional level (at least in the EU), with the WHO restricted to 'soft law' resolutions (commitments by World Health Assembly member states that are not legally binding) which were used to facilitate policy developments and governmental and non-governmental cooperation and collaboration. By the mid-1990s, widespread acceptance of the idea that no one country can single-handedly deal with the tobacco problem led to the search for an alternative form of governance. This acceptance was based on a 'cascading' of events: the accumulation of scientific knowledge on tobacco use, exposure to SHS and economics of tobacco and tobacco control; increasing awareness that tobacco use and control is a transnational issue; and, changes in the tobacco policies of organisations, such as the World Bank (Lopez et al, 1994; Peto et al, 1994; Mamudu, 2008; Roemer et al, 2005; TFI, 1999b). Unlike similar suggestions in the 1970s that did not gain traction (Derek Yach, Personal Communication, March 17, 2008), proponents in the 1990s succeeded in pushing the idea of global governance through governmental and non-governmental circles, which resulted in the initiation of the development of the FCTC.

Between 1995 and 1999, when the FCTC negotiations started, the choice of the appropriate form of governance was a subject of intense discussion among legal and public health experts (WHO, 1997; Roemer and Taylor, 1996; TFI, 1999b). The options considered by designers of the FCTC were (a) non-binding instruments, or 'soft law,' such as intergovernmental resolutions and codes of conduct, and (b) authoritative and prescriptive legally binding instruments by parties, or 'hard law,' such as comprehensive treaties or conventions, convention-protocol approaches and international regulations. Non-binding instruments were considered as the first step. Resolutions, particularly through the UN General Assembly, with the support of some prominent states leading to a binding convention, were deemed most appropriate and effective. However, codes of conduct were discounted because of the 'entrenched interests of the global tobacco conglomerates and adverse experience of numerous nations with voluntary agreement with the tobacco industry' and the likelihood that it would 'obstruct effective national and international legal actions to control the tobacco epidemic' (Taylor and Roemer, 1996). Non-binding instruments were considered as a mere stopgap towards the development of a treaty or convention, while legally-binding instruments, particularly convention-protocol approaches that divide the negotiation of separate issues into separate agreements, were favoured. The rationale was that the FCTC would create 'an institutionalised forum for cooperation and negotiations for implementing protocols containing detailed obligations' and 'be more likely to secure political consensus and significant action on tobacco control than any other form of binding instrument' (Taylor and Roemer, 1996). Subsequently in 1996, the World Health Assembly adopted the idea to develop the FCTC, making the convention-protocol the choice of the form of governance. This prompted the continuous development of protocols through the Intergovernmental Negotiating Body and guidelines through the Conference of the Parties (WHO, 1996c). In effect, the FCTC signifies a notable transition from an era in which policy change was voluntary and policy developments were under the sole purview of states.

Agendas: How important is tobacco control as a policy issue? How is tobacco framed?

The rise of tobacco on the policy agenda, and the reframing of the tobacco problem at an international level, went hand-in-hand with this long process of institutionalisation. During the state-centric era, particularly the 1970s, there was no dominant frame for policy actions because some WHO member states were still driven by political economy concerns and others by the public health impact of tobacco. The WHO became the venue for finding a common frame for policy choice. This goal was accomplished with a combination of long-term knowledge gathering and relatively short-term interventions by WHO leaders. We outline the accumulation of the scientific knowledge below and, in this section, focus on the role of leadership.

The experience of the WHO suggests that leadership matters. Between 1970 and 2003 (when the FCTC was adopted), the WHO had four directors-general, all with medical backgrounds – Marcolino Gomes Candau from Brazil (1953–1973), Haldan Mahler from Switzerland (1973–1988), Hiroshi Nakajima from Japan (1988–1998), and Gro Harlem Brundtland from Norway (1998–2003). These terms correspond roughly to phases of WHO tobacco policy development: tobacco control entered the WHO agenda for the first time during Candau's term; the WHO expanded its activities through the Tobacco or Health programme to become an agent for tobacco control during Mahler's term; the development of the FCTC was initiated during Nakajima's term; and, the WHO led the development of the FCTC under Brundtland.

While it is true that the level of knowledge on tobacco use and control was different in the 1970s and 1980s, it is also true that both the Candau and Mahler administrations focused more on infectious diseases than on non-communicable diseases, hence the incremental changes in the WHO's role in governance in global tobacco control. During this period, even as the WHO expanded its role in tobacco control, the onus was mostly on the member states to develop their individual policies instead of a collective approach. This situation changed in the early 1990s during Nakajima's administration as WHO became increasingly interested in forging collective action (Mackay, 2003; Roemer et al, 2005). Further change occurred during the term of Brundtland as she forged alliances with states, UN agencies, and other international organisations, including the EU and NGOs, for the development of the FCTC.

Brundtland's leadership was critical to efforts to develop the FCTC. The idea of a global treaty for tobacco control first emerged in the early 1990s from conversations among academic researchers and was subsequently presented at the 9th World Conference on Tobacco or Health

(WCTOH) in Paris, France, in 1994. It was accepted there as a conference resolution (Mackay, 2003; Mamudu and Glantz, 2009; Roemer et al, 2005). In 1995, the World Health Assembly adopted resolution WHA48.11, an international strategy for tobacco control (WHO, 1995b) based on the WCTOH recommendation, to begin the process towards the development of the FCTC (WHO, 2003). This process was slow until 1998, when Brundtland became WHO Director General and subsequently put in place an accelerated plan (TFI, 1999b) that the World Health Assembly adopted in 1999 (WHO, 1999). Brundtland gave international salience to tobacco control and the development of the FCTC. She made tobacco control a top priority of the WHO, created and elevated responsibility for the WHO Tobacco Free Initiative to a cabinet position, and brought in tobacco control professionals, thereby marking a shift of attention from infectious diseases to tobacco and global public health (Yach and Bettcher, 1998). Further, unlike her more cautious predecessors (Sir Richard Peto, Personal Communication, October 2006), Brundtland took numerous ambitious steps to develop the FCTC, including: working with the World Bank leadership to publish *Curbing the Epidemic*; working with UN Secretary-General to transfer the UN tobacco or health programme under the UN Focal Point to the WHO; mobilising NGO support for the FCTC; and drawing attention to tobacco company activities to promote tobacco use and undermine policy worldwide. Under Brundltand's leadership, the relationship between WHO and the tobacco industry became increasingly adversarial as she successfully marginalised the TTC role in WHO policy processes, starting with the FCTC and subsequently extended to global health governance more generally, as in the resolution of the First UN Ministerial Meeting on NCDs in April 2011 (WHO, 2011) and the UN General Assembly in September 2011 (UN, 2011; Glantz and Gonzalez, 2011).

Networks: Has there been a shift in power between pressure participants?

In each empirical chapter we track the extent to which anti-tobacco groups replaced pro-tobacco interests as the dominant source of information and advice to governments. In most cases, the evidence for this shift is not unequivocal (for example, tobacco company influence may still be substantial behind the scenes). In the case of the WHO, we actually find attempts to exclude the tobacco industry from any formal involvement in the FCTC. In fact, the guidelines for Article 5.3 formally close the door to the participation of tobacco interests in the FCTC process. We can also identify an interesting shift in group attention, from domestic governments to international organisations, to reflect the change in power in global tobacco control.

Figure 9.2 International Networks for Governance in Global Tobacco Control

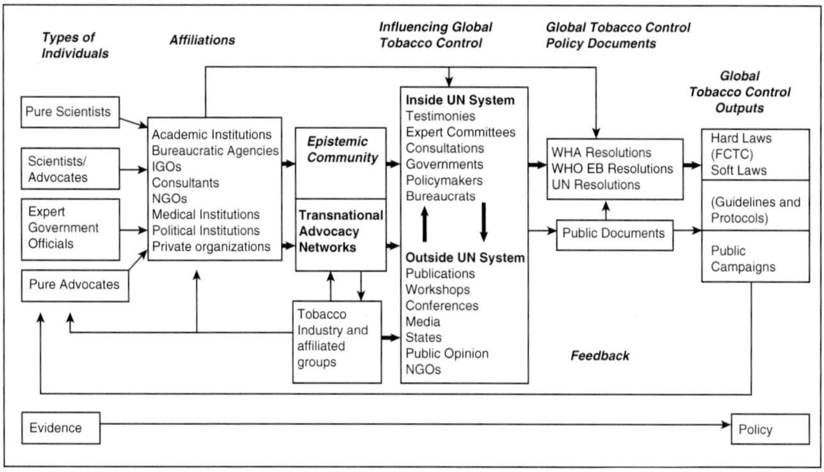

Tobacco networks: The tobacco industry and allied groups

The role of the industry has been to protect its smoking-promotion activities by promoting an economic frame of reference within government. While this strategy had some success within branches of the UN, it has been least effective within the increasingly-influential WHO. Attention to tobacco industry activities to promote tobacco use (in particular, towards young people and developing countries) prompted the 1978 World Health Assembly resolution that called on states to develop policies to combat it (WHO, 1978). The 1987 resolution called on tobacco companies 'to refrain voluntarily from all publicity activities in all countries, especially in developing countries' (WHO, 1987b), perhaps contributing to the worldwide proliferation of the tobacco industry agreements and voluntary codes in the 1990s.

At the same time as the WHO's role in tobacco control was expanding in the 1980s, the tobacco companies changed their low-profile role, in undermining tobacco control at the state-level, to work against the WHO and anti-tobacco individuals and organisations (BAT, 1980). By the late 1990s the relationship between the WHO and the tobacco industry became increasingly adversarial (WHO, 2000b). Evidence from the industry's formerly secret documents suggest that the companies had worked to undermine the WHO and its member states' work on tobacco control through several strategies, including: using various strategies to gain access to WHO-related information; encouraging disputes between the WHO and other UN agencies; challenging the scientific evidence on the effects of exposure to SHS; portraying tobacco control as an issue for developed countries; and, encouraging groups, such as the International Tobacco Growers' Association, to challenge WHO tobacco control programmes (Mamudu, 2008; Mamudu and Studlar, 2009; Mamudu and Glantz, 2009; McDaniel et al, 2008; Ong and Glantz, 2000; Otanez et al, 2009; WHO, 2000a).

Adversarial relations between the tobacco industry and the International Tobacco Control Network date back to the late 1960s when people, such as US Senator Robert Kennedy said (during the first WCTOH) that the companies were 'peddling a deadly weapon' (Kennedy, 1967). They peaked during the FCTC when the WHO declared the industry to be the 'vector' of tobacco-induced morbidity and mortality (WHO, 2000b). Indeed, efforts were made to keep the companies and their allies out of the negotiations. This strategy was undermined by companies who participated covertly in the process by working through states to sabotage and weaken the FCTC provisions (Mamudu and Glantz, 2009; Assunta and Chapman, 2006; Otanez et al, 2009). However, the tobacco companies sought unsuccessfully to influence the FCTC in a number of ways: to discredit *Curbing the Epidemic*, which was used as economic justification for the FCTC (Mamudu et al, 2008b); to develop an industry-wide voluntary code to divert attention from the FCTC (Mamudu et al, 2008a); to challenge European Union competence to negotiate the FCTC on behalf of its member states (Mamudu and Studlar, 2009); and, to influence negotiations on the relationship between trade and public health (Mamudu et al, 2011a). The tobacco industry also worked against anti-tobacco groups supporting the development of the FCTC by trying to create discord among them (mostly by courting alliances with some of them) (Carter, 2002; Mamudu and Glantz, 2009). In the end, Article 5.3 of the FCTC required states not to involve the tobacco companies in the policymaking process, and subsequent guidelines have been published to meet this aim (WHO, 2011c).

Anti-tobacco network: International tobacco control network

The beginning of an international tobacco control network, consisting of NGOs, advocacy network (Mamudu and Glantz, 2009; Farquharson, 2003) and an epistemic community (Mamudu, 2008; Farquharson, 2003; Mamudu et al, 2011b) can be traced at least as far back as the gathering in New York in 1967 for the first World Conference on Smoking and Health (Mamudu, 2008; Mamudu et al, 2011b). It was particularly significant during the 1970s and 1980s when the WHO was preoccupied with issues on infectious diseases and many member states were concerned with political economy issues in tobacco use and control. In the absence of a global governance agenda, this community was responsible for spearheading the production and worldwide dissemination of knowledge and ideas on tobacco control. Indeed, since the 1970s, experts (and policy entrepreneurs) within the international tobacco control network have been travelling across the world to engage in tobacco control activities, including legislative testimony, media advocacy, capacity building for governments and NGOs, and challenging tobacco industry activities (Studlar, 2004). In particular, the international tobacco control network contributed to making tobacco use and control a transnational issue by revealing tobacco companies' activities to promote tobacco use (Mamudu et al, 2011b).

The WHO has long recognised the value of collaboration with anti-tobacco individuals and organisations. Almost all 20 of the World Health Assembly resolutions on tobacco control before the adoption of the FCTC called for collaboration with NGOs. The WHO has relied on members of the international tobacco control network for the production and dissemination of knowledge and ideas on tobacco use and control (Table 9.2), the development of its plans and programmes on tobacco control, and the mobilisation of individuals and groups around the world for policy development (WHO, 1982, 1987a, 1988b, 1991, 1992b). The international tobacco control network effectively introduced public health activism to the WHO and helped transform the WHO from a passive actor to an agenda setter and a key tobacco control advocate.

From the early 1990s, members of the international tobacco control network played central roles in the development of the FCTC (Mackay, 2003; Mamudu, 2008; Roemer et al, 2005). Some members of the international tobacco control network lobbied their governments at the state-level (Lencucha et al, 2010), while others participated in the negotiations as state delegates and representatives of intergovernmental organisations. Individuals and NGOs within the international tobacco control network coalesced under the Framework Convention Alliance (the offspring of Brundtland's efforts to involve anti-tobacco groups in the FCTC negotiations), which disseminated expert information, provided media advocacy and lobbying, and challenged those supportive of the tobacco industry position (Collin et al, 2002; Farquharson, 2003; Mamudu and Glantz, 2009). The long-term impact for the members of the international tobacco control network is in stark contrast to tobacco interests; international tobacco control network involvement in the FCTC was institutionalised in Article 4.7 which made anti-tobacco groups formal participants (observers) in the FCTC process.

Socioeconomic factors

Economic benefits of tobacco

Political economy concerns dictated inter-state relations on tobacco control until at least the 1980s. The tobacco industry and its allies have worked persistently to focus attention on the economic benefits of tobacco. By the mid-1990s, however, there was enough evidence to suggest that tobacco has a negative effect on the economy in terms of direct and indirect health costs and other impacts, including increased poverty and environmental degradation (Barry, 1991; Chapman and Wong, 1990; Panos Institute, 1994; WHO, 1995a). Conflict over the economic benefit and socioeconomic cost of tobacco started in the 1980s (BAT, 1980) then came to a head in the early 1990s, symbolised by the World Bank decision not to support tobacco programmes (Mamudu et al, 2008b).

The balance of the conflict shifted following the production of analytical works on the economics of tobacco and tobacco control, mostly by economists affiliated with the World Bank (Abedian and van der Merwe, 1999; Barnum, 1994; Jha and Chaloupka, 2000). These analyses provided the background for the 1999 World Bank *Curbing the Epidemic* (Jha and Chaloupka, 1999), which concluded that while tobacco control is good for health *and* the economy, except in few tobacco-dependent economies, notably Malawi and Zimbabwe. The study, and subsequent country-specific analyses, provided evidence on the socioeconomic costs of tobacco that influenced the development of the FCTC in three main ways (Mamudu and Glantz, 2009; Mamudu et al, 2008b). First, the WHO used it as an economic justification for the development of the FCTC. Second, it became a source of mobilisation of states, the WHO, World Bank, the UN, and anti-tobacco groups for global collective action in tobacco control. Third, the evidence undercut the economic-benefit argument that the tobacco industry and its affiliates used to dissuade governments from enacting tobacco control policies.

Public opinion

The issue of public opinion became salient in the development of the FCTC, when the WHO Tobacco Free Initiative in 2000 solicited opinion on the FCTC, and the WHO held public hearings in Geneva (WHO, 2000a, 2000c) and collaborated with Environics Research Group Limited of Canada in October 2001 to conduct a survey to determine the support for the FCTC in five countries (Argentina, India, Japan, Nigeria, and Russia) (Environics Research Group Limited, 2001). A total of 514 submissions were received from around the world and representatives of 144 organisations, including the tobacco industry and affiliated groups, testified during the public hearings (WHO, 2000c). Analyses of these submissions by the WHO (WHO, 2000c), academics (Montini et al, 2009), and pro-tobacco groups (Vecchiet, 2000) showed that the overwhelming majority favoured the FCTC. Similarly, the survey by Environics showed that 87% of all respondents supported the FCTC (Environics Research Group Limited, 2001). The WHO introduced findings from the public hearings and submissions into the negotiations – marking the first time that public opinion has been used in an effort to create global governance arrangements (WHO, 2000c). However, while the findings made negotiators aware of the global support for the FCTC, they had little impact on the detailed negotiations themselves (Mamudu and Glantz, 2009; Mamudu et al, 2011a). Instead, the evidence became relevant in mobilising global public health support for the FCTC as whole (Mamudu and Glantz, 2009). The minimal opposition from other segments of the general public suggests the same 'permissive consensus' discussed in the earlier chapters (Mamudu and Glantz, 2009).

The role of ideas: Scientific knowledge

All six empirical chapters highlight a significant gap between the scientific knowledge on tobacco-related illness and the adoption of tobacco control policies. In this light, the role of knowledge production at the WHO level has been to bridge that gap. The earliest role was played by its ad hoc expert committees, consisting of public health experts and advocates from academia, NGOs and government (Mamudu et al, 2011b). The WHO used at least eight major expert committees on tobacco-related issues between the 1970s and when the FCTC was developed (Table 9.2). These committees established that tobacco use and control is a public health issue and that there are transnational dimensions that require inter-state cooperation. The WHO relied on them for scientific information on tobacco use and control, and their work formed the basis for World Health Assembly decisions that incrementally expanded the WHO role in tobacco control. According to a 1986 report prepared for a tobacco company:

> Early on, the WHO program was dictated by the Member States of the Organization. In spite of their concern about smoking and health, these states have much higher priorities in health than smoking. With the appointment of the Expert Committee in 1974, however, the position of the Organization took a very aggressive turn. Management of the issue had fallen into the very hands of 'specialists' with a deep commitment to anti-smoking activities (Devon Management Resources, 1980).

Until the emergence of expert committees, 'Member States have not seen fit to vote any budget to anti-smoking activities' but 'through the Expert Committees and a network of 'collaborating centres' on smoking and health among Member States, WHO brought to the smoking issue not only outside expertise, but also broader interest in its programme' (Devon Management Resources, 1980). This assessment is consistent with the view of participants, such as Lars Ramstrom of Sweden and Mike Daube of Australia (who served on WHO expert committees in the 1970s and 1980s), who said that the committees helped to change the WHO and the member states' orientations on tobacco use and prompted them to commit resources for tobacco control (Personal Communication, 2006, 2007). The involvement of the epistemic community (Mamudu et al, 2011b) in WHO's work transformed its tobacco control programme.

Table 9.2 Activities to Build the Knowledge-base for Global Tobacco Control

Year	Experts	Tobacco Activities	Policy Impact
1969	Sir George Godber, the UK Chief Medical Officer	Lectured on 'Smoking and Self-Inflicted Injury'	Attached to the of Pan American Health Organization (PAHO) report on measures taken in the Americas to control advertising of cigarettes, and considered in the adoption of WHA23.32(WHO, 1970b)
1970	1. Charles M. Fletcher, Secretary of the Royal College of Physicians in the UK 2. Daniel Horn, Director of the National Clearinghouse on Smoking in the US	Prepared a report on 'Smoking and Health' summarizing all the evidence linking smoking to diseases (WHO, 1970a)	Attached to the annex of the PAHO report and WHO Director General submitted it to the 23rd WHA. The WHA23.32 made direct reference to it (WHO, 1970b)
1974	WHO Expert Committee on Smoking and Health	Created as a result of WHA23.32 (WHO, 1970b) and it examined scientific evidence on the health effects of tobacco use.	Produced Technical Report Series No.568 'Smoking and Its Effects on Health' (WHO, 1975) and the 3rd WCTOH recommendations served as basis for the adoption of WHA29.55 of 1976.
1976	Nigel Gray, head of International Union Against Cancer (UICC) tobacco program	Held UICC workshop on Smoking and Lung Cancer to examine evidence on tobacco use and control	Developed the first UICC/WHO report, 'Guidelines for Smoking Control,' in 1980 (Gray and Daube, 1980)
	The WHO	Conducted a survey on legislative actions on tobacco taken by the states.	Produced a report that highlighted effective tobacco control policies and programmes around the world (WHO, 1976) for guiding WHO activities.
1977	Nigel Gray and the UICC	Collated tobacco control policies into the UICC report, *Lung Cancer Prevention* (Gray, 1977)	Authored with Mike Daube the WHO/UICC *Guidelines for Smoking Control* in 1980, (Gray and Daube, 1980) first report on tobacco control that highlighted six specific policies for tobacco control

Table 9.2 Activities to Build the Knowledge-base for Global Tobacco Control – *continued*

Year	Experts	Tobacco Activities	Policy Impact
1978	WHO Expert Committee on Smoking Control	Created as a result of WHA29.55 and examined evidence on tobacco control from developed countries	Produced Technical Report Series No.636 'Controlling the Smoking Epidemic' (WHO, 1979). Considered in the adoption of WHA33.35 (WHO, 1980) that created the WHO Tobacco or Health programme.
1982	WHO Expert Committee on Smoking Control in Developing Countries	Examined the problem of tobacco use and control in developing countries and recommended the transfer of policies and programmes in developed countries	Produced Technical Report Series No.695 'Smoking in Developing Countries' (WHO, 1983). Became a basis for the adoption of subsequent World Health Assembly resolutions and for WHO activities on tobacco control
1982 and 1993	Ruth Roemer and the WHO	Assembled tobacco control policies around the world for the WHO.	Published *Legislative Actions to combat the World Tobacco Epidemic* (Ruth Roemer, 1982, 1993), which served as basis for World Health Assembly discussions and guide for WHO actions.
1986	Advisory Group on WHO Global Action Plan on Tobacco or Health	Developed the WHO 1988–1995 Global Action Plan on Tobacco Control (WHO, 1988b)	The report of the Advisory Groups (WHO, 1988b) considered in the passage of resolution WHA41.25 in 1988 (WHO, 1988d) and guide for the WHO Tobacco or Health programme
	WHO Expert Committee on Community Prevention and Control of Cardiovascular Disease	Examined and identified effective ways to control the use and spread of tobacco and the community level.	Produced Technical Report SeriesNo. 732 'Community Prevention and Control of Cardiovascular' (WHO, 1986a)to guide the WHO and Member States ' action on tobacco control
	International Agency for Research on Cancer (IARC)	Evaluated evidence on the health effects of tobacco use, particular cancer.	Produced Monograph 'Evaluation of Carcinogenic Risks to Humans ' (IARC, 1986) that was used to develop the 1988–1995 WHO Global Action Plan for Tobacco Control(WHO, 1988b)
1988	WHO Study Group on Smokeless Tobacco Control	Examined the evidence on the health effects and control of smokeless tobacco	Report on the effects of smokeless tobacco use and control (TRS No. 773) (WHO, 1988a)

Table 9.2 Activities to Build the Knowledge-base for Global Tobacco Control – *continued*

Year	Experts	Tobacco Activities	Policy Impact
1990	Expert Committee on Prevention in Childhood and Youth of Adult Cardiovascular Diseases	Examined effects of the issue youth smoking and how to prevent it.	Produced Technical Report Series No. 792 'Prevention in Childhood and Youth of Adult Cardiovascular Diseases: Time for Action' (WHO, 1990a) to guide the WHO and Member States.
1993	Conference of tobacco control experts in Harare, Zimbabwe	The WHO and NGOs collaborated to provide forum for expert presentations on economics of tobacco and tobacco control	Served as a catalysts for World Bank's work on economics of tobacco control that provided background for the *Curbing the Epidemic*
1998	70 Public health experts met in Vancouver, British Colombia, Canada	Developed a four-year accelerated plan for the development of the FCTC (TFI, 1999a)	The plan adopted at the 1999 World Health Assembly as resolution WHA52.18 (WHO, 1999) and guided the FCTC negotiations.
1999	A team of over 40 experts affiliated with the World Bank	Prepared the World Bank report *Curbing the Epidemic: Government and Economics of Tobacco Control*	Used by the WHO as economic justification for the FCTC, basis for UN Economic and Social Council resolutions, and for lobbying countries (Mamudu and Glantz, 2009).
	WHO Expert Committee on Tobacco Industry Documents	Investigated the tobacco industry activities to challenge the WHO and member states work on tobacco control (WHO, 2000a)	Produced report 'Tobacco Company Strategies to Undermine Tobacco Control Activities at the World Health Organisation' that was used in the adoption of resolution WHA54.18 (WHO, 2001) Report also introduced as part of the negotiations on the FCTC.
2000	Scientific Advisory Committee on Tobacco Product Regulation	Examined effective ways of regulating tobacco products	Produced several reports on how to regulate tobacco (WHO, 2004). Work introduced into the FCTC negotiations.
2002	IARC	Examined scientific evidence on the health effects of exposure to second-hand smoke	Produced monograph 'Tobacco Smoke and Involuntary Smoking' to affirm evidence on the effects of tobacco use and exposure to second-hand smoke (IARC, 2002).

The WHO collaborating centres on tobacco control helped further the knowledge-base and garner states' interest in the issue (Devon Management Resources, 1980). By the late 1970s and early 1980s, the WHO started to create these centres when it became a clearinghouse for information on tobacco use and control (WHO, 1985; WHO, 1988e). As of September 2011, there were nine centres in four WHO regions – Africa, Americas, Europe, and Western Pacific. Over the past decades, the WHO relied on these centres for scientific information on tobacco use and control, building the knowledge-base for global tobacco control and support for WHO tobacco control activities.

The transfer of ideas

The FCTC effectively represents a global tobacco policy diffusion project. The WHO and its partners have developed what they deem to be the best practice from around the world and are now asking every country to adopt a comprehensive package of measures. The search for appropriate and effective policies for global governance in global tobacco control began in the 1970s, when the WHO became involved in tobacco control and began to examine and identify legislation on smoking (WHO, 1976). It conducted a survey on tobacco control legislation around the world (WHO, 1976) and established expert committees to examine and identify effective policies and programmes or best practices (WHO, 1975, 1979) in the 1970s. The result was that the WHO basically borrowed policies from some countries for others to adopt and domesticate. The WHO has worked from the 1970s to identify best practices around the world, but the idea of a 'comprehensive' approach, where controlling the use and spread of tobacco requires a combination of certain policies and programmes, only entered the lexicon of tobacco control when it collaborated with the International Union Against Cancer in the mid-1970s to publish the *Guidelines for Smoking Control* (Table 9.1) (Gray and Daube, 1980). Until that point, 'there was no consensus policy' and the term 'comprehensive approach' appeared in the tobacco control literature for the first time (Mamudu et al, 2011b). The process has also thrown up a number of contradictory effects, with some regions acting as sources of lessons for the WHO but then proving to be reluctant global partners. For example, the EU and some of its member states served as good examples of best practice in several of the provisions but the major European tobacco control laggard, Germany, was a reluctant partner, along with the US, China, and Japan in the FCTC negotiations (Mamudu and Glantz, 2009). Additionally, even though tobacco control policy is lagging in developing countries, they played leading roles in the development of the FCTC (Mamudu and Glantz, 2009; Mamadu et al, 2011).

Conclusion

To a large extent the FCTC now represents global tobacco control policy, or at least a manifesto for a truly global approach. It covers the major aspects of tobacco control, including measures to provide smoke-free environments, health warnings on packaging, bans on sales to children, bans on advertising tobacco, tax increases to discourage smoking, and programmes to find alternative sources of income for tobacco growers. Given the relatively limited tobacco control in most developing countries (WHO, 2008), and very slow progress among laggards in the developed world, the FCTC represents a sea change of policy choice. Minimal intervention has been replaced by, at least a written commitment to, comprehensive tobacco control.

We can explain this shift in much the same way that we explain policy change in individual countries or regions. First, the responsibility for tobacco control has shifted. Tobacco control was once the sole preserve of individual countries, with organisations, such as the UN and World Bank actually providing support for tobacco as an economic product. This emphasis shifted as the role of the WHO changed, from a hub for the accumulation of the scientific evidence, to the key international organisation responsible for the coordination of the global tobacco control policy response, aided by the IARC, UN and World Bank. Over time, global tobacco control policy became 'institutionalised', culminating in the production of the FCTC and widespread support for it to represent a source of 'hard law'. Second, the rise of tobacco control on the policy agenda, and the reframing of the tobacco problem at an international level, went hand-in-hand with this long process of institutionalisation. When tobacco was the sole responsibility of countries, it was often low on the policy agenda and many countries still furthered the political economy frame of reference. The involvement of the WHO was also rather limited initially, with tobacco competing for attention with issues, such as infectious diseases. This competition changed over time as the scientific evidence accumulated, the role of the WHO increased, and it was headed by directors-general, such as Brundtland who were more likely to promote the issue internationally.

Third, the WHO provided a new venue for international public health influence. The WHO is one of the few organisations to try to exclude pro-tobacco groups from the formal decisionmaking process. At the same time, it has encouraged (and indeed relied on) the positive contribution of the international tobacco control network. Fourth, attitudes to the socio-economic context have shifted over time. The main form of tobacco company influence has come from the economic benefits that tobacco growing and manufacturing provide to countries in need of jobs and tax and export revenue. This benefit is now increasingly challenged by reports (most notably from the World Bank, previously an ally of tobacco growing) that highlight the economic ill effects caused by tobacco use. Such analysis has contributed to movements in public opinion, with surveys demonstrating a clear majority in favour of the FCTC and global tobacco control. Finally, the role of ideas has proved to be crucial. The main driver for WHO involvement, and perhaps the main source of its power, has been the accumulation of the scientific evidence linking tobacco to ill health. Subsequently, the WHO has become a key source in the dissemination of ideas regarding best practice in tobacco control, culminating in the FCTC.

The FCTC's short-term effectiveness can be gauged using the number of parties adhering to the treaty, which was 174 in September 2011.[10] 192 participants approved the treaty in 2003, and it came into force once 40 had ratified it in February 2005. The number of countries with tobacco control legislation was about 30 in 1976 (WHO, 1976). By 2003, when the FCTC was adopted, almost all the member states had at least one tobacco control policy. Even such a recalcitrant state as China introduced a partial smoking ban in 2011. The long-term effectiveness of the FCTC is harder to measure. Countries that have signed the FCTC must now demonstrate that they are willing to translate its measures into legislation and other regulatory measures, and then implement those measures. That process has just begun.

10
Conclusion

Chapter 10 brings together our theoretical framework and empirical conclusions to consider how best to interpret and explain global tobacco policy change. It considers theories and approaches that address one or more aspects of the policy processes we describe – such as institutional change, governance, and federalism – and outlines in more detail some of the main theories of the policy process – such as punctuated equilibrium theory, the advocacy coalition framework (ACF), and multiple streams analysis – that attempt to explain the interaction between the five explanatory factors we identify. It provides two key conclusions that challenge us to be clear on the value of contemporary theories of public policy.

First, our main concern has been to measure, characterise and explain policy change. Yet, an overall picture of change has proved difficult, partly because change varies by country or region. This outcome prompts a number of conceptual problems. In some, we identify profound change in the space of 50 years but perhaps in the absence of a crisis, shock or 'big bang' that marks the end of one era and the beginning of another. This absence of a clear event, or series of events, prompts us to consider the rate and nature (and cause) of change: is it incremental or radical, or can it be both? In others, we identify more modest changes, a picture made more complicated by limited policy implementation. In particular, it will take some time to gauge the long-term effect of policy (formulation) change in countries that have only recently made a commitment to deliver on the promises contained in the FCTC. This development raises a further issue of policy transfer success. We may view the FCTC as a successful global project in terms of commitment but have to reserve judgement on its long-term effect.

Second, we may find that most theories of public policy are somewhat useful in our analysis of the policy processes of developed countries. Yet, in most cases, a discussion of policy transfer is necessary to gain a full understanding of the developing country picture. We may be moving towards an era of 'global governance' in which the policies of domestic countries are supplemented by international agreements that all signatory parties are expected to fulfil. This requires an understanding of the role and effect of policy transfer, as well as some clarity on the meaning of 'governance'.

To address these points, this concluding chapter presents a broad overview of our empirical findings, identifies key theories of public policy and considers how they inform the empirical material. In particular, it considers explanations based on multi-level governance and federalism, as well as the various (and often competing) explanations related to new institutionalism, to provide a broad narrative of change related to the role of institutions and multiple venues. Then, it considers how some of the main theories of public policy help us characterise and explain policy change. It considers the relative value of theories to explain tobacco policy processes and outcomes in developed and developing countries. Focusing on the importance of the transfer of ideas, it considers the importance of 'policy transfer windows' when tobacco policy solutions are imported within political systems. Finally, it suggests that we have entered a meaningfully new era of 'global governance' and considers the future of tobacco control.

Empirical conclusions

Theories of public policy explain major policy change with reference to five key factors:

- Institutions change, or the institution responsible for policy is transformed.
- A change occurs in the definition and understanding of the problem, and therefore a shift in the basis for considering policy choices.
- An alteration takes place in the balance of power between group participants within subsystems.
- Socioeconomic factors change and facilitate new behaviour.
- New ideas are accepted within, and transferred across, political systems.

We make the simple distinction between developed and developing countries and find that this broad process of change differs markedly. In the former, we generally find that profound policy transformation has taken place over five decades, reflecting change in each of the five main factors. Government departments and other organisations focused on health policy have taken the main responsibility for tobacco control, largely replacing departments focused on finance, agriculture, trade, industry and employment. Consequently, the rules of decisionmaking have changed.

The definition of the problem now takes place through the lens of public health, often with moral overtones. Tobacco was once viewed primarily as a product with economic value, and tobacco growing and manufacturing was often subsidised or encouraged. Now, it is largely viewed as a public health problem; an epidemic to be eradicated aggressively or, at the very least, a problem to be minimised. Periodically the public health dimensions have also been affected by strong moral fervour, at times even overwhelming the health concerns. In particular, the 1980s saw the rise of 'secular morality' or appeals for the value of healthy lifestyles based on government regulation and individual choices (Leichter, 1991; Brandt and Rozin, 1997). While tobacco control is an issue dependent on science, in the public debate this has sometimes been de-emphasised in favour of arguments about the morality of manufacturing and selling lethal products. The greater simplicity of morality arguments has often broadened public appeal, a critical ingredient in opposition to the political power of the pro-tobacco network, particularly in fragmented political systems.

The balance of power has also shifted among interested participants. The tobacco industry was, for decades before and after World War II, an ally of government. Tobacco companies were most consulted when policy was coordinated by finance and other departments. Now, public health or anti-tobacco groups are more likely to be called on for information and advice, and tobacco companies are often deliberately excluded from major consultations, most notably during the FCTC process. The socioeconomic context has changed markedly in most countries. The economic benefits of tobacco production and consumption have fallen; for example, tax revenue is less important to finance departments once protective of the industry. The number of smokers has sharply declined in many developed countries, and opposition to tobacco control has been replaced by a passively supportive public willing to accept comprehensive tobacco control.

Finally, the role of ideas is crucial. The production and dissemination of the scientific evidence linking smoking (and now passive smoking) to ill-health has been accepted within most government circles, while the most effective policies to reduce smoking are increasingly adopted and transferred across countries.

Change in these five factors has generally been a mutually reinforcing process. For example, increased attention to (and acceptance of) the scientific evidence has shifted the way that governments understand the tobacco problem. In turn, the framing of tobacco as a health problem allows health departments to take the policy lead. Tobacco control and smoking prevalence also go hand in hand: a decrease in smoking rates reduces the barriers to tobacco control; more tobacco control means fewer smokers. However, the policy change caused by this process has also taken some time to occur. Tobacco control now seems like an 'idea whose time has come' and the scientific links between smoking, SHS and illness now seem to make tobacco control inevitable. However, such conclusions can only be reached with the benefit of hindsight. In most developed countries, this understanding took decades to come to fruition. The gap between the initial identification of smoking-related (and then passive smoking-related) ill-health and a comprehensive policy response was considerable. In most cases the response took 20–30 years.

In other words, policy change is never just about the role of ideas, however strong they appear to be, and however accepted they are within government. Instead, policy change is also about the power and the motivation to translate broad ideas into concrete policy proposals that can be introduced, promoted and accepted within political systems. The developed country experience suggests that this process took place over five decades as the scientific evidence accumulated, the socioeconomic context changed and governing institutions became more receptive to tobacco control ideas.

The developing country experience is rather different, as there is limited change in the five main factors. Health departments are key players, but their voices are often drowned out domestically by other departments, such as agriculture, finance and trade. Instead, health departments have played a stronger role in the FCTC process (Mamudu, 2008; Mamudu and Glantz, 2009). Tobacco policy arises on the policy agenda rarely and, when it does, the public health frame still competes with attempts to frame tobacco as an economic good. Tobacco companies are still powerful within subsystems, and the level of development of anti-tobacco groups is often low. Tobacco growing and manufacturing is an important source of jobs, exports and revenue, and smoking prevalence is often rising, particularly among women, and when wages rise. Finally, the medical-scientific knowledge has had less of an effect on the policy agenda than one might expect. While most governments have similar access to the scientific knowledge and also information on the policy response in other countries, the knowledge-response gap is still considerable. In short, domestic anti-tobacco groups have the motivation but not the power to ensure the acceptance of tobacco control ideas within their political systems.

This limited policy response in developing countries has prompted an unusual degree of international cooperation, based on four main arguments: the tobacco problem is too large to ignore (causing one in ten premature deaths worldwide); it is transnational in scope; there is a relatively limited policy adoption in developing countries; and, powerful tobacco companies are becoming increasingly entrenched in these countries and impeding policy change. Our findings suggest that international efforts to bridge this gap between the problem and the policy response have accelerated the long-term processes that are required to make major policy change. The FCTC was produced in 2003, but the WHO has had a tobacco control remit for three decades and has concentrated its tobacco control efforts on developing countries for most of that time – working with health departments, challenging the economic frame by disseminating evidence on the economic costs of smoking, providing an alternative venue for public health groups, challenging tobacco companies, and identifying and encouraging the transfer of best practice in tobacco control.

The FCTC is effectively the logical conclusion to a much longer process of policy change. In Schattschneider's (1960; discussed in Chapter 1) terms, the WHO and its supporters now represent the 'audience' for disputes between powerful tobacco companies and the relatively powerless anti-tobacco groups in developing countries. The international agenda has helped 'socialise' the issue and challenge the attitudinal and institutional barriers to policy change identified in classic discussions of power (see Bachrach and Baratz, 1970 in Chapter 1). Yet, the FCTC also represents the *initial* stage in a process of policy legitimation and implementation. The success of this international agreement depends on developing countries being able to have their tobacco control policies leapfrog their social and economic conditions. It also requires sustained levels of domestic and international attention, since the adoption of the FCTC is just the beginning of the process.

Using theories of public policy to explain tobacco policy

Multi-level governance and federalism

Both multi-level governance (MLG) and federalism have common concerns. While federalism studies are drawn particularly (but not exclusively) from the US experience, and MLG from studies of the EU, both identify the absence of a single centre of government. Elazar (1971: 6), describing federalism, identifies 'the diffusion of power among multiple centers which must cooperate in order to govern' while Rhodes (1997: 1), describing governance, suggests, 'there is not one but many centres linking many levels of government'. Much of the federalist literature takes the dispersal of power as its starting point for the analysis of intergovernmental relations, examining how governments negotiate with each other. MLG takes this one step further. Drawing on policy networks analysis, it identifies a further dispersal of power to quasi and non-governmental actors, blurring boundaries between formal and informal sources of authority. It suggests that the policy process is messy: many actors may be involved at various levels of government and their relationships vary across time and policy issue. This makes policy outcomes difficult to predict because the formal responsibility for policy issues changes over time, different actors may become involved, and there may be scope to influence and change policy at different stages of the process.

A key theme in recent studies (Studlar, 2010; Asare et al, 2009) is the comparison of experiences of tobacco policy change based on the MLG and federalist literatures. This can involve formally federal systems, such as the US, Canada, and Australia, as well as quasi-federal systems with devolved responsibility for tobacco control, such as the UK, supra-state organisations, such as the EU, and international treaties, such as the FCTC. In each case, MLG and federalism studies help us understand how agendas are set and policy is adopted and implemented. Formally, there may be 'higher' and 'lower' levels of government, but the political economy and public health frames of tobacco policy can be pursued at multiple venues at different levels.

The meaning of governance and 'global governance'

Perhaps the main obstacle to such comparisons across literatures is that 'governance' has multiple meanings. Indeed, it has been used in this book at least two (albeit complementary) ways to identify different processes in different regions. First, as some Chapters (4–7) have discussed, governance in the MLG literature (referring mainly to studies in the developed world), refers to (1) multiple and shifting levels of government responsibility for policy; (2) multiple institutions of government at the same level often pursuing somewhat different policies; and (3) the blurring of the distinction between formal governmental power and non-governmental influence in policy. The third point is especially important, as the history of tobacco policy shows how non-governmental actors, ranging from tobacco manufacturers and growers to anti-tobacco advocates and tobacco control researchers, have become intertwined with governments to the extent that it often becomes difficult to disentangle their authority. Some central governments have provided financial aid to anti-tobacco groups as 'public interest groups', or 'licensed critics', and some also have provided funds for public health research into tobacco control. The relationships between governments and interest groups can be so close, over an extended period of time, that it is difficult to distinguish their perspectives and power. This has been true both during political economy and public health dominance eras. It can also be apparent in sub-central jurisdictions. In these terms, the MSA in the US was an unusual example of a 'governance' strategy within a federal system; a countrywide tobacco policy was made between states and localities on the one hand and private tobacco companies on the other, without the formal endorsement of the central government.

Second, as Chapters 8 and 9 indicate, the concept of 'global governance' refers to the ability of international organisations, backed by certain countries, to influence the policy behaviour of sovereign states, especially those in the developing world. There are different variants of global governance, which the Commission on Global Governance (1995) categorically points out 'does not imply world government or federalism' and Rosenau (1997; Rosenau and Czempiel, 1992) refers to as 'governance without government'. Our use of the term emanates from the 'liberal internationalist' perspective in international relations studies. It suggests, rather broadly, that state behaviour is influenced by systems of international cooperation (Barnett and Duvall, 2005; Held and McGrew, 2002; Moravcsik, 1997; Taylor, 2002; Young, 1999). Under this approach, global governance refers to rules, norms, and principles used to regulate global tobacco use and to discourage the export of the tobacco epidemic to low- and medium-income countries that in many cases have an increasing prevalence rate. In particular, the spread of knowledge (accompanied by norms regarding how best to interpret and respond to that knowledge), through the international system about the hazards of tobacco use (and SHS), helps states to define their interests and identities. It also helps institutions, such as the WHO, with constitutional powers in certain issue areas, such as international public health, to become advocates of certain kind of policies. Global governance occurs through a loosely tied network of multiple actors, states, functional agencies, and non-state actors who interact frequently (Haas, 2002; Keohane and Nye, 2000; Held et al, 2001).

Since 1970, developing countries have participated in the pursuit of global tobacco control through the World Health Assembly (the decision-making body of WHO) and UN resolutions. The most important influence on developing countries is the FCTC, which creates a regulatory framework for parties through its provisions, protocols, and guidelines, putting tobacco control on their policy agenda. In this respect, we found that the FCTC contributes to tobacco control in developing countries by making it a policy priority similar to that in developed countries, and facilitating lesson drawing and transfers of policies to other jurisdictions via transnational actors. In other words, due to the limited availability of tobacco control measures in developing countries, we observed more impact of global tobacco control on developing countries' policy priorities.

The two concepts, MLG and global governance, are clearly related. Global governance involves multiple tiers of government, adding a further international dimension to the local, provincial, central and supranational levels (even to the EU, which had delegate status in the FCTC as a jurisdiction with tobacco control authority). Global governance also entails unclear boundaries between formal responsibility and wider informal influence in two key ways. First, international organisations use various techniques, including persuasion, the encouragement of norms and the dissemination of information, to supplement their limited enforcement powers. Second, central governments and international organisations have fostered anti-tobacco NGO participation (for example, in the meetings leading to the FCTC) to the extent that their respective activities are now difficult to disentangle.

The new institutionalisms

Our findings on the role of institutions go to the heart of a potential competition between traditional studies of comparative politics and the emphasis of public policy theories, perhaps exacerbated by a disciplinary inability to define 'institution' clearly. A strong component of the former is comparing the formal characteristics of political systems and other institutional forms to explain similarities and differences in political outcomes. A strong component of the latter is that many factors that influence policy outcomes transcend formal institutions. A useful compromise may be to suggest that the existence of multiple venues (for example, allowing interest groups more chances to pursue the redefinition of policy) may be more important than the specific institutional characteristics of political systems.

In several chapters we identify a varying potential for venue shopping and variations in veto points within political systems. Chapter 4 appears to support the argument (in Wilensky, 2002; Marmor and Lieberman, 2004; Studlar et al, 2011) that decentralised, pluralist systems have more comprehensive tobacco control than their unitary counterparts. The greater scope for venue-shifting (for example, to the courts or jurisdictions at another level in decentralised systems) makes some policy change more likely than in more centralised unitary states, especially if the latter are corporatist in interest group structure. Chapter 6 also attributes most change in the US before the 1990s to state (provincial) level initiatives (often with the support of policy entrepreneurs) and an unusual degree of recourse to the courts, suggesting that the US would have been a policy laggard if not for federalism (particularly since central institutions, most notably Congress, were relative laggards). However, Chapter 7 is less clear on the institutional effect on tobacco policy. Indeed, the Canadian experience is one of minimal provincial activity over long periods. Further, Chapter 5 on the UK shows that a unitary state with a smaller (albeit rising) number of venues can produce similar levels of policy change. The situation is less clear in federalist countries in the developing world where the central government wields enormous policymaking power over tobacco control similar to a unitary state, except in a few cases, such as Argentina (Asare, 2009; Sebrié and Glantz, 2010) and Mexico (Crosbie et al, 2011).

In effect, the role of formal institutions becomes an empirical question, with particular arrangements generating uncertain expectations of policy outcomes. Indeed, the more important 'institutional' dimension in our study relates to levels of economic and political development. We find the greatest policy divide to be between developed and developing countries, a distinction that may not best be served by a focus on the formal institutions of political systems.

In public policy studies, the analysis often goes beyond formal structures to look for common policy processes and factors that transcend political systems. The approach comes in several forms. As Chapter 2 discusses, a section of the literature rejects the argument that different institutional arrangements produce different policy styles. Instead, we often find common policy styles based on the importance of consultation with pressure participants and constraints on policymaking associated with incrementalism. This theme has been extended to cover processes, associated with the term 'punctuated equilibrium' (Baumgartner and Jones, 1993, 2009), that were once thought to be caused by the US' separation of powers (True et al, 2007; Baumgartner et al, 2006) but really relate to wider processes of bounded rationality and agenda-setting that transcend political systems. Boundedly rational policymakers cannot consider all policy issues. Instead, they ignore most and promote a few to the top of their agenda. This point applies in all political systems (Cairney, 2012: 196).

Our approach reflects this emphasis on comparative public policy in two main ways. First, while our framework includes a discussion of varying institutional factors, our most significant finding is a common institutional element: the shift from Department of Health marginality to centrality in the policy process (and, therefore, a change in the rules of decisionmaking). Second, we relate this change to factors that transcend political systems, such as a transformation in the definition of the tobacco problem.

A similar point can be made about historical institutionalism, which defines institutions as 'the formal rules, compliance procedures, and standard operating procedures' that 'structure conflict' (Hall in Thelen 1992: 2). Thelen and Steinmo (1992: 10) link the attractiveness of historical institutionalism to 'the theoretical leverage it has provided for understanding policy continuities over time within countries and policy variation across countries'. Our findings suggest that it is just as valuable to identify institutional *similarities* across countries and variations over time within countries. Many countries had broadly similar 'critical junctures' (key points at which events and decisions were made which led to the development of an institution) in the early 20th century: tobacco consumption remained legal and tobacco growing and manufacturing was encouraged as a growth industry. The governmental response was to treat tobacco policy as a matter for finance, agriculture and trade departments. The relationship was often cemented when tobacco companies were called upon to ensure the supply of cigarettes to troops during World War I and World War II and, by the post-war period, stable institutions could be identified in which the 'standard operating procedure' was to maintain close industry-government links, generally at the expense of medical interests and the ministry of health. In this context, our common research question is: how did this institution break down, to be replaced by new procedures in which tobacco became a health problem, administered by the ministry of health in cooperation with anti-tobacco groups?

The trend within parts of the institutionalist literature is to go beyond explanations based on 'punctuated equilibrium', or long periods of institutional stability punctuated by a radical change (but note the two uses of 'punctuated equilibrium' in the literature – there is surprisingly little crossover between discussions of punctuated equilibrium in new institutionalism, and the punctuated equilibrium theory produced by Baumgartner and Jones, 2009 and discussed below). Instead, we may also identify 'incremental change with transformative results' (Streek and Thelen, 2005: 8–9; see also Durant and Diehl, 1989). Or, we may treat institutions as dominant ideas that may be supported and reproduced or challenged and broken down (Blyth, 2002: vii–viii; Hay, 2006: 65). In other words, shared beliefs become 'institutionalised'; they are taken for granted and rarely questioned or, at least, accepted as the starting point when we consider policy problems. As such, institutionalised ideas are not fixed structures. Instead, they are 'constantly in flux, being reconsidered and redefined as actors communicate and debate with one another' (Béland and Cox, 2011: 4; see also Schmidt, 2006: 113; 2010: 3; Schmidt and Radaelli, 2004: 193).

Our findings suggest that this process of ideational change is a better explanation than any structural change based on a small number of profound events. There have been key moments in the production of the scientific evidence on tobacco and illness (such as the first report of the UK Royal College of Physicians in 1962 and the 1964 US Surgeon General's Report, Table 3.2) and on the economy (such as *Curbing the Epidemic*). There have also been, in some instances, key organisational changes, such as the role of the EU in modifying the tobacco policies of accession states. However, there has never been what we would describe as a sudden institutional shift. Rather, the scientific evidence was used to challenge existing ideas, first in relation to how we should define the problem (from an economic to a health frame) and, second, in relation to how governments should respond to it. The shift within governments from a finance or agriculture-led subsystem in which tobacco growers and companies were consulted as a matter of course, to a health-led subsystem in which anti-tobacco groups largely usurped this role did not follow any identifiable big bang.

Characterising and explaining policy change

This point extends to a wider discussion of policy change. We identify change, in most developed countries, akin to Hall's (1993) 'third order' change in which there has been a 'paradigm shift' (Kuhn, 1962; see also Studlar, 2009; Cairney, 2012: 229). The whole basis of policymaking has changed since the post-war period: the goals behind policy (from supporting tobacco production to minimising smoking); the instruments used to attain them (from agricultural support and limited industry control using a small number of voluntary measures, to comprehensive control using many statutory measures); and, the way that policymakers think and act (shifting their main source of information and advice from pro- to anti-tobacco groups; seeking to control, not support, tobacco). Elements of Hall's analysis are relevant to tobacco. There has been a 'first principles' battle of ideas in which the dominant assumptions were challenged and much less is now taken for granted. This battle also ended in many countries 'when the supporters of a new paradigm secure[d] positions of authority over policymaking and [were] able to rearrange the organisation and standard operating procedures of the policy process so as to institutionalise the new paradigm' (1993: 281). Yet, unlike Hall, we do not identify a dramatic policy failure that drove this change. Governments did not suddenly lose public confidence following a tobacco crisis. Nor did previous experts suddenly fall out of favour because they could not explain and solve the problem. Further, Hall's example of a crisis for Keynesian economic ideas in the UK suggests that third order change was so significant because it happened in a relatively short period of time (following the economic crisis in the mid-1970s). In our case, profound (and strongly contested) change occurred incrementally, usually over several decades, as a wide range of instruments were introduced at different times and then strengthened.

Our identification of profound yet incremental change prompts us to consider how best to characterise and explain it. In effect, we assess the tempo and substance of change and seek to 'integrate gradualism and quantum change' (Durant and Diehl, 1989: 195–6). For example, Durant and Diehl (1989: 180) identify this combination in Kingdon's work (see Chapter 2). The potential for non-incremental change comes from the agenda-setting process, in which there are lurches of attention. Policymakers often shift their attention to policy issues suddenly and disproportionately, opening up the potential for non-incremental change. However, this change does not happen in the absence of a feasible policy solution. Such solutions do not just suddenly appear, and they cannot be produced at short notice. Rather, they evolve over a longer period of time – years, or even decades, rather than weeks or months. Kingdon's evolutionary metaphor describes the time and effort it takes for feasible policy solutions to develop; they whirl around in the 'policy primeval soup', evolving as they are proposed by one actor but then are reconsidered and modified by a large number of policy participants (although compare with Durant and Diehl, 1989: 201–3). Policy change therefore only occurs when there is a window of opportunity that combines three independent streams: there is a brief lurch of attention to the problem, a policy solution has evolved and is available, and policymakers have the motive and opportunity to adopt it (Kingdon, 1995: 165–6; Lieberman, 2002).

This approach has an intuitive appeal, and can help explain a number of our identified policy changes in a broad way. For example, Chapter 9 draws implicitly on Kingdon to discuss the coming together of a range of factors at the same time to produce a new global governance agenda in the 1990s: the increasing status of scientific evidence on tobacco use and control; increasing awareness that the use and spread of tobacco is a transnational issue that requires concerted efforts; and, political will on the part of governments to cooperate and collaborate on tobacco-related issues, perhaps with (WHO Secretary-General) Brundtland acting as the 'policy entrepreneur', or someone who used her knowledge of the political system to exploit the window of opportunity. Similarly, Chapter 7 describes the development of an international policy community effectively with reference to three policy streams. The problems have long been recognised, and various groups inside and outside governments have recommended policies to deal with the problem. Nevertheless, given the strong position of the pro-tobacco network and the permissive consensus in public opinion that was not demanding that action be taken, it took a confluence of circumstances, especially pertinent official reports, active and coordinated anti-tobacco NGOs, and a strong health minister and health bureaucracy, backed by international evidence and support, to provide the necessary 'policy window', motive and opportunity for action.

There are two unresolved issues with such an analysis. First, the explanation relies on the identification of an element of serendipity and it is difficult to generalise across cases. Second, the approach does not help us characterise the overall process of change. Instead, we have a decision to make: does the window of opportunity refer to the chance to introduce a *whole new approach* to policy or to adopt specific (major) policies? Our two examples in Chapters 7 and 9 suggest the former, with more policy changes arising from the new agenda set following the first successful window of opportunity. Yet, Kingdon (1984) himself, and examples in the literature (such as Zahariadis, 2003), focus on more specific policy measures or instruments. Indeed, multiple streams analysis has been used by Cairney (2009a) to focus solely on smoking bans in the UK. The latter approach suggests that a *series* of windows have to open up to ensure longer-term change.

Perhaps we can say, as a combination of both approaches, that when a window of opportunity first arises for a policy (or set of policies) that signals a radical new direction, then it is more likely that subsequent windows will open in the future and that the conditions will be more conducive to change: solutions are now available and policymakers have shown that they are receptive to this approach to policy (particularly in our field, where tobacco policy is often less subject to policy reversals following a change of government). Yet, this has an unintended analytical consequence: it obliges us to pinpoint the time that policy suddenly went in a major new direction. In effect, we have to identify the major policy punctuation or, at least, the first major policy change that opened the floodgates.

The latter point is explored by Baumgartner and Jones (1993, 2009). The term 'punctuated equilibrium' describes long periods of policy stability (incremental change) interrupted by major, non-incremental change – but can we identify the punctuation and would we even know it if we saw it? An intuitive approach would be to try to identify a key event or series of events that set policy on a different path (much like the focus on critical junctures). This is the aim of Givel (2006a, 2006b: 453–4), who argues that no such punctuation took place in the US in the 1990s because major policy decisions, such as the MSA (and state tobacco tax rises) have not been implemented effectively enough to change the course of tobacco policy. Yet, the more subtle aim of Baumgartner and Jones (2009) is to identify a shift in attitudes to policy over a longer period. In tobacco policy, they identify a shift in media and congressional attention, from low levels of positive attention to high levels of negative attention. While there is no single date or event to pinpoint, their graphs portray a clear dichotomy between the two eras. In turn, these shifts of attention can help explain shifts in the way that policymakers framed and acted on the tobacco problem. Looking back across this time period, we come to the conclusion that there was a clear punctuation. Policy change may have been largely incremental, but at some point it went on a strongly different path.

Which measures capture best this new policy direction? For example, media coverage becomes high and majority-negative from the 1980s (media coverage in the 1950s may also have been a major cause of a drop in smoking prevalence) and Congressional attention follows the same path from the late 1970s – although both are relative policy laggards in some respects, particularly since the media coverage seems to focus largely on government actions (Baumgartner and Jones, 1993: 116). Perhaps more illuminating is the figure showing the changing tone of government reports (as reported in the media), from more positive to industry in the 1950s (2 to 1 positive) to hugely negative by the 1980s (3 to 1 negative) (Baumgartner and Jones, 1993: 116; 2009: 116). This figure gives us a barometer of change, highlighting a shift from mostly-positive to mostly (and increasingly) negative from the mid-1960s. They are supplemented by Worsham (2006), who identifies two major shifts in congressional attention. First, the (pro-tobacco) agricultural committee began to be replaced as the main venue for tobacco policy from the mid-1960s (2006: 441–2). Second, a shift in policy tone – from promotion to regulation – and in the balance between pro/anti-tobacco witnesses began at the same time (2006: 443–5). Worsham (2006) then links policy change to this change in tone and attention. While there was no comprehensive policy that can be pinpointed to the shift in the 1960s, the new tone became conducive to a series of incremental tobacco control policy steps that would not have taken place under the majority-positive era, including mandatory, changing health warnings on cigarette packs (in 1965, 1970, 1984 and 2009) and bans on advertising in 1970 and 1972 (2006: 441).

In effect, Givel's (2006a, 2006b) focus on the post-1990 period is too late because the major shift in policy approach had already taken place. Further, this shift does not relate to a single punctuating event. Rather, it refers to 'fitful bursts of mobilisation that change the structure of bias for decades to come' (Baumgartner and Jones, 1993). In other words, it relates to the beginning of a new era in which policy changes incrementally in a new direction.

However, Givel raises a more fundamental question about how we assess change. His important point is that tobacco policy change is often symbolic and not followed through. He argues that, in the case of the US states, overall tobacco taxes remained low and regulations were still limited while the MSA had not been fully implemented. We suggest that such a conclusion can only be reached if Givel is careful to select a small number of measures that demonstrate the least progress towards tobacco control. Taken as a comprehensive set of measures at different levels of government (outlined in Chapter 6), US policy is a far cry from the largely symbolic measures we could identify in the early reaction to the 1964 Surgeon General's Report. Further, these examples of partial policy failure are less apparent in countries, such as the UK, Australia, Canada and New Zealand. Givel's point may be more pertinent to the early implementation of the FCTC (below).

The identification of major change is also a focus of the advocacy coalition framework (ACF). There are three main sources of change in this framework. First, coalitions adapt continuously to their policy environments and engage in policy learning to remain competitive. This process often produces incremental change because policy learning takes place through the lens of deeply held policy beliefs. In other words, coalitions learn on their own terms, selecting the information they consider to be most relevant and acceding only to change which does not undermine the coalition's main source of cooperation. Second, 'shocks', such as the election of a new government with different ideas or the effect of socioeconomic change, affect the positions of coalitions within subsystems. Shocks may produce major, non-incremental, change as coalitions are forced to question the fundamental nature of their beliefs in the light of new evidence and/or one coalition's source of dominance is undermined by a competing coalition. Although less powerful coalitions can enhance their positions through learning and seeking new allies, they are unlikely to challenge a dominant coalition successfully without the help of a major event (Sabatier, 1993: 35). These shocks 'can foster change in a subsystem by shifting and augmenting resources, tipping the power balance of coalitions, and changing beliefs' (Weible et al, 2009: 124). For example, a competing coalition may adapt more readily to its new policy environment, gain the favour of the subsystem's 'sovereign' and push successfully for legislative change, perhaps by exploiting a 'window of opportunity' to gather short-term support from allies elsewhere (Sabatier, 1998: 119). Or, there is an internal shock when an event prompts the dominant coalition to revisit its policy core beliefs, perhaps following a realisation that existing policies have failed monumentally.

The third source, based on the 'alternative dispute resolution' literature, is major policy change that results from negotiated agreements between 'previously warring coalitions'. Sabatier and Weible (2007: 205–7) identify the conditions required for this to occur: a previous 'stalemate' that suits no one; a negotiating process that builds trust, involves frequent meetings and minimal turnover of staff, gives 'all relevant groups of stakeholders' the power of veto and is chaired by a 'respected "neutral"'; and a realisation that there is no better alternative. The issue also has to be amenable to resolution through empirical research, rather than issues, such as abortion that are too mired in normative beliefs to allow participants to engage with each other in a meaningful way.

The ACF seems well placed to explain incremental changes. In the post-war period, subsystems were dominated by pro-tobacco coalitions. Their positions came increasingly under challenge by anti-tobacco groups presenting new information on the health effects of smoking (and SHS), but the effect was a series of policy responses that addressed the problem while maintaining the dominance of the pro-tobacco coalition, including filter tips on cigarettes, phasing out high tar brands, limiting advertising spending (a move that protected the market shares of existing companies) and voluntary agreements. Indeed, the latter were often still in place in the 2000s, with tobacco companies selling the idea of ventilation rather than bans on smoking in public places. In other words, the ACF helps us explain why it took so long for anti-tobacco groups to get the policies they wanted when tobacco control seemed like an 'idea whose time has come'.

However, it is less able to explain major change in this way because the suggestion is that (unlike in the punctuated account) the incremental changes are all designed to maintain the pro-tobacco position rather than set policy on a new path. The importance of negotiated agreements also seems limited because tobacco is an issue infused with normative beliefs (and the demonisation of tobacco companies). That leaves the role of 'shocks' but, in our case, it is difficult to pin-point their role. It is difficult to identify a single shock that tipped the balance between pro- and anti-tobacco coalitions. Rather, we may identify a *series* of shocks that shifted the balance of power within the subsystem over time, with the pro-tobacco coalition able to slow down the shift before a tipping point in which voluntary and limited measures began to be replaced by tobacco control measures that found favour in the public health community. If the aim is to identify a series rather than a single shock (perhaps, given the ACF timeframe, every decade or so), we have plenty to choose from: from the first publication of the scientific evidence on smoking in 1950, to major governmental proclamations (notably the US Surgeon General's reports of 1964 and 1986), the litigation that led to the MSA in the US and the development of the FCTC (Table 3.2). However, this still perhaps overplays the role of lurches of attention at the expense of more gradual shifts in smoking and attitudes that took place over decades (for more analysis of the ACF and tobacco see Sato, 1999a, 1999b; Farquharson, 2003).

In each case, there is a clear methodological implication: the analysis of policy may require periods of several decades before we can identify profound change in the sense we describe. This is partly because tobacco policy is actually a collection of multiple policy instruments. In the absence of a sharp replacement of all instruments at the same time, it will be difficult to pinpoint a single game-changing punctuation, major shock or third order change. Instead, we may be identifying sharp changes in some instruments that, while significant (and worthy of detailed research – e.g. Cairney, 2007a), are qualified by the bigger picture of incremental change along a fundamentally different path.

Explaining change in developed and developing countries

Thus far, these theories have been useful for the study of policy change in developed countries, but how do they apply to the developing countries that generally have experienced less radical change? Our discussion of developed countries suggests that policy transformation was long term and based on the mutually reinforcing process of institutional, problem definition, network, socioeconomic and ideational change. As such, it is conducive to explanation by the most prominent theories of public policy, which generally derive from studies of the US and have been applied to most developed countries (Cairney, 2012). In developing countries we find a notable absence of this source of domestic, long-term change. In its place, we find that many countries are embracing the FCTC as a means of transforming their tobacco policy regimes. In these cases, their adoption of the FCTC represents a sea change in policy from minimal to comprehensive tobacco control, suggesting that the role of policy transfer is a necessary element of any account. The question arises, how relevant are the most established theories?

These theories are most useful in explaining why policy has been slow to change for so long. As we highlight in Chapter 1, the identification of power to minimise attention to a problem, and hence maintain policy continuity and subsystem stability, is a particular feature of tobacco policy. In this light, we can understand developing country policy trajectories well because their tobacco policy subsystems resemble subsystems in developed countries in the 1950s: the main institutions responsible for policy are often geared towards finance, agriculture, trade and employment rather than tobacco control; political economy is the dominant frame; pro-tobacco interests dominate consultation; smoking prevalence is rising and the economic role of tobacco valued; and the scientific evidence alone is not persuasive enough to cause change.

Most developing countries therefore had (or still have) a subsystem dominated by pro-tobacco interests. In punctuated equilibrium theory terms, tobacco companies were able to construct and maintain a policy monopoly for almost all of the 20th century: tobacco was viewed positively and raised few issues beyond economic ones for governments to solve. Instead, tobacco activity was something for governments to support, an approach that limited participation to tobacco growers and manufacturers. Our current research question focuses on the ability of the global tobacco control agenda to challenge this monopoly and cause a period of subsystem instability and/or to represent a powerful new venue for the formulation of policy. This is by no means inevitable because the conditions are not the same as in developed countries. In particular, unlike our discussion of punctuated equilibrium in the US, we cannot identify the same long-term process of problem redefinition, as media, governmental and legislative attention shifted from a positive, low attention position to a more negative, higher attention one (WHO, 2008).

Instead, those changes took place at the international level, outside of the domestic policy domain. Perhaps ironically, the FCTC represents a clearly identifiable policy punctuation (as we discuss above, in developed countries the punctuation is there but generally hard to locate), but it is one that was generated from outside the political system. The role of punctuated equilibrium theory may be to analyse the longer-term domestic consequences: does it mark a major challenge to the existing policy monopoly, based on a redefinition of the problem and a challenge to previously insulated actors? If so, then the international system has provided an additional venue for policy on what has heretofore been considered a domestic issue. This happens rarely but is not unprecedented, especially for issues that can be defined in 'morality' terms sufficiently to generate a cross-country coalition for change, such as slavery and women's suffrage (Nadelman, 1990; Keck and Sikkink, 1998).

In ACF terms, the pro-tobacco coalition has remained dominant. The ACF may, in particular, help explain why the impact of the scientific evidence has been surprisingly low in many developing countries. It suggests that coalitions interpret new evidence through an existing lens and adapt accordingly, ultimately to maintain their position within the subsystem. In the case of tobacco, the pro-tobacco coalition has pursued two successful strategies: first, to challenge the veracity of the scientific evidence, either directly or by drawing attention to different (largely economic) frames of reference, and, second, to produce policies that address the problem on their terms, largely by introducing voluntary agreements or rather weak policy instruments not acceptable to anti-tobacco groups. An emerging research question focuses on the extent to which we can treat the widespread adoption of the FCTC as an external shock that will alter the balance of power within subsystems radically. The ACF suggests that this requires that the minority advocacy coalition has the means and opportunity to exploit its new context, something that is not inevitable in countries with an underdeveloped domestic tobacco control capacity. Unlike in ACF discussions of developed country policy change, we cannot identify a process of meaningful incremental policy change, as the dominant coalition maintains its position by learning and adapting but also gives some policy concessions. Instead, domestic anti-tobacco coalitions have been relatively powerless and unable to exert significant pressure within the subsystem, providing pro-tobacco coalitions with minimal incentives to adapt. The global tobacco policy agenda may represent a major shock to the subsystem, one that shifts the balance of power between pro- and anti-tobacco coalitions. Alternatively, the ACF may prove valuable at explaining why the FCTC is taking a long time to implement. In other words, we can only assess the magnitude of the shock when we analyse the process over the longer term: was the FCTC sufficient to ensure that the anti-tobacco coalition became powerful?

In multiple streams analysis terms, there have been few (if any) windows of opportunity for major policy change at the domestic level. While tobacco control solutions now exist and most have been adopted in some form in many countries, focused attention to the tobacco problem is unusual, and few policymakers have the motive and opportunity to adopt new policy measures. Instead, the confluence of multiple streams has taken place at the international level. A new research question relates to the effect of this major international change: does it cause a window of opportunity to open at the domestic level?

Hybrid theories: The policy transfer window

In each case, we may need to adapt these theories to account for the heightened significance of policy transfer. To some extent the theories can accommodate the importance of policy transfer because this is really about the diffusion of ideas – as knowledge, ways of understanding problems, and policy solutions. However, there is also an added element of coercion in some discussions of transfer (compare Rose, 1993, 2005 with Dolowitz and Marsh, 2000). In the case of tobacco, the question relates to the role and extent of 'indirect coercive transfer' (Chapter 2) – when the importing country perceives the need to change policy following the effect of 'externalities' (Dolowitz and Marsh, 1996: 348–9). As Chapter 2 suggests, countries often react to a range of external pressures in the shape of norms, embarrassment and economics. Yet, there are some interesting qualifications in the tobacco field. First, the externalities involved may, in some cases, reduce the likelihood of transfer – for example, tobacco control in one region means a higher potential for tobacco jobs and income in another, and therefore no incentive to emulate that policy. Second, transfer may be more about norms of best practice than forms of coercion. International norms or expectations may be *exploited* as a resource by certain domestic groups, organisations or departments within government to help them challenge other groups within existing subsystems. While the WHO may put pressure on *some* reluctant countries to keep up with the international agenda, in other cases it may help anti-tobacco groups within countries reform their own systems.

One solution to our analytical problem is to combine existing theories of policy change with accounts of policy transfer. The 'policy transfer window' is one such attempt (Cairney, 2012: 269). It adapts Kingdon's (1984) focus on the role of problems (how is the policy problem defined?), policies (which ideas or solutions are available?) and politics (how receptive are policymakers to these ideas?). In Kingdon's original model, while multiple streams come together to produce change, policymaker receptivity seems to be the key stream. In the policy transfer window the power to be more or less receptive to new ideas often gives way to the power to oblige importing governments to consider one policy problem and its solution more than another. The window of opportunity now depends on the ability of other jurisdictions to set the agenda of an importing jurisdiction, the applicability of their ideas, and the level of domestic receptivity to those ideas (or the ability to resist transfer).

The particular value of multiple streams analysis is that it shows that policy change is not inevitable, even when several favourable conditions are in place. The FCTC has raised tobacco control on the agenda of 192 countries and helped many countries redefine the tobacco problem as a major public health epidemic. The WHO has produced policies that are available for adoption. These policies have emerged from the 'policy primeval soup' (in this case, they have been refined following their adoption by many countries) and can be introduced at short notice. All that remains is the desire and opportunity for policymakers to turn solutions into policies. The FCTC provides the opportunity, but more research needs to be done to track the varying goals of policymakers in domestic settings.

In particular, we may be interested in the continuing, and varying, role of policy entrepreneurs. In the transfer literature, a policy entrepreneur is an individual or organisation (such as an NGO, think tank or international organisation) that successfully promotes a policy to an importing government. In the case of tobacco, it may be the WHO that has persuaded countries to think about tobacco control. In multiple streams analysis, entrepreneurs are actors with detailed knowledge of the domestic policy process that, 'wait in and around government with their solutions at hand, waiting for problems to float by to which they can attach their solutions, waiting for a development in the political stream they can use to their advantage' (Kingdon, 1984: 165–6). In some cases, the entrepreneur may be an elected politician, while in others it may be the leader of an interest group, think tank or merely the unofficial spokesperson for a particular cause. The entrepreneur is someone with the knowledge, power, tenacity and luck to be able to exploit windows of opportunity and heightened levels of attention to policy problems, to promote their 'pet solutions' to policymakers. In the case of tobacco, the FCTC process may have opened the window of opportunity, but domestic policy processes of each country may still require an entrepreneur to bring the three streams together. This stage of policy development, beyond the broad decision to adopt a tobacco control agenda, has been slow to unfold in most developing countries.

In turn, this conclusion raises the issue of policy transfer success. We may view the FCTC as a successful global project in terms of commitment and the development of new governance arrangements (below), but we have to reserve judgement on its long-term success using other measures. For Dolowitz and Marsh (2000: 17) policy success refers to the extent to which a policy was adapted properly. Failure can relate to one (or a combination) of three factors: uninformed transfer (when the borrowing country has incomplete information about the crucial elements that made the policy a success in the lending country); incomplete transfer (when those crucial elements of policy are not transferred); and inappropriate transfer (when not enough attention is paid to adaptation, or the differences in policy conditions, structures and aims of the lending country). These elements reinforce the idea that the transfer of policy is effectively the first of several stages. This combines with elements from the wider evaluation literature that suggests that success is difficult to measure. Marsh and McConnell (2010: 571, 580) discuss seven main factors. They consider practical issues, such as how long we should wait before evaluating a policy, how much information there is, how we can separate the effects of this policy from others, and what the benchmark should be (e.g. the government's intentions, past outcomes, the success of other countries?). They also consider the more fundamental questions. For example, *whose* success are we measuring primarily – the government, its stakeholders or its target group? Further, how should governments measure their own success? *Process* measures include a focus on a policy's legitimacy, *programmatic* measures refer to implementation success, and *political* measures to the effect of the policy on the government's credibility.

For our purposes, we can say that policy transfer has been successful in terms of commitment, but we may have to identify how adaptable each policy instrument is, when derived from a developed country and applied to a developing country (see also Evans, 2005). We may also explore the short term and ultimate aims of the FCTC and related tobacco control policies. Short-term success is apparent in the number of 'parties' (174 as of September 2011). Longer-term success may relate to the problems we identified in Chapter 1: does the process represent a successful challenge to the power of tobacco companies? Will it lead to a solution to the tobacco problem? Will it reduce smoking prevalence and act as a brake on the next stages of the tobacco epidemic in developing countries? And which instruments will be the most significant? Do the elements of the WHO-endorsed comprehensive tobacco control policy need to be revised, based on evidence of the results?

Conclusion: Global tobacco futures

While most of this book has concentrated on the domestic politics of tobacco control within countries, the future of tobacco policy lies in the multi-level contest between anti- and pro-tobacco forces within and outside of governments. This conflict has now moved to the international level while still being fought on various tiers within countries. In developed countries, the anti-tobacco forces have become increasingly successful over the past half century but, even in leading tobacco control countries, such as Canada there are battles still to be won and the international agenda is an important resource. The FCTC still serves as a model of 'best practices' to which officials can be held to account in their policies (Global Tobacco Forum, 2008, 2010). Increasingly, the battleground between these forces will be in the developing world, which contains the greatest growth potential for tobacco markets and the most significant tobacco control opportunities. It is here that the struggle for the alternative frames of tobacco policy, political economy or public health/morality, will be joined at its fiercest, and where the outcome is most uncertain.

What we have tried to do in this book is to produce for readers the tools, theoretical and empirical, to analyse this policy conflict, with its enormous economic and health consequences. It is an open question whether policy changes will lead to revisions of the existing categorisation of eras in tobacco policy; for instance, whether the tobacco epidemic model will inspire a foreshortening of the consequences of tobacco use in the developing world or whether tobacco prohibition or harm regulation/minimisation will win out. Similarly, which explanations of tobacco policy, either individual or in combination, will prove to be most valuable depends on forthcoming as well as past events and policy developments. But there is little doubt that the conflict has broadened into one best addressed through the lens of concepts, such as global or multi-level governance.

In this final section we introduce some alternative scenarios for a global tobacco policy future. The Tobacco Epidemic Model (Chapter 1) has a normative goal, namely that knowledge of the previous course of the epidemic in the developed world can lead to interventions that prevent a similar epidemic elsewhere. The FCTC is a product of this viewpoint. The major issue in the developing world, therefore, concerns two related questions: (1) how well the FCTC will be implemented and (2) how effective even a thorough implementation would be in reducing or eliminating the tobacco epidemic. These are early days on the implementation front, with considerable variation across countries in the developing world. While developing countries play leading and supportive roles in the adoption of the FCTC and almost all have been willing to sign it, only a few have been eager implementers, with others adopting a 'wait and see' attitude, sometimes based on further guidance and financial subsidies from developed countries. The overall issue, therefore, amounts to whether normative commitment will be backed by practical measures, and whether these measures will work adequately to secure the goals of the Tobacco Epidemic Model and the FCTC.

On the positive side is the power of leading examples and the diffusion of ideas, backed by the WHO as a respected intergovernmental organisation and supported by the fact that smoking rates remain low in most developing countries. Further, in countries, such as Nigeria and Argentina, recently considered to be safe havens for tobacco companies, heavy investments in financial and human resources from the international community combined with active domestic involvement produced countrywide tobacco control laws. In this context, it is difficult to foresee circumstances under which tobacco companies could return to their dominant global position. Tobacco control policy may also inform international policies on other non-communicable diseases (Beaglehole et al, 2011; Mamudu et al, 2011).

On the negative side is the fact that tobacco companies have made strong inroads in many developing countries and have immense resources to offer incentives for increased smoking and weak tobacco control policies. Tobacco companies are very inventive and adaptable, and they have the advantage of immense resources and an addictive, legal product. The political institutions in developing countries are often fragile and there is an ongoing struggle over the definition of tobacco policy, with the political economy perspective having immense attractiveness in poor countries. When tobacco control policies are introduced, their sustainability is not certain, even though population-based policies, such as smoke-free environments have enjoyed increasing support once implemented (Borland et al, 2006; Hilton et al, 2007; Hyland et al, 2009). Further, tobacco has to compete with other issues (such as obesity) for policymaker attention and scarce resources (Nugent and Feigl, 2010; Schroeder and Warner, 2010). A full scale 'prohibition regime' (Nadelman, 1990) is a remote prospect.

A key factor is uncertainty about the role of China. It is difficult to underestimate China's impact on how well tobacco control fares in the developing world. China's rise as an economic power enhances its influence over other developing countries and if it uses its power to encourage popular adherence to the FCTC, it would change not only its domestic situation but also the international dynamic. Yet, the conditions do not seem conducive to such change: smoking is high; there is a state-owned industry that provides 10% of total tax revenue; and, tobacco control policy is weak in terms of institutions, ideas, and the struggle over the policy agenda. Further, despite some limited moves to limit sales and the consumption of cigarettes, there is no more than a nominal commitment to FCTC goals (Branigan, 2011). The China National Tobacco Company is also well placed to build on its monopoly on the Chinese market and to produce cheap cigarettes for poor smokers around the world.

If we assume that prohibition will not occur in the mid-range future, what are the main options? The first option is an incremental, probably erratic, movement toward what we have called a 'neo-prohibitionist' regime, with laggard countries adopting stronger policies, continued decreases in smoking, more public health measures, such as plain packaging and new ratings for movies with smoking scenes (WHO, 2009), backed by stronger institutional support, the public health/morality perspective achieving greater dominance, and anti-tobacco groups gaining power at the expense of the tobacco industry. As the smoking population dwindles, the struggle between a population-based (Chapman, 2009) and an individual-based (Britton, 2009) approach to tobacco control may be more fully joined. The appeal of certain policy approaches to tobacco control may increasingly be questioned when the smoking population falls below a certain percentage. Inasmuch as tobacco excise taxes will remain a major instrument for tobacco control, its attractiveness to policy-makers may diminish as the population of smokers dwindles and the habit increasingly become concentrated in the poor (although anti-tobacco groups have proved adept at turning these images round, to highlight health inequalities). The palatability of tobacco excise tax may be challenged with the issue of fairness and equity, especially if tobacco tax revenues are not used directly to finance programmes for the addicted few to quit. In this respect, there is the need to begin contemplating how to deal with the stigmatisation of tobacco users, a major public health concern. If a breakthrough in the search for a vaccine to inoculate current smokers against the addiction would be discovered, then neo-prohibitionism would acquire a potent new instrument (Quenqua, 2011).

The second option is an increased focus on harm minimisation or reduction. This strategy aims to reduce the harm to smokers through their consumption of traditional cigarettes by encouraging alternative nicotine delivery mechanisms, even if these have not been demonstrated to be completely harmless. The search for alternatives to the traditional consumption of addictive, toxic cigarettes continues in several ways, including the development of snus, electronic nicotine delivery systems (ENDS, e-cigarettes), the ongoing search for the 'holy grail' of a safer cigarette and the proposal to remove nicotine from tobacco products (Felderbaum, 2011; Jacobs, 2011; Gray et al, 2005). The goal would be not to eliminate smoking but to make it less harmful and reduce it to a 'hard core' of perhaps licensed addicts in the interests of improving the health prospects for the rest of the smoking population. De-commercialisation is more likely to be a large part of the latter approach, not only in the form of plain packaging but also through changes in cigarette product design, price and profit controls, and/or the state-controlled distribution of cigarettes (Cunningham, 1996; Borland, 2003; Callard et al, 2005; Malone, 2011).

The main complication to this scenario is the reducing likelihood that pro- and anti-tobacco forces can work together in a meaningful way. Harm reduction might involve working with tobacco companies to develop new products rather than working against them. Such a stance has generated considerable controversy on moral as well as practical grounds within the tobacco control non-governmental movement. It is difficult to denormalise the product, behaviour, and the industry if one is working with them to reduce the toxicity and addictiveness of tobacco products. Those opposed to harm reduction argue that 'safer' products would only be used to induce consumers to smoke stronger cigarettes. Thus far, the lack of truly safe, well-tested alternative delivery products on a large scale has left this argument unresolved. Yet, even if a safer means of alternative delivery can be demonstrated to be effective, the development of a global tobacco harm reduction regime would probably be a slow and uneven process.

The future of tobacco policy is complicated and uncertain. The safest prediction is always 'minimal change on the current trajectory', but, as the weight of evidence in this book indicates, the past half century of tobacco policy has been one of incremental change in multiple countries, which in the longer-term perspective have resulted in cumulative, major change, including consensus on the FCTC, that would have been considered wildly improbable in the 1950s.

Notes

Chapter 1 Political Science and Tobacco Policy

1 The distinction between developed and developing countries is useful but problematic, particularly when we combine discussions of economic and social or political development. We follow the framework, outlined by the United Nations Statistics Division, which lists developed countries as the US, Canada, Japan, New Zealand, Australia and certain (generally Western, not Eastern) European countries. In Chapter 4 we make the distinction between developed EU member states (and associate countries) and developing or 'transitional' Central and Eastern European countries (including the new EU accession states). See http://unstats.un.org/unsd/methods/m49/m49regin.htm#developed

Chapter 2 Theories of Policy Change

2 We use the term 'pressure participants' because not all participants are pressure or interest groups. They may also be businesses, organisations, such as Universities, government agencies or different levels of government. See Jordan et al (2004).

Chapter 4 European Countries and the EU

3 OECD Health Statistics http://www.oecd.org/document/16/0,3343,en_2649_34631_2085200_1_1_1_37407,00.html

Chapter 5 The UK: A Case Study

4 At the time of writing, £1 equals US$1.6.

5 Note the effect of the EU common market which allows for the mobility of people and goods across the UK and makes the enforcement of policy on tobacco smuggling more difficult.

6 Townsend (1996) suggests that tobacco cost £610m to the national health service, £20m to the fire service, a net of £190m in social security payments and 50 million working days lost per annum in 1996. ASH (2010a: 2) puts the NHS cost at £2.7bn (as does the Department of Health, 2010: 5), attributes 1600 deaths in ten years to cigarette-related fires, highlights similar working days lost and estimates that making workplaces smoke-free would save £2.3–2.7bn. See also ASH (2010a: 2) on the debate regarding the net economic cost of tobacco in the Czech Republic.

7 The UK has the highest tobacco taxation in the EU (ASH, 2010c: 3). According to the TMA (2010b), the amount of tax on the RRP of a pack of 20 cigarettes was 73% in 1990, rising to 80% in 2001 and falling to 77% by 2010. For a comparison of prices in the EU, see Aspect Consortium (2004: 79).

8 ASH 2010c: 3 has an estimate of 22%; the Department of Health, 2010 suggests a figure of £3bn in 2006. This is a rather contentious area because tobacco companies have often been blamed (most notably by the WHO) for much of the untaxed, smuggled market – see the Tobacco Control Atlas http://www.who.int/tobacco/en/atlas20.pdf

Chapter 8 Tobacco Control Policymaking in Developing Regions

9 'Parties' (174) refers to all countries that have ratified the FCTC, making them observers to the Conference of the Parties. There are 168 signatories (including the US), making them members of the COP.

Chapter 9 The WHO Framework Convention on Tobacco Control (FCTC)

10 There have been five progress reports (important to gauge FCTC effectiveness) produced by member countries from 2007–11 – see http://www.who.int/fctc/reporting/summary_analysis/en/index.html

Bibliography

Abbott, K. W. and D. Snidal (2000) 'Hard and Soft Law in International Governance', *International Organization*, 54(3): 421–56.

Abedian, I. and R. Van der Merwe (eds) (1999) *The Economics of Tobacco Control: Towards an Optimal Policy Mix*. (Applied Fiscal Research Center, University of Cape Town).

Advisory Commission on Intergovernmental Relations (1977) *Cigarette Bootlegging: A State and Federal Responsibility* (Washington: Advisory Commission on Intergovernmental Relations).

Advisory Commission on Intergovernmental Relations (1985) *Cigarette Taxes and Tax Avoidance: A Second Look* (Washington: Advisory Commission on Intergovernmental Relations).

Agranoff, R. (2004) 'Autonomy, Devolution and Intergovernmental Relations', *Regional and Federal Studies*, 14(1): 26–65.

Aguinaga, B. A. and S. Shatenstein (2002) *Profits Over People: Big Tobacco Industry Activities to Market Cigarettes and Undermine Public Health in Latin America and the Caribbean* (Washington, DC: PAHO).

Albæk, E. (2004) 'Holy Smoke No More? Tobacco Control in Denmark', in E. A. Feldman and R. Bayer (eds) *Unfiltered: Conflicts over Tobacco and Public Health* (Cambridge: Harvard University Press).

Albuja, S. and R. A. Daynard (2009) 'The Framework Convention on Tobacco Control (FCTC) and the Adoption of Domestic Tobacco Control Policies: The Ecuadorian Experience', *Tobacco Control*, 18(1): 18–21.

Alter, K. and S. Meunier (2009) 'The Politics of International Regime Complexity', *Perspectives on Politics*, 7(1): 13–24.

Amos, A. and H. Margaretha (2000) 'From Social Tobacco to "Torch Freedom": The Marketing of Cigarettes to Women', *Tobacco Control*, 9(1): 3–8.

ANRF (American NonSmokers' Rights Foundation) (2011a) Overview List – How many Smokefree Laws? http://www.no-smoke.org/pdf/mediaordlist.pdf.

ANRF (2011b) Local 100% Smokefree Laws in all Workplaces, Restaurants, and Bars: Effective by Year http://no-smoke.org/pdf/current_smokefree_ordinances_by_year.pdf.

APACT (1995) 950000 Apact Conference Chiang Mai, Thailand 951122–951124 Report 3 (Part 2) http://legacy.library.ucsf.edu/tid/alf97d00. 16 Nov 2009.

Asare, B. (2009) 'Tobacco Regulation in South Africa: Interest Groups and Public Policy', *African Journal of Political Science and International Relations*, 3(1): 99–106.

Asare, B., P. Cairney and D. Studlar (2009) 'Federalism and Multilevel Governance in Tobacco Policy: The European Union, the United Kingdom and the Devolved UK Institutions', *Journal of Public Policy*, 29(1): 79–102.

Asare, B. and D. Studlar (2009) 'Lesson-Drawing and Public Policy: Secondhand Smoking Restrictions in Scotland and England', *Policy Studies*, 30(3): 365–82.

Asare, B. E. (2007) *Tobacco Control: Comparative Public Policy in the United Kingdom and South Africa* (Saarbrücken, Germany: VDM Verlag).

Asbridge, M. (2004) 'Public Place Restrictions on Smoking in Canada: Assessing the Role of the State, Media Science and Public Health Advocacy', *Social Science and Medicine*, 58(1): 13–24.

ASH (1998) Tobacco Explained: The Truth about the Tobacco Industry in its Own Words http://www.who.int/tobacco/media/en/TobaccoExplained.pdf.

ASH (2005a) Basic Facts: One. Smoking Statistics http://www.ash.org.uk/.

ASH (2005b) Key Dates in the History of Anti-Tobacco Campaigning http://www.ash.org.uk/files/documents/ASH_741.pdf.

ASH (2007) The UK Tobacco Industry http://old.ash.org.uk/html/factsheets/html/fact18.html.

ASH (2009) ASH Financial Statements: 2009 http://www.ash.org.uk/files/documents/ASH_717.pdf.

ASH (2010a) The Economics of Tobacco http://www.ash.org.uk/files/documents/ASH_121.pdf.

ASH (2010b) Smoking Statistics: Who Smokes and How Much? http://www.ash.org.uk/files/documents/ASH_106.pdf.

ASH (2010c) UK Tobacco Control Policy and Expenditure – An Overview http://www.ash.org.uk/files/documents/ASH_667.pdf.

ASH Scotland (2005) *The Unwelcome Guest: How Scotland Invited the Tobacco Industry to Smoke Outside* (Edinburgh: ASH Scotland).

Ashton, P. L. (1993) 'UICC Regional Tobacco Control Efforts in Latin America', *Tobacco Control*, 2(4): 343.

Aspect Consortium (2004) *Tobacco or Health in the European Union – Past, Present and Future* (Luxembourg: Office for Official Publications of the European Communities) http://www.europeancancerleagues.org/DOSS/uploaded/182_tobacco_fr_en[1].pdf.

Assunta, M. (2004) 'Unfiltered: Conflict over Tobacco Policy and Public Health', *Tobacco Control*, 13(4): 455.

Assunta, M. and S. Chapman (2006) 'Health Treaty Dilution: A Case Study of Japan's Influence on the Language of the WHO Framework Convention on Tobacco Control', *Journal of Epidemiology and Community Health*, 60: 751–6.

Axelrod, R. (1986) 'An Evolutionary Approach to Norms', *American Political Science Review*, 80(4): 1095–111.

Bache, I. and M. Flinders (eds) (2004) *Multi-level Governance* (Oxford: Oxford University Press).

Bachrach, P. and M. Baratz (1962) 'The Two Faces of Power', *American Political Science Review*, 56(4): 947–52.

Bachrach, P. and M. Baratz (1970) *Power and Poverty* (New York: Oxford University Press).

Baggott, R. (1988) 'Health vs. Wealth: The Politics of Smoking in Norway and the UK', *Strathclyde Papers on Government and Politics*, No. 57.

Baier, G. (2008) 'The Courts, the Division of Powers and Dispute Revolution', in H. Bakvis and G. Skogstad (eds) *Canadian Federalism: Performance, Effectiveness and Legitimacy* (2nd ed.; Toronto: Oxford University Press).

Bailey, C. J. (2004) 'From Informed Choice to Social Hygiene: Government Control of Cigarette Smoking in the U.S', *Journal of American Studies*, 38(1): 41–61.

Bakvis, H. and D. Brown (2010). 'Policy Coordination in Federal Systems: Comparing Intergovernmental Processes and Outcomes in Canada and the United States', *Publius*, 40(3): 484–507.

Ballard, J. (2004) 'The Politics of Tobacco Control in Australia: International Template?', in E. A. Feldman and R. Bayer (eds) *Unfiltered: Conflict Over Tobacco and Public Health* (Cambridge: Harvard University Press).

Bansal, R., S. John and P. Ling (2005) 'Cigarette Advertising in Mumbai, India: Target Different Socioeconomic Groups, Women, and Youth', *Tobacco Control*, 14(2): 201–6.

Barnett, M. and R. Duvall (eds) (2005) *Power in Global Governance* (Cambridge: Cambridge University Press).

Barnum, H. (1994) 'The Economic Burden of the Global Trade in Tobacco', *Tobacco Control*, 3(4): 358–61.

Barr, C. (2010) 'Cigarette Factories Suck in €1.5m of Funds', *Financial Times*, 2 December.

Barry, M. (1991) 'The Influence of the US Tobacco Industry on the Health, Economy, and Environment Of Developing Countries', *New England Journal of Medicine*, 324: 917–20.

BAT (1980) 'Africa Public Affairs Conference: The Changing Policies of WHO and their Implications for BAT Companies in Africa', *British American Tobacco*. Accessed 2 Aug. 2010. http://legacy.library.ucsf.edu/tid/sgn26a99.

BAT (1995) 'Key Issues Council: Supranational Anti-Smoking Groups – Analyse and Develop Programme'. 17 Jan. 1995. *British American Tobacco*. Accessed 11 Aug 2011. http://legacy.library.ucsf.edu/tid/hmm24a99.

Baumgartner, F. R., C. Green-Pedersen and B. D. Jones (2006) 'Comparative Studies of Policy Agendas', *Journal of European Public Policy*, 13(6): 959–74.

Baumgartner, F. and B. Jones (1993) *Agendas and Instability in American Politics* (Chicago: University of Chicago Press).

Baumgartner, F. and B. Jones (2009) *Agendas and Instability in American Politics* (2nd ed.; Chicago: University of Chicago Press).

Bayer, R. and J. Colgrove (2002) 'Science, Politics, and Ideology in the Campaign Against Environmental Tobacco Smoke', *American Journal of Public Health*, 92(6): 949–54.

Bayer, R. and J. Colgrove (2004) 'Children and Bystanders First: The Ethics and Politics of Tobacco Control in the United States', in E. A. Feldman and R. Bayer (eds) *Unfiltered: Conflicts over Tobacco Policy and Public Health* (Cambridge: Harvard University Press).

BBC (2009) Assad Decree Syria Smoking Ban. Retrieved November 1, 2009, from http://news.bbc.co.uk/2/hi/middle_east/8302794.stm.

Beaglehole, R. (1991) 'Science. Advocacy and Health Policy: Lessons from the New Zealand Tobacco Wars', *Journal of Public Health Policy*, 12(2): 175–83.

Beaglehole, R., R. Bonita, R. Horton et al (2011) 'The Lancet NCD Action Group and the NCD Alliance. Priority Actions for the Non-communicable Disease Crisis', *Lancet*, 377: 1438–47.

Béland, D. and R. H. Cox (2011) 'Introduction: Ideas and Politics', in D. Béland and R. H. Cox (eds) *Ideas and Politics in Social Science Research* (New York: Oxford University Press).

Bellagio Conference (1995) Bellagio Statement on Tobacco and Sustainable Development. Retrieved November 16, 2009, from http://www.idrc.ca/en/ev-84113-201-1 DO_TOPIC.html.

Bennett, C. (1991) 'What is Policy Convergence and What Causes It?', *British Journal of Political Science*, 21(2): 215–33.

Benzie, R. and R. J. Brennan (2009) '$2 billion in Tax Revenue Up in Smoke', *Toronto Star*, 15 November.

Berridge, V. (2004) 'Militants, Manufacturers, and Governments: Postwar Smoking Policy in the United Kingdom', in E. A. Feldman and R. Bayer (eds) *Unfiltered: Conflicts over Tobacco Policy and Public Health* (Cambridge: Harvard University Press).

Berridge, V. and K. Loughlin (2005) 'Smoking and the New Health Education in Britain 1950s–1970s', *American Journal of Public Health*, 95(6): 956–94.

Berry, F. S. and W. D. Berry (1999) 'Innovation and Diffusion Models in Policy Research', in P. Sabatier (ed.) *Theories of the Policy Process* (Boulder, CO: Westview Press).

Bettcher, D., C. Subramaniam, E. Guindon, A.-M. Perucic, L. Soll, G. Grabman et al (2001) *Confronting the Tobacco Epidemic in an Era of Trade Liberalization* (Geneva, Switzerland: World Health Organization-Tobacco Free Initiative).

Bingham, P. (1988) Tobacco Strategy Review Team – EEC Single Internal Market: 1992. http://bat.library.ucsf.edu//tid/hmb08a99.

Bishop, D. (1998) Plan 1998. Accessed 17 October 2011. HYPERLINK 'http://legacy.library.ucsf.edu/tid/ynx71a99'.

Blank, R. H. and V. Burau (eds) (2007) *Comparative Health Policy* (2nd ed.; New York: Palgrave Macmillan).

Blanke, D. D. (2002) *Towards Health with Justice: Litigation and Public Inquiries as Tools for Tobacco Control* (Geneva: World Health Organization).

Blomquist, W. (2007) 'The Policy Process and Large-N Comparative Studies', in P. Sabatier (ed.) *Theories of the Policy Process*, 2nd ed. (Boulder, CO: Westview).

Blyth, M. (2002) *Great Transformations: Economic Ideas and Institutional Change in the Twentieth Century* (New York: Cambridge University Press).

Borland, R. (2003) 'A Strategy for Controlling the Marketing of Tobacco Products: A Regulated Market Model', *Tobacco Control*, 12(5): 374–82.

Borland, R., H. H. Yong, M. Siahpush et al (2006) 'Support for and Reported Compliance with Smoke-free Restaurants and Bars by Smokers in Four Countries: Findings from the International Tobacco Control (ITC) Four Country Survey', *Tobacco Control*, 15(1): 34–41.

Borrás, S. and K. Jacobsson (2004) 'The Open Method of Co-ordination and New Governance Patterns in the EU', *Journal of European Public Policy*, 11(2): 185–208.

Börzel, T. A. (2002) 'Pace-Setting, Foot-Dragging, and Fence-Sitting: Member State Responses to Europeanization', *Journal of Common Market Studies*, 40: 193–214.

Bozicevic, I., A. Gilmore and S. Oreskovic (2004) 'The Tobacco Epidemic in South-East Europe: Consequences and Policy Responses', *HNP Discussion Paper, Economics of Tobacco Control Paper No. 18*, World Bank: www.worldbank.org/tobacco.

Brandt, A. M. (2007) *The Cigarette Century: The Rise, Fall, and Deadly Persistence of the Product That Defined America* (New York: Basic Books).

Brandt, A. M. and P. Rozin (eds) (1997) 'Introduction', in A. M. Brandt and P. Rozin (eds) *Morality and Health* (New York: Routledge).

Branigan, T. (2011) 'China Bans Smoking in Indoor Spaces – But Won't Penalise Puffers', *The Guardian* http://www.guardian.co.uk/world/2011/may/01/china-bans-smoking-without-penalty.

Britton, J. (2009) 'In Defence of Helping People to Stop Smoking', *Lancet*, 373: 703–5.

Burstein, P. (2003) 'The Impact of Public Opinion on Public Policy: A Review and an Agenda', *Political Research Quarterly*, 56(1): 729–45.

Cairney, P. (2006) 'Venue Shift Following Devolution: When Reserved Meets Devolved in Scotland', *Regional and Federal Studies*, 16(4): 429–45.

Cairney, P. (2007a) 'A "Multiple Lenses" Approach to Policy Change: The Case of Tobacco Policy in the UK', *British Politics*, 2(1): 45–68.

Cairney, P. (2007b) 'Using Devolution to Set the Agenda: Venue Shift and the Smoking Ban in Scotland', *British Journal of Politics and International Relations*, 9(1): 73–89.

Cairney, P. (2008) 'Has Devolution Changed the British Policy Style?', *British Politics*, 3(3): 350–72.

Cairney, P. (2009a) 'The Role of Ideas in Policy Transfer: The Case of UK Smoking Bans since Devolution', *Journal of European Public Policy*, 16(3): 471–88.

Cairney, P. (2009b) 'Tobacco Control Policy Analysis in China: Economics and Health (Review)', *China Quarterly*, 200: 1106–7.

Cairney, P. (2012) *Understanding Public Policy: Theories and Issues* (Basingstoke: Palgrave).

Califano, J. A. (1981) *Governing America: An Insider's Report from the White House and the Cabinet* (New York: Simon and Schuster).

Callard, C., D. Thompson and N. Collishaw (2005) 'Transforming the Tobacco Market: Why the Supply of Cigarettes Should be Transferred from For-profit Corporations to Non-profit Enterprises with a Public Health Mandate', *Tobacco Control*, 14(3): 278–83.

Campbell, J. (2002) 'Ideas, Politics and Public Policy', *Annual Review of Sociology*, 28: 21–38.

Camilleri, L. C. and M. Stanley (2009) Philip Morris International: Unpublished paper.

Cancer Council of Victoria (2008) *Tobacco in Australia: Facts and Issues*, 3rd ed. www.tobaccoinaustralia.org.au.

Cancer Research UK (2010) 'Smoking Statistics', http://info.cancerresearchuk.org/cancerstats/types/lung/smoking/#tobacco.

Corrao, M. A., G. E. Guindon, N. Sharma and D. F. Shokoohi (eds) (2000) *Tobacco Control Country Profiles* (Atlanta: American Cancer Society).

Carr-Gregg, M. (1993) 'Interaction of Public Policy Advocacy and Research in the Passage of New Zealand's Smoke-free Environments Act 1990', *Addiction*, 88: 35S–41S.

Carter, S. M. (2003) 'Cooperation and Control: The Tobacco Institute of Australia', *Tobacco Control*, 12 (Suppl III): iii54–iii60.

Carter, S. M. and C. Simon (2003) 'Smoking, Disease, and Obdurate Denial: The Australian Tobacco Industry in the 1980s', *Tobacco Control*, 12 (Suppl III): iii23–iii30.

Castles, F. G. (ed.) (1993) *Families of Nations* (Brookfield NH: Dartmouth).

Castles, F. G. (1998) *Comparative Public Policy* (Northampton MA: Edward Elgar).

Castles, F. and U. Wagschal (2008) 'Worlds, Families, Regimes: Country Clusters in European and OECD Area Public Policy', *Western European Politics*, 31(3): 321–44.

CDC (1999) Preemptive State Tobacco Control Laws – United States, 1982–1998.

CDC (2007) Best Practices for Comprehensive Tobacco Control Programs – 2007. Atlanta: U.S. Department of Health and Human Services, Centers for Disease Control and Prevention, National Center for Chronic Disease Prevention and Health Promotion, Office on Smoking and Health.

CDC (2009) Global Adult Tobacco Survey: Fact Sheet: Thailand, 2009. Retrieved December 11, 2009, from http://cdc.gov/tobacco/global/gats/countries/sear/fact_sheets/thailand/2009/pdfs/thailand_2009.pdf.

CDC (2010) 'State Preemption of Local Smoke-Free Laws in Government Work Sites, Private Work Sites, and Restaurants – United States, 2005–2009' http://www.cdc.gov/mmwr/preview/mmwrhtml/mm5904a4.htm?s_cid=mm5904a4_x.

CDC (2011) Global Tobacco Surveillance System Data http://apps.nccd.cdc.gov/GTSSData/Ancillary/DataReports.aspx?Option=1.

Chaloupka, F. and A. Laixuthai (1996) US Trade Policy and Cigarette Smoking in Asia. *Working Paper Series paper 5543*. Cambridge, MA: National Bureau of Economic Research. Accessed 31 May 2011. http://www.impacteen.org/fjc/PublishedPapers/w5543.pdf.

Chapman, S. (2003) '"We Are Anxious to Remain Anonymous": The Use of Third Party Scientific and Medical Consultants by the Australian Tobacco Industry, 1969 to 1979', *Tobacco Control*, 12 (Suppl III): iiii31–iii37.

Chapman, S. (2007) *Public Health Advocacy and Tobacco Control: Making Smoking History* (Oxford: Blackwell).

Chapman, S. (2009) 'The Inverse Impact Law of Smoking Cessation', *Lancet*, 373: 701–3.

Chapman, S. and W. L. Wong (1990) *Tobacco Control in the Third World: A Resource Atlas*. Penang, Malaysia: International Association of Consumer Unions.

Chapman, S. and S. M. Carter (2003) 'Avoid Health Warnings on All Tobacco Products for Just as Long as We Can: A History of Australian Tobacco Industry Efforts to Avoid, Delay and Dilute Health Warnings on Cigarettes', *Tobacco Control*, 12 (Suppl III): iii13–iii22.

Chapman, S. and P. Fahey (1989) *Cigarette Smoking and Economic Prosperity: The Relationship of GNP Per Capita and Cigarette Consumption in 103 Countries* (Sydney Australia: Department of Community Medicine University of Sydney).

Chapman, S. and M. Wakefield (2001) 'Tobacco Control Advocacy in Australia: Reflections on 30 Years of Progress', *Health Education and Behavior*, 28(3): 274–89.

Chapman, S. and W. L. Wong (1990) *Tobacco Control in the Third World: A Resource Atlas* (Penang, Malaysia: International Association of Consumer Unions).

Chitanondh, H. (2001) *Defeat in Trade-Victory in Health*. Bangkok (Thailand: Thailand Health Promotion Institute and The National Health Foundation).

CICAD and OAS (2008) Guiding Elements for Public Policy on Drugs in the Subregion: First Comparative Study on Drug Use and Associated Factors in the General Population 15 to 64 Years of Age. Retrieved November 26, 2009, from http://www.cicad.oas.org/OID/NEW/Research/ExecutiveSummary-2008subregional.pdf.

CICAD Anti-Drug Strategy in the Hemisphere. Retrieved November 26, 2009, from http://www.cicad.oas.org/EN/basicdocuments/Strategy.asp.

Cm 4177 (1998) Smoking Kills: A White Paper on Tobacco (London: The Stationery Office) http://www.archive.official-documents.co.uk/document/cm41/4177/4177.htm.

Cm 6374 (2004) Choosing Health: Making Healthier Choices Easier (London: The Stationery Office) http://www.dh.gov.uk/assetRoot/04/09/47/60/04094760.pdf.

Cnossen, S. and M. Smart (2006) 'Taxation of Tobacco', in S. Cnossen (ed.), *Theory and Practice of Excise Taxation: Smoking, Drinking, Gambling, Polluting, and Driving* (Oxford: Oxford University Press).

Cohen, M., J. March and J. Olsen (1972) 'A Garbage Can Model of Organizational Choice', *Administrative Science Quarterly*, 17(1): 1–25.

Collin, J., E. LeGresley, R. MacKenzie, S. Lawrence and K. Lee (2004) 'Complicity in Contraband: British American Tobacco and Cigarette Smuggling in Asia', *Tobacco Control*, 13(1): 104–11.

Collin, J., L. Kelley and K. Bissell (2002) 'The Framework Convention on Tobacco Control: The Politics of Global Health Governance', *Third World Quarterly*, 23(2): 265–82.

Commission on Global Governance (1995) *Our Global Neighborhood: The Report of Commission on Global Governance*. Oxford, UK: Oxford University Press.

Connolly, G. and T. Chen (1993) 'International Health and Tobacco Use', in T. P. Houston (ed.) *Tobacco Use: An American Crisis Final Conference Report and Recommendation from America's Health Community: January 9–12*. Chicago, IL: American Medical Association, pp. 72–4.

Cook, B. J. (1996) *Bureaucracy and Self-Government*. Baltimore, MD: The John Hopkins University Press.

Cooper, A. H. and P. Kurzer (2003) 'Rauch ohne Feuer: Why Germany Lags in Tobacco Control', *German Politics and Society*, 21(3): 24–47.

Corrao, M. A., E. Guindon, V. Cokkinides and N. Sharma (2000) 'Building the Evidence Base for Global Tobacco Control', *Bulletin of the World Health Organization*, 78(7): 884–90.

Corrao, M. A., E. Guindon, N. Sharma and D. F. Shokoohi (eds) (2000) *Tobacco Control Country Profiles* (Atlanta, GA: American Cancer Society).

Council Recommendation (2009) Council Recommendation of 30 November 2009 on Smoke-free Environments. *Official Journal of the European Union*. December 5.

Crenson, M. (1971) *The Un-politics of Air Pollution: A Study of Non-decisionmaking in the Cities* (London: Johns Hopkins Press).

Crofton, J. (1990) 'Tobacco and the Third World', *Thorax: Journal of the British Thoracic Society*, 45(3): 164–9.

Crosbie, E., E. M. Sebrié and S. A. Glantz (2011) 'Strong Advocacy Led to Successful Implementation of Smokefree Mexico City', *Tobacco Control*, 20(1): 64–72.

Cunningham, R. (1996) *Smoke and Mirrors: The Canadian Tobacco War* (Ottawa: International Development Research Centre).

CRUK (Cancer Research UK) (2010) 'Smoking – Statistics' http://info.cancerresearchuk.org/cancerstats/types/lung/smoking/#tobacco.

Dagfin, H. (2003) 'Norwegian Minister of Health Speaks to Eurohealth: Interview by David McDaid', *Eurohealth*, 9(2): 5–10.

Dawson, R. and J. Robinson (1963) 'Inter-Party Competition, Economic Variables and Welfare Policies in the American States', *Journal of Politics*, 25(2): 265–89.

Dean, G. (1959) 'Lung Cancer among White South Africans', *British Medical Journal*, 2(5156): 852–6.

Dearing, J. W. and E. M. Rogers (1996) *Agenda Setting* (London: Sage).

Deeks, J. (1992) 'Who's Choking Smoking? Advertising, Sponsorship and Government Regulation of the Tobacco Industry', in J. Deeks and N. Perry (eds) *Controlling Interests: Business, the State and Society in New Zealand* (Auckland: Auckland University Press).

Department of Health (2002) Tackling Health Inequalities: A Programme for Action http://www.dh.gov.uk/en/Publicationsandstatistics/Publications/PublicationsPolicyAndGuidance/DH_4008268.

Department of Health (2008) Tackling Health Inequalities: 2007 Status Report on the Programme for Action http://www.dh.gov.uk/prod_consum_dh/groups/dh_digitalassets/@dh/@en/documents/digitalasset/dh_083472.pdf.

Department of Health (2010) A Smokefree Future http://www.dh.gov.uk/prod_consum_dh/groups/dh_digitalassets/@dh/@en/@ps/documents/digitalasset/dh_111789.pdf.

Department of Health, Social Services and Public Safety (DHSSPS) (2002) Investing for Health, A Five-Year Tobacco Action Plan: Consultation Document.

Derthick, M. (2001) 'Federalism and the Politics of Tobacco', *Publius*, 31(1): 47–63.

Derthick, M. A. (2002) *Up in Smoke: From Legislation to Litigation in Tobacco Politics* (Washington: CQ Press).

Derthick, M. A. (2005) *Up in Smoke: From Legislation to Litigation in Tobacco Politics* (2nd ed.; Washington: CQ Press).

Devon Management Resources (1980) Anti-smoking Program of the World Health Organization. Interim Report. Accessed 27 Jul 2009. http://legacy.library.ucsf.edu/tid/vmb29d00.

de Zwart, K. M. and J. D. Sellman (2002) 'Public Knowledge and Attitudes Regarding Smoking and Smoking Cessation Treatments', *New Zealand Medical Journal*, 115(1153): 219–22.

DG Sanco (2007) *Towards a Europe Free from Tobacco Smoke: Policy Options at the EU Level* (European Commission Green Paper).

Doll, R. and A. B. Hill (1950) 'Smoking and Carcinoma of the Lung: Preliminary Report', *British Medical Journal*, 2(4682): 739–48.

Dolowitz, D. P. and D. Marsh (1996) 'Who Learns What From Whom: A Review of Policy Transfer Literature', *Political Studies*, 44(2): 343–57.

Dolowitz, D. and D. Marsh (2000) 'Learning from Abroad: The Role of Policy Transfer in Contemporary Policy-Making', *Governance*, 13(1): 5–24.

Doron, G. (1979) *The Smoking Paradox: Public Regulation in the Cigarette Industry* (Cambridge MA: Abt Books).

Drew, E. B. (1965) 'The Quiet Victory of the Cigarette Lobby: How it Found the Best Filter Yet – Congress', *Atlantic Monthly*, September, 76–9.

Duina, F. And P. Kurzer (2004) 'Smoke in Your Eyes: The Struggle Over Tobacco Control in the European Union', *Journal of European Public Policy*, 11(1): 57–77.

Durant, R. F. and P. F. Diehl (1989) 'Agendas, Alternatives and Public Policy: Lessons from the U.S. Foreign Policy Arena', *Journal of Public Policy*, 9(2): 179–205.

Easton, B. (1995) 'Smoking in New Zealand: A Census Investigation', *Australian and New Zealand Journal of Public Health*, 19(2): 125–9.

ECOSOC. E/1993/ 79. Multisectoral Collaboration on Tobacco or Health. 30 Jul. 1993. Accessed 31 Jul 2009. http://legacy.library.ucsf.edu/tid/acu08d00.

El-Awa, F. M. S. (2003) 'Regional Summary for the Eastern Mediterranean Region', in O. Shafey, S. Dolwick and G. E. Guindon (eds) *Tobacco Control Country Profiles* (Atlanta: American Cancer Society, WHO, International Union Against Cancer).

El-Awa, F. M. S. (2003) 'Middle East: Religion Against Tobacco', *Tobacco Control*, 12(3): 249–50.

El-Awa, F. M. S. (2008) 'Tobacco Control in Eastern Mediterranean Region: Overview and the Way Forward', *Eastern Mediterranean Health Journal*, 14(Special issue): S123–S125.

Elazar, D. (1971) 'From the Editor: The Themes of a Journal of Federalism', *Publius*, 1(1): 3–9.

Elinder, L. S., L. Joossens, M. Raw, S. Anreasson and T. Lang (2003) *Public Health Aspects of the EU Common Agricultural Policy* (Stockholm: National Institute of Public Health).

Eller, W. and G. Krutz (2009) 'Editor's Notes: Policy Process, Scholarship and the Road Ahead: An Introduction to the 2008 Policy Shootout', *Policy Studies Journa*l, 37(1): 1–4.

Environics Research Group Limited (2001) Public Support for International Efforts to Control Tobacco. Retrieved August 6, 2009, from http://erg.environics.net/english/5countriesenglish.pdf.

Environmental Protection Agency (1992) *Respiratory Health Effects of Passive Smoking: Lung Cancer and Other Disorders*. Washington: Environmental Protection Agency, Office of Research and Development, Office of Air and Radiation. EPA/600/6-90/006F.

Eriksen, M. P. and R. R. Cerak (2008) 'The Diffusion and Impact of Clean Indoor Air Laws', *Annual Review of Public Health*, 29: 171–85.

European Commission (1982) Actions against Smoking in the Member States of the European Union. Report EUR 7531. Brussels and Luxembourg: Directorate-General for Employment, Social Affairs and Education, Direction Health and Safety.

European Commission (2004) *Tobacco or Health in the European Union: Past, Present and Future* (Luxembourg: Office for Official Publications of the European Commission).

Evans, M. (ed.) (2005) *Policy Transfer in Global Perspective* (London: Ashgate).

Ezzati, M. and A. D. Lopez (2003) 'Estimate of Global Mortality Attributable to Smoking in 2000', *Lancet*, 362(9387): 847–52.

Falkner, G., O. Treib, M. Hartlapp and S. Leiber (2005) *Complying with Europe: EU Harmonisation and Soft Law in the Member States* (Cambridge: Cambridge University Press).

FAO (1990) *Tobacco: Supply, Demand and Trade Projections, 1995 and 2000*. FAO Economic and Social Development Paper 86, editor (Rome: FAO).

FAO (2003) *Projections of Tobacco Production, Consumption and Trade to the Year 2010* (Rome, Italy: FAO).

Farquharson, K. (2003) 'Influencing Policy Transnationally: Pro- and Anti-Tobacco Global Advocacy Networks', *Australian Journal of Public Administration*, 62(4): 80–92.

Farrelly, M. C., K. C. Davis and M. L. Haviland et al (2005) 'Evidence of a Dose – Response Relationship Between "Truth" Antismoking Ads and Youth Smoking Prevalence', *American Journal of Public Health*, 95(3): 425–31.

Farrelly, M. C., K. C. Davis and J. Duke et al (2009) 'Sustaining "Truth": Changes in Youth Tobacco Attitudes and Smoking Intentions after 3 Years of a National Antismoking Campaign', *Health Education Research*, 24(1): 42–8.

Featherstone, K. and C. M. Radaelli (eds) (2003) *The Politics of Europeanization* (Oxford: Oxford University Press).

Felderbaum, M. (2011) 'E-cigs: No Smoke, but Some Areas are Banning Them', boston.com, 4 June http://www.boston.com/business/articles/2011/06/04/e_cigs_no_smoke_but_some_areas_are_banning_them/.

Feldman, E. A. (2001) 'The Landscape of Japanese Tobacco Policy: Law, Smoking and Social Change,' *American Journal of Comparative Law*, 49(4): 679–706.

Feldman, E. A. (2004) 'The Limits of Tolerance: Cigarettes, Politics and Society in Japan', in E. A. Feldman and R. Bayer (eds) *Unfiltered: Conflicts over Tobacco Policy and Public Health* (Cambridge: Harvard University Press).

Feldman, E. A. (2006) 'The Culture of Legal Change: A Cast Study of Tobacco Control in Twenty-First Century Japan', *Public Law and Legal Theory*, University of Pennsylvania Law School, Research paper No. 06-10. http://ssrn.com/abstract=898466.

Feldman, E. A. and R. Bayer (2004) 'Introduction', in E. A. Feldman and R. Bayer (eds) *Unfiltered: Conflicts over Tobacco Policy and Public Health* (Cambridge: Harvard University Press).

Feldman, E. A. and R. Bayer (eds) (2004) *Unfiltered: Conflicts over Tobacco Policy and Public Health* (Cambridge: Harvard University Press).

Ferrence, R. (1989) *Deadly Fashion: The Rise and Fall of Cigarette Smoking in North America* (New York: Garland Publishing).

Finkelstein, L. (1995) 'What is Global Governance?', *Global Governance*, 1(1): 367–92.

Fishman J. A., H. Allison, S. B. Knowles, B. A. Fishburn, T. A. Woollery, W. T. Marx, D. M. Shelton, C. G. Husten and M. P. Eriksen (1999) 'State Laws on Tobacco Control – United States 1998', *Morbidity and Morbidity Weekly Report*, 48 No. SS-3: 21–62.

Fong, G. T., K. M. Cummings, R. Borland, G. Hastings, A. Hyland, G. A. Giovino, D. Hammond and M. Thompson (2006) 'The Conceptual Framework of the International Tobacco Control (ITC) Policy Evaluation Project', *Tobacco Control*, 15 (Suppl. 3): iii3–iii11.

Frankenberg, G. (2004) 'Between Paternalism and Voluntarism: Tobacco Consumption and Tobacco Control in Germany', in E. A. Feldman and R. Bayer (eds) *Unfiltered: Conflicts over Tobacco Policy and Public Health* (Cambridge: Harvard University Press).

Frey, S. R. (1997) 'The International Traffic in Tobacco', *Third World Quarterly*, 18(2): 303–19.

Friedman, K. M. (1975) *Public Policy and the Smoking-Health Controversy* (Lexington MA: Lexington Books).

Frisbee, S. J. (2010) *Comprehensive Tobacco Control Policy Regimes and Population Health: Assessing Causal Loops* (Unpublished Ph.D. dissertation, West Virginia University).

Frisbee, S. J., D. T. Studlar and K. Christensen (2009) 'The Impact of Tobacco Control Policies in the EU: Comparing Old and New Member States', Paper presented at EU Studies Association, Los Angeles.

Fristchler, A. L. and C. E. Rudder (2006) *Smoking and Politics: Bureaucracy Centered Policymaking* (6th ed.; Englewood Cliffs NJ: Prentice-Hall).

GAO (2011) 'Illicit Tobacco: Various Schemes Are Used to Evade Taxes and Fees'. Report to Congressional Committees (Washington: Government Accountability Office).

Geva-May, I. (2004) 'Riding the Wave of Opportunity: Termination in Public Policy', *Journal of Public Administration Research and Theory*, 14(3): 309–33.

Gilmore, A. and M. McKee (2002) 'Tobacco Control: The European Dimension', *Clinical Medicine*, 2(3): 335–42.

Gilmore, A. B. and M. McKee (2004a) 'Moving East: How the Transnational Tobacco Industry Gained Entry to the Emerging Markets of the Former Soviet Union – Part I: Establishing Cigarette Imports', *Tobacco Control*, 13(2): 143–50.

Gilmore, A. and M. McKee (2004b) 'Tobacco-Control Policy in the European Union', in E. A. Feldman and R. Bayer (eds) *Unfiltered: Conflicts over Tobacco Policy and Public Health* (Cambridge: Harvard University Press).

Gilmore, A. and W. Zatoński (2002) 'Free Trade v. the Protection of Health: How Will EU Accession Influence Tobacco Control in Poland?', *Eurohealth*, 8(4): 31–3.

Gilmore, A. B., E. Österberg, A. Heloma, W. Zatoński, E. Delcheva and M. McKee (2004) 'Free Trade Versus the Protection of Health: The Examples of Alcohol and Tobacco', in M. McKee, L. MacLehose and E. Nolte (eds) *Health Policy and European Union Enlargement* (Maidenhead: Berkshire: Open University Press).

Gilmore, A. and M. McKee (2005) 'Exploring the Impact of Foreign Direct Investment on Tobacco Consumption in the Former Soviet Union', *Tobacco Control*, 14(1): 13.

Givel, M. (2006a) 'Neoliberal and Public Health Impact of Not Adopting OSHA's Proposed National Secondhand Tobacco Smoke Rule', *International Journal of Health Services*, 36(2): 137–55.

Givel, M. (2006b) 'Punctuated Equilibrium in Limbo: The Tobacco Lobby and U.S. State Policymaking from 1990 to 2003', *Policy Studies Journal*, 34(3): 405–18.

Glantz, S. A., D. E. Barnes, L. Bero, P. Hanauer and J. Slade (1995) 'Looking Through a Keyhole at the Tobacco Industry: The Brown and Williamson Documents', *Journal of American Medical Association*, 274(3): 248–53.

Glantz, S. A., J. Slade, L. A. Bero, P. Hanauer and D. E. Barnes (1996) *The Cigarette Papers* (Berkeley: University of California Press).

Glantz, S. A. and E. D. Balbach (2000) *Tobacco War: Inside the California Battles* (Berkeley: University of California Press).

Glantz, S. and M. Gonzalez (2011) 'Effective Tobacco Control is the Key to Progress in the Reduction of Non-communicable Diseases', *Lancet*, 6736(11): 60615–16.

Global Smoke-free Partnership (2009) *Global Voices Report: Rebutting the Tobacco Industry, Winning Smoke-free Air, 2009 Status Report* (Naples Italy: Pixel Entropy).

Global Tobacco Control Forum (2008) *The Framework Convention on Tobacco Control: A Civil Society 'Shadow Report'*. http://smoke-free.ca/eng_issues/global/content/global-forum-shadow-report-2008-final-web.pdf.

Global Tobacco Control Forum (2010) *Canada: Implementation of the Framework Convention on Tobacco Control: A Civil Society Report*. http://www.smoke-free.ca/pdf_1/FCTC-Shadow-2010-Canada.pdf.

Goetz, K. H. (2006) *Territory, Temporality and Clustered Europeanization* (Vienna: Institute for Advanced Studies, Political Science Series 109).

Gordenker, L. and T. Weiss (1996) 'Pluralizing Global Governance: Analytical Approaches and Dimensions', *Third World Quarterly*, 16: 357–87.

Gray, N. (1977) *Lung Cancer Prevention: Guidelines for Smoking Control* (Geneva: International Union Against Cancer).

Gray, N. and M. Daube (eds) (1980) *Guidelines for Smoking Control* (Geneva, Switzerland: UICC).

Gray, N., J. E. Henningfield, N. L. Benowitz, G. N. Connolly, C. Dresler, K. Fagerstrom et al (2005) 'Toward a Comprehensive Long Term Nicotine Policy', *Tobacco Control*, 14(2): 161–5.

Green-Pedersen, C. and M. Wolfe (2009) 'The Institutionalization of Environmental Attention in the United States and Denmark: Multiple- versus Single-Venue Systems', *Governance*, 22(4): 625–46.

Griffith C., C. Welch, A. Cardone, A. Valdemoro and C. Jo (2008) 'The Global Momentum for Smoke-free Public Places: Best Practice in Current and Forthcoming Smoke-free Policies', *Salud Publica de Mexico*, 50 (Suplemento 3): S299–S308.

Grüning, T., A. B. Gilmore and M. McKee (2006) 'Tobacco Industry Influence on Science and Scientists in Germany', *American Journal of Public Health*, 96(1): 20–32.

Grüning, T., C. Strünck and A. Gilmore (2008) 'Puffing Away? Politics of Tobacco Control in Germany', *German Politics*, 17(2): 140–64.

Guevara, M. W. (2008) 'Tobacco Underground: The Booming Global Trade in Smuggled Tobacco', Retrieved November 24, 2009 from http://www.publicintegrity.org/investigations/tobacco/pages/introduction

Guindon, G. E. and D. Boisclair (2003) 'Past, Current and Future Trend in Tobacco Use', Retrieved October 31, 2009 from http://repositories.cdlib.org/context/tc/article/1118/type/pdf/viewcontent/.

Gupta, P. C. and H. C. Mehta (2000) 'Cohort Study of All-cause Mortality Amongst Tobacco Users in Mumbai India', *Bulletin of the World Health Organization*, 78(7): 877–83.

Haas, E. (1975) 'The Obsolescence of Regional Integration Theory', Berkeley: University of California, Institute of International Studies, Research Series: No. 25.

Haas, P.M. (1992) 'Introduction: Epistemic Communities and International Policy Coordination', *International Organization*, 46(1): 1–3.

Haas, P. (2002) 'UN Conferences and Constructivist Governance of the Environment', *Global Governance*, 8: 73–91.

Hall, D. R. (1969) *Cooperative Lobbying, The Power of Pressure* (Tucson: University of Arizona Press).

Hall, P. (1993) 'Policy Paradigms, Social Learning, and the State: The Case of Economic Policymaking in Britain', *Comparative Politics*, 25 (3): 275–96.

Hameed, A., M. A. Jalil, R. Noreen, I. Mugha and S. Rauf (2002) 'Role of Islam in Prevention of Smoking', *Journal of Ayub Medical College Abbottabad*, 14(1): 23–5.

Hammond, R. (1998) *Addicted to Profit: Big Tobacco's Expanding Global Reach* (Washington, D.C.: Essential Action).

Hammond, R. and C. White (2001) 'Voices of Truth, vol. 2: Multinational Tobacco Industry Activity in the Middle East: A review of Internal Documents', Retrieved May 31, 2011 from http://repositories.cdlib.org/tc/whotcp/WHO6/.

Hanauer, P., J. Slade, D. E. Barne, L. Bero and S. A. Glantz (1995) 'Lawyer Control of Internal Scientific Research to Protect Against Products Liability Lawsuits: The Brown and Williamson Documents', *JAMA*, 274(3): 234–40.

Hargrove, G. C. and INFOTAB (1981) *Developing Countries Group* http://legacy.library.ucsf.edu/tid/ghr25e00. 22 Nov 2009.

Harrison, K. (2005) 'Follow the Leader and Dominoes: Games Provinces Play in Tobacco Taxation', in K. Harrison (ed.) *Racing to the Bottom? Provincial Interdependence on the Canadian Federation* (Vancouver: UBC Press).

Hausegger, L., M. Hennigar and T. Riddell (2009) *Canadian Courts: Law, Politics, and Process* (Toronto: Oxford University Press).

Hay, D. (1993) 'The Rise and Fall of Smoking in New Zealand', *Journal of the Royal College of Physicians of London*, 27(3): 315–19.

Hay, C. (2002) *Political Analysis: A Critical Introduction* (Basingstoke: Palgrave).

Hay, C. (2006a) 'Constructivist Institutionalism', in R. Rhodes, S. Binder and B. Rockman (eds) *The Oxford Handbook of Political Institutions* (Oxford: Oxford University Press).

Health and Welfare Canada (1974) *A New Perspective on the Health of Canadians* (Ottawa: Health and Welfare Canada).

Healthy People (2011) 'Tobacco Use' http://www.healthypeople.gov/2020/topics-objectives2020/objectiveslist.aspx?topicid=41.

Heclo, H. (1978) 'Issue Networks and the Executive Establishment', in A. King (ed.) *The New American Political System* (Washington: American Enterprise Institute).

Held, D. and A. McGrew (eds) (2002) *Governing Globalization: Power, Authority and Global Governance* (Cambridge: Polity Press).

Hilton, M. (1995) '"Tabs," "Fags" and the "Boy Labour Problem" in Late Victorian and Edwardian Britain', *Journal of Social History*, 28(3): 587–607.

Hilton, S., S. Semple, B. G. Miller, L. MacCalman, M. Petticrew, S. Dempsey et al (2007) 'Expectations and Changing Attitudes of Bar Workers Before and After the Implementation of Smoke-Free Legislation in Scotland', *BMC Public Health*, 7: 206.

Hirayama, T. (1981) 'Non-smoking Wives of Heavy Smokers Have a Higher Risk of Lung Cancer: A Study from Japan', *British Medical Journal Clinical Research Edition*, 282(6259): 183–5.

Hirschhorn, N. (2006) 'Research Reports and Publications Based on Tobacco Industry Documents, 1991–2006', Retrieved November 23, 2009 from http://tobacco.health.usyd.edu.au/site/gateway/docs/pdf/Hirschhorn_publications_list.pdf.

HM Treasury and Department of Health (2002) 'Tackling Health Inequalities: Summary of the 2002 Cross-Cutting Review' http://webarchive.nationalarchives.gov.uk/+/http://www.hm-treasury.gov.uk/media/1F8/DC/Exec%20sum-Tackling%20Health.pdf.

Hoberg, G. (1991) 'Sleeping with an Elephant: The American Influence on Canadian Environmental Regulation', *Journal of Public Policy*, 11(1): 107–31.

Hogwood, B. and B. G. Peters (1983) *Policy Dynamics* (New York: St. Martin's Press).

Holden, C., K. Lee, G. J. Fooks and N. Wander (2010) 'The Impact of Regional Trade Integration on Firm Organization and Strategy: British American Tobacco in the Andean Pact', *Business and Politics*, 12(4) Article 3.

Hooghe, L. and G. Marks (2001) *Multi-level Governance and European Integration* (Lanham, MD: Rowman and Littlefield).

Hooghe, L. and G. Marks (2003) 'Unraveling the Central State, but How? Types of Multi-level Governance,' *American Political Science Review*, 97(2): 233–43.

Horgan, G. (2004) 'Inter-institutional Relations in the Devolved Great Britain: Quiet Diplomacy', *Regional and Federal Studies*, 14(1): 113–35.

Horn, D. and C. M. Fletcher (1970) Smoking and Health http://legacy.library.ucsf.edu/tid/ect36a99. 01 Nov 2009.

Hu, T. W. (ed.) (2008) *Tobacco Control: Policy Analysis in China* (London: World Scientific Publishing Co. Pte. Ltd).

Hyland, A., C. Higbee, R. Borland, M. Travers, G. Hastings, G. T. Fong et al (2009) 'Attitudes and Beliefs about Secondhand Smoke and Smoke-Free Policies in Four Countries: Findings from the International Tobacco Control Four Country Survey', *Nicotine & Tobacco Research*, 11(6): 642–9.

IARC (1986) *Tobacco Smoking*, IARC Monograph on Evaluation of Carcinogenic Risks to Humans: Volume 38 (Lyon, France: IARC).

IARC (2002) *Tobacco Smoke and Involuntary Smoking*, IARC Monograph on Evaluation of Carcinogenic Risks to Humans: Volume 83 (Lyon, France: IARC).

Inamura, Y. and T. Koizumi (2010) 'Workplace Smoking Ban Likely Next Year', *Daily Yomiuri online*, December 25 http://www.yomiuri.co.jp/dy/national/T10122400-3393.html.

Industries Assistance Commission (1987) *The Tobacco Growing and Manufacturing Industries*. Report No. 405 (Canberra: Australian Government Publishing Service).

Industry Commission (1994) *The Tobacco Growing and Manufacturing Industries* Report No. 39 (Melbourne: Australian Government Publishing Service).

INFOTAB (1984) Infotab Board of Directors Meeting Brussels. http://legacy.library.ucsf.edu/tid/cxv75d00. 22 Nov 2009.

INFOTAB (1990) Key Activities & Key Products. http://legacy.library.ucsf.edu/tid/yym40c00. 23 Nov 2009.

INFOTAB and Advisory Group (1983) 62. Following Discussion, the Chairman suggested that the Secretary General and the Advisory Group prepare an Action Plan to Progressively Improve the Quality of NMAs. http://legacy.library.ucsf.edu/tid/ptd88d00. 18 Nov 2009.

Inter Matrix Group (1981) A Study on the Public Policy Process. http://legacy.library.ucsf.edu/tid/fcc44a99. 31 Oct 2009.

International Consortium of Investigative Journalists (2001) Tobacco Companies Linked to Criminal Organizations in Lucrative Cigarette Smuggling. Retrieved November 23, 2009, from http://www.corpwatch.org/article.php?id=898.

IOM (Institute of Medicine) (2007) *Ending the Tobacco Problem: A Blueprint for the Nation* (Washington: National Academies).

Islam, N. (1998) 'Tobacco Control through Imams', *Tropical Doctor*, 28(2): 122–3.

Jabbour, S. and F. M. Fouad (2004) 'Religion-based Tobacco Control Interventions: How Should WHO Proceed?', *Bulletin of the World Health Organisation*, 82(12): 923–7.

Jacobs, R. (2011) 'Pursuit of a Safer Cigarette Gathers Pace', *Financial Times*, 2 June.

Jacobson, P. D. and K. E. Warner (1999) 'Litigation and Public Health Policy Making: The Case of Tobacco Control', *Journal of Health Politics, Policy and Law*, 24: 769–804.

Jacobson, P.D. and J. Wasserman (1997) *Tobacco Control Laws: Implementation and Enforcement* (Santa Monica: RAND).

Jamison, D. T., J. G. Breman, A. R. Measham, G. Alleyne, M. Claeson, D. B. Evans et al (2006) 'Diseases Priorities in Developing Countries', Retrieved October 31, 2009 from http://www.dcp2.org/pubs/DCP.

Jha, P. and F. J. Chaloupka (2000) 'The Economics of Global Tobacco Control', *BMJ*, 321(7257): 358–61.

Jha, P. and F. J. Chaloupka (eds) (1999) *Curbing the Epidemic: Government and the Economics of Tobacco Control* (Washington: World Bank).

Jha, P. and F. J. Chaloupka (eds) (2000) *Tobacco Control in Developing Countries* (Oxford: Oxford University Press).

Jha, P. and F. J. Chaloupka (2000) 'The Economics of Global Tobacco Control', *British Medical Journal*, 321(7257): 358–61.

Jha, P., M. K. Ranson, S. N. Nguyen and D. Yach (2002) 'Estimates of Global and Regional Smoking Prevalence in 1995 by Age and Sex', *American Journal of Public Health*, 96(6): 1002–6.

John, P. (1998) *Analysing Public Policy* (London: Continuum).

John, P. (2003) 'Is There Life After Policy Streams, Advocacy Coalitions, and Punctuations: Using Evolutionary Theory to Explain Policy Change?', *Policy Studies Journal*, 31 (4): 481–98.

Jones, B. (1999) 'Bounded Rationality', *Annual Review of Political Science*, 2: 297–321.

Jones, B. (2003) 'Bounded Rationality and Political Science: Lessons from Public Administration and Public Policy', *Journal of Public Administration Research and Theory*, 13 (4) 395–412.

Jones, B. D. and F. R. Baumgartner (2005) *The Politics of Attention: How Government Prioritizes Problems* (Chicago: University of Chicago Press).

Joossens, L. (2004) 'Effective Tobacco Control Policies in 28 European Countries' http: //www.ensp.org/files/effectivefinal2.pdf.

Joossens, L. and M. Raw (2006) 'The Tobacco Control Scale: A New Scale to Measure Country Activity', *Tobacco Control*, 15(2): 247–53.

Joossens, L. and M. Raw (2007) 'Progress in Tobacco Control in 30 European Countries 2005–2007', Paper presented at 4th European Conference of Tobacco or Health, Basel, Switzerland, 11–13 October http://www.cancer.dk/NR/rdonlyres/7976C5B7-0608-429D-9E94-B0E93274E22E/0/Sammenligningafrygeforebyggelsei30europ%C3%A6-iskelande.pdf.

Joossens, L. and M. Raw (2008) 'Avancees du control du tabacdans 30 pays europeens, de 2005 a 2007', *Bulletine Epedemiologique Hebdomadaire*, 21(2): 198–200.

Joossens, L. and M. Raw (2011) 'The Tobacco Control Scale 2010 in Europe'. Paper presented at European Conference on Tobacco or Health, Amsterdam.

Joossens, L., D. Merriman, H. Ross and M. Raw (2009) 'How Eliminating the Global Illicit Cigarette Trade Would Increase Tax Revenue and Save Lives', Retrieved November 24, 2009, from http://tobaccofreecenter.org/files/pdfs/en/ILL_global_cig_trade_full_en.pdf.

Jordan, A. G. (1981) 'Iron Triangles, Woolly Corporatism and Elastic Nets: Images of the Policy Process', *Journal of Public Policy*, 1(1): 95–123.

Jordan, A. (ed.) (2002) *Environmental Policy in the European Union: Actors, Institutions and Processes* (London: Earthscan).

Jordan, A. G. and W. A. Maloney (1997) 'Accounting for Subgovernments: Explaining the Persistence of Policy Communities', *Administration and Society*, 29(5): 557–83.

Jordan, G., D. Halpin and W. Maloney (2004) 'Defining Interests: Disambiguation and the Need for New Distinctions?' *British Journal of Politics and International Relations*, 6(2): 195–212.

Jordan, A., R. Wurzel and A. Zito (2000) 'Innovating with "New" Environmental Policy Instruments: Convergence or Divergence in the European Union?' Paper presented at meeting of American Political Science Association, Washington.

Katz, S. (1997) 'Secular Morality', in A. M. Brandt and P. Rozin (eds) *Morality and Health* (New York: Routledge).

Keck, M. E. and K. Sikkink (1998) *Activists Beyond Borders* (Ithaca NY: Cornell University Press).

Kelemen, R. D. (2004) *The Rules of Federalism: Institutions and Regulatory Politics in the EU and Beyond* (Cambridge: Harvard University Press).

Kennedy, R. F. (1967) Address By Senator Robert F. Kennedy, World Conference On Smoking And Health. 11 Sep. 1967. Accessed 06 Sep 2005. http://legacy.library.ucsf.edu/tid/gxi94f00.

Kent, D. (1989) *Local By-laws Restricting Smoking-the New Zealand Experience* (Auckland: Action on Smoking and Health).

Keohane, R. and J. Nye (1971) *Transnational Relations and World Politics* (Cambridge: Harvard University Press).

Keohane, R. O. and J. Nye (2000) Globalization: What's New? Not (And So What?), *Foreign Policy*, 118: 104–19.

Kersh, R. and J. Morone (2002) 'How the Personal Becomes Political: Prohibitions, Public Health and Obesity', *Studies in American Political Development*, 16(2): 162–75.

Kessler, D. A. (2001) *A Question of Intent: A Great American Battle with a Deadly Industry* (New York: Public Affairs Press).

Key, V. O. (1961) *Public Opinion and American Democracy* (New York: Alfred A. Knopf).

Khanna, D. (2001) 'The Defeat of the European Tobacco Advertising Directive: A Blow for Health', in P. Eeckhout and T. Tridimas (eds) *Yearbook of European Law*, 20(1): 113–38.

Kingdon, J. (1984) *Agendas, Alternatives and Public Policies* (New York: HarperCollins).

Kingdon, J. (1995) *Agendas, Alternatives and Public Policies*, 2nd ed. (New York: HarperCollins).

Kluger, R. (1996) *Ashes to Ashes: America's Hundred-year Cigarette War, the Public Health, and the Unabashed Triumph of Philip Morris* (New York: Alfred A. Knopf).

Kooiman, J. (1993) 'Socio-political Governance: Introduction', in J. Kooiman (ed.) *Modern Governance* (London: Sage).

Koop, C. E. (1998) 'The Tobacco Scandal: Where is the Outrage?', *Tobacco Control*, 7(4): 393–6.

Krahman, E. (2003) 'National, Regional, and Global Governance: One Phenomenon or Many?', *Global Governance*, 9: 323–46.

Krasner, S. (1983) 'Preface', in S. Krasner (ed.) *International Regimes* (Ithaca, NY: Cornell University Press).

Kuhn, T. (1962) *The Structure of Scientific Revolutions* (Chicago: University of Chicago Press).

Kumar, S. (2000) 'India Steps Up Anti-tobacco Measures', *Lancet*, 356: 1089.

Lachance, V., K. Kenneth and D. Sweanor (1990) 'Tobacco Control in Canada'. Paper presented at 7th World Conference on Tobacco or Health, Perth Australia.

Laforge, R. G., W. F. Velicer, D. A. Levesque, J. L. Fava, D. J. Hill, P. Schofield et al (1998) 'Measuring Support for Tobacco Control Policy in Selected Areas of Six Countries', *Tobacco Control*, 7(3): 241–6.

Lagiou, P. and D. Trichopoulos (2007) 'Legislative Measures and Tobacco Control in Europe', *Preventive Medicine*, 45: 121–2.

Lam, W. K., N. W. White and M. M. Chan-Yeung (2004) 'Lung Cancer Epidemiology and Risk Factors in Asia and Africa', *International Journal of Tuberculosis and Lung Diseases*, 8(5): 1045–57.

Larsen, L. T. (2008) 'The Political Impact of Science: Is Tobacco Control Science- or Policy-driven?' *Science and Public Policy*, 35(10): 757–69.

Lau, R. R. and M. Schlesinger (2005) 'Policy Frames, Metaphoric Reasoning, and Support for Public Policies', *Political Psychology*, 26(1): 77–144.

Laugesen, M. and C. Meads (1991) 'Tobacco Advertising Restrictions, Price, Income and Tobacco Consumption in OECD Countries, 1960–1986', *British Journal of Addiction*, 86(6): 1343–54.

Laugesen, M. and B. Swinburn (2000) 'New Zealand's Tobacco Control Programme 1985–1998', *Tobacco Control*, 9(2): 155–62.

Leary, W. E. (1994) 'A 30-Year Report Card on Smoking Prevention', *New York Times*, 12 January.

LeGresley, E., K. Lee, M. E. Muggli, P. Patel, J. Collin and R. D. Hurt (2008) 'British American Tobacco and the "Insidious Impact of Illicit Trade" in Cigarettes across Africa', *Tobacco Control*, 17(4): 339–46.

Leichter, H. M. (1991) *Free to be Foolish: Politics and Health Promotion in the United States and Great Britain* (Princeton: Princeton University Press).

Lencucha, R., R. Labonté and M. J. Rouse (2010) 'Beyond Idealism and Realism: Canadian NGO/Government Relations During the Negotiation of the FCTC', *J Public Health Policy*, 31(1): 74–87.

Leonard, Z. and Associates (1981) 'Informational Memorandum International Union Against Cancer (UICC)', http://legacy.library.ucsf.edu/tid/gyo88c00. 18 Nov 2009.

Lewit, E. D. and D. Coate (1982) 'The Potential for Using Excise Taxes to Reduce Smoking', *Journal of Health Economics*, 1(1): 121–45.

Licari, M. J. (2002) *Comparative Policy Effectiveness: Smoking Regulation in 14 OECD Countries* (Paper presented at Midwest Political Science Association, Chicago).

Lieberman, R. C. (2002) 'Ideas, Institutions and Political Order: Explaining Political Change', *American Political Science Review*, 90(4): 691–712.

Lijphart, A. (1999) *Patterns of Democracy: Government Forms and Performance in Thirty-Six Countries* (New Haven: Yale University Press).

Lindblom, C. (1959) 'The Science of Muddling Through', *Public Administration Review*, 19(1): 79–88.

Lindblom, C. (1979) 'Still Muddling, Not Yet Through', *Public Administration Review*, 39(4): 517–25.

Lipand, A. for the World Health Organization Tobacco Free Initiative (2007) *Successful Use of Smoke-free Policies in Tobacco Control in Estonia* (Geneva, Switzerland: World Health Organization).

Lipsky, M. (1980) *Street-level Bureaucracy* (New York: Russell Sage Foundation).

Liu, B. Q., R. Peto, Z. M. Chen, J. Boreham, Y. P. Wu, J. Y. Li et al (1998) 'Emerging Tobacco Hazards in China: 1. Retrospective Proportional Mortality Study of One Million Deaths', *British Medical Journal*, 317(7170): 1411–22.

Lopez, A. D., N. E. Collishaw and T. Piha (1994) 'A Descriptive Model of the Cigarette Epidemic in Developed Countries', *Tobacco Control*, 3(2): 242–7.

Lopez, A. D., C. D. Mathers, D. T. Jamison and J. L. Murray (eds) (2006) *Global Burden of Disease and Risk Factors* (New York: Oxford University Press).

Lukes, S. (2005) *Power: A Radical View* (2nd ed.; Basingstoke: Palgrave).

Lundqvist, L. (1980) *The Hare and the Tortoise: Clean Air Policies in the United States and Sweden* (Ann Arbor: University of Michigan Press).

Mackay, J. and J. Crofton (1996) 'Tobacco and the Developing World', *British Medical Bulletin*, 52(1): 206–21.

Mackay, J. (2003) 'The Making of a Convention on Tobacco Control', *Bulletin of the World Health Organization*, 81(8): 551.

Mackay, J., M. Eriksen and O. Shafey (2006) *The Tobacco Atlas* (2nd ed.; Atlanta: American Cancer Society).

Majone, G. (1989) *Evidence, Argument and Persuasion in the Policy Process* (New Haven: Yale University Press).

Majone, G. (1997) 'From the Positive to the Regulatory State: Causes and Consequences of Changes in the Mode of Governance', *Journal of Public Policy*, 17(2): 139–67.

Malone, R. (2011) 'Imagining Things Otherwise: New Endgame Ideas for Tobacco Control', *Tobacco Control*, 19(5): 349–50.

Mamudu, H. M. (2008) *The Politics of the Evolution of Global Tobacco Control: The Formation and Functioning of the Framework Convention on Tobacco Control* (Germany: VDM Book Publication).

Mamudu, H. M. and S. A. Glantz (2009) 'Civil Society and the Negotiation of the Framework Convention on Tobacco Control', *Global Public Health*, 4(2): 150–68.

Mamudu, H. M., R. Hammond and S. A. Glantz (2011a) 'International Trade vs. Public Health during the FCTC Negotiations 1999–2003', *Tobacco Control*, 20: e3.

Mamudu, H. M., M. Gonzalez and S. A. Glantz (2011b) 'The Nature, Scope and Development of the Global Tobacco Control Epistemic Community', *American Journal of Public Health*, 101(11): 2044–54.

Mamudu, H., R. Hammond and S. Glantz (2008a) 'Project Cerberus: Tobacco Industry Strategy to Create an Alternative to the Framework Convention on Tobacco Control', *American Journal of Public Health*, 98(9): 1630–42.

Mamudu, H. M., R. Hammond and S. A. Glantz (2008b) 'Tobacco Industry Attempts to Counter World Bank Curbing the Epidemic and Obstruct the WHO Framework Convention on Tobacco Control', *Social Science and Medicine*, 67(11): 1690–9.

Mamudu, H. M. and T. Novotny (2008) *Progression of Tobacco Control Policies: Implications for Global Action and for Tobacco Control in Developing Countries* (Washington, D.C.: World Bank).

Mamudu, H. M. and D. T. Studlar (2009) 'Multilevel Governance and Shared Sovereignty: The European Union, Member States, and the Framework Convention on Tobacco Control', *Governance*, 22(1): 73–97.

Mamudu, H. M., J. S. Yang and T. E. Novotny (2011) 'UN Resolution on the Prevention and Control of Non-communicable Diseases: An Opportunity for Global Action', *Global Public Health*, 6(4): 347–53.

March, J. and J. Olsen (1984) 'The New Institutionalism: Organizational Factors in Political Life', *The American Political Science Review*, 78(3): 734–49.

March, J. and J. Olsen (1996) 'Institutional Perspectives on Political Institutions', *Governance*, 9(3): 247–64.

Marks, G. (1993) 'Structural Policy and Multilevel Governance in the EC', in W. Cafruny and G. G. Rosenthal (eds) *The State of the European Community: The Maastricht Debates and Beyond* (Boulder, CO: Lynne Rienner).

Marmor, T. R. and E. S. Lieberman (2004) 'Tobacco Control in Comparative Perspective: Eight Nations in Search of an Explanation', in E. A. Feldman and R. Bayer (eds) *Unfiltered: Conflicts over Tobacco and Public Health* (Cambridge: Harvard University Press).

Marotte, B. (1997) 'Big Tobacco Still Smoking', *Ottawa Citizen*, July 9.

Marsh, D. and R. A. W. Rhodes (1992) 'Policy Communities and Issue Networks: Beyond Typology', in D. Marsh and R. A. W. Rhodes (eds) *Policy Networks in British Government* (Oxford: Oxford University Press).

Marsh, D. and A. McConnell (2010) 'Towards a Framework for Establishing Policy Success', *Public Administration*, 88(2): 564–83.

Mathers, C. D. and D. Loncar (2006) 'Projection of Global Mortality and Burden of Disease from 2002 to 2003', *PLoS Medicine*, 3(11): e442.

Mathers, C. D., A. D. Lopez and C. J. L. Murray (2006) 'The Burden of Disease and Mortality by Condition: Data, Methods, and Results for 2001', in A. D. Lopez, C. D. Mathers, M. Ezzati et al (eds) *Global Burden of Disease and Risk Factors* (New York: Oxford University Press).

McCurry, J. (2010) 'Japan Hits Smokers Where It Hurts', 2 August. http://www.globalpost.com/dispatch/japan/100729/health-cigarette-tax-smoking-and-lung-cancer.

McDaniel, P., G. Intinarelli and R. Malone (2008) 'Tobacco Industry Issues Management Organizations: Creating a Global Corporate Network to Undermine Public Health', *Globalization and Health*, 4(2) http://www.ncbi.nlm.nih.gov/pmc/articles/PMC2265275/.

McGowan, R. (1995) *Business, Politics and Cigarettes* (Westport, CT: Quorum Books).

McKee, M., M. Rosenmoller, L. MacLehose and M. Zajac (2004) 'The Process of Enlargement', in M. McKee, L. MacLehose and E. Nolte (eds) *Health Policy and European Union Enlargement* (Maidenhead: Open University Press).

McLoughlin, D. (1990) 'Behind the Smoke Screen', *North and South* (March): 38–51.

McPherson, A. M. and C. D. Raab (1988) *Governing Education: A Sociology of Policy since 1945* (Edinburgh: Edinburgh University Press).

Meier, K. J. (1994) *The Politics of Sin: Drugs, Alcohol, and Public Policy* (Armonk, NY: M. E. Sharpe).

Mendelowitz, A. I. (1990) *Testimony: Dichotomy between U.S. Tobacco Export Policy and Antismoking Initiatives: Statement of Allan I. Mendelowitz, Director Trade, Energy, and Finance Issues, National Security & International Affairs Division* http://legacy.library.ucsf.edu/tid/ndk98c00. 15 May 2009.

Ministry of Health (1999) *Attitudes Toward Environmental Tobacco Smoke* (Wellington: Ministry of Health, Public Attitude Research Report).

Ministry of Health, People's Republic of China. *China Tobacco Control Report.* Beijing, May 2007.

Mitchell, T. (1991) 'The Limits of the State: Beyond Statist Approaches and Their Critics', *American Political Science Review*, 81(1): 77–96.

Mochizuki-Kobayashi, Y., N. Yamaguchi and J. M. Samet (2003) 'Tobacco Free Japan: Recommendations for Tobacco Control Policy', Tobacco Free Japan and Institute for Global Tobacco Control, Department of Epidemiology, *Johns Hopkins University Bloomberg School of Public Health*, http://www.tobaccofree.jp?E/Full.html [downloaded November 4, 2008).

Mokdad, A. H., J. S. Marks, D. F. Stroup and J. L. Gerberding (2004) 'Actual Causes of Death in the United States 2000', *JAMA*, 291(10): 1238–45.

Mollenkamp, C. A., J. Levy, J. Menn and J. Rothfeder (1998) *The People vs. Big Tobacco* (Princeton NJ: Bloomberg Press).

Montini, T., A. George, M. Martin-Mollard and L. A. Bero (2009) 'The Role of Public Participation in Public Health Initiatives: An Analysis of the WHO Framework Convention on Tobacco Control', *Global Public Health*, March 26: 1–13.

Moravcsik, A. (1997) 'Taking Preferences Seriously: A Liberal Theory of International Politics', *International Organization*, 51(4): 513–53.

Morone, J. A. (2003) *Hellfire Nation: The Politics of Sin in American History* (New Haven: Yale University Press).

Morrow, M. and S. Barraclough (2003) 'Tobacco Control and Gender in Southeast Asia. Part I: Malaysia and Philippines', *Health Promotion International*, 18(3): 255–64.

Mossberger, K. (2000) *The Politics of Ideas and the Spread of Enterprise Zones* (Washington: Georgetown University Press).

MRC (Medical Research Council) (2007a) Smoking Still Kills, Stopping Still Works http://www.mrc.ac.uk/Newspublications/News/MRC003839.

MRC (2007b) Smoking http://www.mrc.ac.uk/Achievementsimpact/Storiesofimpact/Smoking/index.htm.

Muller, M. (1983) 'Preventing Tomorrow's Epidemic: The Control of Smoking and Tobacco Production in Developing Countries', *New York State Journal of Medicine*, 83: 1304–9.

Muller, M. (1978) *Tobacco and the Third World: Tomorrow's Epidemic* (London: War on Want).

Nadelman, E. A. (1990) 'Global Prohibition Regimes: The Evolution of Norms in International Society', *International Organization*, 44(4): 479–526.

Nathanson, C. A. (1999) 'Social Movements as Catalysts for Policy Change: The Case of Smoking and Guns', *Journal of Health Politics, Policy and Law*, 24: 421–88.

Nathanson, C. A. (2007) *Disease Prevention as Social Change: The State, Society and Public Health in the United States, France, Great Britain, and Canada* (New York: Russell Sage Foundation).

National Academy of Sciences (1986) *Environmental Tobacco Smoke: Measuring Exposures and Accessing Health Effects* (Washington, DC: National Academy Press).

Nellen, M. E. A., H. S. Chapman and H. Adriaanse (1995) 'Economic and Social Prosperity as a Predictor of National Tobacco Consumption', in E. Slama (ed.) *Tobacco and Health* (New York: Plenum Press).

Neuman, M., A. Bitton and S. Glantz (2002) 'Tobacco Industry Strategies for Influencing European Community Tobacco Advertising Legislation', *Lancet*, 359(9314): 1323–30.

Nielsen, L. B. (2003) *Stability and Change in U.S. and Danish Tobacco Policy and Politics, 1950–2000* (Unpublished M.A. thesis, University of Aarhus).

Niu, S. R., G. H. Yang, Z. M. Chen, J. L. Wang, G. H. Wang, X. Z. He, H. Schoepff, J. Boreham, H. C. Pan and R. Peto (1998) 'Emerging Tobacco Hazards in China: 2. Early Mortality Results from a Prospective Study', *British Medical Journal*, 317(7170): 1423–4.

No Author. Answers to the Questionnaire – Germany http://bat.library.ucsf.edu//tid/wou63a99.

No Author. Chronology of External Events. 21 Aug. 1994. *British American Tobacco*. Accessed 16 May 2008. http://bat.library.ucsf.edu//tid/tct24a99.

Norr, R. (1952) 'Cancer by the Carton', *Reader's Digest*, December, pp. 35–6.

Nugent, R. and A. Feigl (2010) 'Where Have All the Donors Gone? Scarce Donor Funding for Non-Communicable Diseases', *Center for Global Development Working Paper 228* http://www.cgdev.org/content/publications/detail/1424546.

Nykiforuk, C. I. J., J. Eyles and H. S. Campbell (2008) 'Smoke-free Spaces Overtime: A Policy Diffusion Study of Bylaw Development in Alberta and Ontario, Canada', *Health and Social Care in the Community*, 16(1): 64–74.

Obinger, H. and U. Wagschal (2001) 'Families of Nations and Public Policy', *West European Politics*, 24(1): 99–114.

OECD (2010) Health Data http://www.oecd.org/document/16/0,3343,en_2649_34631_2085200_1_1_1_37407,00.html.

Ong, E. and S. A. Glantz (2000) 'Hirayama's Works has Stood the Test of Time', *Bulletin of the World Health Organization*, 78(7): 938–9.

Ong, E. and S. Glantz (2001) 'Constructing "Sound Science" and "Good Epidemiology": Tobacco, Lawyers, and Public Relations Firms', *American Journal of Public Health*, 91: 1749–57.

ONS (Office for National Statistics) (2009) Opinions Survey Report No. 40: Smoking-related Behaviour and Attitudes, 2008/09 http://www.statistics.gov.uk/downloads/theme_health/smoking2008-9.pdf.

Oreskes, N. and E. M. Conway (2010) *Merchants of Doubt: How a Handful of Scientists Obscured the Truth on Issues from Tobacco Smoke to Global Warming* (New York: Bloomsbury Press).

O'Shea, P. K. (1997) *The Golden Harvest: A History of Tobacco Growing in New Zealand* (Christchurch: Hazard Press).

Otanez, M. G., H. Mamudu and S. A. Glantz (2007) 'Global Leaf Companies Control the Tobacco Market in Malawi', *Tobacco Control*, 16(4): 261–9.

Otanez, M., M. Muggli, R. Hurt and S. Glantz (2006) 'Eliminating Child Labour in Malawi: A British American Tobacco Corporate Responsibility Project to Sidestep Tobacco Labour Exploitation', *Tobacco Control*, 5: 224–30.

Otanez, M., H. Mamudu and S. Glantz (2009) 'Tobacco Companies Use Malawi to Lobby Against Global Tobacco Control', *American Journal of Public Health*, 99(10): 1759–71.

Painter, M. (1991) 'Policy Diversity and Policy Learning in a Federation: The Case of Australian State Betting Laws', *Publius*, 21(1): 143–57.

Panos Institute (1994) Tobacco: Health and Beyond – Developing Countries at the Crossroads. http://legacy.library.ucsf.edu/tid/zye17a99. 31 Oct 2009.

Pertschuk, M. (1986) *Giant Killers* (New York: Norton).

Pertschuk, M. (2001) *Smoke in Their Eyes: Lessons in Movement Leadership from the Tobacco Wars* (Nashville: Vanderbilt University Press).

Peters, B. G. and B. W. Hogwood (1985) 'In Search of the Issue-Attention Cycle', *Journal of Politics*, 47(1): 238–53.

Philip Morris (1981a) Developing Countries Group Progress Report Covering Projects and Action Plans since the Board of Directors meeting on 30 March, 1981. http://legacy.library.ucsf.edu/tid/dhr25e00. 22 Nov 2009.

Philip Morris (1981b) The International 'Conspiracy' Against Tobacco. http://legacy.library.ucsf.edu/tid/znw23e00. 18 Nov 2009.

Philip Morris (1993) The Activist Movement. http://legacy.library.ucsf.edu/tid/glg14e00. 18 Nov 2009.

Pierson, P. (2000) 'Increasing Returns, Path Dependence, and the Study of Politics', *The American Political Science Review*, 94(2): 251–67.

Pollay, R. W. (1994) 'Promises, Promises: Self-Regulation of US Cigarette Broadcast Advertising in the 1960s', *Tobacco Control*, 3(2): 134–44.

Polsby, N. (1980) *Community Power and Political Theory* (2nd ed.; New Haven: Yale University Press).

Pomerleau, J., A. Gilmore, M. McKee, R. Rose and C. W. Haerpfer (2004) 'Determinants of Smoking in Eight Countries of the Former Soviet Union: Results from the Living Conditions, Lifestyles and Health Study', *Addiction*, 99(12): 1577–85.

Press Association (2010) 'Call for 5% Rise in Tobacco Tax', *The Guardian* 6.3.10 http://www.guardian.co.uk/uk/feedarticle/8976577.

Princen, S. and M. Rhinard (2006) 'Crashing and Creeping: Agenda-Setting Dynamics in the European Union', *Journal of European Public Policy*, 13(6): 1119–32.

Princen, S. (2008) *Agenda-Setting in the European Union* (London: Palgrave Macmillan).

Proctor, R. N. (1999) *The Nazi War on Cancer* (Princeton: Princeton University Press).

Pross, A. and I. S. Stewart (1994) 'Breaking the Habit: Attentive Publics and Tobacco Regulation', in S. Phillips (ed.) *How Ottawa Spends, 1994–1995* (Ottawa: Carleton University Press).

Quenqua, D. (2011) 'An Addiction Vaccine, Tantalizingly Close', *New York Times*, 3 October.

Ramin, B. (2006) 'Science, Politics, and Tobacco in the Developing World', *Canadian Journal of Development Studies*, 27(3): 383–401.

Read, M. (1992) 'Policy Networks and Issue Networks: The Politics of Smoking', in D. Marsh and R. Rhodes (eds) *Policy Networks in British Government* (Oxford: Clarendon).

Read, M. (1996) *The Politics of Tobacco: Policy Networks and the Cigarette Industry* (Aldershot: Avebury).

Read, M. D. (2005) 'Anti-Smoking Policy in the UK: A Matter of Political Will?', *Paper for Political Studies Association*, Leeds.

Reich, R. (1988) 'Introduction', in R. Reich (ed.) *The Power of Public Ideas* (Cambridge MA: Ballinger).

Reynolds, C. and S. Woodward (1993) 'Tobacco and Children: What Can We Learn from Early Legislation in Australia?', *Tobacco Control*, 2(2): 152–5.

Rhodes, R. A. W. (1997) *Understanding Governance* (Open University Press).
Richardson, J. J. (1982) 'Convergent Policy Styles in Europe?', in J. J. Richardson (ed.) *Policy Styles in Western Europe* (London: Allen and Unwin).
Richardson, J. J. (2000) 'Government, Interest Groups and Policy Change', *Political Studies*, 48(4): 1006–25.
Richardson, J. J. and A. G. Jordan (1979) *Governing Under Pressure: The Policy Process In A Post-Parliamentary Democracy* (Oxford: Robertson).
Risse-Kappen, T. (1994) 'Ideas Do Not Float Freely: Transnational Coalitions, Domestic Structures, and the End of the Cold War', *International Organization*, 48(2): 185–214.
Risse-Kappen, T. (1995) *Bringing Transnational Relations Back In: Non-State Actors, Domestic Structures and International Institutions* (Vol. 48) (Cambridge, MA: Cambridge University Press).
Rochefort, D. A. and R. W. Cobb (1994) 'Problem Definition: An Emerging Perspective', in D. A. Rochefort and R. W. Cobb (eds) *The Politics of Problem Definition* (Lawrence: University Press of Kansas).
Roemer, R. (1982) *Legislative Action to Combat the World Smoking Epidemic* (Geneva: World Health Organization).
Roemer, R. (1993) *Legislative Action to Combat the World Tobacco Epidemic* (2nd ed.; Geneva: World Health Organization).
Roemer, R. (1995) 'Fighting Threats to Legislative Advances in Tobacco Control', in K. Slama (ed.) *Tobacco and Health* (New York: Plenum Press).
Roemer, R. and A. L. Taylor (1996) Programme on Substance Abuse: International Strategy for Tobacco Control. 00. http://legacy.library.ucsf.edu/tid/ifg30c00.
Roemer, R., A. Taylor and J. Larivier (2005) 'Origins of the WHO Framework Convention on Tobacco Control', *American Journal of Public Health*, 95(6): 936–8.
Rose, R. (1984) *Understanding Big Government: The Programme Approach* (London: Sage).
Rose, R. (1987) *Ministers and Ministries: A Functional Analysis* (Oxford: Clarendon Press).
Rose, R. (1990) 'Inheritance Before Choice in Public Policy', *Journal of Theoretical Politics*, 2(3): 263–91.
Rose, R. (1993) *Lesson-Drawing in Public Policy* (New Jersey: Chatham House).
Rose, R. (2005) *Learning from Comparative Public Policy: A Practical Guide* (London: Routledge).
Rose, R. and P. Davies (1994) *Inheritance in Public Policy: Change Without Choice in Britain* (New Haven: Yale University Press).
Rosenau, J. N. (1997) *Along the Domestic-Foreign Frontier: Exploring Governance in a Turbulent World* (Cambridge: Cambridge University Press).
Rosenau, J. N. and E. O. Czempiel (eds) (1992) *Governance Without Government: Order and Change in World Politics* (Cambridge and New York: Cambridge University Press).
Rosenblatt, R. (1994) 'How Do Tobacco Industry Executives Live With Themselves?', *New York Times Magazine*, March 20.
Royal College of Physicians (1962) *Smoking and Health* (London: Pitman).
Royal College of Physicians (1971) *Smoking and Health Now* (London: Pitman).
RTI International & Harris Interactive (2009) More Smokers Worldwide Support Workplace Bans: Poll. Retrieved November 24, 2009, from http://www.reuters.com/article/lifestyleMolt/idUSTRE5AG45920091117?feedType=RSS&feedName=lifestyleMolt&utm_source=feedburner&utm_medium=feed&utm_campaign=Feed%3A+reuters%2Flifestyle+(News+%2F+US+%2F+Lifestyle).
Sabatier, P. (1998) 'The Advocacy Coalition Framework: Revisions and Relevance for Europe', *Journal of European Public Policy*, 5(1): 98–130.

Sabatier, P. (2007) 'The Need for Better Theories', in P. Sabatier (ed.) *Theories of the Policy Process* (2nd ed.; Boulder, CO: Westview).

Sabatier, P. and H. Jenkins-Smith (1993) 'The Advocacy Coalition Framework: Assessment, Revisions and Implications for Scholars and Practitioners', in P. Sabatier and H. C. Jenkins-Smith (eds) *Policy Change and Learning: An Advocacy Coalition Approach* (Boulder, CO: Westview Press).

Sabatier, P. and H. C. Jenkins-Smith (eds) (1993) *Policy Change and Learning: An Advocacy Coalition Approach* (Boulder: Westview).

Sabatier, P. and C. Weible (2007) 'The Advocacy Coalition Framework: Innovations and Clarifications', in P. Sabatier (ed.) *Theories of the Policy Process* (Boulder: Westview Press).

Samet, J. A. and S.-Y. Yoon (eds) (2001) *Women and the Tobacco Epidemic: Challenges for the 21st Century* (Geneva, Switzerland: WHO, Institute for Global Tobacco Control).

Sanghvi, L. D. (1974) 'Cancer Epidemic in India: A Critique', *Indian J Med Research*, 62(12).

Sasco, A. J. (1992) *Women and Tobacco: The Scale of the Problem in Developing Countries. Proceedings of the First International Conference on Women and Smoking* (Belfast: Belfast Ulster Cancer Foundation/Health Promotion Agency for Northern Ireland).

Sasco, A., P. dalla-Vorgia, Y. Skalkidis, K. Katsouyianni and D. Trichopoulos (1989) *An Evaluation of the Effectiveness of Tobacco-Control Legislative Policies in EEC Member States, 1948–1987: A Report* (Lyon: International Agency for Research on Cancer).

Sasco, A. J., P. Dalla-Vorgia and P. Van der Elst (1992) *Comparative Study of Anti-Smoking Legislation in Countries of the European Economic Community* (Lyon: International Agency for Research on Cancer).

Satcher, D. (2001) 'Why We Need an International Agreement on Tobacco Control', *American Journal of Public Health*, 91(2): 191–2.

Sato, H. (1999a) 'The Advocacy Coalition Framework and Policy Process Analysis: The Case of Smoking Control in Japan', *Policy Studies Journal*, 27(1): 28–44.

Sato, H. (1999b) 'Policy and Politics of Smoking Control in Japan', *Social Science and Medicine*, 49(4): 581–600.

Schattschneider, E. E. (1960) *The Semi-Sovereign People* (New York: Holt, Rinehart and Winston).

Schlager, E. (2007) 'A Comparison of Frameworks, Theories, and Models of Policy Processes' Theory', in P. Sabatier (ed.) *Theories of the Policy Process* (2nd ed.; Cambridge MA: Westview).

Schmidt, V. (2006) 'Institutionalism', in C. Hay, M. Lister and D. Marsh (eds) *The State: Theories and Issues* (Basingstoke: Palgrave).

Schmidt, V. (2010) 'Taking Ideas and Discourse Seriously: Explaining Change Through Discursive Institutionalism as the Fourth "New Institutionalism"', *European Political Science Review*, 2(1): 1–25.

Schmidt, V. A. (2011) 'Reconciling Ideas and Institutions through Discursive Institutionalism', in D. Béland and R. H. Cox (eds) *Ideas and Politics in Social Science Research* (New York: Oxford University Press).

Schneider, N. K. and S. A. Glantz (2008) "Nicotine Nazis Strike Again": A Brief Analysis of the Use of Nazi Rhetoric in Attacking Tobacco Control Advocacy', *Tobacco Control*, 17(5): 289–90.

Schmidt, V. and C. Radaelli (2004) 'Policy Change and Discourse in Europe: Conceptual and Methodological Issues', *West European Politics*, 27(2): 183–210.

Schneider, A. L. and H. Ingram (1997) *Policy Design for Democracy* (Lawrence: University Press of Kansas).

Schroeder, S. A. and K. E. Warner (2010) 'Don't Forget Tobacco', *New England Journal of Medicine*, 15; 363(3): 201–4.

Scoggins, A., H. de Vries, A. Conklin and E. Hatziandreu (2009) Analysis to Support the Impact Assessment of the Commission's Smoke-free Initiatives (Cambridge: Rand Europe) http://www.rand.org/content/dam/rand/pubs/technical_reports/2009/RAND_TR646.pdf.

Sebrié, E. M. and S. A. Glantz (2010) 'Local Smoke-free Policy Development in Santa Fe Argentina', *Tobacco Control*, 19(2): 110–16.

Sebrie, E. M. (2006) 'Mexico: Backroom Deal Blunts Health Warnings', *Tobacco Control*, 15(5): 348–9.

Sebrie, E., J. Barnoya, E. J. Perez-Stable and S. A. Glantz (2006) *Tobacco Industry Successfully Prevented Tobacco Control Legislation in Argentina*.

Shafey, O., S. Dolwick and G. E. Guindon (eds) (2003) *Tobacco Control Country Profiles* (2nd ed.; Atlanta: US Centers for Disease Control and Prevention).

Shafey, O., M. Eriksen, H. Ross and J. Mackay (2009) *The Tobacco Atlas* (3rd ed.; Atlanta, GA: American Cancer Society, World Lung Foundation).

Shibuya, K., C. Ciedierski, E. Guindon, D. W. Bettcher, D. B. Evans and C. J. L Murray (2003) 'WHO Framework Convention on Tobacco Control: Development of an Evidence Based Global Public Health Treaty', *British Medical Journal*, 327: 154–7.

Shimkhada, R. and J. W. Peabody (2003) 'Tobacco Control in India', *Bulletin of the World Health Organization*, 81(1): 48–52.

Shipan, C. R. and C. Volden (2006) 'Bottom-Up Federalism. The Diffusion of Antismoking Policies from U.S. Cities to States', *American Journal of Political Science*, 50: 825–43.

Siaroff, A. (1999) 'Corporatism in 24 Industrial Democracies: Meaning and Measurement', *European Journal of Political Research*, 26(2): 175–205.

Sikkink, K. (1998) 'Transnational Politics, International Relations Theory, and Human Rights', *PS: Political Science and Politics*, 31(3): 516–23.

Simon, H. (1976) *Administrative Behavior* (3rd ed.; New York: Free Press).

Simpson, B. C. and INFOTAB (1983) INFOTAB Board of Directors Meeting Bath 831030–831031 http://legacy.library.ucsf.edu/tid/qcg24e00. 13 Dec 2009.

Simpson, B. and INFOTAB (1985) 'International Scope and Major New Issues', *Latin American Workshop*, Miami, 30–31 July, 1985 http://legacy.library.ucsf.edu/tid/gjq-52f00. 18 Nov 2009.

Slade, J., L. Bero, P. Hanauer, D. E. Barnes and S. A. Glantz (1995) 'Nicotine and Addiction: The Brown and Williamson Documents', *Journal of American Medical Association*, 274: 225–33.

Slade, J. (2001) 'Marketing Policies', in R. Rabin and S. Sugarman (eds) *Regulating Tobacco* (New York: Oxford University Press).

Slaughter, A. M. (2004) *A New World Order* (Princeton NJ: Princeton University Press).

Smith, K. B. (1993) *The New Zealand Tobacco Wars: The 1990 Smoke-free Environments Act* (Unpublished M.A. thesis, University of Auckland).

Smith, J. (2004) *Taxing Popularity: the Story of Taxation in Australia* (Sydney: Australian Tax Research Foundation).

Smith, M. T. and T. Umenai (2000) 'Smoking among Buddhist Monks in Phnom Penh, Cambodia', *Tobacco Control*, 9(1): 111.

Sparks, M. (2010) 'Governance beyond Governments: The Role of NGOs in the Implementation of the FCTC', *Glob Health Promotion*, 17 (1 Suppl): 67–72.

Special Eurobarometer 239 (2006) *Attitudes of Europeans Towards Tobacco*. Brussels: European Commission.

Special Eurobarometer 272 (2007) *Attitudes of Europeans Towards Tobacco*. Brussels: European Commission.

Special Eurobarometer 332 (2010) *Tobacco*. Brussels: European Commission.

Spill, R. L., M. J. Licari and L. Ray (2001) Taking on Tobacco: An Event History Analysis of Policy Entrepreneurship', *Political Research Quarterly*, 54(4): 605–22.

State Healthstats (2011) 'America's Health Rankings' http://statehealthstats.americas-healthrankings.org/#/country/US/2010/Prevalence-of-Smoking.

Streek, W. and Thelen, K. (2005) 'Introduction: Institutional Change in Advanced Political Economies', in W. Streek and K. Thelen (eds) *Beyond Continuity: Institutional Change in Advanced Political Economies* (Oxford: Oxford University Press).

Stone, D. (2000) 'Learning Lessons, Policy Transfer, and the International Diffusion of Ideas', Retrieved May 24, 2008 from http://poli.haifa.ac.il/~levi/res/stone-2000.pdf.

Strünck, C. (2005) 'Mix-Up: Models of Governance and Framing Opportunities in U.S. and EU Consumer Policy', *Journal of Consumer Policy*, 28(2): 203–30.

Studlar, D. T. (2002) *Tobacco Control: Comparative Politics in the United States and Canada* (Peterborough, Ontario: Broadview Press).

Studlar, D. T. (2003) 'Tobacco Control and Loss Imposition: Canada and the United States', in L. A. Pal and R. Kent Weaver (eds) *The Government Taketh Away: The Politics of Pain in Canada and the United States* (Washington: Georgetown University Press).

Studlar, D. T. (2004) 'Tobacco Control Policy Instruments in a Shrinking World: How Much Policy Learning?', in D. Levi-Faur and E. Vigoda (eds) *Public Policy and Public Management in a Globalized World: Policy Learning and Policy Emulation Across Countries and Regions* (New York: Marcel Dekker).

Studlar, D. T. (2005) 'The Political Dynamics of Tobacco Control in Australia and New Zealand: Explaining Policy Problems, Instruments, and Patterns of Adoption', *Australian Journal of Political Science*, 40(2): 255–74.

Studlar, D. T. (2007) 'Ideas, Institutions, and Diffusion: What Explains Tobacco Control Policy in Australia, Canada, and New Zealand', *Commonwealth and Comparative Politics*, 45(2): 164–84.

Studlar, D. T. (2008) 'U.S. Tobacco Control: Public Health, Political Economy, or Morality Policy', *Review of Policy Research*, 25(5): 393–410.

Studlar, D. T. (2009) 'Tobacco Control Policy in Western Europe: A Case of Protracted Paradigm Change', in G. Capano and M. Howlett (eds) *Policy Dynamics and Policy Drivers: European and North American Experiences of Policy Change* (London: Routledge).

Studlar, D. T. (2010) 'What Explains the Paradox of Tobacco Control under Federalism in the United States and Canada: Comparative Federalism versus Multi-level Governance', *Publius*, 40(3): 389–411.

Studlar, D. T. (2011) 'The Paradox of Tobacco Control in the US Revisited: The Role of Multi-Level Governance in Establishing a "National Tobacco Control Regime", Paper presented at American Political Science Association, Seattle.

Studlar, D. T., K. Christensen and A. Sitasari (2011) 'Tobacco Control in the EU-15: The Role of Member States and the European Union', *Journal of European Public Policy*, 18(5): 727–44.

Sugarman, S. D. (2001) 'International Aspects of Tobacco Control and the Proposed WHO Treaty', in R. Rabin and S. D. Sugarman (eds) *Regulating Tobacco* (New York: Oxford University Press).

Sussman, S., P. Pokhrel, D. Black, M. Kohrman, S. Hamann, P. Vateesatokit et al (2007) 'Tobacco Control in Developing Countries: Tanzania, Nepal, China, and Thailand as examples', *Nicotine and Tobacco Research*, 9 (Suppl 3): S447–57.

Swaddiwudhipong, W., C. Chaovakiratipong, P. Nguntra, P. Khumklam and N. Silarug (1993) 'A Thai Monk: An Agent for Smoking Reduction in a Rural Population', *International Journal of Epidemiology*, 22(4): 660–5.

Szilágyi, T. (2006) *Hungry for Hungary: Examples of Tobacco Companies' Expansionism, Case Studies from Hungary* (Erd: Health 21 Hungarian Foundation).

Tate, C. (1999) *Cigarette Wars: The Triumph of 'the Little White Slaver'* (New York: Oxford University Press).

Tax Burden on Tobacco, Historical Compilation (2006) Volume 41. Arlington, VA: Orzechowski and Walker.

Taylor, A. (2002) 'Global Governance, International Health Law and WHO: Looking Towards the Future', *Bulletin of the World Health Organization*, 80(12): 975–80.

Taylor, A. L. (1992) 'Making the World Health Organization Work: A Legal Framework for Universal Access to Conditions for Health', *American Journal for Law and Medicine*, 18: 301–46.

Taylor, A. L. and R. Roemer (1996) *Programme on Substance Abuse: International Strategy for Tobacco Control* http://legacy.library.ucsf.edu/tid/hqt83c00. 11 Jun 2008.

Taylor, P. R. (1984) *The Smoke Ring: Tobacco, Money, and Multinational Politics* (New York: Pantheon Books).

TFI (Tobacco-Free Initiation). Report of the WHO Meeting of Public Health Experts. Geneva, Switzerland: WHO. 1999. Accessed 2 June 2011 http://whqlibdoc.who.int/hq/1999/WHO_NCD_TFI_99.7.pdf.

The ITC Project. Promoting Evidence-based Strategies to Fight the Global Tobacco Epidemic. Accessed 2 June 2011. http://www.itcproject.org/.

The Observer (1985) UICC Developments. Accessed 18 Nov 2009. http://legacy.library.ucsf.edu/tid/hcj44e00.

Thelen, K. and S. Steinmo (1992) 'Historical Institutionalism in Comparative Politics', in S. Steinmo, K. Thelen and F. Longstreth (eds) *Structuring Politics: Historical Institutionalism in Comparative Analysis* (Cambridge: Cambridge University Press).

Thomson, G. W. and N. Wilson (1997) *Resource Document: A Brief History of Tobacco Control in New Zealand* (Wellington: AFPHM).

Thomson, G. W. and N. Wilson (2001) 'Tobacco Control Policy', in P. Davis and T. Ashton (eds) *Health Policy in New Zealand* (Oxford: Oxford University Press).

Thomson, G. and N. Wilson (2002) *The Tobacco Industry in New Zealand: A Case Study of the Behaviour of Multinational Companies* (Wellington School of Medicine and Health Sciences, Department of Public Health, Public Health Monograph Series No. 6).

Thomson, S. (1992a) *Evils of 'The Fragrant Weed': A History of the 1903 Juvenile Smoking Suppression Act* (Unpublished M.A. research paper, University of Auckland).

Thomson, S. (1992b) *Stubbing Out the Social Cigarette* (Unpublished MA research paper, University of Auckland).

TMA (Tobacco Manufacturer's Association) (2010a) 'UK Tobacco Market Summary' http://www.the-tma.org.uk/tobacco-smuggling.aspx.

TMA (2010b) 'UK Cigarette Prices' http://www.the-tma.org.uk/page.aspx?page_id=42.

TMA (2010c) 'Tax Revenue Lost from Smuggling and Crossborder Shopping' http://www.the-tma.org.uk/tobacco-smuggling.aspx.

TMA (2010d) 'EU Cigarette Price & Tax Breakdown – March 2010' http://www.the-tma.org.uk/page.aspx?page_id=47.

Tofler, A. and S. Chapman (2003) '"Some Convincing Arguments to Pass Back to Nervous Customers": The Role of the Tobacco Retailer in the Australian Tobacco Industry's Smoker Reassurance Campaign 1950–1978', *Tobacco Control*, 12 (Suppl III): iii7–iii12.

Townsend, J. (1996) 'Price and Consumption of Tobacco', *British Medical Bulletin*, 52(1): 132–42. http://bmb.oxfordjournals.org/cgi/reprint/52/1/132.

Troyer, R. J. and G. E. Markle (1983) *Cigarettes: The Battle over Smoking* (New Brunswick: Rutgers University Press).

True, J. L., B. D. Jones and F. R. Baumgartner (2007) 'Punctuated Equilibrium Theory: Explaining Stability and Change in American Politics', in P. Sabatier (ed.) *Theories of the Policy Process* (2nd ed.; Boulder, CO: Westview).

Tung, G. J., Y. H. Hendlin and S. A. Glantz (2009) 'Competing Initiatives: A New Tobacco Industry Strategy to Oppose Statewide Clean Indoor Air Ballot Measures', *Am J Public Health*, 99(3): 430–9.

Tyrrell, I. (1999) *Deadly Enemies: Tobacco and Its Opponents in Australia* (Sydney: University of New South Wales Press).

Ugen, S. (2003) 'Bhutan: The World's Most Advanced Tobacco Control Nation', *Tobacco Control*, 12(4): 431–3.

UN (2011) Political Declaration of the High-level Meeting of the General; Assembly on the Prevention and Control of Non-communicable Diseases. Accessed 21 October 2011. http://www.un.org/ga/search/view_doc.asp?symbol=A%2F66%2FL.1&Lang=E>>.

USDA (United States Department of Agriculture) (1994) *US Tobacco Statistics* (Washington, DC: Economic Research Service).

USDA National Agricultural Statistics Service (2010) Tobacco Quick Facts. Accessed 17 October 2011. http://www.nass.usda.gov/Statistics_by_State/Tennessee/Quick_Facts/tobacco.pdf

U.S. Department of Health, Education and Welfare (1964) *Smoking and Health Report of the Advisory Committee to the Surgeon General of the Public Health Service* (D. Van Nostrand Co., Inc., Princeton).

U.S. Department of Health and Human Services (1986) *The Health Consequences of Involuntary Smoking: A Report of the Surgeon General* (Public Health Service, Centers for Disease Control, Center for Health Promotion and Education, Office on Smoking and Health, Atlanta).

U.S. Department of Health and Human Services (1988) *The Health Consequences of Smoking: Nicotine Addiction* (Public Health Service, Centers for Disease Control, Center for Health Promotion and Education, Office on Smoking and Health, Atlanta).

U.S. Department of Health and Human Services (1992) *Smoking and Health in the Americas* (Atlanta, GA: The U.S. Department of Health and Human Services, Public Health Services, Centers for Disease Control, National Center for Chronic Disease Prevention and Health Promotion, Office of Smoking and Health). DHHS Publication No. (CDC) 92-8419.

U.S. Government Accountability Office (2011) Report to Congressional Committee: Illicit Tobacco: Various Schemes are Used to Evade Taxes and Fees.

U.S. National Clearinghouse For Smoking. (1973) Smoking and Health Programs around the World. http://legacy.library.ucsf.edu/tid/hli43f00. 08 Jul 2010.

U.S. Public Health Service (1970) Smoking and Health Programs around the World. http://legacy.library.ucsf.edu/tid/ydr68d00. 21 Jul 2009.

Verkerk, H. G. and INFOTAB (1985) INFOTAB Regional Workshop – Kuala Lumpur, May 13–15, 1985 International Overview of Main Issues. http://legacy.library.ucsf.edu/tid/jjq52f00. 01 Nov 2009.

Viscusi, W. K. (1992) *Smoking: Making the Risky Decision* (New York: Oxford University Press).

Vogel, D., R. A. Kagan and T. Kessler (1993) 'Political Culture and Tobacco Control', *Tobacco Control*, 2(3): 317–26.

Wagner, S. (1971) *Cigarette Country: Tobacco in American History and Politics* (New York: Praeger).

Waldron, I., G. Bratelli, L. Carriker, W. C. Sung, C. Vogeli and E. Waldman (1988) 'Gender Differences in Tobacco Use in Africa, Asia, the Pacific and Latin America', *Social Science and Medicine*, 27(11): 1269–75.

Walker, J. L. (1969) 'The Diffusion of Innovations among the American States', *American Political Science Review*, 63(4): 880–99.

Walker, R. (1984) *Under Fire: A History of Tobacco Smoking in Australia* (Melbourne: Melbourne University Press).

Warner, K. E. (1981) 'State Legislation on Smoking and Health: A Comparison of Two Policies', *Policy Sciences*, 13(2): 139–52.

Warren, C. W., S. Asma, J. Lee, V. Lea and J. Mackay (2009) *Global Tobacco Surveillance System: The GTSS Atlas* (Atlanta GA: The US Centers for Disease Control and Prevention, World Lung Foundation).

Watts, R. L. (2007) 'The United Kingdom as a Federalized or Regionalized Union', in A. Trench (ed.) *Devolution and Power in the United Kingdom* (Manchester: Manchester University Press).

Watts, R. L. (2008) *Comparing Federal Systems* (3rd ed.; Montreal and Kingston: McGill-Queen's University Press).

Weible, C., P. Sabatier and K. McQueen (2009) 'Themes and Variations: Taking Stock of the Advocacy Coalition Framework', *Policy Studies Journal*, 37(1): 121–41.

Weiss, T. (2000) 'Governance, Good Governance and Global Governance: Conceptual and Actual Challenges', *Third World Quarterly*, 21: 795–814.

Wendt, A. (1987) 'The Agent-Structure Problem in Internal Relations Theory', *International Organization*, 41: 335–70.

White, A. (1997) 'Cigarette Marketing in Senegal, West Africa', *Tobacco Control*, 6: 243–5.

WHO Expert Committee (1983) Smoking Control Strategies in Developing Countries. Report of a WHO Expert Committee, Technical Series No. 695 (Geneva: World Health Organization).

WHO Regional Office for Europe (2007) Tobacco Control Database http://data.euro.who.int/tobacco.

WHO Regional Office of Europe (2010). Accessed 11 August 2011. http://www.euro.who.int/en/what-we-do/health-topics/disease-prevention/tobacco/policy/who-framework-convention-on-tobacco-control-who-fctc.

WHO (1970a) Limitation of Smoking: Report by the Director-General. 01 May. http://legacy.library.ucsf.edu/tid/cqg82a99.

WHO (1970b) WHA23.32 Health Consequences of Smoking. Geneva, Switzerland: WHO; 1970 [cited 2009 July 20]; Available from: http://www.who.int/tobacco/framework/wha_eb/wha23_32/en/index.html.

WHO (1975) Smoking and Its Effects on Health: Report of a WHO Committee, WHO Technical Report Series, No. 568 (Geneva, Switzerland: WHO).

WHO (1976) *Legislative Action to Combat Smoking Around the World: A Survey of Existing Legislation* (Geneva: WHO).

WHO (1978) WHA31.56 Health Hazards of Smoking. Retrieved July 20, 2009, from http://www.who.int/tobacco/framework/wha_eb/wha31_56/en/index.html.

WHO (1979) Controlling the Smoking Epidemic: Report of the WHO Expert Committee on Smoking Control, WHO Technical Report Series, No. 636 (Geneva, Switzerland: WHO).

WHO (1980) WHA33.35 WHO's Programme on Smoking and Health. Geneva, Switzerland: WHO; Available from: http://www.who.int/tobacco/framework/wha_eb/wha 33_35/en/index.html.

WHO (1981) WHO Smoking and Health Program: A Report of an Interorganisational Consultation, WHO Document CVD/SMO/81.3 (Geneva, Switzerland: WHO).

WHO (1982) WHO Action Programme on Smoking and Health: Programme Objectives, and how to attain them. 05 Apr. 1982. Philip Morris. Accessed 23 Jul 2009. http://legacy.library.ucsf.edu/tid/ndd81f00 (estimated date).

WHO (1983) Smoking Control Strategies in Developing Countries: Report of a WHO Expert Committee, WHO Technical Report Series, No. 695 (Geneva, Switzerland: WHO).

WHO (1985) WHO Programme on Tobacco or Health: Report by the Director-General, EB77/22 Add.1. 15 Nov. Organization WH. http://bat.library.ucsf.edu//tid/pdp63a99.

WHO (1986a) Community Prevention and Control of Cardiovascular Disease: Report of a WHO Expert Committee, WHO Technical Report Series, No. 732 (Geneva, Switzerland: WHO).

WHO (1986b) WHA39.14 Tobacco or Health. Geneva, Switzerland: WHO. Accessed July 20, 2009. http://www.who.int/tobacco/framework/wha_eb/wha39_14/en/index.html.

WHO (1987) *A 5-Year Action Plan, Smoke Free Europe* (Copenhagen: WHO Regional Office for Europe).

WHO (1988a) Smokeless Tobacco Control: Report of a WHO Study Group, WHO Technical Report Series, No. 773 (Geneva, Switzerland: WHO).

WHO (1988b) Tobacco or Health Report of the Advisory Group on a WHO Global Action Plan on Tobacco or Health. 25 Apr. 1988. RJ Reynolds. Accessed 20 Jul 2009. http://legacy.library.ucsf.edu/tid/clm64d00.

WHO (1988c) Tobacco or Health: Report by the Director-General. 23 Mar. 1988. RJ Reynolds. Accessed 20 Jul 2009. http://legacy.library.ucsf.edu/tid/dlm64d00.

WHO (1988d) WHA41.25 Tobacco or Health. Geneva, Switzerland: WHO; Accessed 20 Jul 2009. http://www.who.int/tobacco/framework/wha_eb/wha41_25/en/index.html.

WHO (1988e) WHO Programme on Tobacco or Health. 26 Aug. 1988. British American Tobacco. Accessed 20 Jul 2009. http://legacy.library.ucsf.edu/tid/hsd00a99.

WHO (1989) WHA42.19 Tobacco or Health. Geneva, Switzerland: WHO. 1989. Accessed 12 May, 2011. http://www.who.int/tobacco/framework/wha_eb/wha42_19/en/index.html.

WHO (1990) WHA43.16 Tobacco or Health. Geneva, Switzerland: WHO. 1990. Accessed July 20, 2009. http://www.who.int/tobacco/framework/wha_eb/wha43_16/en/index.html.

WHO (1991) Interim Report by the Director General of WHO on the WHO Programme on Tobacco or Health: Implementation of Resolutions. http://legacy.library.ucsf.edu/tid/drd00a99. 31 Jul 2009.

WHO (1992) WHA45.20 Multisectoral Collaboration on WHO's Programme on Tobacco or Health. Geneva, Switzerland: WHO. 1992. Accessed July 20, 2009. http://www.who.int/tobacco/ framework/wha_eb/wha45_20/en/index.html.

WHO (1995) WHA48.11 An International Strategy for Tobacco Control. Geneva, Switzerland: WHO. 1995. Accessed 7 February, 2006. http://www.who.int/tobacco/framework/wha_eb/wha48_11/en/index.html.

WHO (1996a) WHA49.16 Tobacco or Health Programme. Geneva, Switzerland: WHO 1996. Accessed July 20, 2009. http://www.who.int/tobacco/framework/wha_eb/wha49_16/en/index.html.

WHO (1996b) Program on Substance Abuse: Tobacco or Health. Geneva, Switzerland: WHO. 1996. Accessed July 30, 2009. http://whqlibdoc.who.int/hq/1996/WHO_PSA_96.5.pdf.

WHO (1996c) WHA49.17 International Framework for Tobacco Control. Geneva, Switzerland: WHO. 1996. Accessed 6 February, 2006. http://www.who.int/tobacco/framework/wha_eb/wha49_17/en/index.html.

WHO (1997) Third Action Plan for a Tobacco-Free Europe 1997–2001 (Copenhagen: WHO Regional Office for Europe).

WHO (1999) WHA52.18 Towards a WHO Framework Convention on Tobacco Control. Geneva, Switzerland: WHO. 1999. Accessed 6 February, 2006. http://www.who.int/tobacco/framework/wha_eb/wha52_18/en/index.html.

WHO (2000a) Secretariat Update: Public Hearings on the Framework Convention on Tobacco Control. Geneva, Switzerland: WHO. 2000. Accessed August 6, 2009. http://www.who.int/tobacco/media/en/SecUpdate.pdf.

WHO (2000b) Committee of Experts Report on Tobacco Company Strategies to Undermine Tobacco Control Activities at the World Health Organisation. http://bat.library.ucsf. edu/tid/jbs62a99. October 12, 2004.

WHO (2000c) Public Hearings on the Framework Convention on Tobacco Control. Geneva, Switzerland2000 [cited 2009 August 6]; Available from: http://www.who.int/tobacco/framework/public_hearings/submissions/en/index.html.

WHO (2001a) *Women and the Tobacco Epidemic – Challenges for the 21st Century* (Geneva, Switzerland: WHO).

WHO (2001b) *Women and Tobacco: Challenges for the 21st Century* (WHO/NMH/TFI/01.1). (Geneva, Switzerland: WHO).

WHO (2002) *The European Report on Tobacco Control Policy. Review of Implementation of the Third Action Plan for a Tobacco-free Europe 1997–2001* (WHO Regional Office for Europe).

WHO (2003) *WHO European Country Profiles on Tobacco Control* (Copenhagen: WHO Regional Office for Europe).

WHO (2004) *Tobacco and Poverty: A Vicious Circle* (Geneva, Switzerland: WHO).

WHO (2006) *Constitution of the World Health Organisation* (Geneva, Switzerland: WHO). Updated March 2004; Accessed 29 Jul 2009. 44:[http://www.who.int/governance/eb/who_constitution_en.pdf.

WHO (2008) *WHO Report on the Global Tobacco Epidemic, 2008: The MPOWER Package* (Geneva, Switzerland: WHO).

WHO (2009) Smoking in the Movies: From Evidence to Action. Retrieved December 8, 2009, from http://whqlibdoc.who.int/publications/2009/9789241597937_eng.pdf.

WHO (2011) First Global Ministerial Conference on Non-communicable Disease Control: Moscow Declaration. Accessed May 31, 2011. http://www.who.int/nmh/events/moscow_ncds_2011/conference_documents/moscow_declaration_en.pdf.

WHO (2011b) WHO Report on the Global Tobacco Epidemic, 2011: Warning about the Dangers of Tobacco. Accessed 19 September 2011. http://whqlibdoc.who.int/publications/2011/9789240687813_eng.pdf

WHO (2011c) *WHO Framework Convention on Tobacco Control: Guidelines for Implementation* (Geneva, Switzerland: WHO).

WHO-EMRO (2004) Tobacco Industry Activities in the Eastern Mediterranean Region: Illicit Tobacco Trade. Retrieved November 24, 2009, from http://www.emro.who.int/TFI/pdf/TFI-019.pdf.

WHO and WTO (2002) WTO Agreement and Public Health: A Joint Study by the WHO and the WTO Secretariat http://whqlibdoc.who.int/hq/2002/a76636.pdf

Wilensky, H. (2002) *Rich Democracies: Political Economy, Public Policy, and Performance* (Berkeley: University of California Press).

Wilks, S. and M. Wright (1987) 'Conclusion: Comparing Government-Industry Relations: States, Sectors, and Networks', in S. Wilks and M. Wright (eds) *Comparative Government-Industry Relations* (Oxford: Clarendon Press).

Winder A. E., T. T. L. Chen and W. C. Mfuko (1993) 'Influence of American Tobacco Imports on Smoking Rates Among Women and Youth in Asia', *International Quarterly of Community Health Education*, 14(4): 345–60.

Wipfli, H. L., K. Fujimoto and T. W. Valente (2010) 'Global Tobacco Control Diffusion: The Case of the Framework Convention on Tobacco Control', *American Journal of Public Health*, 100(7): 1260–6.

Wolinsky, H. and T. Brune (1994) *The Serpent on the Staff: The Unhealthy Politics of the American Medical Association* (New York: Putnam).

World Bank (1989) *Price Prospects for Major Primary Commodities, 1988–2000, Volume II: Food Products, Fertilizers, Agricultural Raw Materials* (Washington, D.C.: World Bank).

World Development Movement (1981) Tobacco Action Paper Number 1. http://legacy.library.ucsf.edu/tid/dep86a99. 01 Nov 2009.

World Health Organization (2011) Tobacco or Health. Resolution WHA39.14 of the 39th World Health Assembly, May 1986. Document No. WHA 39/1986/REC/1, 14, 1986. 1986. Accessed 12 May, 2011. http://www.who.int/tobacco/framework/wha_eb/wha39_14/en/index.html.

Wolfson, M. (2001) *The Fight Against Big Tobacco: The Movement, the State, and the Public's Health* (New York: Aldine de Gruyter).

Worsham, J. (2006) 'Up in Smoke: Mapping Subsystem Dynamics in Tobacco Policy', *Policy Studies Journal*, 34(4): 437–52.

WPRO (1994) Action Plan on Tobacco or Health. http://legacy.library.ucsf.edu/tid/nvr03a99. 16 Nov 2009.

Wu, T. (ed.) (2008) *Tobacco Control Policy Analysis in China: Economics and Health* (London: Word Scientific).

Yach, D. (1996) 'Tobacco or Health: Tobacco in Africa', *World Health Forum*, 17(1): 29–36.

Yach, D. (1999) WHO Tobacco Free Initiative: Statement to ECOSOC 1999 Substantive Session. 22 Jul. http://legacy.library.ucsf.edu/tid/kpj60a99.

Yach, D. (2000) 'Tobacco Control in Europe: Progress and Challenges', *Eurohealth*, 6(1): 18–21.

Yach, D. and D. Bettcher (1998) 'The Globalization of Public Health I', *American Journal of Public Health*, 88: 735–41.

Yach, D. and D. Bettcher (2000) 'Globalization of the Tobacco Industry Influence and New Global Response', *Tobacco Control*, 9(2): 206–21.

Yang, J. S. and T. E. Novotny (2009) 'Policy Coherence in US Tobacco Control: Beyond FDA Regulation', *PLoS Medicine*, 6(5): e1000079.

Yang, T., X. Yang, Q. Lv, Q. Zhao and X. Key (2009) 'Special Communication: China's First Historic Efforts to Develop a Tobacco Control Advocacy Workforce Via Schools of Public Health', *Tobacco Control*, 18(4): 422–4.

Yong, H. H., S. L. Hamann, R. Borland, G. T. Fong, M. Omar and ITC-SEA project team (2009) 'Adult Smokers' Perception of the Role of Religion and Religious Leadership on Smoking and Association with Quitting: A Comparison between Thai Buddhists and Malaysian Muslims', *Social Science and Medicine*, 69(7): 1025–31.

Young, O. R. (1999) *Governance in World Affairs* (Ithaca NY: Cornell University Press).

Zahariadis, N. (2003) *Ambiguity and Choice in Public Policy* (Washington: Georgetown University Press).

Index

Note: Page numbers followed by '*f*' and '*t*' denote figures and tables, respectively.